VIRAGO
CLASSIC NON-FICTION

Claire Harman

Editor of the *Collected Poems* of Sylvia Townsend Warner,
Claire Harman is also author of her biography, published
in 1989, which won the John Llewelyn Rhys award. She
lives in Oxford.

THE DIARIES OF SYLVIA TOWNSEND WARNER

Edited and introduced by Claire Harman

Published by VIRAGO PRESS Limited October 1995
20 Vauxhall Bridge Road, London SW1V 2SA

Reprinted 1995

First published in Great Britain by Chatto & Windus 1994
Random House, 20 Vauxhall Bridge Road, London SW1V 2SA

© Susanna Pinney and William Maxwell 1994

Introduction and Selection © Claire Harman 1994

A CIP catalogue record for this title is available from the British Library

Printed and bound in Great Britain by
Cox & Wyman Ltd, Reading, Berkshire

Contents

Introduction

I don't wonder at your mood of self-questioning, if you have been typing out old journals. Of all Pandora boxes, the worst is the box one keeps journals, letters, unfinished manuscripts in. I have mine, too, and merely to open them in search of some specific thing is enough to send me tossed and ship-wrecked into that strange unchartable sea of Time Past. Sometimes I cannot even recognise the woman who did these things, knew these extraordinary forgotten people, entertained these jejeune great thoughts or these absurd ambitions. But one thing I have pulled out with reasonable certainty: the fact that no journal, no record of one's days, conveys the extent of the garment on which these nose-gays and sodality buttons and crape bands were worn. An old teapot, used daily, can tell me more of my past than anything I recorded of it. Continuity, Alyse, continuity... it is that which we cannot write down, it is that we cannot compass, record or control.

Sylvia Townsend Warner to Alyse Gregory, 26 May 1953

Many writers are moved to keep a diary, and most are self-conscious people, with an eye on posterity. Anything – anyone – you repent of can be edited out at leisure: in the meantime keeping a diary is not simply a record of one's life, but an excellent way of salting down material which might come in useful later on. The very act of putting things into words validates them, and, for a writer particularly, validates one's choice of profession: even if the words you find are not the best ones, it keeps your hand in, and the idea that the events of a dull day might be redeemed on a better one, and put to good use in a novel or story, is comforting.

Sylvia Townsend Warner seems to have had something of this sort in mind when she began her diary in October 1927. It was a time in her life when she had nothing particularly troublesome to deal with, a time when she was busy and successful and young and lonely. A musicologist by profession, she had turned writer in 1925 with the publication of her first book of poems, *The Espalier*, followed the next year by her first novel, *Lolly Willowes*, a highly successful fantasy about a woman seeking liberation through witchcraft. By the end of 1927 she had published a second novel, *Mr Fortune's Maggot*, and started a third, *The True Heart*. She was thirty-three years old, had friends, wit, money, a fairly reliable and undemanding lover and an unstoppable desire to write things down. When her friend David Garnett gave her a handsome and expensive new notebook, she decided to use it as a diary.

The first entry, for 29 October 1927 (a brief description of a trip to Maldon with her friends the Raymonds and Charles Prentice), is casual, practised, slightly dutiful-sounding. It is remarkable because it is cleverly disguised not to resemble a beginning, indeed, my first assumption, reading the surviving diaries on microfilm ten years ago for the purposes of biography, was that some earlier books had been lost or destroyed. An entry in late October 1928, however, scotched that impression: 'It must have been ordained that I should not keep the first year of my diary,' she writes. This slips in unobtrusively enough, and is typical of Sylvia Townsend Warner's reticence about mentioning the mechanics of diary-writing, and her instinctive understanding of how to handle the form. She drops straight in, without any of the checks, exclamations and embarrassing vocatives common to the novice diarist. The only overtly self-conscious remark that appears in fifty years of subsequent diary-writing is on the inside cover of this first notebook: 'N.B. This book is a blank copy of the Apocrypha and given to me by David.'

Christening her diary the Apocrypha was both a disclaimer and a warning to herself, for though Sylvia was a strict lover of truth, she also had her fanciful side, and when asked late in her life why she had refused to write an autobiography said, 'Because I am too imaginative.' She had reason to know what a problem this could be: the biography she was writing in 1927 of the novelist T.F. Powys, her friend and mentor, was not a success because she was tempted to elaborate her material – mostly derived from diary entries. She abandoned the project in 1930 because it was getting out of hand. Yet the flights of fancy which she indulged in the Powys book are absent from the parts of her diary which she was using as an *aide-mémoire*: she eschewed such tricks there as being too distracting. And long before she gave up the Powys biography, she had ceased to refer to her diary as the Apocrypha – indeed, she had ceased to refer to it at all.

Diary-writing is commonly thought to be the most natural type of literary expression, a release from convention and constraints of all kind, from manners and grammar, from self-control. The rhetorical problems of dealing with this kind of liberty are a notable feature of most published diaries, and readers are on the look-out for cracks in the surface, the sort of admission which might seem to invalidate the whole enterprise. Virginia Woolf was puzzled by the unwritten rules of the form: 'One must not talk of oneself etc, one must not be vain etc. Even in complete privacy these ghosts slip between me and the page.' In her diary entry for 17 August 1937, she wrote, 'Do I ever write, even here, for my own eye? If not, for whose eye?'

Sylvia Townsend Warner's diary, which runs in total to almost as many words as Woolf's, is, as I have indicated, curiously devoid of any such speculation, or statements of intent concerning her diary. While Woolf uses her journal predominantly to analyse her life, Warner is much more interested in description, and how to make sense, make something, of everyday things through observation. Warner was intellectually isolated for most of her life, and lonely, despite her deeply contented domestic life with the poet Valentine Ackland. When she wrote her diary it *was* 'for her own eye', as if she were writing letters to herself. If for Woolf a diary was like a 'kindly blank-faced old confidante', the important function which Warner's diary fulfilled was that of a kindly blank-faced correspondent.

Sylvia derived both satisfaction and comfort from writing her diary. At a lunch with Garnett in November 1928, she tried to explain the use to which she had put his gift, and the extent of her enthusiasm for journal-writing. She wanted to encourage him to do likewise, but his astute reply was that he led 'too full a life to keep a diary, also that he would have nothing to put down in it'. Once started, Sylvia kept up the habit of writing her diary every evening with remarkable regularity until the mid-1930s: even falling in love did not stop her, though sometimes the entries are rather briefer than before. But during 1932 all manner of breaks, restarts and patches begin and it is impossible to say how much is missing and how much never written in the seventeen years that follow, until 1949 when the thread is resumed and the diary continued with scarcely a break until a few months before her death in 1978. The regularity of this part of the diary is a great asset: it provides a texture which can be made to hold trivial things without them appearing insignificant. Working up this dailyness is essential to the tone since the diary deals, for the most part, with domestic life in provincial England. If asked to describe the events of Sylvia Townsend Warner's life, one could do so very quickly. They are not dramatic, and she could almost share Powys's dictum: 'I went nowhere, I knew no one, I did nothing.' Yet her diary is fascinating, gripping, and at times extremely moving. Nothing is beyond the reach of her extraordinary descriptive powers, nothing bores her and consequently she is never boring. 'She has the spiritual digestion of a goat,' John Updike once wrote of her, and this is nowhere more true than in her diaries, where she is always alert to what is lively and pleasurable. Even illness can be enjoyed.

Sylvia Townsend Warner's diary surpasses most other published ones in the quality of the writing as well as its range, which is considerable, from the anecdotal early years, to the period when she fell passionately in love with her lifetime companion, Valentine Ackland; through the war, the traumatic charting of her near-breakdown in 1949, through long stretches of everyday, and finally through the extraordinary other-life of her bereavement. This last section contains the two diaries Sylvia Townsend Warner wrote in 1970, documents which graphically represent her state of mind at the time, in parallel worlds of loss and reunion. I have interlinked these two diaries, dealing as they do with the same period of time, and differentiated between them by use of roman and italic script. Often the same incidents appear in the one and the other, written as if experienced by two different women, and, in a sense, this is precisely what had happened. The effect is very odd; the more intimate diary seeming as if it were written *underneath* the more conventional one, as if it were a lower skin of the same form.

Diary-writing is a highly artificial form, or ought to be if it is to sound natural. It is common, certainly in this diary, for the writer to use hindsight on a very short-term basis only, part of the illusion that what is recorded is time passing, not time passed, as if writing a diary could really be a process of continual assessment, could pin down continuity. If a diary is too obviously retrospective, it doesn't work and reads oddly, for the form can't stand too much obvious distance from events. We take it as a mark of bad faith if there is a long stretch of writing up, although writing up disguised as if it has just happened is of course perfectly acceptable. Sylvia Townsend Warner sometimes back-writes through absences from her diary, gets the dates wrong, and then has to re-cast her memories. The results can be self-mocking – as in part of an entry on 16 March 1952, 'Sent to Bank (tomorrow, rather)' – or odd, such as the entries for 10 and 11 May 1961. The 11th is crossed through, and reads:

Fetched the cats from Low Knap, where we first had tea with the Francises'. Unfortunately they saw us as we sneaked past; and when we at last came out, & even then had to pause on our way to inspect Mistie & other friends, it was to the accompaniment of unbelieving howls.

On the preceding day, the 10th, when this actually took place, she writes up the same occasion quite differently:

[W]e fetched the cat[s] a day earlier. Even so, Niou was by his gate; & the moment I got out of the car & spoke to Mr Francis, there was a loud commanding yell of welcome; & then Kit appeared, sleepy & just out of his daybed, dazed & delighted.

This is partly a desire not to be a bore to herself by being repetitive, but the effect on the outside reader is a slight loss of trust, for it shows up the method which is at work all the time in every diary entry.

The intensest moments in one's life, whether of pleasure or pain, are the least likely to be written in a diary. 'One need not write in a diary what one is to remember for ever,' is Sylvia's entry for 22 November 1930, and another time, 'Happy is the day which has no history,' with its interesting variant, 'Happy is the day whose history is not written down.' It can be argued that only untypical experiences are ever recorded by diarists, that they never chart what is normal to the writer, but what is notable. Sylvia, for instance, a keen gardener, often records or plans garden work in note form in her diary, but would never describe how she carried it out, nor suddenly divulge the recipe for her chestnut soup, though she writes of eating it. Similarly, because her unanimity with Valentine was the bedrock of her life, she hardly mentions it, noting instead the setbacks and differences. It builds up into an oddly negative picture of illness and trouble and disagreement, which will not endear any reader to Valentine, though love for her was the be-all and end-all of Sylvia's existence. In the years following Valentine's death, Sylvia constantly goes back through their happiest times, mining the old life for comfort and the remembrance of pleasure. She recovers details of that very dailyness which usually goes unrecorded, as in the detail of a dream on 13 January 1972:

She came & stood behind me, combing my hair: firmly, attentively, steadily; and I said no-one could comb my hair but she. It was my black hair, shoulder length, but also my present hair, shaggy & matted.

The value of this dream-incident to Sylvia is that it is intimate and inconsequential: it evokes the time when such things were unremarkable, part of the fabric of life. Sylvia would never have written such a thing down in her diary at the time when it might actually have happened.

In the last year of her life, Sylvia Townsend Warner drew up a new will and tried to sort all her affairs so as to spare trouble to her executors. She devised an ingenious system for the despatch of bequests, which involved a card-file and personal notes to legatees. She also left a dozen or so folders full of her correspondence with Valentine (which she had spent years sorting, re-typing and annotating) all ready for publication when the conditions were right. This project was the obsession of her later years, and once she had finished it, she felt that her life-work was done. But while she left very clear instructions about the eventual publication of the love letters, her feelings about her diaries were quite different, and she told her executrix, Susanna Pinney, that they were 'too sad' to be published. The estate has nevertheless agreed to the editing and publication of this selection from the diaries on literary grounds, judging that it is the right compromise to make. It seems possible that Sylvia thought her diaries 'too sad' for the very reason I have already noted – that they show Valentine in such a generally poor light. The love letters on the other hand glorify Valentine, and constitute a monument Sylvia was proud to erect to their passion.

The length of the complete diary is considerable and to pare the material down to the size of one volume has required many compromises. I tended to include the following: references to her writing (never very lengthy), entries which contained interesting descriptive passages, and those which showed the variety of her interests, the persistence of her pleasure in life, her remarkable stoicism and wit and the crises of her life, both personal and political. References to some friends have disappeared in the process of editing, and others are represented only flitting through footnotes, but I hope that the overall structure of the complete document has been retained. Among the material which I have excluded are a great many interesting and detailed descriptions of concerts and exhibitions, the lives of her cats, Valentine's family, stories about friends and friends' families, the garden . . . in short, much of the ordinariness which is probably more representative of her life than what remains. What remains is, I expect, more a representation of the workings of her mind.

There are thirty-eight diaries in all, and some material scattered through notebooks. The large gaps which occur in this edition are 'natural', not editorial: I have, if anything, used proportionately more of the material from years of which only a few pages survive. There is some evidence of self-editing: entries which record the destruction of old diaries (which probably accounts for the absence of any diary for 1938–9 and the beginning of 1949 at least), pages torn out (few), and very occasionally a passage crossed through. Up to 1956 Sylvia tended to use plain notebooks, mostly hardback and of approximately A4 size; after that time she used a succession of printed diaries, with the result that the entries became much more regular in length, and, on the whole, shorter than before. There is a tendency in any year for her to neglect her diary towards Christmas, which proves a consistently blank spot. 1 January, conversely, seems to galvanise the diarist into action.

When a diary is published, it ceases in some ways to be a personal document and makes the strange transition into literature. We read as a continuum what was written into uncertainty, and any intense emotion which a diary might provoke in the reader is blunted by the knowledge that the crisis was outlived, the illness cured, and that death will hold off for another hundred pages or so. Publication of a diary puts the reader in charge, and the writer at his mercy, a reversal of the usual order. But the stained notebooks which sit ready to go back into their museum cupboards still contain their pressed flowers and love notes between the pages, still smell of the damp house at Frome Vauchurch and carry their coffee rings, cat's paw marks, traces of cigarette ash, tear stains. The diary retains its privacy and essential meaning, unknowable to us, as Sylvia anticipated. In the front of her 1971 diary she copied out this quotation from William Allingham:

I care for my old diaries for the sake of the past, the sad, sacred, happy Past, whose pains, fears, sorrows, have put on the calm of eternity – mysterious Past, forever gone, forever real, whose footsteps I see on every page, invisible to other eyes.

CLAIRE HARMAN, 1993

A Note on the Editing

All editorial insertions in the text appear in square brackets and references in the footnotes relating to short stories are to first book publication, unless, as in some cases, they appeared only in periodicals, when the month and year of publication are given in brackets.

For ease of recognition, I have amended STW's variants on the name of her aunt, Dorothie Purefoy Machen to either Dorothie or Purefoy as necessary. I have also corrected STW's misspelling of t'other ('tother) throughout.

Sylvia's elegant handwriting allows for few illegible words, and the number of arcane references in this selection is also small. To indicate which entries are incomplete I have underlined the dates of complete entries.

The literary executors of Sylvia Townsend Warner's estate, Susanna Pinney and William Maxwell, made the long task of transcribing these diaries very much easier by leaving them in my care for several years. I would like to acknowledge my gratitude to them, and my thanks to Roger Peers and Richard de Peyer of the Dorset County Museum.

Abbreviations Used in Notes

CP	Collected Poems
CSB	Contre Sainte-Beuve
CTHT	The Corner That Held Them
Esp	The Espalier
GS	A Garland of Straw
IG	The Innocent and the Guilty
KD	King Duffus and Other Poems
KE	Kingdoms of Elfin
LW	Lolly Willowes
MFM	Mr Fortune's Maggot
NY	The New Yorker
OTL	One Thing Leading to Another
Sal	The Salutation
SB	A Stranger with a Bag
SC	Scenes of Childhood
SR	A Spirit Rises
TCM	Tudor Church Music
THW	T. H. White
TI	Time Importuned
WA	Winter in the Air
WDS	Whether a Dove or Seagull

Select Bibliography of Works by Sylvia Townsend Warner

Unless otherwise stated publication in London is by Chatto & Windus and publication in New York by The Viking Press.

The Espalier, London, 1925; New York, The Dial Press, 1925.
Lolly Willowes, London and New York, 1926.
Mr Fortune's Maggot, London and New York, 1927.
Time Importuned, London and New York, 1928.
The True Heart, London and New York, 1929.
Some World Far from Ours, London, Woburn Books, 1929.
Elinor Barley, London, The Cresset Press, 1930.
A Moral Ending and Other Stories, London, Furnival Books, 1931.
Opus 7, London and New York, 1931.
The Salutation and Other Stories, London and New York, 1932.
Whether a Dove or Seagull (with Valentine Ackland), New York, 1933; London, 1934.
More Joy in Heaven, London, The Cresset Press, 1935.
Summer Will Show, London and New York, 1936.
After the Death of Don Juan, London, 1938; New York, 1939.
The Cat's Cradle Book, New York, 1940; London, 1960.
A Garland of Straw, London and New York, 1943.
The Museum of Cheats, London, 1947.
The Corner that Held Them, London and New York, 1948.
Somerset, London, Paul Elek, 1949.
Jane Austen, London, Longman, Green & Co., 1951.
The Flint Anchor, London and New York (under the title *The Barnards of Loseby*), 1954.
Winter in the Air, London, 1955; New York, 1956.
Boxwood, London, The Monotype Corporation, 1957; enlarged edition, London, Chatto & Windus, 1960.
By Way of Sainte-Beuve, translation of *Contre Sainte-Beuve* by Marcel Proust, London, 1958.

A Spirit Rises, London and New York, 1962.

A Stranger with a Bag, London, 1966; New York (under the title *Swans on an Autumn River*), 1966.

T. H. White, London, Jonathan Cape and Chatto & Windus, 1967; New York, 1967.

King Duffus and Other Poems, Wells and London, Clare, Son & Co. Ltd, 1968.

The Innocent and the Guilty, London and New York, 1971.

Kingdoms of Elfin, London and New York, 1977.

Twelve Poems, London, 1980.

Scenes of Childhood and Other Stories, London and New York, 1981.

Letters, ed. William Maxwell, London and New York, 1982.

Collected Poems, ed. Claire Harman, Manchester, Carcanet Press, 1982; New York, 1982.

One Thing Leading to Another, ed. Susanna Pinney and William Maxwell, London and New York, 1984.

Selected Stories of Sylvia Townsend Warner, ed. Susanna Pinney and William Maxwell, London and New York, 1988.

THE DIARIES

1927–32

Sylvia Townsend Warner was born in Harrow on 6 December 1893, the only child of George Townsend Warner, a housemaster at Harrow School, and his wife Nora. Her upbringing was conventional for girls of her class and time, with no formal education and a series of nannies and governesses, but the influence of her intelligent and eccentric parents and access to the best minds on the staff of the school produced a highly individualistic and scholarly young woman, whose range of intellectual expertise was considered phenomenal. She began composing music in her teens, and was already known as an expert on the history of musical notation when she was asked to join a committee sponsored by the Carnegie UK Trust. The project was to edit and publish a vast body of English sacred music which finally appeared in the Oxford University Press's ten-volume Tudor Church Music, under the general editorship of R.R.Terry. This work began in 1919 and lasted for more than ten years, during which time Sylvia Townsend Warner published her first two volumes of poetry and the novels which brought her fame, Lolly Willowes and Mr Fortune's Maggot. At the time when the diary begins in October 1927, Sylvia was thirty-three years old and living in a flat at 121 Inverness Terrace, Bayswater, with her black chow dog, William. She was preparing her second volume of poetry, Time Importuned, and had started another novel, The True Heart, and a biographical portrait of the novelist T.F. Powys. She met Powys in 1921 on a visit to his home in East Chaldon, Dorset, and it was partly through her agency that his novels, including Mr Weston's Good Wine and Mr Tasker's Gods, began to be published. Since 1913 she had been the mistress of Percy Carter Buck, director of music at Harrow School and a fellow member of the Tudor Church Music committee. The affair was kept strictly secret.

1927

December

3. Lavenham, Suffolk.

I caught the 10.3 at Liverpool St, and found Vera and Chatto.[1] Bea[2] appeared when we changed at Mark's Tey, with a suitcase like an ottoman.

The Barn[3] has a lot of beams, but they are so indigenous that they are not objectionable. There is a little garden at the back with apples, chrysanthemums and violet leaves. Mrs Parker[4] has red hair, and a shiny face, like soap-stone. After lunch we went to meet Charles[5] who we hoped might be arriving by the 3.16. But as there was no 3.16 this hope was vain. We looked at Lavenham. It is a compact town on a hill and at the end of each street one looks into damp grey-green fields. The houses are washed pink or yellow. They are mostly timbered, and have carved doors and beams. The church is very large, it has a tower like a pilon [sic]. It was nearly dusk when we came to it, but the church-mouse was cleaning it. She let us in and showed us round with a taper. To be inside a church in dusk light is to see it[s] shape as one never could by day. It is to be walled in with darkness and half-darkness. Back to the station and met Charles. After tea I began to read Under the Bondage of Fear aloud.

4. Very cold and grey. We sat before the fire and Charles read letters of Fitzgerald. To look out on a wide green with some geese on it, sometimes traversed by the butcher boy or the washerwoman. A name 'sequestered in a sigh'. We walked before lunch, up a gentle winding valley, a greenish lead landscape embossed with copper hedges and iron trees.

1 Vera Raymond and her husband Harold (1887–1975), STW's publisher at Chatto & Windus.
2 Bea Howe, close friend of STW and an aspiring author, then twenty-seven years old.
3 Gerald Rivington's house in Lavenham, which he let to friends. Rivington was a publisher and an old Harrovian.
4 Housekeeper at The Barn.
5 Charles Prentice, the distinguished typographer and editor, of Chatto & Windus.

An afternoon of complete coma. I read Paul Valéry *Variété*, which I think very good, a mind like Pascal's – for it was only Pascal's soul which was Christian. After tea I went out and Charles came with me. We went to see the church in the dark. It was lit up like a factory. The tower was very grey and unreal above. Presently the bells began to ring and rang for quarter of an hour. I thought how like the changes were to the Athanasian Creed, and how all the systems of the school-men are now to us like a peal of bells rung in a winter's night. They finished ringing off two by two, a major third, a minor third to the dominant (a beautiful bell with an overtone like a flute, so round), a tone; then the A♭ bell went on alone, saying over and over again – 'Deum, Deum'. The organ began to play and the Salvation Band to flourish. It made a nice counterpoint on a ground.

5. Sight-seeing. First the Guildhall, in which's dungeon the Rev. Taylor spent two nights before being burnt on Hadleigh Heath. It was he who on his way to execution got off his horse and danced at the wayside, for to show his joy that so soon he would be in heaven. Then we were shown the Lavenham Belfry. First, the ringing chamber, hung all round with accounts of celebrated ringings. It has to be five thousand changes before it can be a peal. Before that it is a method. Then the belfry itself, the bells balanced on large beams, with great wheels to pull them round. The man rang the B♭ bell for us. It wheeled over abruptly, and the noise clanged, swelled, grew outward on the air, trembled and then settled on the third. The evening before I had expected to see the sounds fly out at the top of the tower like black cannon-balls, but this was like a wave breaking everyway outwards, thinning, ebbing back again. Then we went up to the top of the tower to look at the view. There were to have been four pinnacles, but the architect fell off the tower.

After lunch we drove to Long Melford – a red village all round a long green, like a stately Hilton.[6] It has a great House (Hyde Parkers) with ogival towers, like Hampton Court. There are also alms-houses to match. In the west end of the church are two fifteenth-century windows, with quantities of fashionable donors, and a rather embarrassed archangel in the central light of each. A guide with a terrible voice like a tin basin seized on the Raymonds and Bea: Charles and I sculked [sic] firmly among the Rectors and benefactors at the west end

6 Hilton, Huntingdonshire, the home of David Garnett.

till he was out of earshot. Then we went round the church alone, and were nearly locked in with the Martyn family – Roger and Richard, their brazen wives and families.

9. Spent the morning seeing over the websters, where women weave horsehair on hand-looms. The left hand holds a hank of horsehair, the right pulls out a hair at a time and feeds the shuttle; the left foot works the machine: i.e. sends the shuttle-arm back and forth. The right, moving over a pedal-board, works the order of the warp threads, so that each stamp of the left foot sends the shuttle through a different arrangement of the warp. At the tail of the loom, all the warp threads are knotted together and weighted down with a large stone, to keep the web taught. The noise is a sort of rattle and thud, it seemed a blot in an otherwise reasonable workshop that each loom should be lit by an unshaded gas-jet. One woman told me that green was the least tiring colour to weave.

Downstairs was the store-room, full of cotton twist on large wooden spools, and tails of horse-hair. The hair comes to England in tangles, and is combed straight on a sort of spiked mat. In the passage was an enlivening representation of the different stages of an anthrax sore.

About four I set out by myself along the Bury Road. I turned off along a dead straight footpath running across two enormous ploughed fields. The sky was plain grey, the earth was plain brown. On the horizon about a mile off was a domed city of ricks. I wanted nothing else. I walked on till it grew quite dark, and then walked back again. On the way back I saw a cat sitting on the cross-bar of a telegraph pole, as calm as you please. Coming past the factory I saw the weaving women still at it. The silhouette of the upright jolting back and forth, the women's heads and shoulders moving to and fro above the fixed hands, the lights flaring. The young man who has taken a passionate farewell of his young woman, who for some reason he must give up. As he leaves the town he passes the factory and looks in. He sees her, one of a score, at the window, part of the mechanism, and watches, fascinated, lulled, de-personalised, admiring and acceptant. Phoenix[7] in the evening.

15. [London] Wobb[8] came to lunch, looking very neat in a black suit

7 Poem, *TI*.
8 Geoffrey Webb (1886–1962), scholar of architecture and fine arts and later Slade Professor of Fine Art at Cambridge.

for his father. He is staying with H. Avray Tipping[9] 'an amiable old paederast with one eye', and was full of accounts of all the grand and romantic mansions he had been visiting. Mr Lloyd in Kent, so period that he, his wife and four children all sleep in the same chamber. In the evening Mrs Lloyd dresses like Mrs Ferrers, dove-grey with fair linen oddments, and Wobb very nearly mistook her for the parlourmaid. This was a change from Stourhead where Lady? worships Voltaire and keeps an autograph in a silver photo-frame of the Edwardian period.

He told me of his hopes to get a lectureship at Cambridge, and also of the Pratt Mss turning up (kept by Roger Pratt, architect), which firmly remove the possibility of the only undoubted Inigo Jones house (Carles Hill, Berks) being by Inigo. Inigo will be like Giorgione: the less he has left, the greater his name. We spoke sadly of the prayer-book measure,[10] and decided provisionally to hold Great Snoring, Norfolk and Steeple Ashton, Wiltshire in plurality, spending July – December at G. Snoring, the remaining six months in Steeple Ashton. A quick way of serving tables will be to have a boiler for soup mounted on a motor-bicycle.

In the evening I dined J.A. Westrup[11] at Martinez.

17. Intolerable hard frost, my pipes frozen in this morning, and my bath draped with icicles. Corrected proofs, wrote letters. In the evening I went to see the Machens,[12] driven from 12 Melina [Place] to 28 Loudon [Road]. A very poor substitute; for the house is large, cold, excessively refined, with an airy basement full of blackbeetles. Whenever Arthur went to fetch another shovelful of coal we heard him crunching. Poor Dorothie had dug up her plants from 12 Melina, and while they were waiting to be transferred they were snapped up by the dustman and carried off to the Urban and District Tophet. Arthur is writing a short memoir of Frank for Cape's edition of GJB.[13]

18. In the afternoon to hear Beecham conduct the Messiah, which he

9 Co-author (with Christopher Hussey) of a study of Vanbrugh.
10 The House of Commons rejected a revised Book of Common Prayer in February 1927, but a modified revised edition came into use the following year.
11 (1904–75), music scholar, writer and conductor, knighted in 1960.
12 Dorothie Purefoy Machen (née Hudleston) was STW's aunt. She had married the writer Arthur Machen (1863–1947) in 1903, and they had two children, Hilary (b. 1912) and Janet (b. 1917).
13 Frank Hudleston, STW's uncle, had died in November. He was Librarian at the War Office and author, among other works, of *Gentleman Johnny Burgoyne*.

did admirably, with most irreligious fervour. The angels of the Lord really clashed their golden wings, and hopped off like ballet dancers at the close of the gloria.

21. When I went to bed it was raining, and apparently thawing. In the morning the air was all a thick mist, glimmering with the throbbing and chirping of sparrows, and everything was covered with a thick sheet of ice. Poor Mrs Keates[14] fell flat coming to me, and was picked up by a cripple. Edie, Anthony and Philip[15] crept cautiously out of a taxi about 11.45 and had coffee and exchanged gifts. Geoffrey's[16] long-looked-for clarinets have arrived – hopelessly out of tune! In the afternoon it began to rain and thaw. I went to Bea's birthday tea, and met Christopher Hussey,[17] and Mrs (Gracie) Foster, 'Miss to the late King'. She is very beautiful in a shop-girl way, and her conversation was such that I expected her to call me *Modom*. On my return I was greeted with a noise like Niagara, and a large flood of water running down the steps. Poor William, who had been left to look after the house, was much agitated. My bathroom and part of my bedroom flooded; but the worst burst with [illegible] Miss Hossack overhead. I seduced a policeman from point-duty, and made him break open the bottom flat to turn off the water from the main. N.B. in the Street Offences enquiry that morning Sir W. Harwood remarked: The question of bribing the police is one which need not trouble us – and indeed, I found it perfectly easy. After we had turned off the water and waded about in the flood examining ceilings by a spluttering candle, the poor policeman looked at his hands and asked for water to wash them. I explained sadly that in this swamp water was the one thing I could not provide, and we laughed together, and washed in two inches left by chance in the kettle. After he had departed, two ludicrous officials from the water-works came, stop-cocks or turnkeys. Both were deaf, both were imbecile and one had fallen down that morning and sprained his shoulder. All they could do was to wag their heads, and drop the candle into the flood.

All this over, and after some bailing and mopping I went over to Vera to spend the night there.

23. The plumbers at 121, two large rents mended. '*Now* we will turn

14 Florence Keates, STW's Cockney charwoman.
15 Sturt, family friends from Harrow.
16 Geoffrey Sturt was a past lover of STW.
17 (1899–1970), writer on houses, architecture, monuments and gardens.

the water on'. Mrs Keates and I stood waiting in an admiration for the water to gush out of the taps. A sinister sound . . . The water was gushing through the kitchen ceiling. Another and most intricate rent discovered. I was distracted by Barker's van, and found myself opening a Christmas present of a raw beefsteak. But it was for William, from Charles. Back to 15, Launceston,[18] where I trimmed a Christmas tree and listened to Chatto reading aloud[.]

28. A hard frost, the road crusted with ice and snow. I was weak enough to put on a woollen vest and scratched all day, feeling as though I were fermenting. However I buckled to, and settled three stanzas of the *Fern Harvest*,[19] but got bunkered in the last. Thus, damning and itching, to bed at 1.30. A contented day, never the less.

29. I overslept myself till noon. As cold as ever, and no sign of a thaw. I sat by the fire working at Sukey.[20] Tomorrow she must and shall leave New Easter and go to Southend. When she gets there, God help us both. A letter of ten thousand pages from Fox Strangways,[21] all about proslambanomenos, and perfect time, and hexachords, and tetrachords, and right angled triangles whose sides are integers, and 'if you have your Coussemaker handy' and the Lord knows what else. It makes me so thankful I have shut up that shop; but how am I to answer it, politely implying that I never cared a damn for such things, and now don't even pretend to. Well, it's a judgement on me for pretending.

18 15 Launceston Place, the Raymonds' home.
19 Poem, *TI*.
20 Her novel, *The True Heart*.
21 Arthur Fox Strangways, then music critic of the *Observer*.

1928

January

7. Roused at 8.30 by Violet Hunt ringing me up to say that the Tait Black prize had gone to *Adam's Breed*.[1] I could not feel as annoyed as I might have done because I was so amused by her officious desire to break the bad news; and yet I believe the woman likes me – I'm sure she thinks she does. In the evening I finished the phoenix. During the night 6–7 the Thames overflowed in the city, flooding Thames St. and Bankside. I am worn out with writing poetry.

8. Early in the morning the Thames broke through in several places and flooded river London. The worst flood was in Grosvenor Road by Lambeth Bridge, there were floods in Hammersmith and Putney, Battersea, Blackfriars and Rotherhithe. Fourteen people were drowned in basements, poor souls, and a fish was caught in the kitchen of Battersea police-station. The basement of the Tate Gallery was filled, which may help to settle the question of the 20,000 Turner sketches.[2] In the basement also were some Rowlandsons, and I suspect my Callow of Venice.[3] Very watery and homelike for it.

9. Vera sent over a rose-coloured negligée as a love-gift while I was hurriedly concocting a T.S. Eliot lyric to father on Bunny.[4] In the afternoon I did odd jobs, and commissioned Victor[5] with £200 to invest for me. It is a grand sensation to ring up one's bank to ask what one's balance is, and to await the answer in smug serenity. I find the pleasure of money entirely momentary. I like spending it, I like disposing of it – in between I never give it a thought. In the evening I read my grandmother's diary with a view to an article. I also arranged the

---

1 By Radclyffe Hall.
2 The question of where to house them.
3 On loan to the gallery.
4 David Garnett, [1892–1981] author of *Lady Into Fox*, *Aspects of Love*, among many others.
5 Victor Butler, a distinguished mathematician and son of the Governor of Burma. He was an Old Harrovian.

wine-cupboard. Altogether a rich day, and a very fatuous one. I wish I could be a grandmother. It is wanton extravagance to have had a youth with no one to tell of it to when one grows old.

10. In the morning a note from Mary Somerville,[6] announcing that she is to marry Brown. A gusty day, turning to rain, so in the afternoon, having tried on clothes I decided to go down to the river to look at the high tide. On Westminster Bridge there was a large crowd watching the water lapping against the lawn under Big Ben, and hawkers were selling Old Moore's Almanack, declaring that he had prophecied the flood. Very probably, as he is as inclusive as an all-in insurance policy. Thence I walked to view the damage in Grosvenor Road, very smelly and low-tide looking, and through the warren of streets behind the Tate, where there were quantities of broken basements. A large flock mattress, saturated with Thames, was lying flop on the pavement outside one house, a lugubrious object.

The Tate announced that the only picture likely to be badly damaged is Blake's Nelson. Now I suppose, having damaged it irreparably they will have it irreparably repaired.

In the evening I wrote the first installment of *Flora*.[7]

12. Proofs and ten thousand letters. Thomas Hardy has died. Dorset will mourn — a more rare and antique state of things than England mourning.

13. Hardy is to be buried in Westminster Abbey. I have no objection, he won't mind what the Dean says over him.

14. Hardy's heart is to be buried at Mel[l]stock (Stinsford). This is becoming ludicrous. A hideous day with Sukey at Southend and everything turned sulky and refusing to budge. I wrote like an old flock mattress.

15. In the afternoon I went to the Zoo and saw Reptiles and small Cats. The boa was hanging in majestic loops from his cross-piece, as comfortable as a pussy-cat. The rattlesnake gave a faint sighing movement as it lay torpid; then I saw a pole stretched in to prod it up. It flounced across its den, very angry, and then curled up again, but wakefully rigid, *still* with rage and resentment, with its tail erect. I was sorry for

6 Mary Somerville joined the BBC in 1925. She married Ralph Penton Brown in 1928.
7 A piece of writing about her grandmother, Flora Moir, worked on for a number of years. A story called 'Flora' was eventually published in *NY* (December 1977).

it, I have seldom seen anything look so *purely* furious. The cats were charming to me, the little leopards and the ocelot dancing on their hind legs for meat. When I fed the Caracal he purred. I do love those animals, I don't know how most; whether they are frank and forthcoming, flirtatious carnivores, or whether they are proud and distant, as was the little civet, couched on its shelf with an expression of cultured sour-grapes; though when I left the gobbet on the bar and walked away she came bouncing down. As for the coatias, they were almost guttersnipishly loveable. As I was walking away I saw a girl tickling a tiger behind his ears. He stood pressed to the bars, holding his head to one side with a smile of treacly sentiment, all limp and baggy, dissolved with gratification. The Bob-Cat has died. Stomach troubles, due to his admirers who fed him with bad sprats and jam sandwiches.

I dined with the Sturts; and coming home despatched the Lytton Strachey lampoon.

17. Bad news from Violet.[8] Francis[9] is dangerously ill with complications on top of a bad chill, congestion, I suppose. She has gone to Gillingham to nurse him. It is agonising to me to think that if they were rich she would have gone over before, and perhaps averted all this. But if they were rich, Francis would not have been shivering in lodgings at all. I have wired some money, and offered to go down there as a stand-by. An exquisite morning, 'winter slumbering in the open air wears on his smiling face a dream of spring'; and I walked in Kensington Gardens feeling that too-familiar mask of anxiety clamped down on my face once more. To wait, to walk about waiting, to be able to do nothing . . . but with the Powys's [sic] I can at least avow my anxiety, illness there slams no door in my face.[10]

20. Charles [Prentice] took me to dine at Boulestins. Oysters, red mullet grilled with a slip of banana laid along it like a medieval wife on a tomb, lamb with a myraculous [sic] and undiagnosable sauce, and the best peach I have ever eaten. He began to ask about my music and I felt curiously as though I had this secret past which I was rather proud of being so inalienably mine by renunciation. Every harlot was a virgin once, nor canst thou ever change Kate into Nan. He knows me very well, I think, and perhaps I scarcely know him at all. N.B. To send him

8 Wife of the novelist T.F. Powys.
9 Younger son of T.F. and Violet Powys, b. 1909.
10 An oblique reference to the secretive nature of her affair with Percy Buck.

Chéri[11] to read in the train. He doesn't know it. That extreme gentleness excites me, and I find myself behaving with him as though I were alone out of doors. It is almost unnerving to be so freed of self-consciousness. What he thinks of me I cannot imagine, because I know myself apart from my books, I do not see them as integrally part of myself; but he, I fancy, is giving the peach to Lueli,[12] taking Mr Fortune[13] in the taxi, picking up Nelly Trim's[14] handkerchief. Yes, I feel sure of this; that accounts for my lack of self-consciousness. As an artist I am not self-conscious, and when I am with him my mind flows as though I were my full artist-self, not the naked Sylvia that wears clothes, and is met by people. Suddenly I do something clumsy or idiotic and Sylvia is in torment. But I soon forget her again, she is no more to me than the woman reflected in the mirror opposite.

February

18. To Cambridge, leaving my William behind at the Raymonds. Dined in Corpus with an air-marshal whose name I can't remember and then on to *King Arthur* by the Cambridge Operatic Society. Dryden simply could not go wrong when he wrote for the stage. There is no corner of the cheek his tongue was unacquainted with – the scene where Emmeline recovers her sight is almost Barrie-ish; yet over the whole is the nobility of a Godlike and rational technique. The music is neither Godlike nor rational – perhaps only Gluck's is: but O Lord how lovely and how English it is, English in its inadequacies, for Purcell's small-talk is all about the weather, and in its excellencies, its extraordinary poetry and eccentricity, queerness, authenticity of imagination. [. . .]

At the end a speech from Rootham,[15] involving a compliment to Dent.[16] Dent retaliated from the house, and for one happy moment they both spoke at once, with the utmost civility and loathing in their tones. Young men in plus-fours and pull-overs walked onto the allegorical scene offering wreaths and brown paper parcels to the cast, and to Rootham a bowl of tulips, an unsuccessful bribe to make him leave

---

11 By Colette.
12 A temporary Christian in *MFM*.
13 Eponymous hero of the same book.
14 Subject of a poem by STW, *Esp*.
15 Cyril Rootham (1875–1938), organist and composer. He was a lecturer in music at Cambridge University from 1913, and college organist of St John's.
16 Edward Dent (1876–1957), Professor of Music at Cambridge from 1926 to 1941.

off talking. Talked to Clement and Mary[17] about the usual Cambridge stratagems, especially who is to succeed Q[uiller-Couch] as professor of Literature. ? T. S. Eliot.

24. A house for sale in Inverness Terrace. I want to share it with the Oliver Warners.[18] I went to see him in the afternoon, and he was so young that I forswore my annoyance at his captions.

25. Inspected 113 with Mrs Oliver. The basement is terribly dingy, but I think one could redeem it, and the ground floor rooms are charming. I felt so limp that I spent the whole afternoon asleep.

26. A ravishing spring day, the Kensington Gardens holy thorn quite green. In a final tidying of *Time Importuned*[19] I completed *The Visit* and then went mad and wrote *The Mortal Maid*. Made an offer for 113, as the Warners have decided to come in.

29. I looked at a small cold house in Stanford Road, consisting entirely of rooms which the house-agent said would do for servants' bedrooms; by the third floor this excuse had worn a little thin; and a charming but too small and too expensive house in Bedford Gardens. Home to hear 113 had come down to 1250. [. . .]

Chatto doesn't approve of leaseholds, and chilled my feet considerably. So tomorrow I shall start freeholding – viz. Pembridge Crescent and Victoria Road. I am getting rather bitten with this house-hunting game, and quite enjoy the prospect of a move. Though God knows, my bowels yearn to stay in Inverness Terrace and walk over the same paving-stones to the same shops.

March

17. Roused by telephone message about 113. I went up to 1150, the rival offer, and I hope secured it. Signed the official offer. Then I went to have lunch with Mr Oppenheimer[20] at the Spanish; he was very talkative and frisky. I took him to Rotherhithe to see the grammar school children, and trying to find my way into the church corner I happened on Prince's Street, a street of the purest eighteenth century, doors, windows, panellings, everything quite unaltered. One door stood

17 The Rev. Sir Edwyn Clement Hoskyns, Dean of Corpus, and his wife Mary, of Newnham College.
18 Oliver Warner (1903–76) and his wife Dorothy. Warner worked at Chatto & Windus, and was later the author of a number of books on naval history.
19 Her second collection of poems.
20 Of the *New York Herald Tribune*.

open and I asked if we could just look inside. The lady of the house was extremely friendly. She had lived in Rotherhithe for seventy years. When she was a little girl she would never have dared to come up P. Street, because of the Captains. If you as much as touched their doorsteps they'd bounce out on you. She wouldn't change her captain's house though, in spite of the rats which she called rottens. She was extremely local, so was her daughter, and they spoke with unmeasured rage of the Rotherhithe tunnel which enabled people from the other side of the river to come ravaging in and take the Rotherhithers' jobs. In her young days, the captains' houses had large gardens; they still have sizeable yards, and later on there were fairs, with booths all along the tunnel and merry-go-rounds performing at its mouth. She was heavenly, I could have listened to her for ever. As for L.C.C. flats, you mightn't even drive a nail in – 'so you couldn't as much as hang yourself even'. She did my heart good.

Home by Bankside. Very tired and stiff.

22. Solomon[21] at the Philharmonic in the evening. Good performance by the choir. Beecham conducted by memory, and I hear he conducted the rehearsal by heart also. Two especially fine choruses, 'Let no rash intruder' – almost Purcellian, & 'draw the tear from hopeless love'. One amusing example of prudery. Solomon should remark in a brisk recitative. 'Arise my fair one, come away. My love admits of no delay'. But Clara Serena sang from a bowdlerised text which gave as the second line: 'In sweet seclusion let us stray.' Immediately followed by 'Let no rash intruder', all about pillows and nightingales. I was reminded of Parry altering O spare the husband and return the wife into *restore the wife*'. Such nice feeling for the Married Woman's Property Act.

24. Tea with Edith Sitwell, who was speechless with a cold. Degrading afternoon, the room full of young male poets and old female rastas, Anita Berry among them. The only pleasant person a Japanese woman, who had never seen a sheep till she came to England. Eikon Animae[22] for the Almanack in the evening.

31. A most surprising evening with John Ireland,[23] an evening out of D. H. Lawrence. He was ordinary and conversible at dinner, and had

---

21 Oratorio by Handel.
22 The provisional title of STW's biography of T.F. Powys, never completed.
23 (1879–1962), composer and pianist. His *6 Songs Sacred and Profane* (1929–31) includes settings of three poems by STW.

an amusing description of 'Aunt' Holst as a young man with a trombone in one corner and a wash-stand in the other. Then to his studio, where I admired his taste in pictures. He was about to play me his sonatina when he suddenly went off into what a devil of a time he'd had. First a boy growing up and marrying, then his own reaction of marrying a girl of seventeen. They quarrelled horribly; and with a ghastly exactitude he recalled one quarrel, the girl sitting on the piano and swinging her legs, and singing a rag-time – he stopped, musicianly, to give a rather incorrect musician's rendering of 'I want to be happy', and how he had wanted to strangle her. He raged across the room strangling a ghost, and then when I jumped up and told him to have done with such tormenting nonsense, he stood quite still and dazed. Afterwards he was like Tommy[24] on the worst evening, speaking like an automaton, and saying the same thing over and over again. Perhaps he was a little drunk, I tried to think so, for if he were not, it was creepier still to be alone with this demented stranger.

April

18. Into Fleet St (lunched at Cheshire Cheese) to see Mr Prescott about 113. Caught a chill waiting in his damned anteroom, P.C.B.[25] came to dinner, and remarked that he felt respect for me. I was rather surprised, and forgot to ask why.

19. Byrd schedule.[26] In the evening to the BBC John Ireland evening. Trio – 1919, too noble for my taste, songs by Hardy, Dekker (very good, an excited talking vocal curve, almost like hens) and the love and friendship set. Then the Sonatina, with a Sabbath last movement based on Lolly.[27] This I really liked. It has an excitement of the wild brain, instead of the usual wild body orgy. Then two songs from A.E. Houseman [sic] with a piano epilogue and a cello sonata that I should enjoy on a second hearing, but they were playing against time, and it didn't emerge. A very beautiful serious child named Perkins, who

24 Stephen Tomlin, the sculptor (1901–37). His close friendship with STW began when he was a schoolboy at Harrow, and ended acrimoniously in 1926 or 1927.
25 Percy Carter Buck (1871–1947), organist, music scholar and composer, was Director of Music at Harrow School from 1901 to 1928, and held chairs of music at Dublin and London. He also taught at the Royal College of Music and led the Tudor Church Music committee of which STW was a member. He and STW had been clandestine lovers since 1913.
26 For *Tudor Church Music*.
27 *Lolly Willowes*, her first novel.

reminded me of Bea ten years ago, turned over, tense with anxiety to turn over right. Her hands were ice-cold with nervous exhaustion when I talked to her afterwards. She, I, Ireland and Edward Clark went on to a late dinner. There was a wireless in the restaurant, and we listened to a very good Blues. I thought how close the analogy is between Jazz and plainsong: both so anonymous, so curiously restricted and conventionalised, so perfectly adapted to their metiers, both flowing with a kind of devout anonymity. Talked of Holst, and how the beginning of Egdon Heath is like Holst improvising with his thumb. Ireland drew a horse with smoke and a water-butt, a fire engine, three aeroplanes and God regardant on the table-cloth with creative seriousness. I liked him this time, perhaps he was only drunk that evening.

26. Lucia[28] and I lunched with Cecil Beaton and discussed her working for him on his photographs. He was terribly evasive, just as I should have been. [. . .] The Maze[29] – a pull of it with a lovely god's eye frontispiece by Ceri Richards – came from Stanley Morison with £10.

27. P.C.B. in the afternoon. I was very frayed with being motherly and found it soothing to be reduced to my common denomination again and to be treated just as an ordinary accustomed Sylvia, and to have 'my life-long convictions recognised as extempore. Committee[30] in the evening.

May

3. During the morning I thought about thought, and decided it would really be easier to believe in the divinity of Christ than in twice two making four. Somehow the very frequency of twice two etc seems to invalidate it as a concept.

5. Sukey. In the evening I walked through a long after sunset to the Machens. Every house I passed was a story, and in the streets near the canal there was a smell of water and a sound of trees. Shall I ever be able to write about London?

12. Jobs in the morning, collated *Te Deum* and *Te Matrem*[31] in the

28 The abandoned young French wife of one of STW's Harrovian friends.
29 A short story by STW published in a limited edition by Stanley Morison, later included in *The Salutation*.
30 For *Tudor Church Music*.
31 Both by William Byrd (?1543–1623).

afternoon. Not only is *Te Matrem* the earlier text, but I believe it is the earlier composition. [. . .] Dined at Sorrani's with Victor [Butler]. A little piece of lobster shell gave me the reading of a delicious sauce – white sauce thinned with lobster consommé. Petits-fours again revealed me as being sensuous and practical. Then on to the BBC to hear Oedipus Rex by and conducted by Stravinsky. A great deal of the choral writing was almost pure Taverner, the construction that of an early passion. It is really impressive music, it sounds old and cold, a chilly shadow that has never lifted from man's mind. Two incidents disturbed our listening. First a man stole in and with portentous clattering of keys unlocked a cabinet, taking out a soda-water syphon and a decanter of whiskey; then my cigarette case of synthetic jade burst into flames with overpowering stench of camphor. Home, talking about climate and religion. The blues I admired on the 19th is by Gershwin called *The Man I love*. Victor also under its spell. I have been more pleased with Oedipus than with any of the recent Stravinsky I have heard. It is quite dislocated at last, miles beyond *Les Noces*; and it *is* so old and cold.

June

On Monday 11th as I was walking by the Round Pond a cream-coloured chow strung to a district messenger boy fell upon William, and got me in the right leg with his second. I felt a violent pain and the next I remember is sitting in a pool of blood, with a crowd like cows all round. A kind woman came who helped me to my feet and led me to the gate of the Broad Walk and into a taxi and to a chemists where she saved my self-respect with sal-volatile. My chief feeling was of acute annoyance at bleeding out so much of my private personal blood before strangers. Poor Mrs Keates was washing out 113 when she was summoned to boil water and find brandy. She was very brave but she might – I thought – have brought the brandy with less ceremony. I rang up Sinny[32] – couldn't get him, got Dr Glass – supplied by Providence I suppose to minister to me in scrapes. He said a fortnight in a nursing-home. I rang up 15, Launceston, went off in a taxi, found the admirable Annie had got the bed ready and collapsed into it. Charles came after dinner with a large bunch of dark red batiked carnations and chose me an assortment of books, including Pepys,

32 Presumably her doctor.

Wyndham Lewis, the Percy Reliques and Cowper's poems. He also got William out. Poor William was much more upset than I. He lay under my bed sighing heavily, the picture of misery. [. . .]

Wednesday and Thursday were visited by Bea and Charles and P.C.B. I can't remember much else, for by then I was really feeling the shock. [. . .]

Tuesday [19th] P.C. came in the afternoon to support me through a counterpoint of Parsley.[33]

Wednesday an invalid chair came, and of all hideous experiences this was the worst. Charles dined and wrote neat tickets for Vera's stall of charity while Chatto gibed.

Thursday evening was the last reading of T.C.M. proofs. [. . .]

Thursday [28th] evening I went to Boris Goudonov. Chaliapin with a bad Italian company. Chaliapin a more terrific actor than ever. Just as the curtain fell at the end of the fit scene I saw him turn his head – still watching that ghost in case it should pounce again. This was superb. One felt that he was doomed to madness for the rest of his days. Geoffrey H[art] took me.

Friday I went to Elsworth to Wobb. His cottage is charming, the front garden is full of Malmaison, La France, Gloire de Dijon and cabbage roses. It was a brilliant evening after a violent storm (in which the motor-bike broke down) and we lay in the meadow at the back of the granary looking at a green and gold oak tree, a Gainsborough grouping, and a willow welcoming dusk to its slender arms. Wobb spoke of the noise of poplars, a roar that suddenly ceases as you approach it and then disintegrates into whispers. He is very happy and I heard him in the kitchen telling Mrs Desborough his femme de menage about Mme du Deffand. Then we went in and had a fire.

July

3. [T]o 113 for good. P.C.B. came and took me out to dinner at Paddington and came back to inaugurate me with my first evening and my first Bach. The red field in Africa, guarded by red-hot poker plants. How far away you go in thought, but this is the nearest I have ever been to Africa. I must write that poem of the *Sailors Return* since it has come so truly.

33 Osbert Parsley (1511–85).

16. Very tired and leg-aching. Went on scratching [wallpaper] and distempering. P.C.B. dined, and buttled with curious care, perfectly accurately and yet with a total disresemblance to all butlers.

28. To Stanley Morison to sign The Maze, to look at prawn's whiskers, to be asked if I would design a plain-song fount. Civily refused, grinning inwardly at the thought that three years ago I should certainly have accepted. Dined with the Chetwynds[34], Randolph and Betty and the pretty young Farquar. Very gay and delightful evening. N.B. to suggest to the next Labour government a bill for including some vitamins in the gum of stamps.

August

8 to 21. At Little Zeal,[35] Chief works, carried Sukey from Half-Acres to Cov. Garden. Laid out a stately patchwork. Bought, from a mariner home from the Persian Gulf, two rugs, one sea-blue, one magenta. Also at a junk-shop in Plymouth [. . .] a book of flower-paintings – 1818 – for Nora – a lacquer box. Expeditions: to see a travelling company of *Yellow Sands* (Eden Phil[l]pot[ts]) no go. Good works, nil: except to remove several inches of ancestral well-born ge-hereditary dust from Nora's wardrobe. Read. Queen Victoria's letters mostly and a great many old Vogues with pregnant bellies and waists under our armpits, 1919. Flowers in the garden: dahlias, Zéphirine Drouhin (very sweet), phloxes, evening primroses, hollyhocks. In greenhouse besides the convolvulus, many balsams, described by N. as being the colours of mixed sweets. Chief features. The extreme tidiness of garden. R.[36] laid out a great many continuous cloches. N. 'continuous crashes, I should think'. A new sundial and a new gardener. [. . .]

In short, a peaceful fortnight of ladylike behaviour.

22. I reached Penally[37] rather flat at 6.45. It was raining so hard I could scarcely see a row of smiling Machens. Climbed a precipice to Giltar Terrace, sought to appease Mrs Cole[38] about William, dined and spent the evening with the Machens.

---

34 Friends STW had met through Chatto & Windus.
35 STW's mother's house in South Brent, Devon.
36 Ronald Eiloart, STW's stepfather.
37 The village on the south Wales coast where Arthur Machen and his family were on holiday.
38 The landlady.

Remark of a Scotch lady in the train: it must be very terrible for people with intemperate friends in these days of motor traffic.

23. Woke by odd sounds in large strange bed. Thought it might be the Atlantic but decided against that on remembering I was in a back bedroom. Then reflected that the Atlantic might get round to a back bedroom if it tried. I thought more about Swansea and was sure I would rather live there than in Hampstead Garden Suburb. Better to have what you know you don't like than what you think other people think you ought to like. Rain ceased by breakfast, so I walked along the beach to Tenby, passing a monkey, sitting on a mackingtosh and gazing out to sea with a human fascination and mistrust. In the afternoon picniced with the Machens on Giltar Head, looking at Caldee Island [sic] and St Margarets Island (old convent of six Benedictine nuns) and the tide breaking over the rocky causeway between them. A piercing wind blowing from the rocks against our backs besides all-round drove us to scramble down some very steep and slippery paths to a peaceful pit. During the descent Arthur moaned in a dramatic Welsh manner, and Hilary hiccupped with no manner whatever.

24. Morning arose stormy and pale. I blew the organ in conjunction with Janet while Hilary practised Bach. We were waiting in the porch and reading about St Teilo when Arthur strolled up in the rain. He took us round the churchyard: two palms, two Celtic crosses. Small iron shutters on the outer wall of the church discovered to correspond with Arthur's hypothesis – they were to keep the air from the ventilators. I heaved and urged something cruel over Sukey, then went out for a wet blow on the links. [. . .] Evening at Machen's, where Arthur described drinking raw Absinthe as like swallowing a Bengal tiger.

28. Very hot and heavenly. Bathed at length and lolled on the dunes. After lunch the Machens took me to their ashgrove or ashpit. We climbed over the Ridgeway and swarmed down muddy and leafy lanes to a plain green field. Swooping down from this was a secret green valley with ash trees standing in tiers along the slopes and one green ash alone in the middle. It was absolutely silent. The trees were tall and lavish and looked classical. On the way back as we neared Penally Dorothie who had a sore toe burst into loud lewd song to hearten herself. A woman coming in the opposite direction began to grin. Arthur, walking a little in front, saw this, supposed her to be an acquaintance and ceremoniously saluted her.

September

5. An onshore wind, rather rough. A superb bathe, being shuttlecocked from one steep hummock to another. I Sukeyed during a drizzling afternoon, then we went to have a bonfire and roast potatoes in the Giltar quarry hole. We gathered a great deal of uncared for hay, which we stuffed into mackingtoshes and bore like the rape of the Sabine women, and Janet and I collected a few salt-blasted twigs from a bush. It began to rain almost immediately, and rained harder and harder as we sat stifling and kippering round the fire. When we had eaten our mealies – Dorothie complained with hysterical laughter that I said in a polite voice 'Here's your plate', handing her a shred of sopping news-paper – we trudged home, wet to the skin. I was pleased to sit by Mrs Cole's fire, talking of the small secure comforts of a winter's evening. After dinner more Sukey. She has her Bible and is away with it.

6. Lord Beaverbrook, reviewing The Promised Land (Gilbert Parker) in the Daily Express 6:ix:1928. 'There is no shadow of excessive frankness in dealing with David's love affairs. The murder of Amnon by Absalom, after the Tamar episode, is so treated that the casual reader would hardly know what it is all about.' N.B. The Daily Express has been very much on its toes about the withdrawal of Radclyffe Hall's Well of Loneliness after an attack by James Douglas in the Sunday Express. It was backed up by the Spectator, Lord knows why.

My last day at Penally.

11. Nora sent me Russie's[39] watch in a green case. Very strange to hear it ticking and to remember it ticking from him. P.C.B. came to tea and dinner, complete with preface to a new book. We argued passionately about the aesthetic emotion, the league of nations, whether animals masturbate, whether there is an essential difference between lyric and epigram, whether Mr Stuart was an honest man or a married man – it seemed to come to that, and the Lord knows what else besides. He said one excellent thing: that the difference between classical and romantic music was whether one said: this *is* beautiful, or: that was beautiful. He also asked all unsolicited about my book, and all unsolicited patted William. William and I both flat-headed with emotion – at having our worth properly realised.

21. To Southminster with Charles by the 2.25. To be carrying a ruck-sack and going to the marshes so transported me back to the early

39 'Russie' was a pet-name for STW's father, George.

purity of my manners that Charles found me eating a meat-pie with my fingers on the platform. We found rooms at the Kings Head: a nice kind-hearted inn. After tea in a yellow-washed stable-yard with hanging gardens and a beautiful trellis of tomatoes hanging in swags and garlands we went out past the village War Memorial to the marsh. It was a still sunset, the marsh was dotted with cattle, William chased hares and fell into several ditches to come out garlanded in duck-weed. After dinner we had a long argument as to whether I was right in condemning knowledge as another form of capitalism, about equally damning and deadening; and in the middle of it − I can't remember how it came along − Charles told me the plot of Philoctetes with the foot. 'All art is cheating'.

22. It was perfectly clear and blue and we walked up the village street extremely pleased with ourselves to send Dorothy [Warner] a telegram to wind my watch. After breakfast we filled the rucksack with lunch and walked into the marsh. The road left trees behind after one plantation − then came ditches and low thorn-hedges, fat ochred sheep feeding, sloe-berries and hips and haws. At Middle Wick the road ended all pretence, we saw the sea-wall before us. We watched six teams ploughing an enormous field. Charles said they were like ships. We planted an acorn, carried from inland. The wall-ditch was lined with michaelmas daisy in flower. We lunched on the wall, said little, ate a great deal, lay on our backs looking at clouds, occasionally sitting up to look at William sampling sea-water and sicking it up. The tide was coming in, running round the corner into the crouch, very blue and gay. [. . .] Then we walked inland by a broad chaseway where they were swaling the ditch-sides. Curious to see the fire moving under the reeds, burning its way along as methodically as if a man were there to keep its nose to the grindstone. Then we lost our way through not being sure if Coney Hall wasn't Dean Hall. At last home by a detour to the north of the road, Plumbo-rough, Bovill's Marsh, Ray Wick. These older marsh farms poor and decrepid, compared to the younger lands. Their track scarcely rutted, their big barns empty. The fertility of the sea worn out of their lands.

October

7. Lunched with Victor [Butler] who is setting The First Evening of April. I found it hard to convince him that I really liked the idea of

annihilation. [. . .] In the evening continued struggles with Sukey's epilogue. Wrote like a verbose guinea-pig.

10. Early in the afternoon I had a fit and finished Sukey finally. Then feeling very sick I went to have tea with Dorothy[40], all tempting, fine and gay in my new hat and re-hashed red and black dress. Strange to feel a skirt against the calves of the legs again. At 6.10 I leapt into a taxi and arrived at Wittons in time to eat oysters – Whitstable and Cornish, the Cornish are salt – drink champagne and choose a house with Charles from the framed London Advertiser of the year 1742 on the wall. I wanted a brew-house at Norton Folgate, but Charles inclined to the Manor of Hogstock in Nottinghamshire 'very improveable'. It would be fun keeping it in that state. Then to the Albert Hall to hear Aimée Semple Macpherson.[41] It began with hymnsinging, very flat, but they roused up when they were given a Moody and Sankey, and waved their hymnsheets like a race-meeting – only a wet one with the bookies winning. After the proper degree of Hallelujah had been worked up, A.S.McP came forward. She is very beautiful with a positively baroque golden coiffure, all knops [sic] and curls, and a voice like Australian Burgundy. She told us the story of how she began with a tent in Canada and went on through other tents to the Angelus Temple in California. She also told us her version of the scandal: how she was beguiled from bathing on an errand of immediate mercy – to lay hands on a sick child – wrapped by bandits in blankets and carried off to ransom in New Mexico. How she escaped with her poor feet all prickles and coming at last to a house was told by a man in a night-shirt that it was a slaughterhouse. How on her return vile scandals were spread abroad: and how as a result the membership of the Elim and foursquare Gospel was doubled. O and I mustn't forget her first words. 'I believe in the risen Lord, don't you?' with a conversational twang, just as if he were a really reliable patent food. I adored her. She reminded me of St Paul and Semiramis and realtors. Charles was not so enthusiastic. He would not even grant that she was perfectly artificial, pointing out – shrewd little beast – that when she climbed on a chair – as she did at one point – her face lost the spot-light.

19 After seeing Dorothy I came home to receive Herr Kurt Fiedler,

40 At the nursing-home where she had given birth to a daughter, Bridget, on 5 October.
41 The American revivalist.

of the Insel-Verlag. A tall, lean, fair-haired hollow-eyed young man. At first his politeness slightly overcame me, for when I had drunk a little sherry and was thinking of another sip, he sprang from his feet, took the glass kindly and firmly from my hand and set it on the mantelpiece. At first we politely talked literature, but by seven-thirty we had started on the war; and it was curiously as though we had not seen each other for years and there was a great deal to tell. Yet we had been near enough. For he was a prisoner in a hospital at Dartford while I was making shells next door at Erith.[42] He escaped from Donington Hall by forging pass-ports, but his friend with strident scars caught the station-master's eye at York Station and they were nabbed. His armistice day. Everyone down with influenza, the noise of children shouting, the sergeant-major coming in to say – Well Captain Fiedler, we can shake hands now. Influenza clouding everything, and very ill and miserable he lay writing poems of hate against England. Other things: the excitement of flying over the English lines and seeing the enemy, almost like seeing a rare unseeable animal; the awful embarrassment of taking prisoner a covey of English officers playing cards in a dug-out. 'We looked at each other and could think of nothing to say'. His mother was an English woman, married to a long line of German pastors: when he got back she was dried up, past feeling anything, bewildered and fussed by starvation, regulation and deflation. His theory of the war: that it is like a work of art, unstayable, obeying its own laws, a master-piece to itself; and live men and dead men and courage and rancour all powerless but to one purpose: to be constructive units in that work of art. We dined at Martinez, and talked and talked. And about England too: and he liked my explanation that England was an old gentleman who married late in life and married his cook; and our colonies are the fruit of that marriage, which is why we can't abide nor abear them. Then we came back, and talked still. It was amazingly satisfactory to empty out so much and to receive in its stead. He wants to do Theo[43] for the Insel-Verlag, and I gave him my spare copy of Mr Weston. Just as he went he suddenly became a foreigner again, clicked his heels, bowed from the small of the back and gripped my hand till it hurt. And so departed a really well-met hailfellow.

---

42 STW worked as a shell-machinist at the Vickers munition plant in Erith, 1915–16.
43 T.F.Powys (1875–1953), author of *Mr Tasker's Gods*, *Mr Weston's Good Wine* and *Unclay*, among others. He was the third son of a family of eleven children which included the novelist John Cowper Powys and the writer Llewelyn Powys, and lived in East Chaldon, Dorset.

November

20. I must not forget Naomi's[44] proposed evidence (called but not chosen) in the Well of Loneliness case. Do you consider this a suitable book for general reading?

I do. I consider it most valuable. I was for many years mistress in a girls school, and if this book had then been available I should have given it to read to any girl inclined to sexual perversion. I should have said to her, 'Let this be a warning to you, first, as to what sort of treatment the world will mete out to you if you go on like this; second (Naomi wriggled and bridled) as to what sort of book you may end by writing.'

23. Naomi Royde-Smith and Doffles[45] came to lunch, and the King is ill. Naomi attributed this to the gale having blown off Richard Coeur de Lion's sword outside the Houses of Parliament. After they had gone I planted 36 wallflowers, three ribes, two syringas and two forsythias in a hurricane. The sky was swept with inky blackness and frantic sunsets, and the wind blew the trowel out of my hand, and as fast as I patted earth down the rain washed it away. The height of the gale drove me indoors, but only to rush onto the balcony to bale out my window-box with a tea-cup. I worked into the dark, with one unblown-out star sometimes looking on. When I came in I suddenly realised what a debauch of emotion I had been having, and how I am changed. For when I was young I got my emotion from having things done to me . . . by art or by love or by eloquence, now, by doing things myself.

24. I grew a tail to my red evening dress, and arranged flowers to greet Dorothy [Warner] and Bridget, who arrived rather travel-worn at 6.30, having left Shropshire at 10. We drank sherry in the nursery, while poor Bridget wailed on mother's milk. Sherry in the nursery seemed so very Victorian, with a high fender and a smoky chimney and all, that it occurred to us that we must be the last of the Victorians. But later in the evening at the Chetwynds' party I met a purer specimen . . . the little Countess of Seafield, so like Victoria that as I sat by her on the sofa I felt myself growing more and more like Lord Melbourne. Betty Chetwynd is going to Ireland for a month's repose, with a Bible and a box of gingerbread nuts. The first puss-willow

44 Naomi Royde-Smith (d. 1964), the novelist and then literary editor of *Westminster Gazette*.
45 Dorothy Wadham, a friend of STW from the Bach Cantata Club.

boughs for sale. Very shocking to have them at this end of the year, but I bought them all the same. Talking of Charles, Oliver said that his college – Oriel – is renowned for its civility. It is a lovely thought to think of them all passing each other the port and conversing with traditional urbanity. Oliver fried sausages, and I said it was the one useful thing every man learnt at his public school; but Dorothy said they also learnt to poach eggs in condensed milk over a gas-jet. I have more medlars than I can eat. It seems a waste that I cannot have Schiller too.

26. Beautiful morning. I went for my first walk with D. and the pram. In the afternoon I finished my lesser patchwork and entertained Augusta Chetwynd to tea. Milford[46] has turned down the Whyte Magnificat. I looked up the contract and found, as I thought, that he had no right to. I *should* like to fight this, but with these men on my hands I don't suppose I have a chance of rousing them from their club armchairs. Bridget upset in the evening. A thought on death. I can reconcile myself to believing in a time when I shall not make tea, listen to Bach, etc; but scarcely to a time when no one will. I suppose this is why one wants an heir . . . it is a grateful response to all the things one has loved. 'Here is someone to go on loving you', one would hope to say.

29. I lunched with Bunny at a nice quiet public in Theobalds Row [. . .]. He was wearing a dark suit which gave him a slightly rakish air as if he had been to a funeral. I told him about this diary kept in his apocrypha, and he said he led too full a life to keep a diary, also that he would have nothing to put down in it. No Love[47] has reached 1914 – six more chapters must bring it to 1924 and that by January. 'Then I shall re-write it'. [. . .]

Then I went to Bumpus's[48] to see the Everard Meynell library. The book I wanted, The Saints Nosegay, was sold, but they still had the G.M. Hopkins letters to Coventry Patmore. They are written on all sorts of paper, and most curiously inconsistent in layout. Sometimes he will jump from 1 to 4, then down the inner leaf; or up the inner leaf, or 1, 4, 3, and 2 sideways. An odd disorder. They are mostly very long, very eloquent, with many author's erasures. He writes with great thoroughness and conscientiousness. No contractions, even *infra dignitatem*. In the middle of pages of line by line comments on the Angel[49] –

46 Music publisher.
47 David Garnett's novel.
48 The bookseller.
49 Patmore's *The Angel in the House*.

very minute, commas, and what not – he will go off into long soliloquies on vanity in women, prosody, impiety, obedience in the marriage service, cases of conscience – or produce flashes like this, which I copied from a letter about C.P. and Newman. 'We are rational and reasoners by our false reasoning as we are moral agents by our sins.' Apparently Newman had had a fit of 'I am a worm and no man' and said man was not a rational creature. G.M.H. didn't like Newman. He is very unsparing – rates C.P. for Honoria's vanity in A. in H., and even more severely – for saying in a letter about a dead Master Patmore, that he hadn't worked hard at college but had got his degree quite easily none the less. Nothing to boast of, says G.M.H. Do not say it, unless as an act of reparation. After these thorough dealings, each successive letter opens with a most humble and exquisite I was afraid I had offended you for life.

They are the letters of a wild lonely mind, soliloquies – harping on like his own lark, an angel in a cloud even among his 500 examination papers. But an angel with a vial: a ruthless Catholic, a passionate priest. The more I read, the less I liked, the more I loved, the less I esteemed, the more I revered. But above all, lonely, talking to himself with the fluency of thought long practised in solitude. He composed too – and found the piano so unsuitable to his polyphonic leanings. 'Perhaps you know that the Latin writers exchanged and misapplied the words areis and thesis (his greek hand ever lovelier – very round and silk-twist, very drawn) Areis is properly the rise of the foot in dancing or of the conductor's arm in beating time, thesis the fall of the same. Areis is therefore the light part of the foot, I call it the *slack*; thesis the heavy or strong, the stress.' He quotes Purcell, Full fathom five, in a very clear musician's hand.

I was fascinated by these, and longed to buy them. Instead I went to Woolworths and bought nails and a tea-pot. When I got back, I found my pass-book, so its as well I didn't. Spent the evening on Sukey's proofs: six octaves.

December

2. Woke very late and immediately proceeded to prepare lunch for Victor. He brought me two new songs – *In the Valley* and *The Maiden*. Technique. I said people only needed it to do things that they didn't feel were worth doing; which is more or less true. In these days when everyone has so much, it is positively dowdy to be brilliant. We

had lobster omelet and chicory in cheese sauce. Then I rushed William out to Kensington Gardens just as the keepers began to cry 'all out!' We had great fun in the dark by ourselves, carefully shying away from gates, but we were shepherded out at last and nearly run over.

22. Shopped for Dorothy in the morning, having got up late. In the afternoon I suddenly found myself with poem. I have not written one since April 29th. It was odd to be shot into that feeling again, that deliberate trance, without a word of warning. After I had finished I sat up and took notice. First, that though I thought I was writing it fast, at any rate without any discontinuities of thought, I had sat at it for over three hours. It had seemed about three quarters of. Then, how it sprang. A week ago, I took Aline[50] to Charing Cross, did notice the Cross, did think of Eleanor, but said nothing. This afternoon I took down Eleanor Brougham's book and opened it at E. of Castille. At the first sentence the whole scheme of my poem leapt at me.[51] But the root idea goes back much further, fifteen years or so, to Teague's[52] letter about the procession at Fontevrault, how they don't notice: 'ghosts of the future we are to them'. Afterwards I was consumed with thirst, and drank tea and lemonade in the evening with Dorothy, who said of her stepmother in Beckenham: 'She doesn't only know all the best people. She *is* them.' Children carry to either parent for understanding the side of them they have inherited from [the] other. The inherited father turns to the mother, and vice versa. I think this is true. And I should have put down yesterday a lifelong conviction to Teague that love is impossible between equals. One must have a little condescension or a little awe.

25. A heavenly morning, clear and golden. I went to church at St Marks Marylebone to please the Machens. A very high church, and the goings on at Mass reminded me of nothing so much as of charades, for they kept on hurrying into the vestry and coming out in new clothes, a pea-green tippet, or father's bowler. Suddenly at the Incorporation six or seven dregs of humanity went up – female, aged, decrepid, halt or maimed, to kneel humble and grotesque among the three priests in their plump white vestments. It had the beauty of a Rousseau painting, and I was extremely delighted with it: so even from the Christian point of view I suppose I did not church-go quite in vain.

50 The Warners' Danish au-pair, a granddaughter of the painter Gauguin.
51 'Queen Eleanor', *CP*.
52 Teague was her pet name for Percy Buck.

1929

January

14. Packed, went to the White Star and filled up 36 questions,[1] including Can you read – which moved me to a purely irrational fury – Have you a hare-lip? Are you an Anarchist? etc. Sat in the evening with Dorothy.

15. P.C.B. took me out to lunch, and comforted me for going by sincerest sorrow at losing me. In the middle of final packing I suddenly sat down and wrote a poem. [. . .] Dear Apocrypha,[2] I must leave you behind. Like everything I love best I cannot take you to America.

March

8. I woke with a thud to discover the gale over, the ship speeding. A sunny, blowing day. Elling Aanestad[3] and I picniced, leaping up with sandwiches and claret to see land, the high French coast-line. Presently we saw towers, buildings, a beech-clump, a hay-rick – and were at Cherbourg. There was a smell of land in the wind, sea-gulls flew round us, weed and wisps bobbed in the water, fishing-boats were around, the sun shone on the yellow limestone breakwaters and remembering the word 'jetty' I had a sudden sensation that I was in some way returned to my native language. We sighted England about 5.30. – Dartmoor, a grey dome, with hairy rain-clouds streaking up from it. It was dark by the time we got into the Solent and running in on low tide to save her prestige and arrive to the day, the Aquitania ran on a mud-bank. Long pause, enlivened by looking at the Leviathan and Majestic but not much enlivened. I felt like a dreg struggling to escape down a blocked pipe. The customs dreary and dreggish. I could find

1 Preliminary to a two-month visit to New York City as guest critic of the *New York Herald Tribune*.
2 STW's name for her diary. See introduction p. viii.
3 An editor with W.W. Norton & Co. They had met on board ship.

no porter and Mr Clarence Terhoun's ten-foot back in a musquash coat seemed to be ever before me. But a forward young Canadian official saw my plight and put me through. In the train I began to loose my worries. I thought of everyone dead in turn and then massacred the lot. Broke down and waited for an hour at Wimbledon. Remembered Wordsworth sonnets. Waterloo at 12.15, very dark and difficult. When I got to 113 the house was dark. Frozen with despair I opened the door. Nothing. 'But I will sleep' I thought, and gestured like Siddons to the taxi-driver. Then William barked, ran downstairs, looking so like himself as a baby that he seemed almost a changeling. Then Dorothy, then Oliver. [...] We sat in their bedroom and I heard all, Bridget in a home, the Dane returned with a nervous breakdown, the pipes all bursted, sufferings unspeakable. At intervals I exclaimed: How heavenly to be home!

17. Teague to lunch, most suitably to S. Patrick's day. We had a small lunch and a large fire, the room smelt of hyacinths, I felt at last as if I were really and truly home, not just hurrying through a dream of it to wake in New York. There was leisure to stretch oneself, feel idle, agree that Colles[4] profited nothing, admire one's happiness. Yet the poor Teague's statistics of his days sounded dreary enough, wandering about Plumsted [sic] in the rain, waiting for another board-school to open to his inspection. [...]

28. [Chaldon, Dorset] I left my suitcase at Mrs Way's[5] and walked up with my grapes ... a poor missile when the shepherd's dog set on William. Violet appeared looking like Death. Theo in bed with flu, Doris[6] with a septic sore throat. She herself not fit to be up, and the pump dry.

I sat on Theo's bed. Fortunately *The Countryman* had come with the first instalment of the Grave-digger's Diary, and knowing how this title would please Theo I led him on with tit-bits of centenarian scandal till he began to talk about Kindness in a Corner.[7] 'It is really your story, Sylvia, for it was you who told me of Bishops' aprons fastening behind with tapes'. Presently he said 'Do you think it would be proper for me to introduce Death into a story?' 'Very proper', said I. And he talked about his first thoughts for a story to be called *Unclay*.

4 H.C. Colles was the music critic of *The Times*.
5 Where STW was lodging.
6 Violet Powys's niece.
7 T.F. Powys's novel, published in 1930.

Then, having also visited Doris I went downstairs to help Violet with the tea and await Charles. It was with great relief I saw him, staggering under a packing-case. After he had heard the sad news, and unpacked a pineapple saying: 'Here's your Easter hat, Violet', we walked together up to W. Chaldon.

29. [Good Friday] Theo was better, and angelic with a thermometer in his mouth, which declared him normal. Then C. and I walked up to the Five Maries.[8] Scarcely a leaf out, only the elder bushes and the young hemlock sprouts. Angus Davidson,[9] staying at Chideock, turned up to tea. Could he see Theo? Violet explained that Katie[10] was an undesirable visitor, 'dancing and clapping her hands'. 'Well, Violet, I am not likely to dance and clap my hands', said six foot of mild languor. So up we went. Charles and I saw him to the Rats Valley fence, and heard him jolting down among the rabbit holes in the darkness. Then we walked back, slowly, examining the stars. Arcturus opposite Orion, I must not again confuse it with Aldebaran. Nearing the house we heard gulls screaming on the coast, and a strange noise that we thought might be a cliff-slide; but it recurred and recurred, it was only the sea.

31. Angus to tea. Conversation turned to the Stranger's[11] funeral. Theo explained how he had brought back cousin Father Johnson to wash his hands. The spareroom door locked, as Molly[12] and Doris had hidden there from the mourners. 'I said, after trying the door for some time: "Just now we *do* have locked doors in this house." And it shows how well-trained they are in that religion. He took it as some very ordinary matter.'

April

1. Very cold, and trying to rain. I darned some enormous holes in Theo's stockings. Finishing with pride I showed the mat to Theo.

---

8 The five ancient tumuli on a ridge to the north of the village.

9 (1898–1980), a close friend of the Woolfs, who worked for the Hogarth Press 1924–7 and was later Secretary to the London Artists' Association.

10 Katie Powys and her elder sister Gertrude lived at Chydyok, an isolated farm labourer's cottage in the downs, about a quarter of a mile south of Chaldon.

11 'The Stranger' was Walter Franzen, an American friend of Llewelyn Powys and Alyse Gregory, who died on 26 May 1927 after falling into the sea from Bats Head.

12 Valentine Ackland (1906–69). Her baptismal name was Mary Kathleen Macrory Ackland (shortened to Molly), her married name Mrs Richard Turpin. Valentine Ackland was the name she adopted in the late 1920s, when she began to be known as a poet.

Very nice, my dear. I believe I have just such another in the pair I have on, said he encouragingly. Francis and I fetched the beer, admiring the ship's portrait nailed to the bench at The Sailor's Return. While we were out, Theo suddenly exclaimed to Charles: That old rogue, Dickens with his Pickwick Papers! No doubt he thought he had a coarse brandy there which would suit all tastes! N.B. Theo always refers to writers as 'that old rogue'. That old rogue Powys! Walked up the green valley and home over Rats shoulder before tea. After I retired with Francis and his poems, which are very promising.

Theo by today was beginning to air all the whims and languors of convalescence. Making him eat was like beating up the prices at an auction.

3. After breakfast I went to Winfrith to telephone to Francis, and then home (the longest way home) via the heath. It was burned black as Sodom and Gomorrah and a great many cows were walking about as restless as picnicers. In the afternoon Theo would walk with me. A cart came through the field-gate just as we were started. Theo turned like a hunted animal into the rickyard, saying: Aren't you afraid of those terrible great horses? I said, Suppose I was afraid of those terrible great mangolds ... And those shouting voices – would you pass them? I had never before quite realised that Theo's caution is based on true fear. We talked of fear – the fear of death. 'I never go to bed without thinking of my death'. You, said I, should rather pray:

> Teach me to live that I may dread
> My bed as little as my grave.

I believe you are right, said he. Then we talked of *Unclay*. What would I do with it. I began with death's scythe hung at the inn door, flashing in the summer sun. 'Unfortunately I have begun the book in October.'

17. [London] Teague came, worn out, he declared, with finding room for my five books. So I told him of the 'bumper' volume of Jane Austen, which had caused the Homeric[13] to list 25 degrees to port. He took me to dine at Paddington, where we had the most delicious apple fritters. We fought about the St James Station statues,[14] and about foreshortening. In the end, it was relief to turn to Einstein and Eddington, whom I could pretend to argue about. Un-relative time = cause

13 The boat on which she had gone out to New York.
14 The controversial Epstein figure groups, *Day* and *Night*, commissioned by the London Underground.

preceding effect. And if the hammer must strike the nail before the nail goes in, that is irreversible. But I did floor him once. For he was saying that women always argue to prove a theory true or untrue, rather than to find out truth. Nothing would delight him more than to be convinced that everything he thought wrong was right. Even religion, says I. I should be overjoyed to learn that Christ was God. And would you be overjoyed to learn that God spoke through the Bishops? But it was a poor single bullseye.

22. I spent the afternoon and evening painting, and ironing curtains, which came out all wobbly at the hems. Then Oliver and Dorothy came in from the play, and we had a long discussion which began with feminism and ended with copulation. And before this I had a lovely interlude of idleness, drinking coffee and reading Northanger Abbey like a lady. (N.B. Elinor Morland in her tomboy stage played baseball.) I was very tired, and so I changed my clothes and tidied myself 'to earn my coffee'. That was my thought, and for a moment I was pleased to reflect how strongly my self-respect can drive me on to that kind of act; and then on its heels came the thought: 'As I grow older I shall feel more and more tired. Shall I go on self-respecting, will it be an arid habit, an effort, a thing of the past?' It is things like that that make old age a frightening thought.

24. Cooked with great zeal, finished and despatched an article on Stendhal to the H.T.[15] and began Erich Maria Remarque's Western Front.

Today I saw an advertisement of water-cress – a picture of a little girl thrusting some into the maw of her grandpapa at table. Underneath were these mysterious words: A True Incident. And in the Times was a snip about some workmen repairing a church in Gosport who broke unwittingly into a vault. Smoke was seen coming from it, the fire-engine sent for. When the vault was opened a coffin burst into flames and vanished in ashes and powder. Things like this make life very pleasant.

May

2. Committee at R.C.M.[16] Ram[17] indisposed, and not there. Fellowes[18]

15 The *New York Herald Tribune*.
16 Royal College of Music.
17 The Rev. Arthur Ramsbotham, a fellow member of the Tudor Church Music Committee.
18 E.H. Fellowes (1870–1951), musicologist, choirmaster of St George's Chapel, Windsor, and editor of the complete works of William Byrd. His scholarship and industry were largely responsible for the revival of interest in the composers of the English Madrigal School.

unfolded portions of his American guarantor, and was very anxious that everything should be done for efficiency's sake: which meant one ms. going the round for criticisms, and four people fighting over it at the meetings. I obstructed for all I was worth, and nothing was settled. [. . .] Then home to finish Wooldridge[19] chap iii, which I did at 11.30. Then I had a rapturous meal of tinned salmon, salad and cider, and fell into bed.

9. In the morning a very serious letter from Bunny, saying the blue dog in The True Heart had led me astray, but inviting me to lunch. It was a dreadful moment to walk into the Verdi restaurant and behold him quite grey. He smote me very friendly . . . and produced the image that the reader is a top, whipped round by the writer. If there is a flaw in the surface the top wobbles. He wobbled slightly when Mrs Seaborn struck Sukey but recovered himself – the Covent Garden wobble almost unseated him. He hated the Melhuishes, didn't think much of Queen Victoria and as for dogs, they will be my undoing. 'Why are you looking at me so naughtily?' 'Because I am being convinced of my sin. It shows in my face, my naughtiness.'

A sad set-out in the Graves–Laura Riding Gotts[c]halk menagerie. She had set her affections on one Geoffrey Phipps [Phibbs], who took refuge at Hilton. One day Mr Hardy transmitted five telegrams. Cannot live without you, Laura, etc. G.P. went off for a last night in the old bed. Robert and Nancy[20] brought them early morning tea, Laura followed this up by some Lysol. Phipps was so sleepy he confused it with Milton. 'You can drink as much as you like of that.' 'Oh. It only hurts, does it?' said she, and jumped out of the window – followed from the floor below by Robert Graves. The next telegram was to Bunny. 'Laura dead. Arriving 1.15.'

11. Cold and grey. Spent the day looking for the Machens's rooms in Amersham, and could find nothing suitable. The beechwoods were a vivid watery green, all the larks were singing, and I felt in one of God's greyest moods as I sat in a cornfield eating cold ham with William.

[. . .] Rigel – a star infinitely brighter than the sun, and *blue*. I should like to see it. Today I heard the cuckoo. So obliging to have one bird that everybody can hear for the first time.

19 STW was helping Buck revise H. E. Wooldridge's *The Polyphonic Period*.
20 Robert Graves and Nancy Nicholson, his first wife.

13. Teague came to dinner, and listened with admirable meekness to my attempts to expound Mr Eddington's views on limited space. Lo and behold, astronomy was a witheld love . . . so witheld that I had never stumbled on the secret passion. Rigel came in most conveniently, for there is never any privacy about my intellectual amours.

26. [Elsworth, Cambridgeshire] Another lovely day. We drove into the fens and lunched by the New Bedford River, where Wobb read aloud Mr Thorpe's poor opinion of Ruskin's views on church towers. [. . .] Then through Sutton in the Isle [. . .] to Ely, an enormous ghost on the horizon. The Norman nave and transepts are marvellous. The absence of balustrading to the clerestory and triforium gives a sense of giddy and ruthless height. But while I was still enjoying the octagon Wobb murmured that I mustn't suppose jaunting about to Cathedrals was all pleasure, and led me firmly through the chancel and the two little chapels – the second one has renaissance bawdry, very well at home with the stone-cutters. It pullulates and festers with ornament. Disgusting overgrown traceries sprouting out of three gas-pipes, vesicas with so many tucks and rumples round them as to look like a pattern of guts, everywhere carving put on with the greatest possible extravagance of handiwork and the least possible expenditure of thought. It gave me an acute eye-ache; and I had to be taken out, to look at the green park they keep for a close, the little chapel with the tiled floor of Adam and Eve boxing with the serpent, and the beautiful Bishop's house. The Lady chapel is whorish too; but its proportions are fine, and the trimming isn't quite so all over the place.

We stopped again by the Bedford river, and lay in the sun. Mrs Tomlinson and her sister came to dinner, and I discovered that dinners follow the order of creation – fish first, then entrées, then joints, lastly the apple as dessert. The soup is chaos.

28. Mrs Keates came, after a collapse from too much holiday-making, poor darling. I dined with Daphne Muir, and wrote two thousand letters. Ian Parsons[21] wrote to tell me of a friend of his dining with A.E. Housman. He (the friend) deplored modern novels. A.E. said: S.T.W. writes good novels, and added that mine were the only modern novels he cared to read. Such a compliment left me feeling perfectly quelled.

21 (1906–80). He began work at Chatto & Windus as art editor in 1928, became a partner in 1930, Director in 1953 and Joint Chairman in 1954 until his retirement.

June

22. In the evening I went to the Machens – the last night in the old home. The producer of Porgy was there – a charming creature who reminded me a little of Padraic Colum, but he was a Padraic that hadn't finished fermenting. Then Augustus John came, and I could have no other eyes. He is very long and lean, his hair is grey, his eyes are bright, he was rather drunk, he is the Ancient Mariner. I told him as we walked away he must go back to Wales. He was born in Tenby, but he can't go there, he explained, because his father is still living, and a little difficult. He was still afraid of him. He is perfectly young still, and with a sad drunken youthfulness and guilelessness he embraced my waist in the taxi, and begged me to go to Wales with him. He has been so busy painting that he has never had time to leave off this childishness. I loved him terribly, he is so simple, intent in the true world, astray in the real. It is awful to think that this youth must go down quick into the pit of senility.

25. Teague arrived with a large bouquet of yellow roses for colour and white carnations for smell, and also, alas, for a farewell lunch.[22] I told him about the Dublin prints at Ken. House, and he asked about my youthful visit to Ireland. It rained continually, I said, and we were always being driven in waggonettes to see things. Waterfalls, I suppose, said he. He was tired with cramming all the L.C.C.[23] sourness up into a ball, and needed a longer time to be uncrumpled in than there was time for. We ended with a rather agonising walk along the Park to Marble Arch on the way to his next job. The best night stroll in London, he said, was his letter-posting beat past Buckingham Palace, over the flamingo bridge in St James's Park and home along to Queen Anne's Mansions. It is just like the English to keep some grass at what is the heart of their Empire.

26. I went down to see the Machens at Amersham. We had tea in Shardeloes Park. It was a perfect day and the hay was pink lustred. William chased young pheasants and stared at the swans. Walking up the hill in the evening the haywains were moving about the field, and the children in bright dresses stood watching then. How sorry I am for people who must leave England. Janet remarked on how nice country sparrows were. We saw a young missel-thrush, plump and silvery-speckly.

22 Buck was going to South Africa, where his son ran a fruit farm.
23 The London County Council, for whom Buck worked as a schools music examiner.

July

1. A day of doing jobs, redeemed by the White[24] service at the Abbey in the evening. My precamur, the Magnificat – it was entertaining to hear my added cantus part careering about that roof on 18th cent. wings – the Miserere, and O Praise God. Hearing my version, done for them, incorporating both 4 and 8 p[ar]t versions absolutely clinched my conviction that the 4 pt is an adaptation, and very base at that. It was pleasant to see the Abbey all glorified for Robert's honour, and I liked the procession with the banners walking above the heads of the congregation like giants, flowing down the ambulatory and dipping their heads under the arch. [. . .] The White sicut erat beginning with that low F in the bass is exactly like the world beginning to turn round in chaos and hum like a great top. It spins faster, and the pitch rises. I also examined the new St. James's Underground buildings.[25] The Epstein Night is superb, Morning I am not so sure of. The projection of the lower part of the belly and the receding thighs gives one an uneasy feeling that the foreskin has been stuck onto a sketch elevation of a behind by accident. I like the building extremely. There was a crowd looking at Morning, it had only just gone up today (been unveiled rather) and I was pleased to hear several of the critics were men on the job, and taking a craftsman's interest in it.

9. [Lavenham] While I was in the post office, the machine beat out a telegram announcing the Garnetts. I walked up the fields to the drift before lunch, and smelt tailors needles and saw marestails growing in a fallow field. After lunch they arrived very brown in their new Ford. I took them to the church, to see Ray's[26] ancestor, Thos. Spring, and did the honours of the scaffolding and the tower. Dear Mr Slippertoe performed for us on the handbells, and rang an illegitimate summons to church. The view was very large and pale, it was exciting to see the wind rippling over the cornfields. Looking down on the churchyard, the graves seem very few, and far between: the flat grey back of the nave-roof. [. . .]

They were extremely funny in church, walking about with an air of the utmost suspicion, as though at any moment a Bishop might appear and lay violent confirming hands on them. Indeed, as we were about

---

24 Robert White, the sixteenth-century composer whose music STW edited for vol. v of *TCM*. From 1570 to 1574 he was organist and choirmaster of Westminster Abbey.
25 See note 14, page 33.
26 Ray Garnett, née Marshall, David Garnett's wife.

to enter and the Reverend Flabby's voice was heard addressing some tourists, they started back as though a lion roared. Going up the tower, Bunny asked me if the tower were consecrated; 'for if it is, I shall have to hold my hat in my mouth.'

19. We [STW and Geoffrey Webb] put up a picnic lunch and drove west. First Long Melford, where I noticed for the first time, and the third time of seeing, that the scroll pattern with the writing on it in the Clopton chantry is exactly repeated in the lady chapel, only there the poetry has been washed off. Then Cavendish. Three bells were lolling on churchyard grass, the treble bell hung from a scaffold and is very sweet and round with a spit in tune fourth harmonic. However it must have taken some getting, as the rim is much scratched. The tenor (I imagine) bell was cast by John Warner in London. 18th cent. The church was well-kept except for a very scurfy choir-boy's comb and brush, lying like a votive offering under the photographs of the late rectors. [. . .] Then we drove up hill and down dale to Stansfield. It has a ravishing churchyard on the further slope, with a view into the valley in between some very old ash trees with trunks like strands of grey hair. A pathway of black yews leads past two tarred black barns. Inside was a young man in his shirt-sleeves practising the organ. He only took his hands off the keyboard once, and that was to scratch his head. A very old man was silently blowing for him, his behind sliding in and out of sight. In the churchyard we passed a man who said it was hot. It was. Then we came to Wickhambrook, and drove for a very long way along a very rough road waiting for the drive of Giffords to begin. It is own[ed] by a gentleman called Foss, to whom Wobb had a card of introduction. But Mr Foss was not at home, and while Wobb went in to write a note I looked at the brick and timbered house, and at the dog-kennel, and at the apple-trees, and listened to the silver poplars making a noise like rain. The flowers are very gay, the lawn cut in stripes. Everything bespoke it the house of a single gentleman.

Then we drove to Lidgate, looking for a brick butt end of a cottage Wobb wished to photograph. I watched him nervously, prancing on the extreme edge of a deep ditch with his head in a black bag. Then back to Wickhambrook church, so poor it had never been restored, inside it had a roof (wooden) which Wobb said was late, and I wished it had been too late to ever arrive. Wobb did another photograph, of its ribs, and I sat in a holy hay pook, like underneath are the everlasting springs.

20. In the evening as we were sitting in the garden, the sky began to darken, the tops of the trees to stir. Then the taller flowers began to sway, and a horse whinnied. The colour of the cloud was a fierce pale intent copper colour, and it was curious to see how it bleached the lilies, and made the roses look a silly pink. As the storm improved we drove down to the bridge and watched it. It extended two thirds round the horizon, and every now and then the lightning would fling out further like a hit behind the wicket. There was both sheet and ribbon lightning, both very gay, leaping like lambs and whisking like fishes.

21. During the night William was overcome with the heat and at three-thirty I took him for a cooling down walk. It had rained a little. The sky was clouded, there was no visible sunrise, light seemed to be inherent in the air. The cornfields were sleeked over with a film of mist, the trees very still and remote, the birds' voices very loud and shrill – and incisive. The whole effect was sensuous and heathen and wicked. I have never smelt meadowsweet and mustard so strong, and a steaming hayrick almost forbade me to go nearer. When I got back William was much restored, and quite prepared to undo the rector's bitch, and we both fell asleep. The morning paper told us of a tidal wave on the south coast.

August

1. [London] Still raining passionately at intervals, a s.w. wind and no guardian grasp on blood and brain at all, which pleased me, for I am happier without it. I did contrive to enjoy the day a lot, in spite of devoirs d'escalier all the morning and devoirs social all the afternoon. Having Betty White[27] a little on my mind I took her down to Amersham in the afternoon, and walked her into Shardeloes where the hay was all cut and the trees extremely noble and navy blue in the rain. Then to the Machens. Hilary had just caught a pike, with an expression, he said, like a church worker. I dined there, and admired the water butt and drank some very strong sherry, so that the other occupants of my carriage had to run after me reminding me of my umbrella . . . The world is full of people like that. [. . .]

Theo's commendation of my pine-apple 'Almost as good as tinned pineapple.'

27 Elizabeth Wade White, b. 1906, a young American woman STW had met on her trip to New York. She was engaged for many years on a study of the poet Anne Bradstreet, and published a book on that subject in 1971.

5. [Wayford, Somerset][28] A hysterically fine morning, bright blue and bright silver. I drove by Mr Spurdle – who is getting quite reckless: every now and then he went all out and overhauled a bicycle, to Chaldon. Theo, Francis and Violet all looking well, the front kitchen repapered and marbled with a feather by Mr Miller, Theo in a new grey suit, Francis in an orange shirt, four young geese behind a new wire fence. Theo walked me up to Middle Bottom by Rat's Valley. Wolf Solent; he thought John[29] kept teasing his characters, not like 'an honest Sadist' but lecherously. [. . .] We lay in the sun, talking of stars and atoms. 'When did you read this book, Sylvia? Was it at night?' I also told him a little about The Vain shadow,[30] that it would be grim. 'Quite right my dear. It is time you wrote a grim book.'

On the way back we talked of Mabel[31] whose Littleton had left her on the morning of her silver wedding day, to go jaunting. Theo had consoled her with some remarks – so he said – on the hard lot of wives whose husbands stay hale and hearty whilst they wither. Had Mabel still a mind to be merry, did she in thought follow Littleton into his clubs and hotels. (He spoke as if educational conferences were one round of bawdy-houses.) How can such a woman look in her glass and still expect to be desired? Ovid and Montaigne. I said that I now was beginning to wonder if I should be any better. Theo faced about – 'You will never be like that, Sylvia. You could not be.' Why, Theo? 'You are broad-minded. You are interested in the stars.' He thought it better for the wife to be much younger, for one can make allowances to a child. With my mind on my own affairs I said, What happens when the child is grown into a disappointing woman like another. 'But she will always keep some childish tricks, some absurd way of behaving. He will recognise that.' Then we came into the sheepfold at Rat's Barn, full of fat young lambs like impudent cherubs, and I wondered if to any shepherd a sheep kept some lamb's tricks.

After lunch we sat in the garden and Theo began to speak of *Unclay*. 'Do you think one could be prosecuted by the law of England for saying that Lord Bullman had a poet among his ancestors?' I admitted the gravity of the libel, but begged him to take the risk. He told me the plot – an honour he has never paid me before. He also spoke of that

---

28 Where STW was staying with the Raymonds.
29 J.C. Powys (1872–1963), the novelist, Theodore's elder brother and author of *Weymouth Sands*, *Wolf Solent* and *Autobiography* among others.
30 A novel, in progress but never completed.
31 Mabel Powys, wife of Theodore's brother Littleton.

sad Mr Taylor. 'It is a little terrible to be with him. One sees him in his pit of despair and feels that one has but to take a step to be in it too.' Mr Hayhoe is to heal the harlot by reading her Jane Austen. It was old Mrs Pitman who told Theo he should grow a beard. Why? 'I daresay she had a fondness for beards. Perhaps one of her husbands had had a beard. Then she died, and I cut it off.' 'Did you lay it on her grave.' – No, my dear. She was buried in Southampton.' The gentleman who drove Tommy to Chaldon and immediately drove him away again. 'Tucker? – No, not Tucker. Violet would remember . . .' but Violet was out of the room. 'Well let's call him Tucker.' 'It is too good a name for him.'

Someone had sent a copy of Genesis[32] to a learned rabbi, who said: 'Either this man has read all that has been written about the Bible, or he has read nothing.'

26. [Little Zeal] Finished *Practical Criticism*.[33] I think he boggles rather unnecessarily over the business of accepting the poet's doctrine – i.e. the resurrection in the Donne sonnet. He makes the distinction of accepting emotionally, rejecting intellectually. I think the process is more of an identification. The reader must for the space of that sonnet *become* the writer: for this accounts for much subtler digestions, matters of tone, Cowper and Herrick and so forth, cases where no amount of accepting one way and rejecting another will run. I think the most indigestible poets are the purely lyrical, poetical ones. Very few people can swallow Herrick. He is so small they bolt him in pellets, c.f. Rose Aylmer, too. But if the reader can more than less become Herrick, he has swallowed the poem, has it, momentarily, in his belly.

28. In the afternoon I put on a spurt and murdered my husband[34] to the tune of nearly two thousand words. I had done some of it before, but in spite of that it left me rather breathless. When she was in bed Nora became rather concerned that I don't keep any accounts. I said it would be a waste of time, and as I should have to buy an account-book it would be waste of money too. She doesn't either, bless her heart. Then she began to wonder how Hope[35] contrived to have young men offering her marriage the third time they saw her. I said that ingenuity could do anything though personally I directed my ingenuity to ward

32 *An Interpretation of Genesis*, by T.F. Powys.
33 By I.A. Richards.
34 In her story 'Elinor Barley'.
35 A female relation.

them off from doing it. Still, said she, the third time. Oh, said I, that's nothing. I have often had young men who didn't propose to me the third time they met me. Then she became reminiscent and spoke of a Mr Rice (a Mr Wilkinson) who proposed to her the fifth time he met her – so she ought to have some idea how it's done. What's more, he came to tea with his trousers unbuttoned.

September

3. Finished *Building in Stone*[36] as far as Christendom is concerned, but just at the end it turned nasty and threatened to extend to Karnak and Beth-El. Otherwise I haven't a word against it – it came as slick as cream, and twelve lines all in the subjunctive gives it an *air noble*. Subjunctives are noble; they wear their antique blazonries of *be* and *were* as having a right to them; like armorial bearings where they belong.

9. [London] It was very hot and clear. I sat down under the plane-trees where Teague had refused to visit the Albert Memorial; and suddenly I saw their trunks and branches all mottled and serpentine where they had cast away the works of darkness. This enraptured me into a seventh heaven within me; and I lay on my back looking at blue sky, red-gold and pure green leaves, lime-coloured new flesh and purple and tête de nègre old, while the wind blew down happy days next year on to me and I was too certain of this present joy to mind trying to catch them. There like a bird I sat and sang. An antidiluvian old lady with a bow streaming from the back of her hat sat sketching nearby, two little girls played dodge round a tree, and I heard the swish-swish of dead leaves sweeping. It was a moment for ever. Spring cannot bring me the same ravishment. Spring is strictly sentimental, self-regarding; but I burn more careless in the autumn bonfire.

10. In the afternoon a frenzy of more poetry fell on me, and I was still writing when the telephone awoke me to the fact that I was dining out with Charles in twenty minutes. I was dressed by the time he came, but perfectly demented, and told him I was like the Victorian ladies who hurry home from a lover to meet a husband's eye and pour out the children's milk, still quivering, with not a grain of powder to veil their shameful radiance. We dined at Boulestin's to bon voyager the

36 Poem, *Modern British Poetry*, ed. Louis Untermeyer, 1936.

Raymonds. Sole, delights of partridge, peach Melba and Meersault. It was a pleasant party, and by some cataclysm of nature both Raymonds were well. The story of Blanche[37] collecting an author. She emerged from her private bathroom in a grand neglect of pyjamas and said: Now, Mr Deeping, I want you to put your English end in my hands.

21. A slightly grubby day, dealing with Wooldridge. In the evening I finished the text, and began on the illustrations. Looking for one from the *Gradualia* I happened upon *Quotiescunque manducabitis*; and at the bass entry on *mortem* Domine I was cast into such a rapture of knowing the man's mind that I was ready to count all the damnations of scholarship as nought for the sake of that one passage alone. O William, my dear, I said. And William chow woke up, not knowing the William I addressed had been bones for three hundred years.

The proof of *Some World Far from Ours* arrived. Quite a decent plain page, and large type, very becoming to my monosyllables.

30. I woke at 6.30 vaguely aware that something was happening; and saw the ship[38] settle down in the dock, and fell asleep again. When I woke it was to think that any perspective as one walks down it, begins to frighten one . . . and a perspective in time does its own walking, absorbing one's detachment in a gradual willy-nilly till at last one is there – at the end. As it had rained, I cleaned the poor drought-stricken garden, remarking that now it had at least the ornament of a meek and quiet spirit, even if everything else has died from it; and then I had my hair washed and spent the evening putting positively the last finishing touches to positively the last t.s. of Wooldridge.

October

1. Teague came to tea. He got himself into the house with the wash, and when I came on him in the hall he appeared so perfectly life-size that I began to feel that I had been in Africa, not he. How are you? said he. Rather dirty, said I, too surprised to be anything but immediate. I should have added that during a great part of his absence I had been perfectly clean. The pheasant-shooting effect[39] was perfectly unnoticed

37 Knopf, the American publisher.
38 Bringing Buck home from Africa.
39 This refers to an entry on 27 September in which STW links the opening of the pheasant-shooting season on 1 October with Buck's return. She seems to have been contemplating breaking off their relationship, which had become problematic.

in the greater shock of discovering how massively intimacy can just sweep one on as before. And there was the reflecting piano-top accepting the umbrella, calm as a glacier; and it was only when he said Kiss me, that absence, his share of it, roared in my ears for a moment. After he had gone I wrote the old dream of the winter thorn into a poem, and got on with the elegy. During the night it poured with rain, and the wind shook autumn into the air.

2. I dealt with jobs and letters all the afternoon, and then fell to work on the quantum in Jeans' Book.[40] For one minute I felt quite alert about atoms in orbits being energy, being a going-round, and so filling the entire orbit. But what I want to know is, why when a superfluous electron is shot off does it get shot into a larger orbit, since there is less of it? Does it take greater energy to go round in the lesser orbit, or what? Perhaps if I read this same chapter daily for seven weeks I shall begin to understand some more tufts of it. [. . .] I forgot to say that yesterday evening I explained economic processes to Dorothy, particularly capital leaving the country of its production, with a speciousness which shocked even myself. My God, I ought to keep a lenten fast from lucidity.

3. I found Bea also enthralled with the new Jeans. We agreed how lucky we were to get in on the ground floor of a science like this, while the discoveries were still so new to the discoverers that they hadn't had time to make them an incomprehensible perquisite. In fact, they are still making them clear to themselves, and the dogs can eat of the children's crumbs.

4. Instead of going to bed I wrote *In Egypt*, and today I was again brought to bed – in Whiteley's, too, of all places, of *More Joy*. My fingers drop myrrh. I really am writing a poem a day. Of course I am doing nothing else, and M. and F.[41] languish, and I have no clothes to face the winter in, and most of my time is spent on the floor. But what fun!

13. Lunched with the upper Warnerium, and stayed on till the muffin-bell and tea. After tea Bridget appeared and romped on my lap like a short stout salmon. It is not a person one feels moving when one holds a baby: it is life, compact, darting, incalculable.

40 Sir James Jeans (1877–1946), the astronomer. His book was *The Universe Around Us* (1929).
41 A lecture on 'Mystery and Fantasy'.

23. My God I have this day: given lunch to Hilary, signed the Woburn Book[42] (530 sheets) prepared damson pickle, washed my hair, and dined with Victor for a Delius concert. Victor was sickening for he knew not what, and the Delius concert rather bored us. The truth is, we neither of us like music enough for that kind of thing. [. . .] Saw Herbert Howells[43] coming away, who pleased me and saddened me all in one by asking what I was working on now 'music or t'other thing'. 'Perhaps you will be composing again when you are eighty-five?' I said that at 85 I should be taking up monumental sculpture [. . .] Delius should never be shown a word. Words dry him up. He was there, blind and paralysed, bowing his rather bird-like head to the applause. The performance was sympathetically encored, and each time I thought he would crash the blind brow into the gallery barrier. We may not be a musical nation, but we *are* so kind to dumb animals. When he was alive and kicking, who gave a damn for Delius?

24. It was a ravishing sou'westerly morning. In the afternoon it poured with rain and I shopped at Barkers, buying a pineapple and half a stilton, and thinking how scandalously easy it was to be kind, when one had money to spend. In the morning I had decided that henceforth I only cared for easy loves. It is so degrading to have to persuade people into liking one, or one's works. Let be. Then I made damson pickle three 2lb pots. Charles fetched me to dine at Boulestin's with Vera, Chatto and Richard Hughes.[44] He is tall, rather over-shouldered, beginning to go bald. He has eyebrows that meet, and eyes the colour of mackerel. [. . .] Then we went back to Charles's where Hughes talked about American children – the five children who on a night-bathing expedition were piqued at not being able to drown him, so they took his pyjamas in the car and left him to walk home naked. [. . .] And in a Chicago taxi they discovered they were sitting with their feet in a pool of blood. But seeing the driver's face they decided not to mention it, tipped him largely, and hurried indoors. I am not quite sure about him, he is just slightly oppressive.

25. We started, Charles and I, by the 2.30 for Chaldon. At Bournemouth I began to invent nouns of collection for the church, a conglobulate of Bishops, a plethora of deans, a hash of curates. It was a

42 *Some World Far from Ours*, no. 18 of the Woburn Books, published by Elkin Mathews & Marrot, 1929.
43 (1892–1983), composer, organist and teacher on the staff of the RCM from 1920.
44 The author of *High Wind in Jamaica*, among other works.

stormy evening, and the yellow aftermath of sunset behind the Pur-
beck hills, with tattered cloud-hills rising above it. We seemed to be a
tighter fit than ever in Mrs Hall, what with Charles's goose in a packing-
case and William's winter coat. Theo was looking extremely well,
Violet very much the better for having Dick[45] home. He is a cross
between them, Violet's eyes and carriage of head, Theo's upper-lip,
and Theo's nose set on at Violet's angle. At tea Theo began to speak
of the customs of the Masai, Dick's African tribe. Their name for a
bastard: the child of the fireplace. Although he is well in on Unclay, he
projects another novel with that title, a story of the early years of
Christ. 'I do not seem to have made enough of him. I shall let him be
married in the end . . . marriage instead of the crucifixion.'

27. Theo, Charles, Dick and I set out for the stone circle by West
Chaldon. Theo remarked how very different the farm was under the
rule of good preaching Mr Cobb. No cursing or swearing, and no
barking dogs. We passed a bull in a field, and came to Holworth and
the haunted valley, and the view of Moigne Down Farm, where Nelly
Trim lived, and then baulked at the stone circle and sat under a stone
wall instead, where Theo asked Charles about war-time rum, and said
how sad it was that Liam O'Flaherty should have to spend all his
money on women in order to have material for his books. Home by the
five Maries and a flock of Mr Duke's thriving Dorset horns. At lunch
the goose and Trinity audit ale. Charles asked Theo if Mr Weston
drank it. 'O no, they wouldn't give it to him. He is not a member of the
college'.

November

1. [London] After dinner I read him [Buck] Modo and Alciphron.[46] He
said it was entirely different to anything I had written before except
perhaps Peeping Tom, 'better-oiled' were his words. I should have
thought 'more-vinegared' myself, but while one can keep some tally
of one's thoughts, one doesn't really know what's happening to one's
technique. Then we began on Jeans. I was being all grand about
discontinuity, when he collared me low with how about imagining a
car travelling discontinuously from one milestone to another. When
he was at Rondebosch he rang up a man in Cape-town and heard just

45 Dick Powys, Theodore and Violet's elder son.
46 Poem, *Modern British Poetry*, ed. Louis Untermeyer, 1936.

before he rang off, the Cape-town twelve o'clock gun. After he'd hung up the receiver he heard it again in Rondebosch. How many guns did he hear? I said, one gun, but two times heard it. He incited me to write to Jeans about electrons being goings-round, which after he left I did.

4. Dorothy's and Charles's birthdays. Mrs Burroughs senior came to cook the dinner, which was: Munzcazine, lobster au gratin, hare stewed my way with prunes, onions and pickled walnuts, baked apples and stilton. Drinks, *Nuits St George*. Arthur came early to mix the punch, but alas without Dorothie, who has a stinking cold, and is rebuked by him for saying there is Peace in Zion when there is no peace ... Diners were Oliver and Dorothy, Charles, Arthur, Bea, David and Vera, vice Dorothie. During dinner Bunny expatiated to Bea about how he flew. Looking down on the 'well-brushed fields' and thinking: How tidily they keep their fields in this part of the world; a spiral above Hilton and the village elms rushing up out of the ground. I also heard something about parachutes, but at the time I was discussing Welsh waggonettes with Arthur. Punch and cake guests were Chatto, Mrs Leyel,[47] Ian and Victor. I talked to Bunny about flying and to Victor about de la Bruyerè, and to the Raymonds about Francis. In the end, when most of the people were gone I complained to Bunny that there was a conspiracy to put us to bed together, our names always appear together, we might have Mr Wells as a bolster. 'You should resign yourself as I do and look on me as your cross.'

7. I finished *The Return*,[48] and had a letter from Jeans explaining that electrons a) are definitely particles once they are outside the atom; and b) that their energy, as dispersed by radiation, can scarcely be reconciled with my going-round theory; though he admits that in the end something like a going-round reading may be found to be the right one. Their outward (radiable) energy greater than the orbital. Now I want to know if a centrifugal kick wouldn't supply this for long enough for the electron-life.

20. I finished the *Woman's Song*[49] and in the evening I took Daphne Muir to the second Courtauld concert. The Bach suite in D. Anton Bruckner's 8th symphony. The conductor was Otto Klemperer. He

47 C.F. Leyel, the herbalist.
48 Poem, lost or re-titled.
49 Poem, *CP*.

was very good and played the Bach overture, as Daphne said, as if it were by Beethoven. Before the air there was an outburst of anxious coughing. He waited, grew impatient; turned and scythed the audience with such a look. Then he went to the air played twice as slow as ever I have heard it before, and extremely ode on a grecian urn-like. The Bruckner I found hard to stomach. It is all mental music, weak and scrappy and forever going up to climaxes and down again like someone industriously practising scales. But the scherzo is good – all the best true wandervögel german romantic manner, a great deal of satisfied repetition and a ravishing oboe slippery tangle in the trio.

As for the slow movement, I thought it would never end. It was like being in such a slow train with so many stops that one becomes convinced that one one has passed one's station.

During this concert I had a curiously strong illusion that I was looking at myself of eight years ago. She was sitting in the upper circle, very white faced and black-haired. She wore horn-rimmed spectacles and a slightly odd severe grey dress, her hands were red and chillblainy: each time I looked up it was a shock to see her still there. She was not good-looking, but she had a kind of disdainful corpse-like vitality which was impressing; and I suppose I was like that au temps que j'étais belle.

December

18. I read Graves' *Goodbye to all That*. It is written in a hectoring tone of voice that makes it rouse all the hairs on the spine of one's prejudices, but the war-part is good, and it has a lot of jokes with a tang. In the evening I dined with the Hendersons.[50] We dined on the model's throne, squatting on cushions. The effect was quite genteel till Keith got up to fetch a plate; then he suddenly appeared to be walking round the table on stilts. Afterwards some more people came in. A very beautiful young creature called Jebb who was entertaining about Victoria[51] and Harold Nicolson passengering to Teheran. V. very grandiose and romantic, driving the car very badly with Shakespearian confidence, and waking up H. – uncomfortably asleep on three restaurant chairs – with 'Hedji I should like a little intelligent conversation'; and Clifford Bax[52] with a chin beard and a voice to match, and

50 The artist Keith Henderson and his wife.
51 Vita Sackville-West.
52 (1886–1962), the playwright and lyricist of many successful West End musicals.

his wife who had just incapacitated her telephone by upsetting Vichy water on it.

27. Sex in literature, pace Virginia's new book.[53] The moment you say how women are to write well, you've given away your case, as a feminist. It should be, how people are to write well. And personally I mistrust this ambivalence of sex idea. The best male authors are undoubtedly the most male, great writing seems to establish itself in periods of marked sexual distinction, periods of sexual fusion produce only good writing. So why aren't the best female authors to be the most female? However, I haven't yet read V. W.'s book.

53 Virginia Woolf's *A Room of One's Own*.

1930

January

7. Charles has three new Wyndham Lewises: a scarabish one, a large pencil drawing of a woman in an upholstered chair, and a ravishing pencil and wash torso, the head tilted back, and a breast dangling like a ripe pear, and all the body curves ranging away like a mountain landscape from the mons Veneris. I liked this the best. It is more vital than his usual work: I almost mean less intellectual.

12. Cold and raw. I lunched with Victor; Lucia and Roger Senhouse[1] the other guests, and we had a very Anglican round of beef. Roger said that the latest theory about cancer was that it was caused by some ultra rays from a star which is moving nearer to us. All right as a theory, but a little careless of the time a star takes to move – it can't have got so much nearer in the last century of cancer getting so much commoner. Still, I'd rather have a wild guess than a tame one, and this is all very like my dear astrology. After lunch we sat over a cross-word with clues from Browning. It did not raise our opinion of Browning's poetry.

13. [To] 44[2] to see Bea's gifts, and say goodbye to Miss Howe. It was curious to be talking to Bea about walls and gas-stoves, and all the rest of the evening I was haunted by the wood in the Chilterns where we lunched long ago – the day of the chestnut avenue and the scrubbed apostolic table in the inn garden. Rather sadly I said goodbye to my nymph. Her wedding-dress was spread in her bedroom – an enormous rectangular ghost, like an aeroplane, shrouded in tissue paper and dust-sheets. Then on to a committee at Charterhouse. 8cto royalties, a limited liability trust for the rotographs, fount, etc; and dealings with providence.[3] I nearly fell asleep several times, and couldn't get my poor old Ludford through. However, I have wedged in Collins I hope.

1 (1900–70), bibliophile. Later a partner in the publishing firm of Secker & Warburg and Lytton Strachey's last great love.
2 The Howes' address in Lowndes Square.
3 Providence, Rhode Island. Fellowes was trying to get backers for further research.

It was a sad clear moonlight night, with a very blue moon on the wet pavements.

22. I spent the whole day with belly ache, trying to keep my mind made up. It was an ornery looking day, just such a day as a thing having begun on, might end on. [. . .] And while I was dressing the bell rang, and I let Teague in to the slaughter. It all began as I had arranged, and I said my piece, staring at some dead freezias on the mantlepiece; and when I had got through it I sat down, and began to sweat and tremble, my temperature going up like a bean-stalk. There was a very long pause, and then he said 'I have never set down' – he went onto say, to think us out, but if I hadn't been beyond all hysteria it would have finished me. He talked for a very long time, very slowly and gravely, and I couldn't make anything out. My own theory of his Freudian distaste he scotched, but there was something that kept mounting; and presently he was saying words like 'complementary' and 'incompatible' and mentioning the Sitwells and Rina and so forth. To think, as I did, that I must lose him for such trumpery smashed all my dignity, and even when he comforted me I still felt it was only pity for the lost one. But [it was] when he had said 'I will try to be less –' and I had answered 'O but it isn't', and heard him laugh at this lucidity, that I began to live again, and felt redintegratio amoris. [. . .] At last we had dinner, and the rest of the evening did justify my instinct in getting down to it, for it had the serenity and kindness I had despaired of. So it is all right for me – but I am not so sure about him, poor lamb, his farewell being 'I don't leave you miserable?' O equity, injurious fiend, as though love were a question of parity like Naval conferences. I can't, though, love less even to preserve our delight. But I don't feel, now, that it is my job to fuss any longer. I have cleansed my bosom – what a lot of quotations – and if I am more loving, he is more affectionate, so there's our parity.

26. At breakfast I began to read Mr Fortune: and suddenly my old fancy of him fetching up at a house in the pampas blew off the page like a wind, and followed me into the park, so that I walked in an easterly cold rain discovering how hot the hour of siesta can be and hearing the sunflower seeds crackle for miles and miles. After tea I sat down and wrote 2000 words – all most injudiciously, everything that David [Garnett] says is, and himself proves to be, so fatal, for I have no notion what will happen, so far I only see him asleep outside the house, and afterwards driving through the rain in a leggy Ford to the church,

where there is a new Immaculate Conception and an old wooden virgin said to be carved from the timber of a ship that came from Spain. Lord help me, what a queer start!

29. Some more Timothy.[4] In the evening I went with Ian [Parsons] to a Courtauld concert. Bruno Walther conducted. Beeth. symphony no 1, the scherzo superbly played, and then Mahler's Lied von der Erde. An interminable dreary soup, mawkish and morbid at once. The last movement was the only one I could have listened to, and by the time it came I was too weary to notice anything except a passage of much-worked downward phrases just before the contralto came in with her unsupported bit about the stirrup-cup. When she had said Euring for the sixth time Ian and I laid our heads on each other's shoulders.

February

4. I can remember nothing of this day except that I have written the whole rhapsody on Spring in Rebecca,[5] and have been shattered by doing so. I am still so moved I dare not think how bad it may be.

5. And I lay awake jumping like a newly-killed trout till 5 or six, when out of the dark I suddenly heard the comforting noises of the milk being set down on the door-step.

7. [Chaldon] There were eggs for tea, the Gilbert Spencer on the wall, Francis looking much smoother and better. After tea we walked up to W. Chaldon, Theo and Charles talking of Lucretius and Epicurus, for Theo had been reading a book about them. I must ask something, 'When did Lucretius live?' C. told me – 50 B.C. or something – adding that he was murdered by his wife when he was about 50. Theo, mezza voce, '43. And she was not quite his wife. Some girl'. A piercing wind faced us when we turned back. It was clear moonlight, but a faint mist was on the shoulder of High Chaldon. At first it seemed to me that the mist was my sorrow and I stared, feeling that this would explain everything if only I could attend. Then the mist was me, transiently obscuring the outline of a lasting grief. I had just settled this when Theo put his arm round me, and carried me back against the wind, still talking to Charles about Lucretius, whom he liked extremely, he and his atoms.

4 'The Salutation', story, *Sal.*
5 Her long poem in heroic couplets, *Opus 7*.

Francis had advance copies of his poems for Charles and me, our names together on the dedication page with a flight of flat fish underneath.

9. When I asked how he [Theo] had slept he said: I was fretted for a little while thinking about that journey;[6] but then I thought that you would not be starting just yet.' During breakfast I felt he might have shown a little similar compassion; but he bore us off on the long walk he had designed. The wind was like a knife, I ached all over with cold, and Charles grew painfully muddy and wore a sort of trench face. Theo between us proceeded at an inexorable saunter, asking our opinions as to the exact quarter of the wind, pointing out the first celandine, and wondering how it came out in such weather (perhaps, Theo, it can't help it). The ice in the brook, the glittering green of the water meadows, the staring white of the flints, the emptiness of Winfrith street. Just before the Red Lion he took off his hat: Charles inclined his face an angle further into the blast and caught my eye. We turned into the heath lane, and passed Mrs Trent's cottage where she sticks pins into bullocks' hearts, and along the Tadnol track. Theo was right, it was warmer on the heath and I began to thaw: but as at the same time I began to faint, and could see nothing except a black zig-zag shot up from the glittering landscape, I do not remember much of all this, till we came to Tadnol, where I recovered enough to see Charles intensely smitten with this watery place.

15. [London] A cold, pretty day, very young – bright sunshine one minute and next everything black and growling. Dorothie Machen to spend the night. We dined off mulligatawney, chicken with almonds and an orange soufflé that was out of breath, but made a good custard. After dinner D.M. and I fell to duets, and the house rocked with our attack of the scherzo and finale of number 5. We also played the scherzo of number 3 a great deal better than most horns do. Unfortunately after an interval of songs and D.M. doing the Bach G mi Fantasia and Fugue with masterly faking, our hands were out and we botched the 1st's Finale like two schoolgirls – Dorothie referring to squemiquavers. In the end we put the little Dorothy [Warner] to bed with a mustard plaster: standing over her like two Lady Southdowns with the black draught.

19. In the afternoon I began an article on Moll Flanders, very much my way with an account of county towns. In the evening a committee. We

6 A proposed trip to Hadrian's Wall.

dismissed the first half of the Byrd Cantiones, most uncomfortably, standing on one leg while Fellowes mastered the ceremonies. Afterwards he told us how Nicholson had got 5000 copies of the Gibbons evening service photographed by Novellos . . . apparently a gratuitous gift of our rights by Mitchell, damn him. Ram was highly indignant. Poor Teague sat bearing it as best he could, he had already had Ethel Smyth for lunch; but he plucked me one rosebud, admiring my black ring. I do hope these wonders will never cease.

20. More domesticity than I meant. Valentine [Ackland] came to tea, and told me how Anna de Benson Barry, an old flame of Theo's, came to tea, and was handed a plate by Valentine in trousers. 'Is this your elder son, Mr Powys?' Theo, just like that, 'No.' Violet, in a loud aside: 'Theodore, you shouldn't have said that.' Nothing more was said and A. de B.B. went off free to think it out as she pleased.

21. I woke thinking how pleasant it might be (presently) to be resigned and middle-aged, and so on. No doubt if I had stayed in bed it would have been. But it was a grim morning, no Mrs Keates, a great deal too much washing-up, icy cold, my hands like nutmeg graters and chaps on my nerves, and Dorothy sore-throated again and very miserable. Applied Tidman's Sea Salt. He has given up the old picture of the strong man in the saucer bath. In the afternoon I strove for hours with Moll[7] and a lead hand. Dined with the Raymonds, feeling ghastly. Home to more Moll. Lord, what a 'orrible day.

March

2. Finished Maurois' Byron – liked it much. I am now almost exactly the age at which he died. I feel very childish in comparison. I envy him, beyond anything else, so thorough an exploration of his own feelings. I sat wondering how it would be if he were to walk into the room. I became more and more dubious of his finding anything to please him till my eye fell on William. He would certainly love William. [. . .] Yet I believe I have felt as acutely as he, but in a much smaller field, and along one line.

4. [D.H.] Lawrence is dead, and The Times sniffed over him like a Sunday school inspector. Joan Hudleston[8] came to tea, and in the

7 The article on Moll Flanders.
8 STW's cousin, daughter of Frank and Winifred Hudleston.

evening I dined with Elling [Aanestad] [. . .] We went to The Applecart. The trouble about it is, it seems to me, that the whole essence of Shaw's mind is reasoning faculty, and applied to politics the thing is a misfit. One knows all the time that politicians couldn't err and muddle as clearly and logically as he makes them err and muddle. It is like turning such a brilliant light onto a tangle of wool that one doesn't see the woollen tangle at all, only some peculiar rhythm of curves. That was why we liked the second scene best. Sex is a more logical subject than politics because in sex people do more or less know what they want.

5. I went with Teague to a board-school children's concert in Wandsworth. We went in a tram, and came to a Wesleyan hall and walked up and down a very respectable dark street of semi-detached residences which frightened me. The children sang folk-songs and a Bach piece, and a Brahms piece. They looked very clean and happy, but there was a curious sort of gravity about them when they sang. When they were allowed to talk they made an extraordinary shindy like rooks or seagulls. There were also a band of fiddle-players from Catford, very good indeed. Then we went back to Victoria and had supper in an A.B.C.;[9] and Teague tried to convince me that there was no difference in kind between the Meistersinger overture or a Shakespeare sonnet and a letter; and I tried to convince him there was; and both of us thought our arguments incontrovertible, and neither of us changed our minds in the least. I find it hard to accept that he should prefer this as an evening's entertainment to coming here; but every day defeats me a little more, and though I am bewildered, I feel that there is nothing to be done, only take it for granted, let go, be silent over the loss of it since I am too sad and middle-aged for whistling. At my door I had a curious moment, looking at the stream of light from a window, and the stream of bulk sweeping up in the trunk of my ailanthus tree and being able to equate them in my mind as being equally substantial. I try and warm my heart at Rigel, but it is too conscientious, and a poor disembodied theoretical heart, not worth warming.

27. I tead with Elling and met the Geoffrey Keyneses,[10] whom I liked extremely. He keeps his radium in the wine-cellar. Teague came and

9 Restaurant.
10 Geoffrey Keynes [1887–1982], surgeon and bibliographer, the younger brother of Maynard Keynes.

took me out to dinner. He had spent the morning at a levee, wearing black velvet with silver buttons and a cocked hat and a sword – hired from the Army and Navy. He must have looked a perfect cherubim. I told him the next step would be a knighthood and then he would have to wear three ostrich feathers on his cocked hat. He believed me, and turned pale.[11] There was nothing to eat or drink, which I call shabby. At least they might have been offered elevenses – a glass of milk and a bun. Talking of all the Handel oratorios he had conducted when he was young he was gravelled for another title, and fell back on Hiawatha. My health improved so rapidly under his attentions that it was slightly scandalous.

April

11. Elling came to say goodbye to England. It was a very beatific warm April day, and we had tea on the balcony. I dined with W. Empson. I had gone a little frightened, fearing it might be a party of intellectual young things; but it was as though he had foreseen that I was a timid grandmother, for when I arrived it was to a very untidy room, with bottles and books on the floor, a delicious smell of frying, a saucepan of twopenny soup on a gas-ring and Mr Empson cavalier seul. So nothing could have been pleasanter. He had learned to cook because his sister runs Girls Guides, which led me to refer to 'the meteor flag of England'. He was extremely flabbergasted with the adjective, no doubt it would seem more striking to a scientist. We argued quite naturally about Eliot, and Windham Lewis [sic] and Richardson, and I found myself making gaffes quite comfortably. The argument was that I complained W. L. had A Message. He was of the opinion that poets should have a message, should be in touch with real life. I didn't see then, but I do know [now] that they should be so much in touch etc. that they don't want to alter it. It is a drawing-room or study contact with real life which wants to move the groundsel off the landscape.

18. [Chaldon] Violet's birthday. Her first act had been to see how the cake looked by daylight. Theo and I went the walk under the Five Maries, as it was blowing hard from the north. I saw the first cowslip in the Drove,[12] the winter turf was a-dazzle with separate blue violets,

11 Buck was knighted in 1936.
12 The road from the village up to the Five Maries.

the blackthorn was coming into its milky-way bloom here and there, otherwise knobbed with those curious tight buds like little pellets of cheddar cheese. Passing the leafed elders Theo reminded me how on our last walk that way I had discovered that even the first knobs of winter bud contain the elder leaf odour. Then he put me through all my relations – a sorry show I fear he thought them, but a mad great aunt raised me slightly in his esteem. Home by High Chaldon. [. . .] At lunch we heard how Katie had quarrelled with the carter at Chydyok. His wife joined in and Katie threw a blacking tin at her. Gertrude rushing to the riot tripped full-length and cut her leg. Then Katie had gone to wail in Valentine's bosom. This made it proper that I should visit Valentine. It was queer to walk into Tommy's cottage[13] and see *Lilies* and *George and Mary* on the wall not a day older, with the palm still sprouting from George's epaulette. The piano was gone, but there was still a mouse in the cupboard.

19. The Silver Wedding-day. A cold rainy morning. Theo and I walked the lower Five Maries again, and sat a cigarette's while in the chalkpit. We talked little, but chiefly of death. Theo described it as falling in a moment into that pit, that abyss beneath the lowest, the earliest forms of life; back to the state of the rock. He spoke also of the pains of death, the struggle to breathe, the suffocation, and mentioned that when he was a little boy he had been half-smothered, experimentally, by a brother with a pillow. I said he might find Death's hand less experimental. For the rest we spoke mostly of the lateness of the spring – no swallow yet. As we neared B. C.[14] we met Valentine going home. 'She'll get wet' said Theo with the satisfaction of a scientist glorying in a certain truth. Meanwhile the sitting room had been dusted, and was closed to the public. Theo began 'Violet, Violet. Have you taken Herodotus? I must have Herodotus.' *Violet*: Theo, you musn't go into the sitting room. Theo: But Violet, I must have Herodotus . . . Violet dear, where is Herodotus? *Violet* Your slippers are under the dinner waggon. Theo was still crying like a lost lamb for H. when I unshoed and crept in in search. He took some finding, and I had decided that if he could not be found I had best take the H. Bible. Lunch was eaten rapidly, and immediately after Theo went for a little walk while Violet and I cut sandwiches. At five the guests came. Mrs Ashburnham, Mrs Lynch, her daughter Eve (who very nicely brought

13 Mrs Wallis's, previously rented by Stephen Tomlin.
14 Beth Car, T.F. Powys's house.

us an apple) Mrs Hardy,[15] like a very sad subdued seal, looking out of her face and then diving under again, Miss Wolsey[16] in a particoloured shawl that made me feel like a timid mad bull, Gertrude, Lulu and Alyse,[17] Valentine – 14 in all. They stayed till 7.15 or so. I talked my way round like an epidemic, and Lulu told me about Jerusalem, how very Christlike it is, and about Pompeii. I quite liked talking to him, because Alyse was at the other end of the room, and could not browbeat us into culture. Theo was very Jovian. V. told me that at one moment he made a rude gesture at the whole roomful, and then immediately looked out of the window, becoming absorbed in High Chaldon.

20. [Easter Day] Immediately after tea we had the regulation cricketmatch – two laths and a walking stick batter's end. The doorscraper bowler's – a very green tennis ball just the colour of the nettles. Rules a catch first bounce counts, a ball over the face is out. The team consisted of Theo, Francis, Doris, Valentine and myself. Theo was superb – he is a cunning slow bowler, with a habit of shouting Ho! just before delivering the ball – very intimidating. In the field he has a Jovian gesture of standing fixed with his arm out, as though compelling the ball to fly into it. He also, as a bat, has a nice way of mentioning to the field while they are scrabbling among the nettles and ash boughs and hens – 'I'm running'. It was a marvellous game, with William in the middle of the pitch, except when I was in. Then, whenever I made a run he bounded beside me. In the midst of it the Wolsey undulated down the steps, announcing that she was going to see the lambs. Violet came out later. Where's Miss Wolsey? *Chorus* Gone to see the lambs – an alibi (obscene) for the rest of time. However, she couldn't find them – but she went to Todd's Barn and heard a cow breathing 'which was very delightful'.

21. Walking up the drove Violet spoke of Miss Green's cottage for sale, and I became so inflamed that we must turn round to get the key from Mrs Goult and go over it. It is very nice inside, sizeable rooms, a good back-kitchen and stairs. No water, but a water-butt. The garden is charming – snow on the mountains, clove carnations, lavender,

15 The poet's widow.
16 Gamel Woolsey (1895–1968), an American poetess engaged in a love affair with Llewelyn Powys.
17 Llewelyn Powys and Alyse Gregory, who at this time lived in a cottage at White Nose, about a mile away from Chaldon on the cliffs.

apple and cherry trees. Valentine and I in independent first thoughts approved the partition which would make it possible for one person to escape upstairs unobserved whilst the other dealt with the door. (This could be perfected by a thick staircarpet and felt slippers always in readiness, as at the door of a mosque.)

25. [London] News that Mr Goult is buying the cottage to sell at a profit. And that twenty-five other people are buying it too. This came in a very pretty letter from Valentine . . . too, and too early, grateful.[18] This habit of being the Royal Family seems to fasten upon me. In the old days when I strove and schemed to please others, I didn't. Now I have apparently but to wag my finger. Alas, it is my means, not me. Then the extent of my goodwill worked out at two and sixpence. It's not that people are mercenary; only that they are human beings, and must butter their parsnips.

May

10. The Machens came in the afternoon, bringing me a bunch of savoury herbs. Sad tales about Hilary's stay with Cousin Lambe, where the housekeeper commanded him to carry all the coals, and accused him of stealing an alarm-clock. I told Arthur my theory why St. Paul speaks as he does of women: that he knew only church-workers. He agreed that St. Paul's language was needlessly restrained.

13. I went to see Valentine, to tell her of Mr Duffett's valuation of the late Miss Green. 'This is a small undesirable property, situate in an out of the way place and with no attractions whatever'. Such words whetted and confirmed my desire (also a valuation of £65), and in the evening I wrote to Symonds telling him to make an offer.

22. In the evening I was rather redeemed by a good beginning to the 5th section of Rebecca. Into my heart an air that kills from that far country blows. I am quiet, I might almost think myself resigned; but it is fear which keeps me quiet, fear of how much more it may hurt. I have lost initiative to be happy, my instincts, my roots into life, decay. I could still be saved at any moment but I shan't be, and I can do nothing about it myself.

18 STW had proposed buying the cottage for Valentine to maintain as her 'steward'. Valentine's landlord had thrown her out on suspicion of his property being sub-let at a profit and Sylvia, who had used it rent-free, felt partly responsible.

31. A rainy day, stuffy and still. I went down to Amersham for tea, and a pair called Haselden arrived for dinner, and left soon after. [...] Arthur talked of books. When one had finished the poor things one must seek out rascally publishers. When I think of him I am almost ashamed of my own easy conditions, with Charles to make all secure and easy for me. I walked up the hill in the almost dark. The may and the Queen Anne's lace were mists of white, swathes, winding sheets, the trees enormous and solid in the heavy green, the air still, moist and sultry; yet there was a whine of a wind somewhere, a frightening sound in that scented unmoving voluptuous dusk. After in the depth of the wood, to be conscious of the tree shapes overhead changing, dissolving, like cloud shapes, as I walked on, I took off my glasses, and D. suddenly saw that I was like her mother. These faces one has never seen that possess and look out of one's own.

June

4. This evening it struck me how odd it was that I haven't taken to drink. Once, I should have supposed it the certain thing for me to do, yet in these six months I have drunk less than for years. As I am now writing the Faithful Bottle passage in Rebecca this thought rather chills my hand.

21. [Lavenham, with Percy Buck] Teague was an instant success with Mr Slippertoe, knew mutual campanologists, said: Any trouble with the parson? – as one says any trouble with greenfly?, and told of the T.C.D.[19] bell, for which's silver the duty alone came to £200. But now I come to remember, all this took place after dinner – before dinner we just sat and I sewed on my quilt, and he thought it very clever of me, and then fell to trying to make theoretical hexagons with the Evening Standard. I cut out several experimental ones, but they all turned out octagons or rhomboids. Of course he did it eventually, but we both felt properly impressed by the New England matrons who found out or worked out how to construct them with one snip. It was a very hot evening, and we sat in and out of dressing-gowns. [...] Then we went to bed. As he fell asleep his breathing under my head lengthened out exactly like the Atlantic showing her paces on the second day out. A blackbird just by the window squirted – there was no other word – into song, then cocks and cuckoos. I stayed till half-past four, then we

19 Trinity College, Dublin.

were really becoming too sleepy. I went out into the garden. It was very sweet, bees humming with a warm noise among the snap-dragons. I lay down on the grass – the dew was so thick and cold that for the first minute it was like going into the sea – and looked at the pear-tree and a sky of pale milky blue mottled with high, pale pewter-coloured clouds. But at last I began to shiver and think of agues, and went in. To lie drowsing in the dark thinking that before long I should see that beautiful austere remembered sleeping-look.

26. In the afternoon I sat groaning my way at the beginning of the last agony of Op. 7. I even got to the stage of getting on to my feet and beginning to pray. And if I am not careful I shall begin to believe in prayer, for in the evening I had an illegitimate riot over the coda. Dear Mrs Parker gave me a tea-pot, and a mortified vase for my cottage, and now addresses me as Miss Warner, dear. O a holy heavenly day, even the agony was enjoyable, since I could have it all so securely to myself. Alas! only one more blossoming isle of solitude!

27. It blossomed, and was too happy to have a history.

July

8. [London] A letter from Anselm[20] suggesting to me once more a seat on the P.M.M.S.[21] Council. The old gentleman who had previously vetoed me as a female had asked Anselm if he might unreservedly recant.

10. All the limes are out, William wades complacently in the round pond, I sit with my windows open hearing the trees rustle as the night establishes itself. Already, for there has been no rain since Ascot week, the dead leaves chatter along the pavement, and it is so late and so still that I hear them. And I have done the burial in Rebecca, and got well past the 1000 mark, and tell people on the telephone with utmost secure calm that I cannot accept any invitations as I am finishing a poem, and laugh when I have them condole with me on my hard life. Two things I have noticed. The way the coping-leaf in the acacia cluster wags independently, almost personally, like the wagging tail of a lamb who sucks; and that singing a turn in the rightly constructed tune is exactly like the feeling of swimming over a wave – one pre-

20 Dom Anselm Hughes, OSB, an expert on medieval polyphony.
21 The Plainsong and Medieval Music Society.

pares oneself to surmount it, and in the same instant feels it slide under one.

23. Ordered pink paint for the Late Miss Green (Mrs Moxon[22] wants to give me blue roses, and as Valentine wrote 'other strange sly plants'). FINISHED REBECCA, except for four lines to be tinkered at.

The flowers of the ash-tree. Like a very fine, very crumpled and dirty, lace handkerchief; and the scent is wild and sour, and wooden.

25. Bought lilac paint and holland and pink linings for the L.M.G.[23] and a tea and dinner set (butter-coloured Titian ware) and some more enamel and tin oddments. It is unexpected, but the Devil has but to bait his trap with an enamel sink-drainer and I walk in.

27. Licked Becky's face and sent her off. Planted Machenian campanulas and sang Handel. Lord, how lovely it is to have a book off one's mind!

28. I awoke from a queerly vivid dream of Teague extemporising, and remembered it was the beginning of the Cambridge bout. We travelled together, and arrived at Kings[24] in time for tea. [...] Even though there was no excuse of dusk they were lighting the candles in chapel. The choir sang a capella a sixpart anthem of Teague's – *Let the peace of God*, the Farrant Mag and N.D. and Tallis Salvator mundi. This they did exquisitely, very poised above a very regular beat. Where a later composer less in the vocal tradition would have augmented the effect of a high note by going one higher in the next sentence, Tallis repeats the same note, knowing that the augmentation will be put in by the increase of tone in the voices. Teague's piece is thirty five years old; in spite of that date, it might have been 305, for it is extremely serene and severe. The other thing I shall remember is the singing of the water of Babylon psalm: a dead pianissimo, wasted with misery; the dying away into the cursing verses really dramatic. We dined in Eric's[25] rooms, with Boris Ord[26] and a choir scholar called Hedley – about 10.30 we went to the chapel. It was quite dark, except for the bicycle lamp, and under that enormous roof one had the feeling

22 Anne Moxon, known as 'Granny', lived across the lane from Miss Green's cottage.
23 The Late Miss Green.
24 King's College, Cambridge.
25 The Very Rev. Eric Milner-White (1884–1963), later Dean of York Minster. He had been one of George Townsend Warner's pupils at Harrow.
26 (1897–1961), composer and then organist and choirmaster of King's College, where he instituted the Christmas Eve Festival of Nine Lessons and Carols.

of being out of doors, and to go into a side chapel was like going into a cottage. The air was warm and sweet with wax candles. We sat at the west end, while Boris Ord played (first something I didn't know, then the Fantasia in G, with the roulades escaping on iron pinions after the pause) and the light in the organ sent an enormous rod of shadow along the roof. Then he called Teague. There was an interval of conversational voices, and he began to extemporise. I thought I should never hear that again, and in that terrific tunnel of dark masonry with its one useless shaft of light piercing the upper dark, it was like a Donne poem and a funeral. Just at the end, or rather just as one felt the end, he let off for a minute and then started the theme on all the most tigerish and domineering reeds – a last jutting-out rock of a mainland – and then away in a pianissimo. Nothing really has altered. I listened with the old obedient ears, the old destined flesh. Only now I hear with a deeper-sounded abyss below me, a more closely-encompassing dark-ness, and both accepted. It was beyond all my dreams, to be listening to music so, in the dark of that ancient and bare building (for the glassiness of perp: gives it by height an austerity which in a way rather frowned down the baroque arabesques of the J.S.B.), and all the day was heavenly; walking on the court lawns, drinking port, listening to bells and stories of Rootham. So to bed at the Bull – ordering early morning tea like a lady.

30. The day began with the choir breakfast in the combination room. When I saw that vast table extending between the portraits of Henry VI and Richard III, glittering with silver, and grapes, and cherries, and all the thousands of admirable young men, and Mary's[27] eye at the other end, and myself on the right hand of the Vice-Provost and Teague opposite I felt myself anonymously in heaven. The V. Provost is short, and grey-haired, and bulky. He has a very short face, large grey eyes, the healthy pallor of someone never exposed to outdoor inclemencies, the relax and twinkle one has waited for to happen in a Gainsborough portrait. I was enthralled by him. Every joke one makes scores a boundary, and swivelling round in his chair he leans towards one with a benevolent coquetry. Lady Castlemaine's pa's cup – a large tankard, was before me, with a punning mottoe on *palma*. There were seven courses . . . The joy of it all was the feeling that it was quite natural: that no one had spat on the silver the day before. Then we adjourned to the fellows garden, and sat in a rustic summer house, till

27 Unidentifiable.

the young men began to play bowls, and Teague, Eric, and I were left talking like grandmothers. But before that Eric had propped his bulk on Ram's wicker chair, and shoved it. 'Wait a minute, shall I change my angle?' Ram examined him. 'But Milner White, where is your angle?' Then we were photographed; then we walked back to lunch in Eric's rooms, while a thunderstorm, the storm of all 18th [century] architectural views, mounted above Clare. Ord lunched too. We talked about Books; Ulysses the Ring and the Book of our days. Then Teague, Eric and I had a long wail about women's colleges, and women in general, during which I found myself obliged to do something for my sex, though the best I could do was to try and keep up an end of an argument. [. . .] The music this evening was another, and very lovely C. Wood Introit, Tomkins' service, Byrd's Haec Dies, and C. W[ood] O gladsome light thrown in as an extra. Then too happy to be sorry, we left, and travelled back together, and Teague came in for tea, and a conclusion of how happy it had all been. It had. So happy as to be almost unearthly. Such pleasant people, such beautiful things, such friendliness ordained to us hundreds of years ago. For we owe this to Henry VI and William Byrd, really. As for Teague, he floated like a water lily.

August

17. Overslept into the ringing of church bells. Wrote Mr Cope[28] all day, and frolicked with the holy ghost. The Church has lost a great religious poet in me; but I have lost an infinity of fun in the church, so the loss is even.

28. My bi-yearly cheque from U.S.A. £3.10. and Lamport and Holt, the shipping firm gone bust. This will be a black winter, if a raven doesn't turn up from somewhere. My Teague has already offered to be that bird, but he will need one himself. The best thing we can hope for, I suppose, would be a good rousing influenza epidemic to carry lots of us off. Meanwhile in default of ravens, Oliver is all afire to keep a goose in our backyard, and take it leashed for walks in Kensington Gardens, and I have finished *Over the Hill*[29] in such a flow that I had to lift myself away by the neck or I should have gone straight on to

28 A poem about the Rev. Joseph Staines Cope, a past incumbent of Chaldon Herring, published in *WDS*.
29 Story, *Sal*.

Mrs Faux and the soldiers. But if I am to be my own raven I must recapture the Lolly manner, and be light and satirical and talk of gentlemen and ladies.

September

3. *Mem*: that man who wanted to buy mss of mine. Here I sit with the wolves howling nearer and nearer, too weak-minded to turn out a cupboard for fear of what I might find in it. I think I have lost his address, too. But of course I have muzzled the wolves since Teague wished to be a friend in need and with such comfortable assurance that he dam well would be, too. Burglar, Banker, Father.

17. I visited every counter of the domestic Woolworth, even to buying boot-polish, and refreshed myself with a sixpenny fish tea – plaice, of course. Cheap low-class meals are such a pleasure, I wonder I don't take to chewing-gum. Then it began to rain and I lit a fire, and Teague appeared with roses from behind an umbrella like the shield of Achilles, but plainer, and walked in and looked round and said 'I hadn't noticed anything so extraordinary about your walls' – by which I was flattered to know he had been reading me interviewed.[30] [. . .] He began to play a bit of one of the organ fugues, and I heard the affinity between his touch and the way some painters float their colour onto the canvas.

20. [Amersham] It rained, we [STW and the Machens] sang Handel and drank pale ale. Charles came by the 3.15 and soon the rain lightened and the fair woke up. The Stonors[31] came too, and an infliction of three painful Yankees: Mr a rich stockexchange New Yorker, who debated every penny with the booth men. After dinner Charles and I visited the boxing booth, and stood in the mud watching the end of a fight. The head man was a very handsome mulatto with a broken nose and head with alternate ripples of shave and hair. Then Hilary took on Slosh Benson of the Whitechapel ring, and was knocked out in the fourth round, while we sat on some wavering staging like geraniums. More merry-go-rounds: as Dorothie climbed onto her dragon the calliope broke into majestic Wagnerian chords. It had a lovely God, with a grimy unshaved face, and a pale blue eye, which once winked at

---

30 By Louise Morgan, in the periodical *Everyman*, reprinted in *Writers at Work*, Chatto & Windus, 1931.
31 The writer Oliver Stonor and his wife.

me. D. and Arthur were so gay and relieved that they played the most absurd games with each other: when she cried to him Nag-pot, Nag-pot, Nag-pot, she swore she saw Charles's spectacles turned nervously on her to see if they would come to blows.

21. The street all bare again, the vans packed and moving. More Handel. In the afternoon I walked the wood path to Farthing Barn, and promised myself to walk that way one windy winter night. Oliver and Dorothy arrived to fetch me away, we dined at The Griffin, and afterwards Dorothie fetched out her grease-paints and made us up. Oliver drove back very drunk, singing the Volga Boatsong in triple time. Lucky we weren't copped, him drunk, conveying two painted whores.

23. Just as I was looking round on my preparations[32] Dorothy came in like a ghost, and bowed herself on my shoulders and began to cry. Bridget was ill: spots, which her doctor could not diagnose. Neither of us realised that the sherry I poured out was cherry brandy. This rather clouded the start, though I can remember Willie[33] in the hall before the jerry-bin, and Valentine saying firmly: Is this wooden thing to go? We went by Guildford and beyond Alton lunched in a nut copse, talking about great aunts. A delicious lunch: cold chicken, beer, pears and madiera [sic]. And midges. And ash-trees. Their green fronds so flatly distinct on a grey sky that they looked like transfer patterns on china. We were late and though we drove fast (by a notice which said Gush opposite the minster) it was seven before we were in sight of home. The clouds broke into a blue and yellow curd sky: Miss Green was in her pink and white, charming, with a geranium on the doorstep and Mrs Moxon clattering a pail. N.B. Where is the backdoor key? —

Supper at B.C. where Violet looked better. After supper Valentine took all but Theo to Portland while he and I drank claret by the fire. 'They (Violet and Doris (!) belong to innocence and happiness. You and I to misery and destruction.' He said this with marked satisfaction. He also said that they had been feeding Francis very carefully, and that he seemed more amenable — a very zoo-sounding policy. At 10.30 the party came back in a rapture, with papers of fish and chips. A foggy dew, the wind rising, and I am in dear Mrs Way's bed.

26. My arm mends.[34] However, I take it for walks in the morning,

---

32 STW was about to leave London and move in to Miss Green's cottage.
33 The Ackland family's chauffeur.
34 It had been bitten by a dog.

tucked into my bosom like a Victorian statesman. After lunch [. . .] Valentine and Francis came to Miss Green, and put the cooker together. Betty[35] and the oil appeared in the midst (n.b. I must pay the coal). Betty was sent off. We hope in time for her flea to be still in her ear, for she lavishes them everywhere.

30. Still waiting on Mr Miller[36] – but I asked Mrs Way to work for me, and she accepted. She then gave me a patchwork quilt made by her aunt-in-law, and we spent the luncheon interval turning out her treasures – a vast paisley shawl, one of the thistle coloured ones, an elegant pewter tea-pot exactly like Mary Shelley, a little flat pewter flask picked up at the battle of Waterloo, an enchanting bohemian scent bottle that Nora must never hear of, and the scrap-screen with a cincture of grapes stuck round Garibaldi's loins. Then to Miss Green with Valentine, where Mrs Moxon lit our first fire, with a gimelled prayer cum incantation of good-will upon us. It burned merrily, the room began to live, like a ship getting under way.

October

3. My arm has had a set-back, but seems better again. It misses Valentine's chaperonage; and so do I.

4. After lunch I moved in. My first act was to have a bath, then I had tea in Mrs Parker's tea-pot. It was gusty and rainy, and I was still damning the oven when Valentine arrived into a black room. The car was lit up inside like a train and there sat Ruth[37] and the jerry-bin. V. and I dined on duck and mushrooms which I had found that morning on the Five Maries, and drank hock and brandy. The large Bible lay on the chest of drawers, and the candles burned down in the mirror sconces, and there was a large mixed bunch of flowers from Mrs Way. It seemed odd that we hadn't been there for years. It was a windy moonlight night, the sound closing one in. From my bed there was a new aspect of High Chaldon.

5. I had always thought my own breakfast fairly abstemious, but Valentine breakfasting off a cup of cold water put me out of countenance. William woke as though he had lived here all his life . . . the moment I began to cook he settled down.

---

35 Betty Muntz, the sculptress, who lived at Apple Tree Cottage in Chaldon.
36 Carpenter and handyman.
37 Ruth Ackland, Valentine's mother.

8. A brilliant tearing gale of a morning. The Trinity[38] had lost all their leaves, the house sounded like engines, and we had to lock the front door to keep the gale out. We walked a very quarterdeck walk along the Maries, seeing the pheasants trying to rise into the gale, but flutter down again. Looking over the heath we could *see* the wind . . . a cloud of sea-spray and earth dust. In the afternoon I made a sackcloth rug like a fallen woman.

11. After lunch we gardened, and set off for B.C. We went over the field, and there was a strange stilled light over the landscape. I said 'Something is going to happen – something horrible.' She was equally sure that something was going to happen, but sure it was something pleasant. So she walked on to the vicarage to inspect for dogs, and I stood watching her, and admiring her legs. At B.C. we heard that the servant had run away again – twice – that day.[39] Everyone said something must be done about it, and suddenly Valentine and I were on our feet, setting out to call on the Vicarage. The dog bayed and padded, we saw it moving like water in the dusky house, then the old woman came, and tried to get our reason for calling from us, but we were firm and sinister, and would call again. [. . .] A rapid dinner, cooked with fury, and eaten with loins girded, and we were walking up for a third time, I telling Valentine what a comfort her pistol was. Miss Stevenson opened the door, and let us into an empty room. [. . .] She shook like a blancmange, and kept on trying to ingratiate herself into our assistance by laughter and uneasy cryings. She got little from me, and nothing from Valentine, who sat white and motionless like Justice, while this execrable woman gave herself away, saying the girl was sent her for special treatment (the whole housework), and had sex mania (and was left alone with Wallace in the cellar), and had the mentality of a child of six (and was shut up all day long with the old hag and that dog), and had actually been comforted and called Miss by P.C. Wintle. But we frightened her, and kept her taken in, and so left her. As we walked from the door, speechless, Valentine shook her stick in the air like a squire. Righteous indignation is a beautiful thing, and lying exhausted on the rug I watched it flame in her with severe geometrical flames.

And then we went to bed. Just as I blew out the candle the wind began to rise. I thought I heard her speak, and listened, and at last she

---

38 A group of trees on High Chaldon.
39 The lady at the Vicarage 'trained' young girls from an asylum by keeping them in service, the conditions of which were notorious in the village.

said through the door that this would frighten them up at the Vicarage. How the Vicarage led to love I have forgotten (oh, it was an eiderdown). I said, sitting on my side of the wall, that love was easier than liking, so I should specialise in that. 'I think I am utterly loveless'. The forsaken grave wail of her voice smote me, and had me up, and through the door, and at her bedside. There I stayed, till I got into her bed, and found love there, and a confidence that could twit me with how rude I had been the first time we met. We heard a screech-owl wing up the valley to the vicarage, and after a while it came back to tell us with a few contemptuous hoots, of its errand there. And we remembered the light in the field, that I had been so wrong about, she so right.

12. My last day, and our first. It was a bridal of earth and sky, and we spent the morning lying in the hollowed tump of the Five Maries, listening to the wind blowing over our happiness, and talking about torpedoes, and starting up at footsteps. It is so natural to be hunted, and intuitive. Feeling safe and respectable is much more of a strain. A final tea at B.C. was called for, and it took three quarters of an hour to go there, owing to there being so many regrets and expostulations to rehearse. We stayed interminably, Francis walked back with us, and I shall never forget Valentine, ginless, standing with her back to the fire, keeping her eye on us lest we should dare to sit down, while Francis sipped with his stick propped on the table, and I weakly made conversation about the poltergeist. It is a fierce creature I have released, though so kind to me. 'Won't you sit down' it said, rather severely, after he had gone. And I sat with relief, as if a permission were given. Dinner was briskly through, and William was allowed once round the green, and my loving leopard took me off to bed.

13. I went away, by Mrs Hall, who surprised us with an early train, but was routed. Looking for a sort in Mrs Johnson[40] for the day, Valentine pointed to: 'He is the God that maketh men to be of one mind in an house, and bringeth the prisoners out of captivity.' Then a glass of gin to rally my spirits, and I was gone, looking back to see her walk, slender, erect, and determined, into our house.

London seemed full of simulacra, and Teague took me out to dinner, and I was torn between 113 where I was, and the cottage, where my ghost walked. Yet I cannot forever besiege the past, there is a

40 A 1787 edition of the Book of Common Prayer.

treachery to the future, too, and perhaps the deadlier, and life rising up in me again cajoles with unscrupulous power, and I will yield to it gladly, if it leads me away from this death I have sat so snugly in for so long, sheltering myself against joy, respectable in my mourning, harrowed and dulled and insincere to myself in a pretext of troth.

16. In the morning I received two small snail-shells, one orange, one lemon-yellow, smelling of Valentine. I shut them firmly into a box with a lid, for one has no defence, no possible counter-sallies against the inanimate. [. . .] In the morning I saw two seagulls, flying high and screeching, from the south-west. It was strange to see them wintering on such a warm secure day, and I thought how in any other year this would have been a threat of winter, but now a promise.

18. There was even more disorder in my black hair than in my thoughts, indeed my thoughts were as secure as trees – the poplar twittering outside, shaking the light off its leaves, like flashes of joy – as I sat on the floor with her looking at me with that lappet of smooth hair, such inequity, hanging over one eye like a very young, fastidious, urbane pirate. Though a pirate with an undoubted vocation. Kensington Gardens was full of St Lukes summer and early morning sun. I tried to write a poem, but was too sleepy and too happy. Then I went to Amersham, and had tea and confidential toast with Purefoy [. . .]. Catching the 10.27 I *ran* up that hill under the beech-trees with a ghost growling round my ears, and as a result waited for ten minutes in the company of drunk men singing bawdy songs, on whom I looked with benign incomprehension. The room[41] was dusky candle-lit: duskier-seeming than when the candles were blown out and the tall pattern from the lamp outside marked the ceiling. I have no idea what time it was when she said, 'I thought we would be vulgar and have champagne.' We had caviar, too, sitting on the floor, a romantic picnic.

19. This new life when day begins in the evening throws out the diarist. [. . .] It is being the most heavenly weather, serene and golden, a bloom on the air – a secret summer hidden in the ageing of the year. My content lasted me till she came again, very taut and fierce, having been kept by one thing and another. We drove – a lap-wing dive round into Constitution Hill – and down into Whitechapel, and through the glittering unconsciousness of the Blackwall tunnel, and so

41 At Valentine's flat, 2, Queensborough Studios, W2.

back by Greenwich. [. . .] She has stillest face I have ever known. Amusement sharpens it slightly into that fox's smile, but it disdains to smile for pleasure, or turn aside from its melancholy beauty. The loveliest thing of all is how, with bowed head embracing me, her arms and neck pour from those narrow shoulders, like a smooth torrent of water limbed as it falls over a rock.

22. I got home and Francis [Powys] arrived, very anxious to please, and to stay. I inflamed him with Winifred Duncan,[42] most successfully. We dined at Romero's, and went to the News movie, where the governor of Labrador spoke a few words of praise, 'we have our magnificent coast line and quantities of – er – trees'. The gyroplane, its windmill horizontally revolving, and landing plum like a cat. A tank charging through a brick wall, and going away draped with it. And a Ward Disney [sic] film with a terrific comic swift close up of a lion's mouth. Then we went home and I wrote the delicate proposal to W.D. and ran excitedly, unchaperoned by William to the studio. There I heard how Bo[43] had been tiresome in a taxi, but it didn't keep us long. In the morning I was shown my ring – a very deep amethyst set in rose-crystals. Friday night hazards. A barrier of the Bible and the fish-kettle. It might perplex visitors a little, but we shall be known to be eccentric. One need not write in a diary what one is to remember for ever.

28. We dined very fast at the studio, with Haru[44] howling round us like a lost soul. At 113 was a telegram from Winifred telling Francis to come C.O.D. So we started,[45] driving very fast, too fast for any thoughts to turn to the left towards Colville Terrace[46] in its black labyrinth. It was raining, that closed us in. Our speed seemed to make our road, calling it up and dismissing it. A lorry on the wrong side of the road buckled our mud guard. We went on. Six mile bottom, and Newmarket, and a mill by a bridge called Bantram Mill where we stopped for petrol. I opened the window and heard the water flowing, and smelt the quality of the night, and heard those clear light footsteps. After that the pursued feeling was gone, and it was secure to stop and eat a great many sandwiches, and walk William, looking exactly

42 An American writer, living in the South of France, who was looking for a secretary/companion.
43 Bo Foster, a friend and former lover of Valentine.
44 Valentine's Siamese cat.
45 For Hill House, Winterton, Valentine's family home in Norfolk.
46 Where Dorothy Warren, another ex-lover of Valentine, lived.

like a hoary small bear in the head-lights, as he carefully sought out the sandwiches thrown out for wayside animals. A tall war memorial near Thetford, a terrible stretch of road where trees on either side had been confounded and turned backward, Wymondham with a comfortable butter-market. Acle Bridge, very narrow, and the car going faster and faster, past the green sleeved trees. A dusky-white tower rising up, and a narrow drive, and the house was before us. It had left off raining, the air was listening to the sound of the sea, it was 1.15, we had got there safe. So there was time to walk all over it, to examine the kitchen and the servants hall, and one of the cats, and the long unreal greenhouses, the naked sexless love whose hair might have been in a little bun, sitting all marble-cold and solitary in the last one.

29. Now there was all the garden to see, the donkey going round the well, the other wicked well in a little jail of trees and nettles, the out-houses, the lavender stocks clipped into tea-tables, their stalks tied up with string, the little wood, and Valentine's room above the stables. It had everything in it, from poems written on the wall to jeweller's scales and microscopic slides, and invisible Love's prayers cut on glass. We walked over the dunes to the sea, I arranged to get my feet wet and walked home barefoot. A village boy called Roger was respectfully waiting about to catch Valentine's eye. After lunch, which was pleasant, and John's[47] most innocent young cauliflowers, in a room like being in a liner, we drove to Yarmouth. The herring girls wear black seaboots and oilskin petticoats, and coloured bodices and headkerchiefs of the brightest and most considered shades. They work flick-flick, the silver running through their red hands. All the fishing-nets hanging up like a strange vineyard.

31. I had made up my mind to tell Teague, and said so. We talked of it, lunching in a very playful wood of birch and sweet chestnut. It was a drive of all moods, but mostly I knew I was being carried back in triumph. London was horrible, the decrease in speed like a physical ill-being, then it took ages to find Bolton St, where Mr Sansom mended two teeth. I bought dinner and a stilton, and waited for a bus, all rather cold and dim. It was not an easy thing to say, but he made it all extremely clear and secure by his magnanimity. My poor Teague, I can scarcely believe it is done; nothing more became it than its ending. Then we talked about Donne, the imagined corners. There was no

47 The Winterton gardener.

dazzle of love in my eyes, no nursed delusion or self-conning. Yet I have never liked him so well, seeing him thus clearly. Alas! . . . but here's nothing but what may quiet me, for it was most perfectly taken, the blow I dealt.

November

7. Caught the 10.30 by layers of teeth being so anxious not to miss it. Polished my nails nervously in the train. [. . .]

Valentine and Mrs Way had made tea to greet me. There was a new chrysanthemum, and a new top to the copper. The walls were very white, we saw our shadows mingled on them. It took a long time to unpack, and I walked alone up the Maries in a darkening dusk, and vowed and prayed that I might never hurt this wild sensitive love. She had written two poems the day before: the rocket, and the weasel, and was rather sniffy when I said weasels could not stand up with their paws on the wall.

11. Six snipe from G.N.C.S.[48] and herbs from Purefoy [Dorothie] Machen arrived. Also Mrs Hall, selling poppies. Seeing us sitting up in my bed Mrs Way exclaimed affectionately 'twins!' We listened for the silence on the wireless, in order to find out the exact time. It went on for so long that we began to think London swallowed in a convulsion of nature. We didn't much mind. I walked on the Maries, after we had dug a herb-bed and planted; tansy, sage, savoury, and tarragon. Asking Valentine anxiously if I snored, (I don't) I found her rather vague about snoring. That noise, I said, one hears in hotels at night if one walks down the corridor. 'That? I thought it was central heating.'

12. It was a brilliant shining day, and there was cold snipe, so we had a picnic under the Five Maries, where we had sat on the violets. This led her to talk of how resolutely she had fallen in love with me when I was still so far and rude, and from that I wrote, in the new kitchen memorandum book which had come for a picnic too, the first complete poem of this house, *Grow as a Tree*. It was amazing happiness to be writing there, full of cold snipe and beer, with my love lying beside me, her lappet of hair trailing into the winter grass.

17. We woke early, and saw our windows frosted over. Breathing holes in them, and thawing them with the nightlight, we saw a pale

48 Geoffrey Sturt.

silver-green world, with a sky a clear faint red. It was icy still, everything most pale and sanctified. We walked out in dressing-gowns to the top of the Knap. (O and I have forgotten gathering the crisped ruined endive overnight, by torchlight.) It was unspeakably beautiful, a new world. And the same excited loss of perspective as in snow, so that the hills look flatly steep. We went to bed again, and lay late.

19. Katie [Powys] came early, and brought two poems, and consulted Valentine as to how to spell immense, and stayed to a dressing-gown breakfast. After she had gone Mr Sansom the oil passed by. We were shamelessly embracing by the door when I heard a click, looked round and saw little Mr S. standing at the gate with his head reverently bowed. So in my blue trousers and bunny coat[49] I frisked out to give polite directions, and had the pleasure of seeing big Mr S. bolt by me as though I were a vampire bat.

26. I walked up the Maries, seeing a terrific blue stormcloud westwards over the sea. As I turned again to it a flash of lightning greeted me. It was the intensest scarlet. A blackbird shrieked, an owl hooted low, everything was afraid. Another flash, a pink one, and then, walking up the drove, pale and spirit-like in that strange light came Valentine to look for me. We got in just before the rain, and lay on my bed watching the storm, but there were only two flashes more. She had a temperature, and a little heart [pain], but was better after dinner, when we weeded again in her book of poems, and had a long talk about poetry. I don't think I can do much to help her, but if I can teach her the necessity for being a charlatan, that conjuror's click which Housman has so perfectly, I shall have done something. It is, perhaps, the peck of dust we must all eat before we die, but eat it we must to show that we are alive.

December

17. [London] A heavy dark fog in the morning. After lunch we went to visit Dorothy Warren. Her house seemed to me to be decorated by Cochran, so smart and artistic: a siamese kitten, a samoyede, a cockatoo, needlework poodles, all the equivalents of the Lord's Prayer in fretwork. We went down to her work-room, where she sprayed a

---

49 An exuberant bed-jacket.

plaster death-cast of herself. She is beautiful: beechen hair, a fierce taut slender shape, but ugly hands and a voice like Ottoline's[50] only more baying. After hours of standing about we started for the galleries. In Cavendish Square Valentine drew neatly to the curb, and collapsed. She was sick, and lay crumpled under the wheel saying – Don't touch me. Send her away. With desperation I at last did so, then got her into a taxi and back to 2 [Queensborough Studios]. Rang up innumerable doctors. [. . .] Earlier in the day her own doctor had diagnosed other attacks as migraine (cf More's Lady Conway), and said you might die of it, so I was none too easy as I sat reading Lawrence's poems, and wondering if the gas-meter was her death rattle. The other thing today was a D.H. Lawrence at D.W.'s[51] – Leda. The swan leaning down its neck between the breasts of a recumbent woman, very beautiful.

50 Lady Ottoline Morrell, Dorothy Warren's aunt.
51 Dorothy Warren owned the Warren Galleries, where the notorious D.H. Lawrence show was held in 1929.

January

7. Telegram to say Unendurable, arriving 11.30 to-night. Also two letters, and a sailor's jersey with a deep embossed pattern round the chest. It was cold, I put it on and went to sleep again. In this, plus a pair of pyjama trousers, I told two firmly and sinisterly smirking Dominican nuns I would not subscribe to their home for fallen women. Looking at me, they can scarcely have been surprised; but it took doing: one is so in awe of that black and white.

12. It was our most completed night, and after our love I slept unstirring in her arms, still covered with her love, till we woke and ate whatever meal it is lovers eat at five in the morning. She said, remembering Lady C,[1] that Lawrence in heaven would be taken down a peg to see us, specimens of what he so violently disliked, loving according to all his precepts, and perhaps the only lovers that night really to observe them. But heaven would be to be taken down a peg – released from string-strain without displeasure. The body, after all, older and wiser than soul, being first created, and, like a good horse, if given its way would go home by the best path and at the right pace.

19. She brought me a number of early photographs of herself, which had been Bo's. A fat baby steering a long-legged car, with a tense competent face, rather grim, and that beldam nanny smirking behind, with Fiend written in every inch of her. This night she was melancholy, and said – the fruit of that wait at Greenwich – that she could mean nothing to me but as a lover. How to house, and yet not to tame, this wild solitary heart, so fierce even in its diffidence. And I, lumbering, so I seem to myself, after, clogged with all this cargo of years and tolerance and mind's dust.

---

1 *Lady Chatterley's Lover.*

February

5. W.[2] still very heavy on us, and being a vampire bat to Valentine all day. In the evening, as she was calmer, we drove her to Amersham. Arthur meeting Masefield (after marriage) at the Café Royal. 'I offered him a liqueur brandy. He said, 'I never drink spirits.' I offered him a cigar. He said, 'I never smoke.' The evening was an unpalatable one, he talked a deal of nonsense. At 9.30 he began to fidget and said, 'I must be going. I never sit up late'. I said to him. 'Sir, your customs are horrible.' Also Winifred very gloatingly describing to him the degeneration into lower forms of the soul-corrupt man in his early story – 'a mass of corruption bubbling and heaving on the bedroom floor'. Arthur rolling about in his chair with an appreciative smile. 'Charming!' I was happy to see how well they liked my dear, Purefoy saying she must make her up. 'You would pay for make-up[3] it would be a great improvement.' And my dear liked them, commenting on their married manners – the slight formality with which they addressed each other – no marital sluttishness there.

10, 11, 12. During these days I tried unavailingly, to write more poems, and finished *Out of your left eye*. I signed 550 sheets of *A Moral Ending*. I lunched with Valentine at a 2/= restaurant, very good. I endured (not very well) a prick from Bo, aimed at me through her, an 18th [century] ballad sheet of an inconstant Lindamira. I dined with her, very festively, on oysters and spent a happy evening turning out drawers of old letters, but it ended in a sudden explosion of our wills, because I tried to manouvre [sic] her into taking two trumpery presents she had disapproved of me buying for her. Tearing up the handkerchief and seeing it flutter limply down among all the rest of the torn up rubbish on the floor I suddenly felt myself turn cold with fear, and gave in. And going back in silence to 113 the first thing I saw, of course, was the calm golden milk-glaze T'ang figure she had given me earlier in the day. But I was comforted in bed, and I suppose in time I shall learn not to make this housewifely fuss over small crusts of differences. It is just like 'my God, I *must* not waste that half tomato –' which is so maddening to her. Also, trying to buy her the Hopkins letters to Patmore (but they are gone to a private buyer in Aberdeen), I had a few words with Mr Wilson of Bumpus's and found he knew Edward Thomas. His settled grave melancholy. 'A drenched man.'

2 Winifred Duncan.
3 i.e. 'It would be worth your while.'

14. We fell on our Valentines. Mine a papier-maché writing-case containing Penelope's mittens, Grinnie's pen, and a tiny little gold heart, and two 18th cent. pieces of bead-work. And while I was still enjoying, the bell rang and delivered a small made bouquet of a daffodil, hyacinths, mimosa, and jonquil-buds. The day before she had filled me with flowers – white stocks, and white lilac, and almond boughs tufted with blossom. We lay in this bower, watching the pigeons at their nest in the plane-tree. [. . .] I had to go to Nettlesnip's⁴ awful party. All the women sitting silent on the window seats, with their feet tucked in as though there had been a mouse, while a plump young woman in scarlet pyjamas did acrobatic dances. Her first entry, feet over hands from between curtains, was accompanied by a crash of broken glasses. No one spoke to me except a Danish lady who asked twice – 'Who is she?' and then, for variety's sake, pointing to one of the few men, 'How old is he?' Home with hysteria, and early to bed.

18. The King of Spain appears to have mastered his revolution by sheer keeping his head, also some tactful acts like going to pray alone before his mother's tomb, and the opportune arrival of Queen Victoria. They kissed at the railway station to the rythmical cheers of six hundred noblemen. Valentine much pleased, and with restraint I refrained from mentioning The Apple Cart.

March

1. 'It's snowed', she said, sitting up suddenly. It was about 7 o'clock, the sky a pale excited blue, snow on all the roof-tops, boughs powdered with snow and pink with sun. With very little expostulation from me we were up, dressing very hastily, and drinking gin. And then, with deep forbidden excitement we walked out, down the lane and up Queensborough Terrace a little to see the park, an early car scattering snow, the launching tree with its new cargo. It was clear cold, the cold of a foreign town, and the hideous houses in the Terrace caught our excitement, glowed yellow in the sun, were unopened boxes of strange new living. Then writing our initials on the snow domes of the dust-bins we went in, and back to bed, to meditate on all we had done and dared.

5. Opus 7 out today. In the evening I was suddenly appallingly tired,

4 Ursula Nettleship, Augustus John's sister-in-law, who had a flat above Valentine's at Queensborough Studios.

and sat on the floor for half an hour gloomily and speechlessly struggling with the cork of a sparkling Burgundy bottle – a sorry sight, watched by her from the cover of the evening paper, too tactful to intervene lest I wept. As the cork was mostly aimed at her, this was courage.

7. We read some Coventry Patmore, who is better than one thinks, but not so good as he thinks himself. To be so very pure and at the same time so very rich in language is rather too like bathroom tiles of a grand description to be perfectly comfortable.

12. [F]or the new census we decided provisionally on 'companion' and 'spinster: annulled.'

23. [Chaldon] Valentine had gone to tea at Beth Car, and I had been planting the roses when a telegram came, just as it was too dark to go on. It said that Ronald [Eiloart] was dead. I walked up and down the lane, after wiring I would come, waiting for my dear to come and rally me. She made all the arrangements, and we went to bed early, very sad for the morrow, loving under this sudden swoop of death's wing.

24. The next morning early I started by car for Little Zeal, still thinking it must be a mistake. Nora came out to meet me, looking as though she had been hit on the head. He had died of angina, in the garden, and she had found him dead.

I was at L.Z. till April 3rd, holding onto my snuff-box, very unhappy nearly all the time. Nancy Eiloart came, and in the next week R.T.W.[5] The funeral was on Thursday 26th, and the clergyman read the service in tones of the deepest and rather disapproving astonishment. Poor old Cranch who did the coffining was very sorry to lose his friend; so were all the people of the village who had known Ronald. He looked very beautiful, dead. A calm, secret look; and, most moving, his large, rough, hard-working hands folded still. Valentine and Ruth came over on Sunday. It had meant a good deal of contention, but when I saw my dear it was worth it. We went to the Sanatorium about a puncture, and walked up and down its cinder drive, with gramophones playing in rabbit-hutches, and those strangers staring at us, all like a painted backcloth. She brought me a new mourning ring. I needed it. All the next week it rained.

5 STW's uncle, Robert Townsend Warner.

April

3. The car came for me after lunch. The weather had suddenly cleared, but a high wind was blowing. We sat waiting in the garden, while the trees tossed and waves of wind rushed over the grass, and the dogs barked at strangers in the lane. She [Valentine] had waited in Brent, when she got into the car she looked so ill, so worn and severe, I felt for a moment it wasn't her. [. . .]

We got home at late dusk. The whole house was full of flowers – lilac and freesias, and flounced pink azalea, and roses and white irises in my bedroom, and the little gallipot of violets and puss willow by my bed. Only then, taking me in her arms, she spoke. It was a voice I had never heard before, gentle and weary, and it almost broke my heart to think how lonely she had been, and tormented with every fear.

4. We woke very early, just after dawn, and heard all the birds singing. The blackbirds first squirt of song, and the lark ascending, and the wren shaking its tambourine. Mrs Way gave us breakfast . . . but before then we had gone down in the early morning to look at the garden, and she, coming back to bed, brought me a little cold damp nosegay of primroses. That day everything came out: the Winterton wallflowers and rosemary, the yellow jasmine, and the new ribes. We walked down the Drove, past the tall palm willow with its powdered torches, and wandered in the field under the Maries. There were cowslips in the hedge, and blue and white violets. The sun shone and we lay and loved under the tree.

14. In the afternoon I went out alone into the cowslip field, and picked a bunch for Mrs Keates.[6] They were in plenty, blossoms feathered out from the firm stout pink stems; and picking them I thought how a year ago I should have been almost embarrassed to be so strewn with pleasures – but now I take them as my right, as a king's daughter would take her needlework, being all glorious within. Alfonso of Spain has abdicated, after the election went Republican. These dowdy republics.

May

15. Started after lunch for Winterton. It was raining, and the drive interminable, a *wet* green, like eating too much unsophisticated salad.

6 Who was coming on a visit to Chaldon with her two daughters.

At Barton Mills I thought of a poem I shan't ever write, moments so like each other, so still, that they become timeless, like mirror reflecting mirror in avenues.

28. [Winterton] At midday there was a thunderstorm. It came darkening up the dunes from Hemsby, a thick, fusty-looking mist, a blot over the sea. We watched ourselves into the middle of it. Constant lightning, but no very spectacular flashes except one, rapidly uncoiling, like a swift rope thrown out. There was also a strong smell of thunder, until it was overpowered by the smell of roast veal. In the afternoon we picked and sent off flowers, and in the evening we watched the Winterton boys tobogganing down the bank, chiefly on strips of tin, or rolled in sacks. After they had gone in we went down ourselves. Valentine bruised her bottom and I grazed my wrist, but we were not deterred by this.

June

7. In the afternoon we went to East Dereham to see Craske.[7]

J. Craske lives at 42, Norwich Road. A red brick cottage in a row, with a front garden. He was lying in bed by the window, a crumpled-faced man with darting eyes, and large pale hands. Mrs C. was short, upstanding, pale sallow. Her knobbed hair and folded hands gave her the air of something by Craske – a model of a woman.

The room was filled with Craske's work, pictures in wool, silk, paint, texts, even the ornaments painted with ships and lighthouses. The most arresting was a long narrow panel in wool representing a beach scene. Wool-foamed waves ran along the bottom, under the narrow skyline were emerald green and purple hills, dotted with red bungalows, and parted with white roads. The road from the beach bisected the panel, on it was a fishladen cart, a man with a creel, and the vicar posting a letter. To the left on the beach was a fish[g]roup – the auctioneer with a bell, buyers running, a full-face policeman to see fair-play. On the right were creels of fish unpacking, a man hammering whelks, children sailing toy-boats. The whole composition was violently full-faced and direct and crackled with vitality. Craske had made all this up, but the parson and the man with the creel had been recognised as taken from life, the creel man acclaiming the resem-

7 John Craske was a Norfolk fisherman who took to painting when ill-health forced him to retire from the sea. Valentine had seen his work by accident and brought it to the attention of Dorothy Warren, who put on an exhibition of Craske's work in London in 1929.

blance. It is not imagination he piques himself upon, but reality – in this fancy piece it is fact he preens over, pointing out the graves in the churchyard.

<u>14</u>. [London] Sunday. We spent the morning rollicking in bed, while the parrot squawked and whistled opposite. We spent the afternoon between rollicking on bed (nice distinction) and a picnic at Black-heath, where we pointed out the beauties of a victorian villa, and saw the Paragon, and Tarnsy's Wren house. A slight interval of virtue after dinner while I mended Ruth's lace dress to The Epistle of the Hebrews, then to bed and rollicked again. A very suitable amorous day for June.

18. Teague had dinner with me. He had met Einstein at a lunch, where Einstein said of his theories, 'When it has been discovered if they are correct – for myself, I do not know – one of two things will happen. If I am right, the Germans will say I was a German, the French, that I was Jew. If I am wrong, Germans will say I was a Jew and the French, He was a German.['] He was, Teague said, an extremely simple man. Perhaps that sort of simplicity which goes with genius is not only a concomitant, but an integral part. For the ordinary mind is teased into complexity by leaving off its thoughts to worry over this and that. A superior intellect may keep its unity by the same strength that enables Carnera to come away unbruised and unscarred. He also spoke of [Robert] Bridges . . . How pleased he had been by the success of his 'scatter-brained' Testament of Beauty. Teague played to me, and we argued about how far one can appreciate Isaiah at this remove, and it was all very peaceful and pleasant. Then I went upstairs and talked to the little Warners. About 2 Valentine rang up, and asked me to go round. I went. Letting me in she said, 'I have had a frightful scene with Dorothy [Warren]. The worst I have ever had'. It looked like it. The room was all upheaved, rugs scratched up, scars on the wooden floor, ink spilt, furniture awry. Valentine herself very flushed and breathless and black-eyed, walking up and down, and staring from the window. D. had gone back there to see the Craskes. Suddenly, while V. was leaning on the mantlepiece, Dorothy launched herself at her and knocked her down. The dog Rudi immediately sprang on her chest, growling, while D. seizing the kettle, threatened to knock her face in. V. struggled, was hit in the side of the head by D's fist, and then had her head knocked repeatedly on the floor. 'So I went limp. And when she slacked off I was up in a flash. I walked over to the window, and

she said, 'I'll throw you out.' Then she offered to fight with me. My first impulse was to say Done, but immediately I was prudent. I am rather ashamed of this. I must be growing old.' Then, since she couldn't fight, Dorothy started abuse, and finally attacked with insults about the poems. She tried to get at them, and was then thrown. After this came tears, laments, recriminations. And even when she had gone shrieking away, vowing to kill herself, she had come back, remarking comfortingly 'You see, when I am angry, I am always violent.' All this came out in spurts (Oh, I forgot. She also seized Valentine's tie and tried to strangle her. One loses oneself in this lavish programme of vile behaviour) while I listened, turned stockish with impotent rage. [. . .] If I ever have a chance to get back on that woman, I will. But meanwhile my hands are tied, as this is Valentine's quarrel, and her pride won't allow anyone else to take it up, and she won't go further herself.

July

13. The car ran over a weasel beyond Buckfastleigh. I saw it crossing the road ahead, it ran like an express train far off, that steady streaking haste. I thought we cleared it, looked back to make sure. As I looked I saw it turn over onto its back and enter its death-throes – writhing and striking with extraordinary savage grace.

15. [Chaldon] I walked alone on the Drove and the Maries, smelling the left-out dregs of hay, hearing a murder behind the impassive hedgerow. Then cooked for Lulu and Alyse, who had dinner with us. Ll. was given his prototype in Evelyn – the man who 'abounded in things petrified'. Also a present of a microscopic Genesis engraved on glass, and Alyse had my humped[8] garnet brooch which she was very prettily pleased with. But they are a sad pair compared to their last visit here: she is far the braver of the two, resolutely enjoying her food, the respite of a party, the relief of walls not stared into her sense by unhappiness. He once spoke echt Llewelyn, about the godless cry of the peacock. They were fetched away by an odious young man called Malhousie [. . .].

After they were gone, Valentine, indulging in one veramon too many, was taken sick – stalking about the house white and grim. I lay awake alone, remembering too well the first migraine attack. In spite of the example of The Ladies[9] I was bundled out of the way.

8 STW was going to write 'snail-shell' here, but crossed it out.
9 Of Llangollen, Lady Eleanor Butler and Sarah Ponsonby, famous for their devotion.

17. About tea time it turned to heavy rain and a wind splashing against the house, almost like a gale. From the kitchen window we saw the top of the elm by the green – its rumpled confused foliage – swaying, and expected at any moment to see it fall out of sight. Charles and Oliver arrived extremely wet just when we were beginning to say they must have stopped for the night. They brought a large crate, a duck, the Craskes, and foie-gras from Dorothy. They were both quite dazed with travelling. Theo came in for dessert, and on the strength of only wanting biscuits very happily consumed melon and strawberries, sitting cautiously in his coat. Intimations that Violet also would not be able to come to tea tomorrow. To bed very late, having stayed up after Charles left to make sardine sandwiches. I walked him to Mrs Way's. The rain had left off, but it was very dark and windy, the air smelling of salt. But once a waft of honeysuckle wrapped me like a kiss.

18. I spoke to Charles about Valentine's poetry, which after lunch he read. While this was going on, all under her nose, V. walked about like a very stately formal cat awaiting her hour of lying-in. He began slowly, with a puzzled face; I saw him reading and re-reading, not quite sure of what he thought, and not quite sure if he was on the right track. But in the lot I chose *The rocket*, and *The roof-tree*, and *hymn-singing child*, and *See you tommorow night*, and *After long travelling*, and *Rack and Ruin* caught him; and he asked if there were more. He liked better among those I hadn't picked out, *Pippity*, and *If you had any love*, which he liked extremely, and *Let the thermos* [sic] and *this heart ordains*. We talked about publishing. I think he would have made a proposal for Ch. and W. were not things in such a bad way now. As it was, he counselled that she should write more, and more let-out-ly. Just before tea, it still raining, I said I was sorry he had had such a dull day. O no, said he. I was really excited by those poems. It was a well-controlled excitement certainly, but I take his word for it.

19. *Sunday*. A grand cooked breakfast, the whole house smelling of bacon. Very hot morning, Charles and I walked along the violet bank, and sat in perfect silence. [. . .] Coming back I found that Valentine had washed up, laid the fire, got the copper going and written two poems – one incomplete and secular, the other the first of her decided-upon private religious poems, and very moving and good, with the untrammelled arrival I have been looking for. But I dared only praise discreetly. Then to the Inn for drinks. In the afternoon it grew dull and rainy, we sat indoors, I showed Charles the jewel-casket. Just as we

had given him up Ben Huebsch[10] arrived. His first act was to beam, his next to plunge into the ditch. Explaining our custom of drinking a little sherry before going out to tea we followed at a stranger's pace him and Charles walking up the village street. Inspected the new grave (old English customs for poor Ben) and still following an invisible hearse to B.C. *Not* a nice tea. Francis insulting and furious, conversation constrained, Violet ill. V. and I escaped early on the wings of a chicken[.]

20. Talk about Charles and the poems. I mentioned his remarks about publishing. She pounced at once – Had I made it perfectly clear . . . etc?

'Yes, absolutely clear. I told him that if there had been any such idea, of course you would not have let him see them while he was staying with us – they would have gone into the firm in the usual way.'

Sour voice from face buried in grass, 'That sounds very thin.'

I said she would pick a hole in a vacuum.

21. Hot day. Constrained by Mrs Way's presence, so conducive to sustained mental effort, I wrote letters, paid bills and filled up forms about lost letters [. . .]. Then gardened. Then had very nearly a quarrel with Valentine about Queen's.[11] It began with her saying she wanted to start serious reading again. I said Piers Plowman. Said she, I was put through that at school. In my fury at any institution having the effrontery to put children *through* an extremely difficult and unimportant masterpiece, and all out of that Beowulf snobbishness I let fly. And she flew back; and tea was consequently constrained, with silent civil offering of buns, until a passage in the Arabian nights – for we have fallen into a good habit of reading at tea – melted her to me again.

25. Rose early, and left the washing up, to drive out. Our first pleasure tour – to Lulworth, and back by the Wordsworths' road, past the House with the Echo and the secret valley. It was strange to go along the Wool to Lulworth road – my first journey in Dorset, made in that early morning waggonette ten years ago. Valentine likes the car extremely, drives it already to the manner born, and is most happy in it.

26. *Sunday*. Rained a great deal. During the night 25–26 Valentine unloosed my iron bridle, and I told her about Teague, who couldn't, and said he couldn't, endure more than three days on end of my company. That was very right of him to say that, very honest and rare,

10 Of The Viking Press, New York.
11 Queen's College, Harley Street, where Valentine had been educated.

said she. This deeply pleased me. Not, I think, that she should commend him − but it was a sanction of my other love which had gone rather weighed in darkness.

August

The Machens stayed with us till August 6th − a delightful visit, but not allowing much diary-writing, as the small house seemed full, and when V. and S. got to Mrs Way's feather-bed we were usually not inclined for anything but falling into it. Diversions of their visit were a lunch of lobsters at Osmington, Bindon Abbey, very green and be-lilied, where V. said the water and the birds were the same sounds the fathers heard, and where Purefoy, snuffing after a real presence, almost got herself turned away from Miss Weld's door, and where the appearance of the pious gate-keeper, and her assistant, 'such a comfort to me, she's almost blind and has fits', provoked the enquiry why devout R. Catholicism always produces withered torsoes; and a picnic under the menace of thunder and Powyses by Rachael's cottage; and a boat-sailing, very slow, with Betty. But mostly we did little, mooched about the garden, and spent long mid-days at the Inn, playing darts and shovehap'ny; and where the incessant vicinity of Moppie and his accordion were almost too much for Dorothie. Janet learnt to drive with Valentine . . . at her fourth or fifth lesson she was driving alone, gears and all. She also played cricket at B.C. (where Theo fielded clasping a kitten), and made the top score and caught Francis out. For this she received a bouquet. Valentine also gave her a ring (bought when they went into Weymouth together), and liked her very much. We three sat on a flat tombstone in Dorchester eating raspberries with the greatest amity one hot afternoon. She was exceedingly handy, and worked like a black. [. . .]

On August 4th I went alone to Todd's Drove field and lay exhausted in the sun, rather upset because Valentine had seemed to snub me. Presently I saw her look over the stile. She came and sat by me, very oppressed and silent; and presently said she thought it would be better if she killed herself. I said, Not alone, at any rate, and tried to discover what the matter was. But there was not time, and sadly we went to tea at Betty's, and got through a long evening not too ill. Then, in the early morning at Mrs Way's I woke to find her awake, and we began to talk. It was her finances − a prospect of things wrong certainly getting worse, and wouldn't it be better to end our happiness rather than live worse – either separately or guttering in London. At last, after about two hours of lame persuasion, and hearing cocks crow, she consented to my expedient of a tide-over cheque.

24. I was at Little Zeal till 24: vii: In that time I wrote a pot-boiler for the XIX Cent.[12] One bad finished poem – the rain – and some unfinished ones; and went once to Totnes where I bought a celestial globe (£1:0:0:) and a very beautiful straw-work cabinet (£5:5:0) and a bunch of flowers painted on a slate (25/=) for Nora, and some smaller oddments. And I saw Mrs Lefanu several times, and Meinie and Mrs Winterbotham once – Mrs W. and I again exchanged glances of, Oh God! must I talk to you again!, and pruned gooseberry bushes, and visited nice sick Mrs Rayner, and sat in the studio while Nora painted, and in Little Vicky[13] every evening. And every day I wrote to Valentine, and every day had a letter from her – also a jade heart in a tiny tortoiseshell chest, and the Koran. And the weather was so-so, and the garden full of phloxes and very overgrown. And then two bitches came on heat, and the dogs raged, and so I left on Monday instead of Wednesday after a visit in which N. and I tried to be nice to each other and succeeded well enough.

October

16. *The Flat, Winterton.*[14]

It was in the houseboat at Thurne that we read of the supplementary Budget, and knowing that it would hit Ruth, began to discuss ways for the winter. Which is why we are here now, with Miss Green tidied away except for Andrew Wordsworth's Christmas tenancy there, and 130 and 113 trying to get themselves let.

[. . .] I have begun to score Howard's *Salve Regina* – much as usual. I am drinking madeira, Valentine sits by the fire reading Plutarch's Morals, and scoring them with an attentive pencil. William has had his first, long-expected set-to with Bunny,[15] which is sad; but otherwise the omens seem good. And presently I shall put on my beautiful new dressing-gown, pleased and companioned by an essay by E. Thomas in which he describes the Harrow of my childhood. I

12 The periodical. STW's friend Reggie Harris was the editor.
13 Unidentifiable.
14 A flat above the Acklands' garage, used by Valentine.
15 An unidentifiable Winterton pet.

suppose I should inevitably feel a little defenceless at the outset of this new sort of winter, for all my happiness and sheltered estate; and Thomas has consequently been a singular comfort to me.

December

1. [Lavenham] Cold and sunny. We went to Bury [St Edmunds] in the car. In a good grocers I saw a whole set of lacquered jars and tins – most exquisite. The shop dates from 1792, and they are probably contemporary. We liked Bury – it has a grand air, and the hunting connection fills it with good leather and queer brands of tobacco. Visited Cockfield church – where an experiment into the font cover, which hangs on a balance, left it swinging like an ominous demonstration of perpetual motion – N.B. by glueing one down, some village atheist with high principals could do a lot to thwart baptisms – and ate our lunch in the lane nearby. Valentine found lambstails. A sudden mist came on afterwards. We mulled the local port after dinner. We set fire to it six times, and even then there seemed to be a fair proportion of methylated about it, though it must have burned for a good ten minutes – a half-bottle, too. Mr Justice McCardie at Leeds has spoken out against the law against abortion, excellent fellow.

1932

16. [Winterton] A ravishing morning. We went down to the beach. The waves were casting up a quantity of foam. I ate it, it tasted bitterly of iodine. Then I must needs paddle, and she did too. Then we played games – running a heart with our foot-tracks, and crashing together as we ran the arrows, morris-dancing like rabbits and grangles, lying together at the sea's edge, and playing at horses – she unseated me everytime. We found a pure white pebble, very small and smooth. 'Sometimes I love you like this' she said – And threw it up against the blue, and caught it, like catching the moon.

20. An announcement of a 'drastically abridged and expurgated' edition of Lady Chatterley. V. wrote protest to Daily Mail and Daily News, I to T. and T.[1] Raged all day.

March

18. Up. My last day. We saw The Shanghai Express, with a small bad part for Anna May Wong,[2] who is exquisite – not a feather's weight of movement wasted or misjudged. Otherwise a boring film. Packing, and sad adieux to delight. I looked up from a book and saw her, standing by the dresser, staring at me – already alone, and desolate, and drooped.

19. Caught the 10.30 for Brent, accompanied by all her cares and provisions. Harmless journey. Nora was well, at first I didn't think she was in the least pleased to see me, afterwards things went better. The waterworks are still tearing up the road, and we had to come via bylanes, all with far too much moss in them. The Blackie money[3] has dwindled. It is only £200 apiece this year.

22. A spring-like day – I sat for a long while in a field by the river

1 The periodical, *Time and Tide*.
2 The film star had been a lover of Valentine.
3 From her father's book royalties.

90

looking at a very large celandine. Nora sits in the evening with a musical-box on her knee, in the brave bright new room she has made for herself since Ronald's death, a picture of all that is admirable in her. I read Shadows on the Rock by Willa Cather, and liked it much. No letter from V.

June

17. [Chaldon] Finished and packed The Salutation, my eighth book. Valentine typed some for me, pestered by Mrs Way. Then we soaped the roses, and William. After dinner I walked alone up the Drove, admiring the sunset, and the smell of the fields, exactly like the smell of cows. Then V. read aloud, The Island of Pines and some Ford, and I patched. A full happy day.

18. Worked, for now it presses, on the Dickens book,[4] and was happy in the Chapel with Stickfast. My little table came, and fell rather flat, she being mournful and I tired. Then Mr Goult with the cider cask; then Mrs G. with a gift of new potatoes. So dinner was late, and I rather sadly writing this, when she came down in the new corduroy trousers made in Dorchester; so handsome, so slenderly swaggering, that my life flared up again in admiration.

July

19. Yesterday my dear told me she must have a blood test, as she suspects herself of T.B. It will be on Thursday. Meanwhile we wait. Last night we sat up late, talking of Dicky;[5] and comforted ourselves with love after. Aeroplanes were flying over the house. The last went over with a fierce metallic clang, like a dragon.

This morning we got up late (V. with a headache), and walked in the hayfield, and picked honeysuckle, and took care to embrace in sight of Beth Car. This afternoon we walked up the Drove, sat under Jacob's hayrick, and strolled over the Maries, and down Lovers' Lane, where the grasses are thigh-high, and the hedges matted with bryony, like green mountain-sides. My dear talked of the elder wands that Bob[6] used to cut for her at shooting lunches (busy killing birds all the morning, and then carving a wand for a child) and cut one for me, and

4 *The Weekend Dickens*, an anthology edited by STW, Maclehose & Co, 1932.
5 Dicky Powys died violently in Africa in 1932. At first it was thought that he had been killed by a lion; later it seemed more likely that he had been murdered by tribesmen.
6 Robert Ackland, Valentine's father, who had died in 1923.

carved it with a running band, a heart, and VA. Helping me with the cooking she put on my Paris apron and looked like a mason with her long legs under the blue nonsense.

31. [I]n the afternoon I had gone over the hill to the heath. All the July flowers: poppy, succory, rampion, millefoil, hemlock, scabious, ragwort, and on the heath centaury and a St John's wort of sorts, and thousands of grass-hoppers, and two lizards; and the up-shot of the walk was my poor darling, who had expected to find me sooner, sitting on a Mary reflecting on adders, murderers, or that it had all been a dream, and she awaking alone.

August

3. We drove Theo all over Dorset. To Piddletrenthide, and up a fierce hill, to a beech-wood, where we lunched, alarmed by wasps and stray dogs. On to Plush, a small valleyed village under high green downs. [. . .]

Home by Blandford, and Bere. We had tea on the heath. Theo spoke of our happiness with great grace and tenderness, and then went into the minor to speak of being alone. Till then he had been in high spirits, thinking that we should find lodgings.[7] But nothing had been found, and we were on the way home, and his happiness was dated. Then, heavily as a tired child, he leaned himself against my knee, and fitted his shoulder into my arm, patting V's hand very gently as he spoke to us.

Later a bee got into the car, and, the windscreen lifted, got out again. Theo exclaimed 'How wise of it! And how kind!'

6. Final (for we leave, alas!) scrimmage in the garden. Theo spent the afternoon. We walked up the Drove and sat on a Mary, it was very hot, a faint blur of sea-mist on the downs – the weather, he said, to make wasps angry. I spoke of his estate. He admitted that he thought more and more of going away, that sometimes such a thought was his only consolation, that he had £5 put away secretly for that need. But not to an Inn. 'I don't think I could ever do anything hazardous. I could not go to an Inn.' We had a very happy tea which my love had prepared, and then all walked up to B.C.

7. *Sunday* and packing. Our last evening walk, too melancholy at farewell to speak of it. The moon enormous and feminine, slinking behind High Chaldon, the mist glimmering. Belly pain (mine) began. For all its business a most happy day.

7 Theodore nursed a strong desire at this time to live by himself.

1933–45

Miss Green's cottage proved too small for a permanent home, and in July 1933 Sylvia and Valentine took a lease on Frankfort Manor, a beautiful seventeenth-century house near Sloley in Norfolk. Less than a year later, however, they became involved in a libel case surrounding the treatment of servant girls at Chaldon Vicarage, the very issue which had brought them together in October 1930, and the subsequent legal costs were so heavy that they were forced to leave Norfolk and take a dilapidated cottage at 24, West Chaldon. This period saw the beginning of their involvement in politics, and in the spring of 1935 both women were admitted into the Communist Party. They became well-known local activists, and Sylvia particularly was a tireless committee member and propagandist. During the Civil War in Spain they worked for a Red Cross unit in Barcelona, and in 1937 were sent as part of the British delegation to the 2nd International Congress of Writers in Defence of Culture. Sylvia's two novels of this period, Summer Will Show *(1936)* and After the Death of Don Juan *(1938) are both based on historical subjects which satirise the contemporary political scene.*

In August 1937 Sylvia and Valentine moved into Frome Vauchurch, a house by the River Frome in Maiden Newton, Dorset, where they were to remain for the rest of their lives. Their struggle to make ends meet had been partly alleviated by the success of Sylvia's short stories in the New Yorker *magazine, which patronised her work for the next forty years. They were dogged by personal unhappiness, however, when Valentine fell in love with a young American woman, Elizabeth Wade White, in 1938, an affair which dragged on through the following year and up to the start of the war. Very little of Sylvia's diary remains for these years.*

$\underline{1933}$

January

12. Our second anniversary[1]. A most brilliant day, with frost and sun
bargaining. In the morning (the proper morning, for already in early
light my darling had got up, seen the moon setting behind Granny,[2]
and sat reading Pocahontas by candlelight, while I drowsed and bur-
rowed beside her) she gave me my aquamarine pendant. An aquamarine, very deep through, cut to a point behind, and ice-burning
blue, dangling from a diamond the colour of a drop of champagne; and
a sleek compact silver cigarette-case, with the falcon; and Mrs Gaskell's
Letters to Ch. Eliot Norton, who must have been the father of my
Mr Norton in New York; and I gave her a new-faced watch, with a
scientific expression, and an inscription in a wedding-ring on the back.

We drove to Dorchester to fetch the oysters. After lunch we walked
to see the lambs in Child's meadow, and then took William as far as
the thorn. Elder, and spindle-berry tree already showing their leaves.
Our ceremonial dinner was oysters, champagne, truffles cooked gently in cream, and coffee.

It is freezing hard, and the night after full moon. The air windless
(so far), the bleached landscape hovering and disembodied. The only
un-supernatural thing the warm light of the lantern carried into
Jacob's shed, where I suppose a cow is calving.

August

23. So long since I have written any diary. So much has changed. We
have left Miss Green and come to Frankfort Manor. We left her very
early in a July morning. The sun was just awakening the air as I went
up the lane to open the garage doors. It was so early that it was cold,
and there was no smell in the air. 'Safely left and sure' I said to myself,

1 Of their private 'marriage'.
2 Anne Moxon's cottage.

looking at the grey plain-headed little house and the ash-trees, which have come to overtop it since we went there first in 1930.

We travelled all day, through Dorset, Wiltshire, Berkshire, Oxfordshire, Buckinghamshire (which was most beautiful – untouched pastoral country) Bedfordshire, Cambridgeshire, Huntingdonshire, Suffolk to Winterton. And from there moved in here on July 10th. It is a most lovely, large and tranquil house, and our bedroom the fairest room in it, as it should be. And I should be very happy here; and am happy. But William failed almost as soon as we arrived; and on July 31st I had him destroyed. From that moment I have been subject to a queer coldness of heart, which makes me feel a stranger here – rootless, unattached; except when I stand by his grave in the meadow, which my darling dug, with the hindrance of a very old man who had that morning appeared in the gardener's stead; and, immediately assuming the sexton, explained that our spade was not the right shape for digging graves.

25. Today which was to have been such a nice full secluded day, my poor darling laid low with a violent eye-ache. Nothing to do but lie limp in bed; and I strove with both cats, auricula-grey Meep and a plangent kitten called Boots: they can't meet; and Boots is pining for his mother, and finds me a harsh substitute; and I also sowed spinach and strove with bindweed. An interminable gloomy day, with nothing to show for it, except reading Sorley's poems, who died in the war: which was to make the world safe for democracy, so very properly killed all the poets it could lay hands on; and then, as Valentine said, finished off a few more in the Irish Rebellion.

If I can I will re-write old 'Flora'[3] and foist it on Chambers' Journal, as something Scotch and sentimental. I have had three acceptances since I came here: which is better than I dared hope; but I must keep on at that rate or better, if we are to have a chance of paying for this place. Try as I will, and live as we do on vegetables, I can't keep within my estimate; and today there was nothing for a poor yowling Meep, and if Irene[4] hadn't wisely breakfasted off Meep's liver, there would have been little for Irene: And she is so charming, and I do so enjoy having her.

It is dark now by nine. I hear an owl crying in our heavy trees.

3 The article about her grandmother she had been working on in 1928.
4 Irene Peake, their maid.

1934

April

29. In the morning it was so hot that instead of a single duteous work we sat on the lawn drinking our specimen bottle of Vin Rosé. And very nice it was, while the bulbs smelled and the cuckoo called.

After lunch we drove to Winterton; and just beyond Stalham saw white smoke rising from the ploughed fields, and ran into a sea-fog – with horses, and young willows suddenly becoming three-dimensional out of the flat pearl-painted landscape.

And on our return we forked the weediest part of the cabbage bed; and ate our own tender broccoli.

Washing and distempering, £1.1.9.

May

1. And rather chilly. The tulips are coming out, and look like Arabian Night brides, so suavely contoured and sleek in such passionate colours. Cherry colour, plum with an almond green slash, scarlet tinged with lime green. V. still limp and Sylvie so-so. But a bottle of champagne recreated us and sent us to our affable bed.

2. 'Summer!' she said; and looking up from the weeds in the fruit border I saw her in an open-necked white shirt, and the broad-brimmed panama in which she mistakenly supposes herself to look like a Colonel. Sent off a great many parcels of flowers and vegetables. But I doubt if two asparagus beds is enough to warrant the bestowal of asparagus by post.

3, 4. Happy is the day whose history is not written down.

7. I did a great heap of the Day of Glory;' and we stretched trip-wires in the meadow and shrubbery against those inroading Baineses and

---

1 An unidentifiable work.

96

Leeses, who have robbed our birds-nests. And weeded the parsnips, and I must say they look as miserable as any other saved souls now we have done them. And shopped in Norwich, where I visited Miss Cowper-Johnson,[2] and was surprised by V. stealing up in the car behind me, gloating over handbills of hangings and dying speeches, glass-cased on the curiosity shop wall. In the morning I had been melancholy, having missed my writing overnight. But roused from weeding by Irene and lunch I realised that I had been so brimming up with an interior happiness that I could scarcely believe myself for joy.

2 A relation of the Powys family on the distaff side.

1935

March

10. [West Chaldon] The snow has come. It was scratching at the door, hard little scrabbling wind-blown pellets, when I went out before dinner – now it is thick and feathery-soft everywhere . . . flattening out the curve of the hill, aging the barton-building by centuries: the whole landscape like a black and white tapestry.

11. And came to some purpose. In the morning Nora rang up to say that her lane was blocked and that the car could not get to the station to fetch me. So I contented myself by sending her a box of odd small presents and lending Harriette Wilson. I felt in a daze all day, the snow was thick, and in the afternoon the sky cleared, and the landscape looked as if it had gone to heaven. The Maries were white breasts; in front of our windows the barton, and the cattle, and the leaning willow made an endless series of Bewicks. V. wrote a very good Country Conditions III[1] about the gentry.

12. Snow still, though the sun shone on it. In the afternoon we picked several bucket-loads of old iron and broken glass from the garden, and pruned. In the evening I began *John and Ivan*.[2] But I am dubious of it, I don't seem able to escape from conveying a lovely sense of fiction.

16. Valentine was sure I had a cold coming on. So I spent the day in bed with Postgate's Revolutionary documents of the 19th century and my patchwork. In the evening Betty came, and brought with her a cheque from R. C. Trevelyan, a cheque for £15, 'because he did not like to see poets victimised',[3] a reason even more likeable than the cheque, which we liked very much. [As] at the same time I got £7:14:10: for 'Without

---

1 For *Left Review*. The articles were later made into a book, *Country Conditions*, Lawrence & Wishart, 1936.
2 An unidentifiable work.
3 Referring to their recent prosecution, see p. 93.

98

Comment' from John;[4] and Valentine heard that we would not be summonsed for leaving the car in Queen's Road, and a penny saved is a penny earned we sent £2 to the Hawker's Aircraft strikers. Germany has announced conscription. Bad black news . . . and who prodded them on with a White Paper?

4 John Robertson Scott, editor of the *Countryman*.

1937

November

20. [Maiden Newton] And I think it is time I kept a diary again. Dorothy[1] died about a year ago, in a nursing-home, saying 'Let there be no remorse'.

It is very cold, snow in the North. We cooked a solemn lunch of pork and greens and large green Winterton pears, the same pears appear in a still life by Courbet which I saw long ago in the Barbizon Gallery. While we were still digesting it a telegram came from Janet[2] saying Sylvia Robert ill. Lice are everywhere. Miserable. [. . .]

All this was very distracting, and led to a great expense of spirit in shame and telephones. It froze, and I went to bed with a cold.

21. And spent the morning tidying a ruined garden. Cleared all the michaelmas daisies, etc, V. lopped apple-trees. Glazed polyanthus look very pretty, even yellow privet is tolerable with an ermine edging. It was a most beautiful morning, everything bloomed with silver, falling rime sparkling, the sun shining, the Sunday smoke of Maiden Newton gently rising, Tom and Toad[3] kissing each other. We lunched off cold pork and then, as bargained, I went to bed.

24. V. up in the morning. Then, with the arrival of the thermometer, down again. I read Boylesve's Young Vigilance. It has one admirable character – particularly where she goes to confront the priest and the house-keeper who have been fleecing an old woman and is downed by them. For the vileness is not the priest's, and not entirely the house-keeper's, but is of the thing they represent, an inherent vileness in religion. But I would like to know if the author meant this. If so, he is a genius at reticence, for it is the only hint he gives.

1 Dorothy Warner. She had suffered bouts of mental illness during the previous decade, and had separated from Oliver. She died on 6 January 1937 from pneumonia following a blood transfusion.
2 Janet Machen was working at a Basque refugee home in Thame.
3 Grey tom-cat and Pekingese dog.

Felicie is another of these grand avarices – clutching at land, clutching at power, the sort of character I deeply disapprove in real life, and invariably like in fiction. In the evening I did a possible New Yorker, based on a catalogue of parlour tricks, found by Valentine.

25. This morning early I looked at the river. It reflected the moon, pale green and metallic in a blue-grey sky. All the birds were twittering, a fine mesh of sound, in the village I heard a man coughing, heavy boots on the frozen road, the rumble of an early lorry. Though it was still freezing it was meek.

After breakfast we went to William's Roman Road and walked there. Dead-nettle and a pale ragged-robin in bloom. Then we discovered a very beautiful field path near Compton Valance, leading through a little wood and meadow to a sloping field that rose to a wind-break, and had ash-trees in it. In the meadow there was a most surprising and inexplicable smell of new hay. Then to the field at the top of the hill, where we found an elder stump rubbed smooth as marble by sheep. When we got back Valentine went to bed. [. . .] I walked to the station to get some automatic chocolate, and was pleased on my way by a white cottage, a large broken white ewer outside, and a child in a white pinafore playing with a black and white dog and a white cat. All Staffordshire mantlepiece figures.

28. A great deal of roasting pork. Face-ache tedious. In the night my darling got up and brewed me tea and brandy. Wrote to Edgell[4] suggesting an enquiry into elementary school history-books for the APC[5] campaign. Sent him details of earnings as a writer. Average for the last four years just over £250.

December

2. Face-ache today definitely better. High time, too. I have been slinking around under it, much too wary to be able to give my mind over to anything. This morning I cleaned the sitting-room (V. did all the passages yesterday, and polished the stairs). And meant to work this afternoon but had a discussion instead in which I seem to have played a poor parochial part. I suppose CP[6] is at once too tight a pot and too draughty for her roots to settle in to their own comfort. She

4 Edgell Rickword, the poet and essayist, then editor of *Left Review*.
5 Arts Peace Campaign.
6 The Communist Party.

feels at once unused and misused. Janet sent me a grand green blanket as a birthday present, and this morning V. gave me a record, most beautiful, of two Monteverdi madrigals, Amor and Ecco mormorar l'onde. A letter from Elizabeth [Wade White]. She has raised $1180 in Waterbury – and incidentally has received invitations to lunch with Mrs Franklin D. Rooseveld[t] and join a nudist colony. Such a pity they could not be combined. That was a good day's work when we fired her. But these are not day's works – which is perhaps the best comment on this afternoon's fraction.

4. A fish-letter from Harold Raymond about New Yorker stories. Little does he know that I have my eye on him for a future one! Finished *Mrs Hazlitt's Divorce* and sent it to Cornhill.[7] And I wait to see if my red has dyed through to that respectable consciousness.

6. Birthday. [. . .] In the morning it was frosty and cold, and we played the gramophone. Janet arrived for lunch, thinner, her cheek-bones showing, which makes her very handsome. Drove to Dorchester in the afternoon. V. brought back my green and sumptuous birthday cake, and gave me a paper narcissus, and lilies of the valley. More music – Lasciate me morire, most lovely: then a grand birthday dinner, and making up Jan's bed, and going to our own. Most of all today I have enjoyed her complaints that we are not alone. Yet Janet is charming, and out of this triangle we have grown much more intimate and affectionate then ever before: which is, I surmise, the normal development whenever there are no children. It is a pity but seems true, that bearing children reduces women to extremes of potential nobility or potential baseness in anything like a crisis. But robs them of the impulse to behave with reason and decency. I suppose a birth is such a shock to the nerves that one never gets over it.

7 *Cornhill Magazine*. They rejected it.

1940

June

13. Paris has fallen – has been abandoned. My father used to make a face at the Schubert Marche Militaire because it was to that tune the Germans marched into Paris in the war of '70. For some days the city has been under a pall of smoke from the burning oil-dumps in the suburbs. One could not see across the Place de la Concorde. During the last night they blew up the factories.

But all day the impression in my mind has been the serenity, the urbanity of Paris, those wide streets, that air of tranquility and civilisation, must have a queerly austere and reproving look to an invading army, confused with triumph and exhaustion. It seems to me that the Louvre and the Place de la Concorde, and Notre Dame and the bridges, all so compact together, all, somehow, so much smaller than their renown, must have a look of saying – Yes, here we are. Et puis? And the people who remain; I suppose their blank faces would have much the same impression.

To invade Paris . . . surely it would give the invaders, those who were not too tired, too brutalised, to have lost all perceptions except pavement, food, drink, a hallucination of being a quantity of tourists, tourists with rather unusual equipment and baggage.

Was fur Plunder. Presumably the Venus of Milo and so forth have been retired. After the statement that Paris had been made an open town in order to preserve it, it was disquieting to read that in the event of the Germans massing troops there we should no longer consider it as such. It is a very limited, very barbarian, frame of mind which limits the class 'work of art' to objects which it is possible to carry away; objects thievable or preservable. So that the Elgin Marbles are works of art which can be removed from the Parthenon. A work of art which is the property of the people can achieve at least the dimensions of the Acropolis. But as works of art become private property they are forced smaller and smaller, and the artist finds himself confounded with the goldsmith and the jeweller. One must take into account the part played by insurance companies in determining the nature of a work of art.

14. Onlooker, speaking on the wireless on the events of the week, urged hearers not to be too much overawed by the Fall of Paris. It was less important, he said, than the steadfast courage of people in this country. In fact

> 'Courage in another's trouble,
> Kindness in your own.'[1]

Probably people in this country are being quite fairly courageous; but it is a courage of incomprehension. The direct military effect of war, just being killed or maimed, does not yet have any meaning for them; and the other aspects, hunger, poverty, famine, slow ruin, are not shown to them by any propaganda. 'Look out for parachutists', say the official spokesmen; and the bulk and blackness of the cloud *behind* the parachutists are – it is hoped – to pass unperceived by people looking out for parachutists. I suppose if a government were to stress the long-term effects of war no country would undertake a war.

Actually, I think people here would be much more frightened if the Germans were the Black Death. Then the news – the Black Death is in Rouen, in the Channel ports, has appeared in Paris, would set people to thinking: soon I may catch it, and die.

But also, I think the giving of news by wireless, which is *non-geographical*, has tended to give the war-news something of the quality of news of a pestilence. It has made it, in a fashion, an atmospheric rather than a territorial phenomenon.

15. The soldiers, who were to have come yesterday, have not come. I say to Valentine that the billeting officer has probably been assured that we are dangerous fifth columnists. What more likely? We were anti-fascists long before the war. And our neighbours, receiving a strong impression that our views were uncongenial and reprehensible, will now remember their impression rather than our views. Accordingly, they will feel convinced we are, and always have been, black-shirts.

17. The French Army has capitulated. Radio-Paris rings with announcements to auditeurs Français about how happy Paris is to be

1 A deliberate readjustment of Adam Lindsay Gordon's lines in 'Ye Wearie Wayfarer'.

released from her oppressors, mingled with *sub-audite* horrors about the collapse of the army, the fall of Verdun. Much the same propaganda as Haw-Haw: old socialist clap-trap about plutocracy, toiling masses, brave soldiers, etc. This afternoon as we were gardening two aeroplanes went over, they were French planes. V. said – There's honesty! What sort? said I. The simple Teuton would not think it so. [. . .]

Later, talking of democracy, it seemed to us that whatever figures or deeds of excellent virtue a democracy casts up are anarchist. It is not enough to think individually to be an anarchist. In a democracy everyone thinks selon ses idées, even when he thinks plumb in the centre of majority thinking. The anarchist is distinguished by doing also, by commandeering responsibility.

Talking again of the inferiority complex underlying fascism we worked out how an inferiority complex of the simplest social nature prepared the ruling classes of Europe to turn fascist. After the last war they emerged, hoping again to be socially what they had been before it: the leaders of society. Instead, they found themselves by-passed through the cultural revival that followed the war. Old Prussia, and Mayfair, and Quartier St Germain, all had their noses snubbed by finding the limelight focussed on the leaders of culture.

V. said that the Left had made a great mistake in underestimating the stupidity of the German people: its vast extent of lumpenbourgeoisie, readers of the Daily Express (we have it too, my God). Victory will not allay their inferiority complex, nor defeat[;] in either, they will still feel inferior to the intelligentsia, will still remain as fascist as ever.

[. . .]

I think I envy the French. Hearing Churchill in a very bad paragraph announce we would fight on, etc, I found in myself a sense not only of exasperation at the numbers more who must be killed and maimed in a war that never reached its purpose but also the frustrated impatience of an experimental scientist. For war – this sort of war – is no way to attack fascism. And I am fretted to think how every day my chances of seeing other methods tried out are diminished. I feel like a scientist who has to wait in a queue to get to the laboratory – while both the laboratory and he are under bombardment.

18. Slept out last night under the apple tree. The nightingale sang from 10 pm till 5 am. And is at it again now. And we shall again sleep out. In the evening the air smells of Mathiola Bicoronis, and in the early

morning the pinks take over. Counterpointing the war is the loveliest summer I have ever known.

Our garden is much fished from. I still suspect we are not bien vus, but the anglers come every evening. The B.E.F.[2] pair have gone – whither I don't know – now we have two children, one from Stoke on Trent, t'other from Perthshire. While V. was listening to Churchill's speech – audit of swings and roundabouts – they were sitting on the lawn, each holding a young rabbit. Perthshire caught a trout – and was much relieved when V. killed it for him.

These are the instruments of the old: as the psalm says: young children are like arrows in the hands of a giant.

19. Soldiers fishing in the garden. In bed I heard a new aeroplane noise, and said it might be a German.

20. And it was: a steady *unrhythmical* engine noise. It flew north, maybe was the one that visited South Wales. On the wireless this evening wounded French soldiers sending greetings to their families in France. It was profoundly moving: the serious voices, the dialects, the unvarying bon santé: one said, firmly: Le morale est bon. Many gave addresses in invaded districts – one, asked what region his village was in said in a tone of unforgettable melancholy: *Nord*. The whole landscape spread out under the word, and the trails of refugees.

Tidying and throwing away all afternoon. So much about Spain. Thinking how vainly I worked, I wish I had worked a hundred times harder. Strange how there was room for one in that war: and in this – none. This war has not issued a single call for the help of intellectuals. It is just – your money and/or your life.

December

10. Philippa [Katie Powys] went to the shop. A woman was buying a plumcake, and as Weston handed it to her he said: 'That's the last of these we'll see. The factory where they are made has been burnt to the ground, and these were saved just in time. Look at the invoice that came with it'. And he pulled out an invoice that was brown with firing. The women in the shop looked unbelieving and unmoved. I think the Westons are doing wisely in trying to make MN realise what bombing of Bristol and S'hampton means to them. But they are working in the stiffest clay.

2 British Expeditionary Force.

Just after lunch we heard a plane flying high, that Philippa & V. said was German. Then the Performing Spitfire came over, and did his usual acrobatics, beautiful tight turns. He vanished over the hill, we returned to coffee. A long distant growl. An explosion? Not till the third of these did we realise it was only a thunderstorm. One of the advantages of a thunderstorm is that one feels no need to locate it. I don't know why not being allowed to know where *noises off* take place should irk one so. If a bomb falls, a bomb has fallen, and that should suffice a contented mind. But it doesn't.

$\underline{1941}$

March

17. The night very noisy with bombers. 8 am news spoke of a heavy raid on a West-Country town. We guessed (it was), unhappy Bristol. So we were not much surprised when the 9.10 did not come in. At 10.30 we waited no longer. It was a misty day, we could not have done the YMCA round[1] in the time, even with the Ford V8: and this was the Fordson. Returned to pick up the day thus unexpectedly dropped into our laps.

19. Valentine continued the trench.[2] We planted onions. The baker's sister explained the national loaf position thus: 'We're supposed to make a government loaf and charge a farthing less for it. But no one scarcely wants it, so we only make a few and charge them the same as ordinary'. Her handsome features were beaming with patriotism, probity and obtuseness.

22. Plymouth again last night. We heard many bombers while we were out fire-watching. One, flying very low, went over and came back, like a dog that has overrun the scent. It was so low that we could hear the noises of the engine as well as the noise. [. . .]

Our train to Dorchester being only 20 minutes late we arrived full of pleasurable anticipations of getting off on time. Dashed by Miss Harrison, who informed us that an official inspection of the Mobiles was due at 11. All the mobiles were to be ranged up: with engines running, she added, so that any defects could be seen at once. She was rosy with self-importance, so we went away. At 11.30 we returned to find our mobile only standing where we had left it, and Miss Harrison saying the inspection would not take place. Debating on megalomania and fantasies of greatness we set off two hours late. Chapman's Pool (where the cliffs were wrapped in dark grey vapour, the sea-line

1 Taking cigarettes and sweets to troops stationed along the coast.
2 Civilians had been encouraged to dig them.

brilliant pure silver, and the men very subdued), Kingston, Kimmeridge and Kimmeridge Hill. At Kimmeridge we found an honest man,
for being asked if the second go of chocolate he asked for was for a
friend he replied No, its for me. Overcome by this phenomenon, and
having a fair supply of chocolate, we rewarded his infant piety.

[. . .]

The Keren battle sounds expensive. Jugoslavia seems to be ripening
in order to coincide with tomorrow's day of national prayer. I found
the resignation of the Croatian Governor difficult to reconcile with
the Serbian resignations. V. diagnosed it as a pan-axis made to bring
down the Government, and this seems perspicaceous. Other news in a
gloomy day is that Blois, Tours and Louviers are badly damaged, and
Caudebec in ruins – besides the devastation of the N. Eastern provi-
nces. Louviers in the moonlight when we first saw the portal – and Blois
reflected in the river. Evreux damaged too, I suppose those windows
are gone. In a mood of architectural vindictiveness I remembered with
satisfaction that we have not damaged any German Gothic.

23. Day of National What-Not.[3] In deference to public opinion we did
not garden. Valentine painted a door green and I waxed the sitting-
room floor. Occasional [word obscured by ink blot] of very small
groups of people going blackly to church. Visited by John Fox, whose
nerves have become very much worse as a result of staying at home
with measles and listening to his bugaboo parents. Country children
need to be evacuated quite as much as town children.

26. An aeroplane crossing us about lunchtime went on and bombed
Yeovil. Instant flare of grape-vine and latest intelligences, reported by
poor John. This much to it, that a balloon barrage was up this evening.
I visited Mary Ann.[4] It rained all day, young Mr Fryer in ecstacies
because of what it would do to the pasture. I was taking in Mary Ann's
milk during this conversation, and said that March and April were the
leanest months – as they are, if you discount flowers. He agreed. 'But
after the second week of April things take a turn. And then its nothing
but delight.'

He said this with absolute sincerity, his face beaming at the thought
of summer near, and not an arrière-pensée of the delights this summer
may bring. Having just noticed the hawthorn, plastered with cement

3 Prayer.
4 An elderly neighbour.

where they laid the tank-traps, but cracking through with green shoots, I liked him for being so much more in tune with nature than with man. Most people achieve an uneasy even temperament and are in tune with neither. The first green pea up. Hyacinths out, grape and grand: bulb onions and shallots shooting. Ribes on the brink of flower. It was a quiet warm evening, and we went for a walk. Curious reflection that half our local Home Guards are probably more afraid of meeting a ghost than of meeting a German. V. says no, their preoccupying fear is of being murdered by some stranger jumping out of the hedge. We heard one whistling. He sounded rather thin. In a letter to Janet I suggested that it would be nice if England could produce a weekly corresponding to *Life*, and with the same pictures of bombings and fashion, and call it *Death*.

29. Van. This time we did Worbarrow properly – under an air-raid warning screaming from Arishmell Gap. We saw a full squadron of Spitfires going over, a handsome implacable pattern in the sky that also, like the Great Bear n'avait pas l'air chretien, O figure fatale, exacte et monotone. Having a little time we drew into the Tadnol lane to warm up with the dregs of tea. And Mr Miller came bicycling by and stopped for conversation. The Daily Mirror carried a little piece about German aeroplanes wirelessing each other with *Achtung, Schpitfeuer*. Very cold.

April

3. [T]he trench flooded. V. strove to drain it, I cleaned flower beds as it was too wet to get on the vegetable ground. Two bombs during the night, two rabbits sold. Rhoda re-mated. Mrs Harper visited us in the evening. During the distribution of sand-bags she got none, on the plea she hadn't a man in the house. She hasn't got a contex to her gas-mask either, presumably for the same reason. A very noisy evening. We have lost Benghazi to the German advance. Today the news that Virginia Woolf, missing since Friday, is now presumed drowned in the Sussex Ouse. I was thinking of her while I weeded, and suddenly received a powerful impression that the reason of her going was the leader in the Times about a fortnight ago, called Disappearance of The Highbrow, and a flood of filthy letters that followed it.

6. Woke into the wireless news that Germany has attacked Jugoslavia. Afterwards listened to Hitler's speeches, and the German news on the

Paris radio. Belgrade is arrosée des bombes. A cold day without, and heavy within. The BBC did the 2nd half of the Matthew Passion in the afternoon. We have taken Addis Ababa, but made little of it. The Germans are fighting on the Thrace frontier. No news comes through. I stare at maps, and think of the wild horses in Thrace that Hercules laboured for. They might be useful now.

1942

January

20. Snow grizzling the hills this morning. Left at 12. caught the 11.45 at 12.30 (wearing to my shame that be-giftet pixie hood and of course met by Mrs Barnes (though nothing to her) because I'd left my Paristient-toujours hat in the car) and stepped into a cold pale mist at Weymouth. Lunched at the Brit. Rest.[1] where a very dandyfied black & white cat rejected the wholesome fare, hinting that if I had been in the kitchen . . . and then went off to mew at other tables. Walked along the esplanade, the sea growling invisibly under a cold wind, and up to the AFS[2] headquarters on V.'s affair. It was a comfortable suburban mansion, singularly, bleakly, tidy: full of celibate camp-beds and deserted helmets and draughts. At last I found a sleeping fireman. Who led me to a black-eyed gent called Adams, at first antagonistic, finally amiable and cigarette-sharing (but a prig) who advised a visit to Jefferies. They have one trailer pump worked by girls and they are excellent. So back, and to the Rechabite Hall, and gave the first of my six lectures to the Weymouth Labour women. They restrained their coughs and listened nicely. Matriarchy, the rice and the shoe, Polynesian Joseph, Jewry's Batchelor Diety, etc. They took the ticklish question of Xtian celibacy better than I dared hope. So did I. I had notes, but spoke without them. About 15 there. Train to Dorchester, met V. oppressed with ear-ache. She dined in bed. A cable from Eliz.W.W. 'Wire how you are Evelyn operated on for appendix Monday' V.'s comment: two at one blow. The doctor's angel daughter brought 6 eggs. [. . .]

Churchill met the House. Feeling about Singapore met with the question of whether to broadcast speeches in the House. Comme hareng c'est assez hareng. Gould brought 4 galls paraffin to replace what was stolen. The hay is now being stolen, and some small cloven-footed animal has eaten a row of early broccoli.

1 British Restaurants were part of the government's emergency measures.
2 Auxiliary Fire Service.

22. V. had a temperature, but insisted on getting up. In the afternoon Mrs E.[3] and I inspected Langton Herring. A nasty affair: Mr & Mrs Sparks, two devoted sychophants[sic] and a rector was all that met us (except that we drove into the backyard, and saw an old bay cart-horse being loaded up to go the knackers: thin, and sad, and very gently resisting with rooted undemonstrative force). Going to the school we were accompanied by the Rector. There we found the schoolmistress, 93% proficiency in 1st Aid exam, with no drugs or appliances beyond her own medicine box, and her point (at the Sparks's) occupied by ARP[4] and general affairs, and out of her control. We also found that the water supply (kindness of Mr Sparks) previously admitted scanty, is also contaminated. A beautiful old world village story, and still for ever new. On the way there Mrs E. asked All about Communism, and on the way back illustrated the subject with telling me about Clan Williams at Bridehead.

Did up for Soviet Aid 100 flower prints mixed.

23. [. . .] 30/= for Soviet Aid came from the Glasgow branch of ASLEF[5] and on the midnight news the Soviet announcement of their advance in the Valday sector, as far as Kholm. Amid our own ignominious news I remember last autumn, and how I knew that the defence of USSR was the defence of my deepest concerns; and I know it still: though I would like to think we would be advancing too. Instead of which that damned clever general, Rommel, has taken Jedabiah.

24. A high wind, and rising. A soft gipsy day. In the afternoon we drove to Dorchester, where V. had a disappointing interview with the Mayor of Dorchester about NFS.[6] The fruit & vegetable shop was disappointing too. She came out of it saying they had nothing but a moss cross.

26. At Boots Library the young woman put into my hands Virginia Woolf's last book. And I received an extraordinary impression how light it was, how small, and frail. As though it was the premature-born child, and motherless, and literally, the last light handful remaining of that tall and abundant woman. The feeling has haunted me all day.

3 Anita Egerton, with whom STW inspected possible Rest Centres for evacuees on behalf of the WVS.
4 Air Raid Precautions.
5 Associated Society of Locomotive Engineers and Firemen.
6 National Fire Service.

27. A whole day at home. I began a short story for the New Yorker. I also cleaned. There seems to be no end to the usefulness of USSR as an ally. Not only does she fight the Germans for us, but she affords every ample reason for why we don't do it ourselves. Shinwell in the H. of C. debate, reckoned we had sent them a thousand tanks. No one contradicts this.

29. A howling cold wind. Cattistock Rest Centre and then Maiden Newton in the afternoon, Miss Clarke attending. Reade[7] also came, *ex machina* as usual. At Maiden N. Mrs Slemeck[8] expatiated a great deal, and most meatily, on her longing to bath babies. A hundred, she averred, would not appease her passion. Subsequently Miss Clarke inspected the (very bad) school privies. Mrs S's zeal for infant sanitation did not go so far. She had never seen them before.

30. Gale and rain, W.V.S.[9] in the morning. I spent some time with Mr Nicholls – who had laid in large stores of sanitary towels, which he called cotton goods. During the afternoon I mentioned this to Mrs E. Musing a moment, she burst out: 'I get so worried about those heroic women in Russia. I think of it a great deal. What will they do, for cotton is so short there?' We did Dewlish – Sir Ernest Debenham's handsome hall, constructed with only one exit, and so arranged that the privy bucket must needs be carried right through the hall to be emptied – and Melcombe Horsey. M. H. lost in sheets of rain, gaunt bare hills standing up out of nothing, squalid hovels, dead trees, and M.H. the picture of a damned soul with a chapel attached. We got wet to the skin, and frozen to the bone, and were not offered tea. On the way back Mrs E. began brooding over the dinner she'd have to cook. She must, she explained, cook dinner every night, whether she feels tired or no: because Wion, so devoted to her, so anxious about her health, would insist on her giving up her WVS work if he suspected it tired her. I told her, after a decent interval, that the Labour Party and Transport House were just as bad. Went to bed early, per. V. who washed up. She had a racking headache all day.

31. Singapore invested, Benghazi and Benina lost, Burma Road threatened, and Pitt-Rivers[10] released. Next week the BBC stars a perform-

---

7 B.C. Reade, Civil Defence Controller.
8 The rector's wife.
9 The Women's Voluntary Service.
10 George Henry Lane Fox Pitt-Rivers, an advocate of the science of ethnogenics, had been held as a political prisoner by order of the Home Secretary since 1940.

ance of the Greeks starving (for six months no child in their children's hospital has put on weight). Why don't we send out our ruling classes as tanks – bigger and more impermeable tanks?

'Being alone as little as possible, and keeping healthy enough to have a slight margin of reserve strength, and that means, by whatever methods are necessary, getting sleep when you need it, and being outdoors in the sun and the air, among fairly decent people with whom you are working at something, just as much as possible.' E.W.W. to J.M. [Elizabeth Wade White to Janet Machen] advice on how to lead a Happy Healthy life – war-time.

February

2. W.V.S. Mr Nicholls approached me about 300 tin hats, which he believes to be in the archives of Colliton House, and if I can get him 150 of them he will be my friend for life. I took him a list of equipment wanted, and felt that should make him my friend for quite long enough, really. Still, I will enquire for his hats.

6. W.V.S. Cold as hell all day. Ordered a hamper for Ruth's birthday from a basket-worker in Durngate. Everything seemed shut, but I pushed open a door into a small yard, and then another door into a bare work-shop, where an old man sat on the floor making a basket of white wands. The living cream white of the peeled wands, the dusky lime-washed walls, the old man's cold hands and face, pallid, made a beautiful arrangement of colours. Then we saw a woman in a fur-coat clasping proudly to her stomach and bosom a burden of naked onions. Oh, to be Daumier!

10. House-worked. In the afternoon with Miss Clarke and Mrs Egerton to Tincleton [. . .] the barren heath dotted with churches, sunday schools, & vicarages built by Miss Yonge. Actually the school, *Christo in pauperibus*, a mere decade earlier. *Christo in pauperibus* very damp and only one bottlenecked exit (like hell). Above the tablet was a coloured wan photograph of some young man dead in the last war, who eyed me with a melancholy recognition, as if we might once have exchanged a few words at a promenade concert in 1913. Then to Chesilbourne – a farmer's wife with a very remarkable head, a head of some heart-of-oak, rum-drinking, man-flogging Admiral of Nelson's day. I could scarcely prevent myself from asking her what she had done at Trafalgar. Then on to a singularly rich tea with some people

called Boyle: butlers, family portraits, sponge cake with eggs – all manner of old empire hospitalities. Home late, because of tea, to a beautiful sunset of green and pure rose, and a dusty look of spring on the wintered landscape.

13. On the morning wireless the news that the Scharnhorst, Gneisenau & Prinz Eugen[11] had gone up the Channel to Heligoland; and that we had lost 6 Swordfish, 20 bombers, 16 fighters attacking them. Bad news for a cold morning.

14. Valentine on this day gave me a canton enamel box and snowdrops and daffodils. I gave her a very industrious exceedingly handmade and regrettably tubular Fair Isle scarf. We spent the morning walking in the valley below New Building; and through the hazel woods, and gathered pinecones where a tall stand of fir-trees caught the wind blowing above the level of the sheltered valley copse, and sang their runic song. It was a cold, sunshining day, with a look of youth, of intensity, of expectancy all over the landscape. In the afternoon V. planted peas and married Joseph & Rhoda.[12] No news of Singapore, except Axis reports.

16. W.V.S. A very cold day. 60,000 men surrendered in the Singapore garrison, Lack of food, petrol, water. Landing in Java. Palembang lost. *Fous l'honneur.*

17. To Weymouth where I discoursed my L.P.[13] women on the Renaissance, which they didn't understand at all, on the reformation martyrs, which they grasped only too readily – but I countered Anne Askew with Margaret Clitheroe, explaining that the goodness of martyrdoms is no warrant for the goodness of causes – and Mrs Ann Turner, who went down nicely. They were totally uninterested in the 6-hour [working day] in Utopia. Then Mr Matthews parted my hair on one side. Then we shopped a little, and drove home. Hellish cold, and Valentine had her hair washed, most unsuitably.

19. An exasperating letter from E.W.W. about Craske's *Window.* Valentine in bed with a temperature and Thomas. Knitted madly, and clung to the fire. The wind is pure east, the moon is in her first quarter, we are losing the war, and the Billeting job shows no sign of coming

11 These three German boats had steamed through the Straits of Dover, taking the Royal Navy by surprise.
12 Table-rabbits.
13 Labour Party.

along in time to save Valentine from returning to the T.A.[14] But not, if I can help it, to that cat-house of a back office.

21. It gets colder and colder. Our pipes freeze, and I begin to write a story about a medieval nunnery: to be entirely taken up with their money difficulties. The Hull boy brought his joseph-coloured doe to mate with Joseph. Mrs Bott to tea. V. lent her Country Conditions[15] (still selling, how proper), Damnable Opinions, and The True Heart.

22. Knitted and unknitted. Smothered rabbits in hay. Valentine collopped the toughest beef it has yet been our lot to munch. The salt and pepper and sauce were delicious. More nunnery[16] . . . shame on me for a gadabout.

24. In the morning I cleaned the sit and bed rooms. In the afternoon Mrs E. & I to Abbotsbury (where a lemon-coloured old lady told us of the cousins blown to bits in Liverpool, and her expression was so proud that it was hard to reply) and looked at the school, late Albert with a bell-tower & leaks. It is so cold the children write in their gloves. Then to W'bourne Abbas, to interview the two Mrs Biggses. An applepie garden behind a garage. When I got home V. had cleaned the kitchen. Tidied letters all the evening and paid bills, and drank iced cider, and looked forward to a hot bath, as the taps seemed to have thawed. Yesterday Margesson, Moors Brabazon outed from the cabinet. Also K.W. & the blameless Greenwood[17] – and Sir J. Reith *exit*. But where to, as V. remarked.

28. Thaw. A cold air, but a south wind breathing upon a bank of violets. Our poor crumpled violets did actually smell. The garden looks a disaster after this month of cold and east winds. In the afternoon we collected fircones. There has been a small parachute landing in France, near Havre. The Burma Road is cut by the advance on Rangoon. Maiden Newton is in an uproar because Mearns's customers have had their milk cut and t'other two dairies go on as usual. We shall get five pints next week.

March

2. I spent an idiot morning acquainting organisers by hand that they

14 Territorial Army. Valentine worked as the local Controller's secretary.
15 See note 1 (1935), page 98.
16 STW's novel, *The Corner that Held Them.*
17 Sir Kingsley Wood, Chancellor of the Exchequer, and Arthur Greenwood, Minister without Portfolio in the National War Cabinet.

might have to lay out mattresses but that nobody would lie on them. An unconscious Dali provided by a large Mexican hat lying on a heap of blankets. I found both Mrs E. & Mrs M. felt as I do that war-savings is the opium of the people. Continued a great deal of the Fair Isle pullover: which I hopefully design for Easter. Prepared for Weymouth.

3. But didn't get there, as the car wouldn't start. [. . .] A gloomy day, a damned gloomy drive. An afternoon pretty much like the only shade of wine colour (old dirty ox-blood) available for dyeing V.'s pretty pink coat for office wear. Heu!

4. Our last day[18]. A warm day with sun and wind. We went for a peramble through fields sloping down below Donkey common, and then in a very symetrical and sighing fir-plantation. In a lane a chinese picture. An old man with a small wrinkled face like Thos. Hardy, standing in a straw-rick. The lane lined with reddish hazel boughs tinkling with saffron lambs-tails. Below the stack a farm-cart drawn by an old white horse whose collar points were bright lacquer scarlet, and a young man with a clear pink face wearing old blue jeans. And a deep blue sky over it. Sadly, sadly, to an early bed. The R.A.F. last night bombed the Renault works at Billancourt.

7. Spent the morning at W.V.S. trying to make up for lost time, but failing. It was the day of the exercise. At 9.30 or so there was a real air-raid warning: but nothing came of it, to my surprise. I cannot understand why not. Since everyone has been talking of the extreme secrecy of the proceedings for the last fortnight surely Berlin knows of it. Presumably our Black-shirts preserve us. We hung about after lunch, waiting for zero-hour. The dive-bombers turned out to be low-flying Spitfires fitted with screamers. They flew very beautifully, but the screamers seemed a mistake to me. Why advertise? It is the *Silent* plane that would frighten me. Guns went off: dogs barked. We drove home, visiting Charminster on the way. Java is falling. And so from hour to hour we rot and rot.

8. Today was Invasion Day.[19] Except for two H.Gs[20] walking quietly home with fixed bayonets, we saw it not. I cleared some of the narrow

18 Valentine was returning to work the following day.
19 An exercise.
20 Home Guards.

border: and knitted a great deal. And felt inclined to keep my feet up. Rangoon gone.

10. At the 6 o'clock news came Eden's statement about the atrocities on the fall of Hong-Kong. 50 men tied hand & foot and bayonetted to death. Wounded men left to die untended; prisoners starving in internment camps; rape; and all the old story. Such a flock of vultures coming home to roost: and as usual, the son atones for the wrath of the Father. Now if Jesus had been the Devil's son, and together from them proceeding the Holy Ghost it might be a Trinity with some hope in it.

11. A mild day, all pearled with sea-fog. Lunched with V. (who had a splitting headache but sufficient spirit to rebuke me roundly for joining in the W.V.S. contingent of the Warship week or washing-day march round Dorchester). Did so: just as we were due to start everyone had sudden doubts as to whether gas-masks were worn to the right or to the left. Like swords, I said: but unheard, for they were all undressing. It was raining hard by now, and an Admiral dressed as an Admiral from head to foot and standing on a makeshift poop, took the salute as drenched as Neptune. Suddenly I remembered the Quatorze Juillet. But kept it to myself, and went musing on Descartes down High East St. Afterwards the office was a den of Screaming Hornbies,[21] and I drafted a letter which I can't approve of to Mrs Balfour, to whom resignation means as little as it did to SS. Cosmo & Damian.

In the evening I finished Valentine's back, and laid the foundation of her front. And looked at Cecil Beaton's *Time Exposure*, and felt much like the old woman whose petticoats were cut off as she lay asleep. But mine on the other hand have had a tuck let out of them.
[. . .]
For God's sake let us sit upon the ground. Now I will put on the slow movement of opus 130.

12. Wrote a short story about scorching English earth.[22] Why do I write about old people when I write about war? Because they have more independence, a freer play of reaction? – or because it seems, down here, so much an old persons' war? Oxley, in the office, suddenly came alive talking to V. about Burma: the people wearing their wild bright colours, the crowds in street & market 'like hundreds &

---

21 Presumably fellow members of the WVS.
22 'Scorched Earth Policy', *NY* (April 1942).

thousands.' Then to Hong-Kong, and shame & fury – that all feel, that none express. To bomb Tokio – or rather, since it is all past, to have bombed Tokio. Too wet to garden. Now, this evening, an easterly gale rises. At first, at the first impact, we thought it was bombing. We turned off the wireless and looked at each other: almost with hope.

16. W.V.S. A woman came from the Blood Transfusion Service. Doctor Saxton (Barcelona) is working with them. Mr Lewis doesn't get, or doesn't read our letters. Mr Lewis forgot, or intentionally neglected, to give the revised Rest Centre figures to the Relieving Officers, who have been distributing the old ones. May Mr Lewis's tongue cleave to the roof of Mr Lewis's mouth.

28. Wrote all the morning, sending the chaplain out hawking.[23] [. . .]
Sometimes my book seems to walk around the room alive: but I wish it were a book of poems. Because this morning Macmillan asked to reprint *Narcissus* in a school-anthology, and this set me to reading Time Importuned. We have done another combined raid: at S. Nazaire.

29. We went a long spring walk through the meadows to Notton; and saw butterflies, puss-willow shining, violets, a bank of withered wild snowdrops, a picnic-party, two fat geese, a pair of wild duck who were wooing. And heard the willow-wrens sing. And, for one finds a new beauty every spring, I saw for the first time the sombre brocade of the *alder*, its clove-coloured cones, its catkins, dull saffron with scarlet powdering, all thick on the dark dense boughs. We also saw Mr Reade out politely strolling with a Piero di Cosimo dog.
Earlier in the morning V. turned on the wireless into the middle of the sustained B♭ of the 9th Symphony. Seid umschlungen, millionen. But in the midst of standing there absorbed, a part of my mind could notice that the chorus singers had the tone of people who had spent a lean winter, and coughed oft – though the soloists were all well-buttered enough. This came queerly back on me, walking in the new green meadows, where the sight of last year's dried bleached rushes pricking from a ditch made me think of ghost-soldiers holding a trench.

31. Weymouth – to talk to my women about the XIX cent, and the far reaching effects of the higher critisism: if Bluebeard had been incor-

23 In *CTHT*.

porated in the O.T. it would have afforded yet another convincing proof that women must never be encouraged to ask questions, or assert themselves. It was nice to see several awakened nods when I asked if any of them had read the Song of the Shirt. Bad news from India: they won't take it, I think. I suppose this will sink Cripps, into the bargain. The air is darkened with sins coming home to roost. In the evening the wireless did Pergolesi's *Stabat Mater*. I find that as I grow old I like this sort of music better and better, and respect it a great deal for being so noble and unassuming and humane. I see why Stendhal thought so well of it. As one becomes disillusioned about people's intellectuals by seeing people so continually fools, one attachs more and more value to people's emotionals. Portico-music. I like porticos and Bernini colonnades, and poplar-tree colonnades too.

April

14. In the evening, Reade's Invasion meeting. Very small attendance. Nixon's speech obligatoed by a snoring dog. Reade is resigning (moving, I hear) and the new Leader is Fryer. Points from Nixon. Bell-ringing for immediate parachutes. *Action station* the button that sets things off. (Dig trench, inspect gas-mask, bury food, *pace* Nixon). Keep in, or keep under. Do not exasperate the enemy. Bury the dead. Boil water. Local evacuation of infirm, old, children. Requisitioning unlimited. Report any signs of private evacuation. Kill rumour. Bull-etins will be issued. Nixon referred to Leningrad as Stalingrad: but is not, we think, a Trotskyist for all that.

15. Gardened in the morning, and extracted banks of couch-grass, now so much valued by V. for her trench. In the afternoon to my first S.L.[24] I was too early, so I sat in a field, admiring how large a landscape becomes when one has time to sit and look at it. At 5.30 I was there; an anxious face looked out of a window, an anxious voice called the Bombardier. A tall blonde man, pale of countenance, appeared in a gentle fluster, and said 'We're having a terrible time with our new cook.' In fact, their tea was late. So I again sat in field and contemplated till 6. At six the cook, penitentially, explained they were all on a job. They appeared all to be on a merry-go-round: the sound locating creature, three great ears surmounting a turn-table. A captain R.A. had a few words with me: a distant Jerry: sound-locating creature

24 Sound Locating.

already out-of-date, superceded by wireless. Then observing that the unit was often called Little Moscow, he left. I had half an hour, so I did the 1929–30 slump, leaving New Deal till next week. (Comparison of start of USSR and start of new New Deal. USSR every handicap, but one: its revolution had liquidated the antagonists.) They listened very well. I spoke too fast, as usual.

On the way back I saw a weasel, and a quantity of loose cows, which an elderly stranger and I humanely herded into a field with a mangold stack. Afterwards a frantic cow-herd arrived from Fratrum, and took them out again. I think I shall like being cultural militia.

16. I ached after so much digging and walking. So with a clear conscience I moved into the sun-parlour, which smelt of quiet and onions, and wrote the prologue to Isle Drury:[25] and was extremely happy.

18. Meditations on vieux singe[26] reinforced by arrival of pass-sheets, and balance horribly registering failure to contact New Yorker since August. Meditations mitigated by thought of P.O. book: but it doesn't *bring in*, alas! merely staves off.

Waited long for the 12.11. Lunched with V. We watched the public tennis courts, she went home, I to a sorry Russia-Today meeting. In the train back the ugly woman with the beautiful golden hair, who remarked on the buttonlessness of the soldier who got out at Frampton, then on the grave in the field (which is just flushing with green) then, in her flat deaf voice, I suppose my son is lying somewhere like that. No news for 18 months. The woman war had laid a hard hand on. Her husband in last war, her second son as a child in a Zeppelin raid, her other son now. 'Giving sugar to people who've got a brickbat ready for you', she said of appeasement, her only emphasis of voice. The silent WAAF[27] in the corner.

20. W.V.S. Where Reade came in, announced his departure from M. N. [Maiden Newton] and spoke of the inhabitants with such nausea that I felt quite drawn towards him.

26. Bath bombed last night. Damn them. Somewhat sleepy during the day, because of noisy night. It was Exeter the night before. Very cold wind, and the noise of midwinter.

25 *CTHT*.
26 Vieux singe ne plaît à personne: a common observation when work failed to please, or seemed to.
27 Women's Auxiliary Air Force.

28. To Weymouth, Setting out to brisk gun-fire (it was Poole). Inspected the not very impressive ruins of Weymouth, and farewelled my women, who gave me a bouquet. The high wind blew the whole smell of mid-channel inland, the sea was violent green and white, the landscape inland its own green and white of blackthorn hedge. I felt extremely gay. Back to Dorchester, where Colonel Oxley, drunk after a wedding, was wearing a white camellia, which did not suit him. Norwich on Monday night. The new campaign is bomb everything three-starred in Baedeker. Enlightened little pets. Bad news from Burma. Lashio bombed, and an unspecified retreat.

May

19. I spent a peaceful morning preparing the third talk on Germany,[28] housing, and getting Ralph to the nunnery.[29] Ruth back in the evening. Valentine's birthday presents in the evening. She was almost asleep when I put the paisley neckerchief in her hand, and thought it was put there by burglars. Finished potato bed.

20. Ruth went into Dorchester to lunch with Valentine. The house smells of white lilac, and a white shrub with small shiny leaves brought by Valentine. To T.P.[30] in the afternoon. A smaller group, but a very good discussion – a small gunner and I striving with Bombadier Arscott, who thinks science is the same as intense industrialism, and wishes he were back in the 15th cent.

27. To Toller where we finished off Modern Germany – and discussed, of course, the Jewish problem. The intellectual would keep on talking of Jews as Jews, but I strove with him about rabbinical and non-rabbinical. A howling gale made striving even harder. The Kharkov[31] news made us all rather glum: they had observed, with disapproval, that the BBC always gives us the German communiqués for USSR hostilities, though not for ours.

31. It is fine again. In the morning I gardened, and V. did the Sunday dinner. In the afternoon we sat on the lawn, where Joseph and Rebecca mated most affably, and Valentine remarked that 'Elgar's orchestra is

28 For her series of broadcast talks.
29 In her book.
30 Toller Porcorum, where she was lecturing to troops.
31 Kharkov was surrounded, and fell to the Germans later that day. A quarter of a million prisoners were taken.

always so very full'. Bevan rang up, and intimated that Charminster[32] is to be weekly. Tant mieux. I like it; and it brings in something. Meanwhile the spring brings in a young blackbird, who will strut into our bedroom. To C. [Charminster] where we did Wren – and I admired their really admirable works, and heard how they hunted out nails for their rustic woodwork (it is functional, to keep the cows off the instruments[)]; and they want USSR next please, and shall have it, bless 'em. Then to the car, where V. had heard on the 6 o'clock BBC that we sent 1,000 bombers to Cologne last night.

Meanwhile it is a most beautiful evening and the sky is like a sapphire: and Thomas was chased up the drive by mother blackbird; and somehow her beating wings seem handsomer than 1,000 bombers, though God knows I was almost on my knees in thankfulness for the news we had done something. But oh the poor bloody army: which is assuming a female role of sheltered domesticity and retirement, broken by bouts of such frightful activity as only women are expected to undertake.

June

1. WVS . . . home to await being fetched for RASC.[33] Large house, belonging to Eldridge Pope. Quantities of stuffed animals, outside one superb copper beech, and quantity of purling rustic woodwork bridges over which I strolled with 2nd Lieut Jones, elderly, stout, tough, anxious, and abounding in madding crowds. Passed through phalanxes of non-coms to an unwilling audience. Talked about USA – full of human sides. It all fell flat and constrained; and after a vindictive glass of sherry in the officers' mess, full of stuffed colonels, I went home in a gloomy dudgeon: for such was not my idea of a educational afternoon.

3. To T.P. boiling hot. We sat outside the hut, and their black kitten passed from paw to paw, and I did the first talk on Russia up to Lenin's exile.

4. Went nowhere. Prepared a volume of short stories for Ch & W.[34] Slept out. We slept out the night before too, and were disturbed by the guns on the raid on Poole.

32 Where she lectured to the Royal Army Service Corps.
33 See above.
34 *A Garland of Straw*, Chatto & Windus, 1943.

8. WVS in the morning. Charminster at 5.30. I arrived with my teeth set, but it was so much less painful than last time that I got them unclenched again. Gun practice in the evening with rumours of official disapprobation (which I had also heard at Reade's ARP meeting in Dorchester where I *viced* for Mrs E.) By some quaint fatality, balancing a gun on a straw-filled sack poised on a very unsteady tripod I sighted it the only bull of the evening. I tried to explain that it must be an accident, but those present were sufficiently in earnest to eye me with sullen unconviction.

21. Last Sunday a year ago.[35] This Sunday Tobruk surrendered. Still no news of the Mediterranean fleet – and no word of evacuation by sea, or of any naval guns taking part in the defence. In the afternoon Alexander's Rape of the Lock on the BBC was a moment of relaxation and human understanding. Then we walked out, and gathered elder-blossom.

24. T.P. on an exercise or something. So I spent a day serenely at home, working on Isle Drury. Judging by the news, days serenely spent at home likely to be numbered.

July

1. Still dry, still hot, though we slept out last night in every expectation of a thunderstorm. Axis 65 miles from Alexandria. Ineffective debate in the House. To T.P. where the new hall was up. A very good discussion after Wars of Intervention (none of them had heard of it). Rumour still about that GB might join with Germany to finish off USSR. And if so? – About 50–50 they said. No one wants to fight USSR. But some are so browned off they would fight with anyone, against anyone, to leave off fighting – or rather to see the war ended. And the others? Then on to talk of Mosley,[36] the boy from Ulster said how disappointing his Belfast visit was. Everyone, Catholics & Orangemen, were lined up waiting to drop him in the dock, but the police never let out a hair of him. General feeling that we are waiting for the end of the war to see what happens next. A bone dry evening, with the mist lying on the fields, and the smell of honeysuckle almost unbearably strong. Rebecca[37] lay in. Some bombs at night.

35 As the day to which this refers is 14 June, it is likely that STW is remembering the fall of Paris on 14 June 1940, though this was not one year before, but two.
36 Oswald Mosley, leader of the British Union of Fascists.
37 Another rabbit.

3. WVS. It began to rain about 11. Excellent for gardens – but the wind, s.w. not so good for a second Front. Horace remarked to Valentine: 'There's one thing. We've still got control of the weather.' [. . .] Lunched with V. and afterwards became so engrossed in the Sten gun shown me by Mr Ingram (full of devices seemingly taken from a typewriter) that I missed my train, and stayed on, placidly putting things into envelopes. The raspberries had ripened in half a day's rain. Slept indoors.

1945

January

13. I dreamed that Valentine, Nancy[1] and I were in France – in a small coast town, as it might be Port Bou. Everything was perishing of hunger and idleness – shops with no wares, not even such wares of the district as fruit and pumpkins. A shopwoman with her French pleasure in exposition said to me that when people grew or found something edible they ate it: it was waste of effort to bring it to a shop, since money could buy nothing better, nothing more solid. When I went back to the quay Louis Aragon[2] was sitting with Valentine and Nancy. So small, so thin, so debilitated, that he had a curious air of being a little girl. He held out to me – not rising – a small cold polite hand. I said how ill he looked. 'My dear, I am dying of England.'

[. . .] This morning we were talking of Asunciòn:[3] how she outstripped Fea on all fours, gambolling across the kitchen; how her garlic breath drove Stephenson[4] from our table; how she walked, light as a bubble, solid as an elephant; how her black eyes, that were grey-brown really, but the long eyelashes blackened them, perused our faces to see if we really understood; how she made herself thin and abject to explain her religious husband, and pompous to express the proudness of the Mothers and the Brothers. How long ago dead, my darling, and how?

15. I did a little more towards getting Magdalen Figge into the fishpond.[5] Sometimes I suspect that I am writing my best book, but we do not seem to notice it.

---

1 Nancy Cunard (1896–1965), poet, translator and publisher of the Hours Press books. STW's long friendship with her began in 1942 or 1943.
2 The writer and left-wing activist (1897–1982). STW had met him when she was part of the British delegation to the International Congress of Writers in Defence of Culture in 1937.
3 Asunciòn was the Spanish woman with whom STW and Valentine lodged while working for a Red Cross unit in Barcelona in 1936.
4 Unidentifiable.
5 In *CTHT*.

18. A letter from Nancy with news, via Raymond Mortimer, that Aragon is well, very thin, trés distingue, very grey: and his address. So I wrote to him. Churchill's filthy statement on Greece, stuffed with lies and sentiment about hostages, and with a large dab of butter for USA in the middle of it. All day, yesterday too, a wandering neuralgia, not improved by a hailstorm this afternoon.

20. Woke up with the thought that Hilary in Silesia[6] may be hearing the Red Army artillery: *must* be hearing it, unless he has been moved. W.V.S. & Report Centre. A little while ago, so Mr Hooper told me, the War Office demanded Boots, Rubber, Urgently, for the army in Holland. Dorchester ARP raised and reported 700 odd. In answer, told to keep them as there was no storage. *No storage*, said he.

21. So cold, so bitterly cold, and both of us so stiff, that we were medieval, and spent the day in bed.

22. Hard frost, the birds in starvation plight. V. brought back a dying blackbird, in the garden a dead bullfinch (his red feathers are red-tipped on grey, his head is Spanish black) and a robin. We nailed up a bone, and saw a tit and a starling pecking side by side. Usually a tit will drive away a starling. More P.G.O.[7] This evening the Red Army is 165 miles from Berlin, has taken Allensteig, is 45m. from the Baltic, 30 from Poznan, and is encircling Bromberg. And today, while Hilary hears their guns, the appropriate authorities returned to me my first letter to him in captivity: addressed to his Italian prison in March 43, intercepted by US before it reached him there, and now here once more.

29. Too cold to keep a diary. Things to remember of this snow, the Bewick wood-cut look of the trees by our gate, the broom-bush all cut-glass in the sun, the full moon rising with the colour and imminence of a harvest-moon. The snow came heavy on Friday night, and stayed, now it is snowing again, and the wind howls and mumbles between its howls.

30. Twisting the wireless tonight in search of Hitler's speech V. got onto the 1st act of Walküre – the finale, as it turned out, of a grand Fuehrer-concert. Given one was a Nazi it would certainly have fine drama and appropriateness tonight; with the Red Army in the Branden-

6 Hilary Machen was in a prisoner of war camp there.
7 'People Growing Old', another working title for *CTHT*.

burg mark, and taking Königsberg, and Berlin raided night & day: the voluntary defiant outlawing, the invocation to Nothung, and all that. They sang as if they meant. So would good artists on any date, and under any circumstances.

It has begun to thaw, though everything is still white, and I believe it's freezing again tonight. Wrote to Anne P[8] and did business letters, and cleared up some of the traces of having our pipes twice unfrozen, and the spareroom floor up.

8 Anne Parrish, the American novelist, whom STW had met in New York in 1929.

1949—69

Sylvia and Valentine remained in Dorset during the war, Valentine working firstly in the offices of the Territorial Army and later as secretary and dispenser to a local doctor, Sylvia working for the Women's Voluntary Service and lecturing to the troops. In 1947 Sylvia published The Museum of Cheats, *a volume of stories about the war, and the following year* The Corner that Held Them, *a complex novel set in a fourteenth-century nunnery, which she had been writing for six years.*

The diary resumes in May 1949, at the beginning of a critical year in Sylvia's life which saw the revival of Valentine's affair with Elizabeth Wade White, and Sylvia's temporary removal from Frome Vauchurch. In the period which followed this crisis, Sylvia began to feel that she would never write again, but while her career as a novelist waned (her last novel was The Flint Anchor, *published in 1954), her output of short stories increased significantly. Two other important projects involved her in years of work; one was the first English translation of Proust's* Contre Saint Beuve *which she undertook in the mid-1950s, the other a biography of the novelist T.H. White a decade later. In 1956 Valentine joined the Roman Catholic Church, towards which Sylvia felt a pronounced antipathy, but despite this setback they remained devoted to each other and the domestic life they had evolved. Valentine's health, which was never very good, declined steadily during the 1960s. By 1968 it was clear that she had cancer, which a series of operations did nothing to halt.*

1949

May

17. She took me for a drive. We dined at the Askerswell Road House,
& drove to the old Bridport harbour because I had never seen it in all
our journeyings. It was an exquisite evening, the young oak-trees
defiantly green, angrily green, against the sea-dusk, and lilacs blooming in all the bungalow gardens, & the sea's colour fresh & gay as an
open wound.

There are two blackbirds in the garden, & it seems to me they sing
over & over 'Going to leave here'.

June

5. At her command we had a long picnic . . . The Pitt-Rivers museum
[in Farnham, Dorset] very philosophising: so many dearest objects,
British, Roman, Etruscan, outliving their cherishers in the cold
ground; so much careful love of life behind us. It was a happy day, &
serene, & almost natural.

20. If this is infatuation, it is the wariest, the most long-sighted infatuation the world has ever seen. No, no! It is generalship before a crucial
engagement. But it is strange, & bizarre et elévé, that I should be her
Chief of Staff.

25. Thomas's ears were bad, & I carried him indoors to clean them. I
don't know how long I stood in my room, looking at it as it will be
when I am gone, and all the time he lay in my arms quite still as though
he had died there . . . But what I cannot begin to imagine is myself
alone. The moment I think of that, I go out like a candle. I see a strange
room. Scattered about it are things I recognise as mine. But that is all.
There is no one in the room.

July

25. Between sanity & madness there is a territory like a darkened moor, full of peat-hags, & mists, with no perceptible water-shed or frontier. The moisture sinks into the ground, is sucked up, & its division, whether it flows to sense or madness, takes place invisibly & underground. But there is a water-shed of mental direction, of choice, apart from the vital, willy-nilly watershed; & that is touched when one's thoughts look towards madness as towards a sheltered valley – still far off & hard to obtain, but [to] which one looks with a wearied longing, as towards a place that *could*, with time & endurance, be travelled to. It is only a few who are transported to madness, the rest have to stumble towards it, over the soggy misleading ground, & through the obstacles of being a nuisance to those who love them, & a laughing-stock to strangers. Philippa [Katie Powys]'s indifference to being comical & conspicuous shows how far she has been along that road, & so did Dorothy [Warner]'s indifference to the sorrow & nuisance she was to Oliver.

28. The last page of this diary. Four months so happy, & three so wretched. It is a strange thought that in time to come I may yet turn back to it for record of better days. For ill or well, I have been with her, slept by her, heard her voice, felt her hand. What she did, she did unwittingly, in innocence & too great trust in me: & since then she has still been the light of my darkened eyes, & the core of my heart, & my strength & comfort, & raison d'être, and all I have.

August

12. I woke good for nothing, and my dear's concern could not quite heal me. For after all, it is this baleful Eliz: that she loves, and awaits. Colin' cleared the garden path by the fruit cage so well that it was as though he had redeemed my soul, and after he'd gone I went on with it. He weeds better than I do. In the afternoon we drove to Dorchester. Alyse wants to change her dates. She invites me to go to Chy[dyok] while she is in London. Valentine said this is the greatest compliment A. could pay me.

In three weeks time she [Elizabeth] will be here. Her foot trailing on the stairs, her glance dawdling over our possessions, her voice & smell

---

1 Colin House, a local boy who occasionally helped with the gardening.

filling the house. I feel a curious defencelessness when I think that while V. is at work she will be here alone, with house & garden to herself. It is not hate that I feel. It is loathing – as though I saw a frightful never-quite-forgotten sore re-opening in my flesh.

15. These are uneasy days. This morning, sitting in our newly-painted chairs on the porch, she began again about the problem of Evelyn.[2] [. . .] After a while of serious silence I said I must make it plain, so that there could be no possible mistake between us, that if or while she lives with Eliz: I cannot fit into a trivet – to do [so] would imperil my love & honour for her, and that being my whole core of life I cannot sacrifice it. She said that was understood. But was it understood without mitigations of hope and opportunity, I wonder?

[. . .]

In the early evening we went for a drive through Abbotsbury & up the sea road. The sea was looking brimful, a gentle endless blue, & wearing its moiré pattern, except for one patch of fiery sparkles, like the moving fire in an opal. Valentine wore her new-made blouse – revised from the green indian dressing-gown of 1938 – & under it her arms were milk-white, slender, timelessly young. I kissed the hollow of her elbow – gentle now under my lips, and no stir beneath the skin. She looks as beautiful now as when she was beautiful with love for me.

The torment of the flesh is so much purer, so much nobler, than the torment of the mind. It keeps an unbruised innocence.

17. Valentine gave me – as an en revanche for the Sevigné of hers, a stout, snuffy, bound solidly in red, S[evigné] in French. 300 odd of them. To P.M.[3] they go with me, to be more than a mother to me. And I shall read that worldly & fleshly madonna as much to my soul's health as V. could read her Eckhart or F. de Sales.

18. I find myself brought morally low by misfortune. I wish I could lay emotional booby-traps for Eliz: and it is an effort to put roller-towels with my large red initials on them below their anonymous brothers. Meanwhile I continue to take care of her feelings – and it is the extreme of moral affectation.

19. [I]n the afternoon she extended herself like a cat over the tool shed roof, catching river-tree apples in a landing-net . . . The plop of apples on ground, and sliding down the roof runnels to plop-splash in

2 Elizabeth's American lover.
3 Pen Mill Hotel, Yeovil, where STW was to stay during Elizabeth's visit.

the river, and the leaves violently rustled, and Valentine looking down through the branches, her smutched face & her sunned hair. Then we sat on the lawn, sorting them, and talking about Pen Mill . . . But Gaster[4] thought she was looking ill, and her glands hurt her, and when I think how dead-fatigued she may be I am ready to wish death on that incompetent exorbitant Moll. Yet Joy may mend all.

21. Sunday. Three weeks ago we went to Miss Green:[5] now, in a fortnight, they will be here, and I at P.M. The date that seemed only a little while ago, so inconceivably far away now seems appallingly near. Last night I dreamed of Eliz: breaking in on me at P.M. & I not knowing whether she brought bad news of Valentine or a piece of her own bad humour. Today, Valentine saying to me not to fret at P.M., grieve, but not fret or be gnawed, I answered that I could not vouch for the last week: it might be hard, I said, & I might be impelled to go to London. My blood stood still at her answer, that it was no use to look so far ahead. All my fears crowd back on me: but this and the dream last night,[6] may be partly because yesterday I opened the re-turned letter to Marchette Chute.[7] I had written it on May 20th: and as I looked through it such a smell of despair & terror rose up from its page that I could not go on. Then, Eliz was still potent, regnant. And presently she will be again?

[. . .] Colin came & weeded. He looks at me with serene eyes, as a tout of gold-crested wrens & pansies. How comfortable a naturalist could be to a wounded spirit! That attentive gaze, seeing, seeking, *Nothing* from the human countenance.

22. Brown is the madman's colour. I had a bad night, seeing a beggar's coat with long skirts hanging on a bare thorn-bush, and Eliz: lying on me like an incubus, and the end of September lying in wait. In the morning she asked me if I were grieving at the window for autumn & old age; and I replied, too straight from my heart, that I was grieving for the old courage I had ten years ago. Then it was valid – or seemed so. But now the cistern is dry, and echoes with terrors. She said again that I am making a bogy of Eliz: but during the morning when I was cleaning bits of myself from the bedroom I found a letter from her,

---

4 The doctor in Evershot, for whom Valentine worked as dispenser.
5 They had gone to look at the site of the cottage, which was destroyed by a bomb in the war.
6 Not recorded.
7 The American biographer and literary historian. She had begun to correspond with STW following the publication of *CTHT*, but at this date they had not yet met.

written in Feb 1941, saying that she was back with me, and securely. And this I had come to believe. [. . .] She gave me some sort of pill for sleeping – and after a long spell of deliberately trudging round the Terrace at Harrow I got to sleep. It was astonishing how much I could remember, groping & stooping to recall each detail out of the dark. For the next week this should be a good exercise, but it is extremely tiring to the back of the head.

26. Two parcels of Eliz:'s books came this morning, & Valentine tumbled them out in her chair. Some, said Valentine, might be presents. I began to look through them, to find embarrassing inscriptions of mutual ownership. So I said so, and went back to finish dressing, & Valentine came in on pretext of Boëthius, and sat gently beside me. These ensueing days are bound to have thorns, and I sat in front of the house, in one of the new-painted chairs, counting how many they were; these days that I almost count to come to the last of them, and yet know that they may be the last days I shall live with her. The bright zinnias she bought for me look at me with their intense late-summer faces, and the pansies that were flowering in the first careless half of May are flowering still.

[. . .] There was a talk by F. Hoyle on the 3rd, about the solar-planetary system. The old theory of planets being matter from the sun is disproved, because of a disparity of hydrogen too great to be accounted for by loss in fission. Now they seem to have established that the sun was originally a double star, whose companion became a super nova, and blew itself to pieces. The widowed sun remains, surrounded by débris of its double, a few cold chips and solidifactions, tethered to it and lightened by its diminished single light.

31. At 6. Valentine brought me to Pen Mill. Now it is 9, and I wonder how I can last out even till tomorrow, when I go back to look after the animals and spend the night. My room looks out on the main road, with buses – behind is the station. I have a view of the laundry, some public trees, and a poor almost real wood. I have a choice of a bentwood chair, an easy one that is not easy, and the window sill, which is best. It is really a nice room, plain, and clean, no pictures; and at dinner there was a great deal of that pathetic English food, so well-meaning, and so dreary. There is a nice waitress, foreign I think. All the other guests are men. And Valentine rang me, and there has been a Mozart qut, and presently there will be the Winterreise. And I feel idiotic with grief, with care, with bewilderment, with exhaustion of

spirit. This is where I have travelled since May. Yet my love left me swearing I was her love, and that it rested with me to save her if again she is whirled away. I see she dreads it. I feel I have not enough strength left even for dread. For one moment in the dining-room, I staggered to life, feeling myself returned to that melancholy saturnine young animal wandering about for Tudor Church Music – at Wimborne, at Norwich, and in Oxford. (In the evening she rang up to say she was lost [.]) And so I think of refugees. (The sudden rain-storm, the water gushing from the gutter, the arc-lamp[.])

September

1. I took a Soneryl, and lay in a bed which was comfortable, listening to violent rain and wondering if it thundered at home . . . it was slow to work – and then after I'd forgotten it, and resigned myself to wakefulness I felt it take me stealthily in its hold, and assault me with sleep like a very slow and impersonal sexual possession. I can see why these drugs have their spell. And this morning I woke without any shock or surprise at all, and opened my eyes on the room, saying 'anti-biotics – remedies against life.'

Yet it was easy to walk in to our house, and Shan's[8] frantic welcome told me what she had told me on the phone – how distracted she felt, and how much severed. There was coffee and wine on a tray, and in my (her) room, a note praising me for mannerly love – and that is how I would wish to be praised, now that it is no longer mistaken for autumnal complaisance – and in my sitting-room, still in the type-writer, a letter, the most love-letter of all she has ever written me, I think, saying that though it were best if she liberate herself, yet, failing that, she calls on me to do it.

Glorified with this I tidied, and sorted, and sewed my last shirt, and ate Anne's pork[9] – and in the evening, after she had rung up from St James' Court [. . .] I finished that G.H.[10] pot-boiler; and went late to bed with Thos.[11] on my bosom.

2. And now I am back again at Pen Mill, having all things done, and seen the dashing local fire-engine leave for a fire at Evershot, followed by a swallow-flight of children on bicycles. She rang up from the

8 A Pekingese.
9 Sent from the USA by Anne Parrish.
10 *Good Housekeeping.*
11 Thomas, the cat.

air-port to say E.'s plane would not arrive till 2.30, and that lunches were only provided for passengers. She sounded worn out with exposure and delay, and it was raining. About 4, just as I was getting ready to go, I had a violent sudden impression of Now they are looking at each other, with passion and desire flashing between them. Strangely enough, it was not in the least painful: too violent, I suppose, too pure. And now I am in my severe little isolation-cell, and – how soon, how tragically soon the feeling of home establishes itself – looking round on it ownerly.

3. The first of my ancient solitary reign. Seeing a bus for Sparkford I went to Mudford, and saw an extremely fine weir across the sulky skulky Yeo, couched at the bottom of its gully among iron-black mud. Came back and wrote to Valentine, since we are to write after all. This morning her letter said there was no doubt, none, none, which way she would turn. In the afternoon I walked at random; a path in the wood parallel to the road so often driven, and up to a strange stone house that must be an annexe for wind-loving owners of the grand house down below, with a pavilion – but now all cabbages and waterworks. A fine stone trough, and a noble view of a park. Then along a road to the Barwick turn; and on my way back I went past two enormous ash-trees into a grove all fitted out with rustic bridges, and waterfalls, and victorian privacies; and so back. Not far, nothing as fine as the morning's weir; but agreeable, and no harm in it.

4. Extremely hot. In the morning I walked to Upper & Nether Compton. [. . .] I had suspected the way to church was down a road labelled Private Cars Only. Now I looked for the nether end of this road, found it, and musing on the private devotions of private cars, walked through an agreeable park, and found the church behind a superlative cedar. It was so hot (so was I) that I went, thereby adding an eighth person to the congregation. A rather Pollocky man, who read the lesson, and had a green wife in an anglo-cat hat, was unable to remove his speculative eyes from me; easier, since he and the wife were occupying a transept. An elderly parson read a sermon about Onesimus – full of details about Philemon and Onesimus that did not, I think, stem from Holy Writ; the moral of which was that the lower classes of Upper & Nether Compton would give a good example to mankind (or was it the universe?) by continuing to work nicely. Cooled, if not much refreshed, I walked home – how red Yeovil is! [. . .] In the evening, after I had fled upstairs to listen to Iphigenia in

Tauris, Valentine rang up, to say that time went very slowly. I defied her to guess where I had been, and she instantly replied, To Church.

5. Woken by lightning and one of the longest and best sustained rolls of thunder I have ever heard – I thought of it as pure unwavering *black* – like the Cézanne clock. But a short storm; and thinking of Valentine, and wondering which room she heard it in, I fell asleep again, to the steady loud purr of a sudden wind. The wind was still about in the morning. I translated the story of the stolen linen.[12] It neatly filled the morning. After lunch I took a ticket to Thorney Halt, and threw myself on West Moor. Burst of brilliant sun, the willows blown sideways and silver, the osier beds swinging. Yet the surface of the rhines was like a solid floor of green marble; and the water lily leaves flapped in the wind like paper-scraps on a London pavement, though the bed-knob flowers stood upright, barely wagging on their thick stalks. And I ate blackberries on a squat stone bridge, and passed a very handsome young red bull, svelte in a solid way; and talked to a flotilla of white ducks, and to a handsome swarthy hook-nosed man who was cutting rushes – Sedgemoor gipsy, I think; and picked rushes for Valentine that were swaying ten foot high out of a hedgerow; and saw the largest and oldest willow possible; and smelt the delicious fragrance of boiling osiers, the steam curling softly through the roof of the shed; and learned that Mr Rogers in the fourth house like a sentry-box makes a very honest basket. An exhilarating two hours. [. . .] And tomorrow I look to see my Love.

6. She came at 2.15 bringing 2 volumes of Lady Holland's diary, and a bottle of black coffee, and a picnic lunch, and vitamins, and her returned day-book – and herself. She is much more tired than she meant me to know. I saw her get out of the car, and all her movements, slightly sleep-walking, spoke of deep fatigue. She even admitted that she was tired. Yet Eliz: is being quiet and reasonable, and, as far as she can be, helpful. And there is pleasure; but between the pleasure, tedium, and the oppression of talk in idleness. We drove to see S. Nicholas,[13] and she wrapped his halfcrown in a piece of paper saying, 'For You', because a naked half-crown might create a painful conflict of conscience, whereas a miracle could not disconcert anyone.

12 From *La Légende de la mort*, a collection of peasant stories from Brittany, which STW was translating as a pass-time.
13 At the church in Nether Compton.

7.   On the forsaken bridge as I crossed over
A dead man stood, looking down on the water,
And as I passed, he laid his hold on my shoulder,

It was here, saying, I thought I would row my darling,
And her white hand would feather the water, holding
A yellow lily, and a long weed trailing –

Or did I indeed bring her? As skies cloud over
And lighten again, I remember and cannot remember.
I wait to hear my oars plash in the river.

I wrote this today, sitting on the yonder side of Pill Bridge, where I
had come on pilgrimage to Llewelyn to thank him for *Love and Death*
– the only book that held me up during that worst spell in May–June,
and that I had pulled out of the shelf as an animal pulls the herb from
the hedge. [. . .]

I lunched there, on Valentine's pie; and afterwards read the canti
spirituali of May 1948;[14] and then, quite suddenly, came to life and
wrote this poem, as one wakes from a deep sleep and turns to the
beloved, and falls asleep again; for ten minutes later I had not a line left
in me. It was very hot, still, mainly overcast. The hedges had blackberries, there was wild peppermint in the ditches, sheep pastured in the
fields. [. . .] Today I feel deeply tired, and melancholy, and fretted
over my Love who looked so ill yesterday. Last Wednesday at this
hour I was driving here with her. This week has had every possible
amelioration, novelty, two days at home, that *really* happy and delighting walk from Thorney – and, above all, her letter left in the
typewriter. Yet I have had to drive myself on through it; and there are
three more weeks to come, and if I wonder how I can last out, what of
my darling?

9. I drove from Dorchester with Gerry, *très dame*, to Daggers Gate;[15]
and walking towards the sea-path I had a strong and grateful impression of Tommy walking beside me. It was a landscape of the fields
completed and contented of which he had spoken and I made a poem
in /22. Then I saw a thistledown halo and it was Alyse: a stern
benevolence shone from her. You sit there, she said, having plainly
arranged everything in an anxious mind beforehand. She questioned a
little – speaking of Eliz: as 'that woman', and so sharply that I found

14 A group of poems by Valentine.
15 About a mile from West Lulworth, and the nearest point to Chydyok by road.

myself beginning to defend my offender. I visited Gertrude, and drank mead, and she, in fact, being quite unconcerned as to my state, was easier; then in a dusking room I listened to the Beeth. fiddle concerto, my mind ill at ease for there had been no answer when I telephoned. [. . .] Later, the moon had risen, I went to my bed in Llewelyn's shelter, and slept in a charm, between the east and the west, feeling the strong soft wind, smelling the haystack (taller than the barn) opening my eyes on bramble wands and the first light of day, and finally on Alyse bringing a tray, as so often to Llewelyn. I had been thinking of him just then, and it was almost as though I saw her with his eyes.

10. After tea I walked again with Alyse to Llewelyn's stone.[16] The dreaming blue sea, the one motionless upright white sail on it.

In the evening Alyse spoke a little of herself. Her chosen epitaph, 'she loved too well, and lived too long.'

11. In the afternoon I walked with Alyse to Rats Barn, and saw the shell pattern in the tank. And in the evening it was chilly enough to light a wood fire downstairs as we supped, again talking, this time more easily of my affair. The extreme counsel: Never cling, Never reproach; Never seek to revenge yourself. I admitted to her, as openly as to a midwife, the curious sense of security and riches it had given me to discover what frankly base and hateful feelings I had experienced about E. 'I can contain this also, and yet be myself.'

12. Mrs Webb's car drove me down the valley and into the Twin Ash Valley and to Winfrith. Bus to Weymouth. Lunch with Janet and Catherine.[17] Hair washed. Donkeys and merry-go-rounds on the sands. Home by train, deeply downcast again, and languishing at the thought of how long lies ahead of me – and what then? Even 2 letters from my Love could not blow away my depression. For 3 days I have had support from someone who has been, is, for all I can be sure, as unhappy as I. The visit was all I had hoped it might be – and now it is over, and I stare myself in the face again. And Chaldon was so beautiful, and its ghosts so living, so much more living than I.

Things Alyse said.

That after Llewelyn's death it was looking at things that sometimes brought her back to life: a bird on a roof, a pond with ducks in it, an

16 A memorial stone, cut by Betty Muntz, which stands in a field overlooking the sea. Llewelyn had died of tuberculosis in 1939.
17 Catherine Davis, Janet Machen's daughter, then nearly two years old.

old man carrying a load of sticks. She would look at them purely, without speculation: and they would become 'lifted out of significance' and then they had power over her mind. [. . .]

Theodore's concern that Mr Jackson[18] spread the communion feast in vain; he persuades Alyse to go with him, to make up the necessary couple. Her scruples, and T.F. bidding her to imagine herself in Africa, among simple natives who worship a black god. 'You would think nothing of it then.' Gertrude's deep passion for animals. 'Gertrude kisses slow-worms.' And Gertrude to the old cat, 'Goldie! you should not *growl* at your grand-child.' Alyse, shocked by nothing else, finds herself shocked by Gertrude's serene grossness, her calm pleasure in watching sexual phases, copulation and birth, of animals.

My myrtle, the Miss Green myrtle, that I gave Llewelyn, is growing in the garden. Strange to see. And the dusky tapestry brown and green of his medlar tree against the hillside.

Den allen schuld recht sich auf erden.

I understood that, this evening, lying in deep misery, thinking of a passage in Valentine's letter about how she in her love with Eliz: can live innocently – and that it is because I am steadfast 'and completely without guile or reservation.' *Recht sich auf erden*. She lives and loves innocently with Eliz: because I am shaken with fears and doubts, ravished with physical and mental jealousy, and steadily murder myself in concealing it. But she tells me she is feeling well; and poor tired touzled Janet, with grey hairs on her forehead, said how beautiful she looked. I know. So she did by me once. Alyse said that it was because of being sure of me that she was able to love Eliz: which is strangely akin to that enigmatic and shocking remark of hers that it was with the me in her she loved Eliz. I cannot understand it. I am still a Manichee far from my home.

13. (11th of A.S.R.)[19] Exhaustion put me to sleep – that old drudge of every prison, barrack, hospital, who will in the end, when doctors and priests have taken their polite selves off, do the same office at every non-violent death-side. And I woke in the minor, and could not pull myself out of it before my love came. She looked as beautiful as Janet said yesterday. It numbed my heart to think that I must have made her look lifeless and almost plain – and that it is Eliz: whom I hate and strive against who renews her beauty. [. . .] Eliz: has got her later

18 The incumbent at Mappowder, where T.F. Powys and Violet had lived since 1940.
19 Ancient solitary reign.

passage, and I shall not see her till she comes back on the 6 o'clock on the 30th from seeing Eliz: off. The thought of one more day as a D.P.[20] was like a thousand; and the thought of Norfolk was dashed by a letter from Katie Rintoul[21] that she could not manage more than ten days, and that only if she could find a companion. I was stupid with melancholy, and a weight on her heart. And I am stupid with melancholy still. Typed two of the Brittany stories, and darned stockings. 13 from 30 = 17.

15. This morning a letter in which she writes of the duality of her mind, which can reconcile my belief in her truth of love, and Elizabeth's corresponding belief, and feel in herself both loves compatible and not conflicting, though to either of us in total war. It is a difficult letter, written in great fatigue and melancholy – and I have been perplexed all day, both how to understand it, and how to act on it ... but I think this September should if possible include no final conclusions, no full stop. For the pattern is not worked out, and finality might unrip what is already woven. I translated La Princesse Rouge. And in the afternoon I followed a suburban road that turned into a lane, and thus became acquainted with the power-station, the sewage-farm, and the rubbish-dump. It rained a little, and the banks of the Yeo had a clothing of nettles and brambles, and willows that spoke of home, and here and there a fringe of purple-flowered rushes, broken by the wind.

16. (14 of a.s.r.) Today is an exact watershed. Eliz: leaves (a day later than first proposed) on Sept 30th. Today, as she is in London, exercising her se[s]quipedalian tact and charm on Ruth, my Love fetched me at 9.45. [. . .] I arrived home between a dazzle of delight and a daze of anxiety. But my Love held me, and charmed me, and Thos: was uncurling from his peat, and Shan in whirls and whorls of welcome; and almost immediately I found myself picking off dead pansy heads, and eating wild strawberries, and quenching the thirst of geraniums. Then my Love – who liked her shirt – gave me her fairings of a small 1825 Hours of Idleness, a pinchbeck neck-piece with a coral stud and a charming little saucer; and playing me Coward's *Don't lets be Beastly to the Germans*, which she had recalled as prophetic. Prophetic it is. We wandered about with coffee, and talked. I asked her why she had read that letter. Tidiness, said she. But after I had asked you not to? –

20 Displaced Person.
21 Who was going to look after their house and animals.

'I thought all that had been annulled by now', she said, with a silken Thomas look that made me fling myself on her in an embrace of pure delight. [. . .] It grew dusky. We had dinner by candlelight. In a last dash of my stay I covered the jelly, and we drove to the station. And here I am. With a hundred cares and one hope, and my head whirling with anxiety, with simple joy, with a kind of derisive attention to the situation, with talk, with flowers, with the odd gaiety of an intrigue swept on by the music of Mozart, with further fuel for my H.M.S. Implacable – and steadied on my Love's love; and that she is coming to tea on Sunday.

17. [I] walked the *'narrow road but pleasant'* to Hamdon Hill, eating blackberries, and considering the alternatives of V. in USA at Eliz:'s behest or Eliz: living nearby, and myself always with one hand on the back door-knob. The latter would be so infinitely preferable that I can't allow myself to think of it. Better a running fight than to sit besieged by fears that can't be telephoned, care that cannot be comforted. I came to Hedgecock, thinking of Llewelyn – and saw a nymph-white cat in a tunnel of beechen green. Then I came out on a drystone quarry landscape, an old quarry face with bushes at its feet that was like the Forum as Goethe saw it, and sat for a long time looking down on a towered church. The particular effect of a church sunk *in* a landscape and looked down on. With its batter and buttress, and its curious trick of having to be looked for when once you have glanced away from it, it is astonishingly like a hunting animal *regardant* and ready to spring. Then home across the Summit, and down by the sliding-steep old fort-side to East Stoke. Wrote to Marchette Chute and to my love and to Anne, and translated Les Bouefs [sic].

18. We had tea together. She looked extremely tired, and the pain in her arm has come back, but Eliz:'s melancholy was dissipated by benzedrene. What a pity we didn't know of this useful drug ten summers ago, when it seemed as though only dynamite could perform that office. She stayed till 5. After she had gone I read the letter written to me on May 1 1944 – a farewell letter, about her poetry, deeply unhappy, speaking of living in a confused despair. It made me unhappy too, and flicked with fears that we may wander into that wilderness all over again. I listed to [a] G.B.S. play about Charles II – poor, with a nonsensical epilogue of a love-scene between Ch: and Katherine of Braganza, a Darby & Joan watered down Man & Superman pair, with

Ch. addressing K. as Beloved, and K. understandingly tidying his
boots. Barrie could not have worsened it.

19. (17 of A.S.R.) I woke to the news of the devaluation of the £ from
the next door radio. 30% – and a 25% rise in the cost of the loaf. And if
this isn't a string-clause I'll eat my hat: for any danger to USA of our
making more £ per $ by export is stymied by the strikes for wages-
raises this will bring on. So at 7 a.m. I said Damn the USA. And now
at 10 I am saying it again.

27. In the a.m. to Thorney and Mr Rogers the basket-maker. After a
mill, working, and the water sliding down as fine as oiled silk into a
great pillow of white foam (and osier-bundles sidling in the pool) I
found Mr Rogers in his little orchard – a most congenial man from
whom I ordered 1 apple basket, 1 wood basket, 2 quarter bushel
baskets (loves!) and a cat basket. His osier wands, the long white ones
and the little buff ones, in sheds and outhouses and steeping in a
narrow tank, and the grey cat who came sliding from a stack of buff
osier-bundles. A withy bed will last 20–30 years with good care, and
he knows one that is fifty years old. Then I walked towards Middle-
ney, and farewelled kind Thorney. p.m. I met Janet in Dorchester, –
You will be glad when it's over, said she, and I agreed heartily. 'Yes.
It's so hard on one's legs.' A discerning comment, and such as Arthur-
cum-Purefoy might have made. Poor little Catherine, adjured to enjoy
E.'s visit, did enjoy it, except for one burst of tears; and said afterwards: 'I only cried once', in an anxious hospitable voice.

29. [Maiden Newton] I was like them that dream when I left Yeovil;
and when Mrs King[22] brought me here I still delayed, talking to Thos:
and then to Shan, combating my feeling that I should find Eliz: upstairs. But the poor thing has gone, on this misty autumn-smelling
morning. I wandered about from room to room, looking out of the
windows. Kitchens, bathroom, small sun-parlour, cupboards all as
tidy as could be. It was not till mid-day that I pulled myself together
after drinking coffee from the Rome cups (the pair was on the rack):
to make the bed, to unpack, to make over the bedroom[.] [. . .] And
now I sit here, home again in my body at any rate. I have just re-read
her letter of July 27. And at nine or so I heard her voice, for she rang
up – saying she felt well, that her arms were better, and that Ruth
might appear at any moment. It is Ruth's talent to do a harlequinade at

22 Mrs King and her husband kept a local garage, and ran a small taxi service.

the end of *every act* of the tragedy. By this time tomorrow she will be back; and then I shall be back too, properly back: though Thos, purring on my knee, seems to think I am back already. (Alas, you sanguine idiot! 9:x:49)

30. When I went up to the station the music of the fair was playing, and its lights were casting odd looks on the village street. It had turned cold, and the wind blew. Not hope, I said to myself – but more trust than ever before. On the station the wind blew cold and steady, and whined along the tracks. She got out of the train, she was there in body; but so completely tired that I seemed to be walking by some ghost or stranger. We had coffee in her room, and talked a little, and she gave me a bag she had got in London – black, with a grey lining – very elegant. Her arm hurt. She said nothing of Eliz: she took a phenobarb, and came to bed, walking in her sleep. She fell asleep quickly, and so did I, but woke for she cried out 'I am so cold' in a despairing voice, and cast herself against me, still in her sleep. I lay with her head on my shoulder, and I tried to warm her; and as she warmed, the smell of love came from her, that smell of corn and milk that I shall never smell from her again except love for another causes it.

October

2. The cable came in the morning, Eliz: having delayed till Waterbury. I gardened, and we both tidied against Zahn.[23] In the evening the smell of the washing-basket overset me so that I went out into the garden to faint or be sick. I was neither, but had to spend a long time with the cold iron rail of the bridge pressed to my face, and my eyes shut. It was as localised a storm as a cyclone – from my heart downwards to my knees. And as I walked back I was terrified at the minute slow step-by-step crawl of my preceding shadow: it was as though I were walking slowly out of my grave. A bad end to a day that had begun with waking from a dream of a rose-flowered camellia tree on a small revolving island – my first coloured dream for many weeks.

5. [At Warren Farm, Horsey, Norfolk.] After tea, thinking she would want to write to Eliz: I walked alone along the familiar road to Waxham. It was too familiar to retrace, so I came back along the sands in

23 The house-sitter.

the dusk watching the tide come up the shelving beach, throwing its cactus blossoms of spray between the sand-colour and the dim hyacinth-blue. When I came in she was pleased because she had begun to write on her Norfolk story again. For a little while I think she was really happy.

6. In the morning we again walked on the beach, and brought back a great deal of drift-wood, and cut our toe-nails, on her theory that the sea would mollify them. After lunch we cleaned the car. Then Ruth came to tea – it went off better than I supposed it would. After she had gone we walked out on the fen, and watched an owl set out on its first dusk-flight. It flew low towards us, and right over our heads, so close that we could see its demure mild face and the sharp nose set in it, and the bright eyes; it was above us before it saw us, and wheeled off on a new tack. In the evening, late, we went out to look at the beach, and watched the subsidence of the waves running southward, the white feathering swallowing up the black smooth tunnel. She has a chill in her stomach. Sorrow comes over me like a mist, and I feel myself lost and fading, and at a touch or a word, the mist thins; but then it comes on again. This place is beautiful, and serene, and the air is mild and allaying; but with its evocations of Lavenham, and Winterton, and the time when she loved me as I still love her, and when I felt myself delighting her, it has also an effect of making me a ghost to myself. To feel myself delighting her . . . that is something I think I shall never feel again; and of all the things I grieve for, it is that I grieve for most.

7. I woke in the night, and heard the sea, and remembered the letter about Dover Beach – and felt I dared not ask if it were still true, for it would be like trying to hold her to her word. The past rushed back at me: and I wept for a long time, and then she woke out of a bad dream and my stifled voice betrayed me, and she took me in her arms. But I dare not speak, I am so much afraid of imperilling what may already be about to fall.

8. Coming in from a before-bed walk she said to me that she thought I was cold, and misunderstanding I answered that I could never be cold to her – but that I hesitated to talk out. Neither could she, she said; she could tell me nothing yet, she must wait for the dust to lie down and her mind to settle. Realising that this must certainly imply some compact or agreement that must be broken to me, I fell into the tranquil sleep of defeat and had a remarkably clear *brown* dream. [. . .] Alas

for my camellia tree and revolving island[24] . . . for I do not want to go mad, and these brown dreams alarm me.

11. After tea she set to copying more of the Norfolk story, and I was reading Michael Howe's Spring Song, when there was a clap of thunder, and a violent rain storm. Suddenly it cleared, I ran out to see if there were a rainbow – there were two, and everything drenched in brilliant low-shafted light, the moss on the thatch, the white ducks gobbling, and we counted seven churches on the horizon, and knew there was an eighth – Horsey hidden in its woodlands, Waxham, Palling, Happisburgh, Ingham, ? Hickling, Somerton, Winterton. And three windmills and two owls.

In the evening the wind blew, the driftwood fire crackled, and I remembered that she had spoken, under that rainbow, of asking for a first refusal of this house. But I remember too, her typewriter crackling before breakfast, and how she left it with a sigh as deep as the Pacific; and it seems to me that this time the disease of Eliz: is working in her far more deeply than in 1939 – when she often resisted it, and tried to throw it off; and in me, I know, it is working like a malaria; and if I am not helped soon I think I shall lose my last power to hold out, it will become such an obsession of helpless anxiety, of impotence, of insignificance. And still, though I have lost all affection, all respect, for Eliz: I am visited with pity for her, for what must be some spark of real feeling amid all that sprawl of emotional verbiage, self righteousness, and chicanery of argument. And in that real feeling there must be an element of horror at all she has brought about. I, who have brought about nothing, who have merely struggled to retain my integrity of love, feel horror. But also, and worst, deep shame at my consenting in /39 in that hell-house at Warren.[25] If I had stood up then, this would not have happened – And I did not – and it has.

12. And yet, in days between, small sprouts of hope begin to grow. A pollarded tree, so I read today, gives more timber than a straight one. [. . .] Pheasants were crying and complaining to each other, the sunset had dyed the brown reeds a dull dead rose colour, and she spoke of how we might suggest to Mrs Howlett that we should spend a winter here. I can think of nothing I would love better. This place has enchanted me, slowly, persuasively, as if with an affinity. And could she speak so unless she had it in her heart to remain? And then, seeing

24 See 2 October 1949 above.
25 Warren, Connecticut, where STW, Valentine and Elizabeth had stayed *à trois* in 1939.

her so ill, and so turmoiled with letters and complications of compassion, I wonder if she can remain anywhere, if she can survive. And yet I put out this pollarded growth of hopes.

13. In the late evening I spent some time walking along the marsh path, watching the strands of mist emerge, and fade out, like long sighs of earth. It is six months today since all this began. A summer, the loveliest in men's memories. 'Nought have I have harvested but a crop of weedie cares.' Or perhaps it is more like a sieve; the juices have gone through my consciousness, and what I seemed to be left with are the stalks and strings on top.

16. Alas – our last day in this endeared place. And in the morning we made our last expedition towards Waxham for wood; and in the afternoon it rained, and we looked at the annexe – and were personally pained to see that the sea-ward wall is damp – though Valentine says that one could always make out with a damp sitting-room; and in the evening we went up to the hills, and saw the loveliest of all the skies we have seen here – for the s.east was full of clouds, and they were all in relief patterns of pale violet against deep violet, above a dull flint-blue sea: or was it obsidian? a chipped-stone sort of colour, anyway, nothing in the likeness of flower or feather; and on the shore there was a Craske group of men fishing. But the colour of the clouds was such as I have never seen before, and untinged by any whiff of pink or gold – a pure solemn purple.

And nothing has been said: so I must suppose the dust is still unlaid. She talks of Eliz: constantly – no, it is more accurate to say that Eliz: is constantly in her talk. Sometimes I bat it back – but I cannot be forever batting. E. was in my dreams again last night. We had driven to a concert, and in the foyer I saw her, inordinately tall, and in black, as massive as an up-ended coffin; and said immediately, I must go away. And we drove away together – but it was a *coloured* landscape we drove through, of blue and green poplar meadows. And now I think I will leave off any more batting-off of the Eliz: motif. For I believe my best hope of overcoming the horror I still feel is to go on, willy-nilly, until I can feel bored. Boredom is a power not often invoked; and it is a dangerous drug, since it marches with obsession; but it is a homeopath and obsession's cure. And though we have a balance still, it will not last beyond Christmas, so somehow when we get back I must cajole myself into being able to write again.

24. And I am at home again – for a couple months more perhaps. For another frightful letter came this morning, saying it must be all or nothing, and full of threats of renunciation. And all that morning we talked of it, and she is rent between us. But Eliz: will certainly destroy her with possessiveness thwarted, and I may be enabled not to harm her if I go away. So in the upshot a clear letter was written, saying that there must be a year's trial in which she lives with Eliz: and after that it may be possible to work out some future expedient. She showed it to me, and I agreed.

But looking back on the letter of July 27, & the letter in the typewriter, and the letters to Yeovil I realised how far, how much further, I am lost. For of the letter in which she said I should be her choice if it came to a choice, she said sternly, 'It can never become a matter of choice.' And in these words I heard the axe at my root.

For now it seems to me that the only way in which I can save her anguish is to love her less: that she can only reach a peace of mind, and a wholesomeness of mind, and retrieve some sort of good out of this calamity, by ceasing to know that she is my only love and my only life. And yet I will not accept this, for it is of an unclean spirit. I love.

26. 'And another day is tucked under my wing'. So I wrote, a month ago, in Yeovil. If I could find a god I would pray to him never to hope again. Valentine this morning gave me an Indian book that I had admired at Baldock, about death and renunciation.

I wanted to carry up the coal-scuttle, and said Let me, while I can. When I came down again I heard her weeping, standing alone by the sink, her hands in the basin, her body shaken and bowed with tears.

30. Sunday. Valentine spoke of how badly she sleeps, heavily, and waking not daring to enquire what dreams she had, for fear. In the afternoon we dug the garden together for a while, but her back would not let her go on. I worked on alone – there is kindness in an autumn garden, though not very much. A sad constrained day – poor Sunday, poor island. It is horrible to consider that she dreads a letter of refusal, and I a letter of acceptance – and yet we love each other.

November

14. No letter.[26] I chored most of the morning, fought at half a page of

26 From Elizabeth, in reply to an urgent letter from Valentine.

Sib.[27] and found the dates all wrong. Phelps from Western BBC rang up to say he liked the Légende, and had a new programme. I told him he should have Valentine's poems in it. After lunch we looked for some. Her poems of this summer. It is curious that I can read them, she watch me read them, discuss them: all the time both of us bleeding life-blood. While she cleaned the car I weeded, on into dusk. When I think of the harm Eliz: has done me already I can't believe she won't finish the job. And she thinks of the harm I've done her, I suppose. Tried to go on with that book. Automatically, like a killed snake, I give a twist of writing well; but there is no connection. I suppose I should be grateful for Phelps, and turn my mind to becoming a BBC hack. I should enjoy the technique, that would still be a pure pleasure. But how am I to comfort my love, my bruised and threatened and bleeding love?

15. The anemone is out – a pink & white one: an exquisite winged insect, with long transparent green wings like mica, and a long green body, was sheltering on the car. Thomas on my bosom as I lay in hers. I put down things at random – not knowing where to place my hope where it will not be indecent. [. . .] Fired by Mr Palmer's bill I am trying a story for the N.Y. . . . myself at Cromer the theme.[28]

16. I went on, and finished it. One is not grateful enough to the *lower* gods; the demiurges, who run out with their vulgar little cups of gin and peppermint when the real Gods turn away the cup of nectar. Writing for money I wrote quite decently, and was rattling out the last sentence when she came in – so pale, so tired, so care worn that I was ashamed of my facility.

18. She [Elizabeth] has shown, as far as I know, no shame on either side about Evelyn: for taking to her, for leaving her. She left that un-abashed parcel for me at the end of Sept. (after I had injured her feelings by going to a hotel); the letter from Evelyn in May that shook her to the core did not shake her into answering it – or remembering it, when she got a similar one while she was here. Again she was shaken to the core. And with this assiduity to collect her dues, Vénus toute entière welded into a tax-collector or a bailiff, she can perfectly well be shaken to the core one day; and go bravely on to collect her dues the next. [. . .] Such woe, such foreboding, and such *nausea* fill me that I

27 'Sibilla', an unfinished novel.
28 'The Sea is always the Same', *OTL*.

can hardly contain myself. I sicken at the thought of this cold poison, this octopus out of a bad sea. Was ever love so true, so burning true, for so cold and calculating a creature?

December

7. I do feel extremely tired; especially whenever the strain slackens, or appears to slacken. [. . .] But I look back to Nov. 7th and am abashed at such an inordinate flippant hopefulness that could look for any renewal at a month from then. While one goes on living all the time, and *because* one goes on living, one does not realise the extremity which one has lived through. My hair is burned black as Dante's with hellfire, and I wonder why it will not lie down in a graceful wave.

9. My Italian *Corner* came this morning – and gave me an unforeseen and deep pleasure – its dustcover with a small *pink* cloister under a blue sky, all a thousand Alps away from Oby.[29] I did Christmas presents, finishing the last card for USA, and in the afternoon, out of a dark sky, small white pellets of snow rattled on the house. I ran down the drive for pleasure, eating them.

28. I felt subdued, and spent the afternoon contentedly translating the portent section of L.de l.M. [*La Légende de la Mort*]. The thrush sang sweetly in the afternoon. The passage in Guermantes Way II about desiring Albertine for the smell and light & sensation of Balbec as well as for her ready *improving* self must be very close to what Valentine felt in May. That tutelary element in love is something I have never felt, and so I incline to disregard its importance.

30. In the evening making a pair of chamois socks for my Love; with tufts at the back, *selon la Nature*. A strange apparition from the Bank acquainted me that I had £390. I thought I had about £150. Nobly resolved to pay my income tax – 1st instal. anyhow – out of currency. I cannot, I still cannot believe that this year's ending sees me here. When I look back at May and see how Eliz: had, it seemed, all the cards in her hands: body, renewal of lust, reparation of what had been wrong, romantic quest, twelve whole years, money, novelty, beauty, a surface undinted by war, two large new ears, the spring, instinct at its liveliest, and determination; and I was old, familiar, the worse for wear, and stupid with shock. How comes it then? Partly Eliz:'s fatal

29 The setting of *The Corner that Held Them*.

rapacity, get-sure quick, poor wretch; partly my truth, which stayed when everything else I had tattered away; but mostly my Love's love, her innocence from all calculation. But no river could be more astonished, after a deluge, to find itself in its familiar bed.

January

18. During a brief conversation in the kitchen, arising from the green teapot I broke on Xmas day, Valentine said I was remarkably unreproachful. I said, after consideration, that I nothing to reproach her about. She was incredulous; only last night, she said, she had lain awake thinking how, if I were to die, she would have no friends except among those older than herself to turn to – and time and place & cause for self-reproaching. I said again, that Eliz: was nothing for me to reproach her with, for one cannot reproach an unconscious injury. And this is true. For that morning, having wanted to look up the two moons entry in her minute book I found that the May pages had been unsealed again – and sat down to read them. From April 11th to May 24th (when my grandmother had forced me to force myself on her notice)[1] there is no word of me. I had vanished from her mind. All that talk about bigamy, and being able to include both Eliz: and me, must have been a façon de parler, a desperate *façon d'adoucir*. And I realised, having discovered this and felt a profound mysterious thankfulness, that to be injured is not irreparable, that what is irreparable is injustice and misprision. If I can steadily retain my knowledge that her façon de parler meant nothing, since the person it was addressed to had at that time been abolished from her mind, I can fight off the poison in my wits, that she had really supposed I would consent to spending the rest of my life in an ignoble hypocrisy. It is relatively nothing to have been dead (though Lazarus must bear a haunted mind). To be dead is better than to have been defiled.

But the days grow longer, the year turns towards Eliz's: determined new assault. I cannot go on expecting miracles (my grandmother was a miracle, and so was the leap of resistance that taught me how to answer E.'s first letter (though I must always regret that I allowed

1 STW is referring to a decisive dream in May 1949 which encouraged her to stand her ground as regards Elizabeth.

myself to be weakened from sending the first plain unsweetened version (there *is* a spot of defilement here)). It will be hard to keep myself unspotted again. If need be I must go. Rather than live falsely with my Love, I must go and live truly by myself . . . not linger out a purposed overthrow. But meanwhile, I will dance and trample on that fallen Dagon, that supposed expedient of a revised mystical Warren.[2] She said it to me, poor Love, out of flurry & compassion: *but not to herself.*

20. Valentine came back from work to a letter from Eliz:. I think it must be about coming in the spring, for she suddenly looks aroused, and combative, and decisive. And now I hear her whistling. Yes. Now I hear the typewriter – it rattles as it did last summer. How quickly one is wrong. She was typing Gaster's income-tax return.

28. Kess[3] came in the p.m. A kind crow, and very amiable, and with beautiful brows and extremely pure honest eyes. After she had got her strength up by a solitary walk, she came in and – so I learned – instantly tackled Valentine on Eliz's: behalf. I knitted by the dining-room fire, dissembling the shock – more than I had expected – of an American voice twined with Valentine's overhead; and got dinner and dawdled [. . .] Kess had asked what chance of a solution that would not havoc V.'s relationship with me. She had said that torments and reproaches made holes in our life together, through which life was lost; but that if she were happy with Eliz: it would be all right with us. This was such a shock to me (for it seemed to be the most out and out denial of any validity or meaning left in my love as it appears to her, and was said with shining confidence, as in May) that I think I showed nothing at all. [. . .] Most of the night I was awake, haunted with an exact recollection of the evening when the moon and I were in the garden, before she came back from London. The evening of Sept. 30th. I saw how full of hope and confidence I was. I had no doubt but that she would be happy in our re-union. Her letters had said so. Why did she write them? Why did I read them? So I said to myself, lying awake with the wind in the east.

29. Very cold still. Blackbirds could hardly lift from the ground as we drove into Dorchester to take Kess for a drive. We went to Wool Bridge House, and along the Lulworth road where I drove with Stephen Tomlin, already setting out for this rapture of love that has

2 See note 25 (1949), page 148.
3 An American friend of Elizabeth Wade White.

come to such sad kindliness; and back by Marley Wood, and on to Weymouth & Portland. A misty iron-coloured day, but at Weymouth the sea was broken and brilliant dark emerald; and then to Portland. We lunched at Kings Arms, and came back here: Kess nerved herself and suddenly began to praise Eliz: before me[.] [. . .] She left on the 4.40.

February

12. A quiet day, till in the evening Mrs Riverel[4] rang up to say Nora had become weaker. I'll come tomorrow, I said, thinking of the 9.25. But I had barely put by the receiver when V. had everything planned that she should drive me.

13. We started at 8. It was clear sky, and lambstails wagging in the hedges, and the sea in the Golden Cap aperture so turbid with storm that for a moment I thought it was an immense ploughed hillside. Sun, and wide views till we got to Torquay. The nurse let me in and without speaking, gestured me to the drawing-room. Matron came in, and told me that Nora had died in her sleep at 4.30 a.m. We went up to her room. Matron had laid her out herself. I thought, seeing her clay colour and her hollowed cheeks and chin, of the peasant death in La Légende. I stayed on alone for a while, looking at her. Her face was composed, stern, not sad; her little nose soared out of it like the dome of St Pauls. It was not like my father's death-mask . . . being so much older, she seemed infinitely more dead, and abstract like a work of art. Only her hair when I caressed it was light and living.

Downstairs the poor little nurse was in bitter grief, swollen and speechless. Matron gave me Nora's turquoise ring, and I gave it at once to the nurse. V. came in from the car, and coffee was produced, and we sat waiting till the undertaker came. A short pale rounded man, with pale grey eyes. Then she drove me to the solicitors for the cremation certificate (where I heard myself reported as 'Miss Warner waiting for an oath') and I ordered a mixed tulip and iris bunch for the funeral at a shop where Valentine had bought flowers for my mother, and for me. After lunch I supposed all was done; but we had to wait till 4 to see the doctors. I telephoned kind Marion Deuchar,[5] explaining about the ashes, and she undertook to get a hole howked out, Evans

4 Matron of the nursing-home in Torquay, where STW's mother lived.
5 The tenant at Little Zeal.

being ill; and Evans;[6] and then on my Love's good suggestion we sat in the car writing letters till the doctors – and so away. The drive back with the sun behind us turned the green fields even more pistachio-nut, and put a green light on the lambstails, and damsoned the woods, and enriched the red plough. I felt strangely unreal, because of the gliding smoothness of all the arrangements: steps of an old dance. We had dinner in bed. All day I had at the back of my mind the thought of what this day would have been if Eliz: had got her will: how harsh, jolted, and dry. And today, at any rate, my Love did not feel a flicker of regret, we were each other's heart.

15. The 9.15 to Totnes – where I lunched with a black kitten, went to Kellock's and read a copy of Nora's will. It is £1500 in legacies, the residue to me.

16. I drove with Hand in a small bowler hat to Efford Crematorium, where poor H. Boucher was wandering among graves like a lost Nelson. Nora's small purple coffin coming out of the hearse; the one bunch of brilliant spring flowers on it. Out of such bare material, out of mere birth and death, we spin the intricate web of love, we distil it from these poor bones and ashes, and with it conceive the tale that is told and ended when we die.

Back to L.Z. and walked up to Brent Moor House in the p.m. Its long sullen sighing drive, and the cave in the rocks – I had forgotten how wuthering it was.

17. [Little Zeal] It is a curious sensation to get one's mother by post; and rather hastily I took her upstairs and unpacked a small violet cloth-covered casket, with a shiny name-plate (good lettering). After breakfast Evans & I buried it with some moss and snowdrops under the cherry-tree – Captain Ferguson had come down to help howk the hole, because of E's bad leg. Afterwards Marion came out to help us talk about the garden, and we had elevenses in the kitchen, and I left for the station, full of sincere regard for that very sensible and upright young woman. A long wait at Yeovil Pen Mill. My knitting failed me, and I sat looking at the fir trees with that September morning traveller beside me for a very mauvais quart d'heure.

19. Lupton snowdrops in a.m. [. . .] On our way back we saw an owl at the roadside, eating. By daylight they are almost the colour of

6 The gardener at Little Zeal.

orange lichen. In the evening I wrote to Alec's[7] possible tenants. Agreeable thoughts on what can be done when wealth to virtuous hands is given – but a motor scythe is £75 so we will turn our minds to painting the kitchen, and giving it a new cupboard, new oil-cloth, and perhaps a wall-paper as in Bo's closet to the spare-room and lobby. In the evening she spoke of her drinking . . . it was that that baffled her about the convoy to Spain.[8] Often I cannot believe it was so at all.

21. After lunch we went out to prune willows . . . and were happy till the post brought me a letter from Eliz: It was only condolence on Nora's death, and required no answer – and she offered to read it for me. But the knowledge that she had told Eliz: (I suppose writing while I was away) called back the shock of my visit to Monica[9] having also been told. Why must I be written of between them? And though we went on gardening, I felt like a ghost, and a ghost that is not left unraised either. Implore pace!

That was not all. By the same post, I heard later, there had been a letter for her saying that Eliz: *is* coming on March 19th, and also containing something – some flout, some infidelity, I don't know – that she found hard to endure. This she told, that evening, and spoke of all the discommodities, the pains and embarrassments of this affair, and of how she is divided in mind as to how to meet Eliz: But when, gathering up what dregs of courage I have left, I said that I seriously asked her to come with me to Paris instead, and not tear everything open again before anything has settled to heal, she said No – as though she had not heard the words.

Afterwards, reading La Prisonnière and looking at a log in the fire that was like a Cézanne rock, I suddenly had an overpowering impression of Charles[10] . . . as though his ghost had come to fetch me, and the taxi were waiting outside, and the kind evening all arranged. In less than 3 weeks Eliz: comes. In a month from now we shall be back again in hellfire.

HONOUR WON'T PATCH

23. We voted – for the Liberal . . . for myself, dubiously, since it is only a negative vote. I saw a cow eating the rose-prunings I had

---

7 Valentine's cousin, Alec Robertson (1892–1982), chorusmaster, organist and music critic. From 1940 to 1953 he was head of music talks at the BBC.

8 In November 1936 Valentine had been asked by the Communist Party to drive a lorry in convoy to Valencia but backed out at the last minute, apparently due to ill health.

9 Monica Ring, whom Valentine first met when working in the TA office during the war.

10 Charles Prentice had died in Africa in 1947.

thrown over the fence on Tuesday afternoon; and saying aloud that it would turn into Apuleius, and hearing my voice in the empty house a sudden sense of helplessness and impending calamity fell on me, and I felt more hopeless than ever before, and as though one or the other of us must be dead, could not be other than dead. [. . .]

Walked up Visitors Walk[11] at dusk, and saw how the sickle moon grew older and younger as the smoke of cloud thicked and thinned. A thicker cloud shuts off the lustre of the inner side of the curve. I came back having resolved most of my sense of helplessness in the dark and the rain, past the last electors: but at the gate was Valentine coming out to look for me in the car. She had been on foot half-way up the village earlier, thinking that my premonition must be that I would be developing influenza. Shan ill. The vet came, and said [it] may be rheumatism. We lay happily hearing election results and light music – a shortened organist etc till midnight. I woke later, she asked if I was worrying about Eliz: I took this as a last chance to say that we seemed to be in just the state she had refused in her letter of November; and that I felt no hope for her or myself in any house built at the mercy of Eliz's false watery instability. It was a mistake. I made her unhappy and did nothing.

26. Three weeks to Eliz: If it begins again what to do? Her recount of what she said to Kess about being happy in love with Eliz: making no difference to our state together rings in my ears. For all I know – for what I must suppose – she really believes this true. Unless some angel of frivolity breathes on me I don't see how I can keep up such a pretence. Perhaps I might sneak off on visits. Bea, the Sturts, Ian perhaps, Little Zeal. It is a small repertory. The Robertson Scotts. Frederic Caunter.[12] Nancy [Cunard] . . . or people staying here would be a help, but nothing comes except Ruth.

Meanwhile she lies sick and in pain and nursing some inner wound, some slight or flout . . . and it is like treachery to have to consider expedients for going away.

27. The first grape hyacinths and white violets gathered this morning. The wintersweet is full of flowers. I supped in bed, and all of a sudden she came out of her cloud, laughed and embraced me, was angry because I tricked her over fetching her lemonade, and threw the coffee-cup at the bureau and broke it to relieve her feelings. After this we

11 A steep and brambly public footpath, recommended to visitors.
12 Unidentifiable.

settled down very happily to hear Anthuil's[13] Antigone (ANTHUIL'S?).
The last of Hoyle's talk on the universe. Galaxies receding at a rate
faster than light ascertained by spectroscopic analysis of light-changes
in atoms. This was Majestic – like a great sweeping change of key in
music.

March

7. A foggy morning, a fine day. I dug some back garden. After lunch,
saying I looked pale, she drove me to Chesil Beach, where I paddled in
a silk sea, and we lay in the sun, in a world where there was nothing,
she said, that would have seemed strange to a Roman soldier, or to
Dante, or to Milton – except, I said, to Dante, who would have
thought it very strange to lie on a shingle-bank, listening to the sea.
Then we drove to see the barn, and the swannery; and in the valley
there is a beautiful ruined house, and I want it. [. . .]

When I look at her as she was this afternoon, I cannot, cannot believe
she will again sell herself into the slavery she repudiated last autumn;
and yet – things being as they will be – what else is to be expected?
Proust – I am reading Albertine Disparue chap. 1 – says so. Besides,
dalla sua pace la mia dipende – and her tenderness to me has an amorous
colour in it. I lick sweetness that oozes from the outside of the vessel.

11. What hinders it, a voice, a cold voice said: and I went and took
Amy[14] from the coffin, and sat down to go on from where I left off,
eleven months ago. And did, to the tune of a dreary page and a half.
Then just before lunch her chimney caught fire. Burning soot like
Christmas decorations fell down the chimney, and she telephoned for
the Fire Brigade – groaning with horror when she saw all the children
attending it. They all looked romantically spruce in their uniform, and
Mr Cox remarked maturely that fire was a good thing but a bad enemy.
He also cherubically pissed by the water-butt, turning his red winking
winter sunset face over his shoulder before he unbuttoned.

12. On a brilliant afternoon we drove to Mappowder, and met T.F.P.
in the lane, with the sleeves of his fine overcoat turned back, and a
strange purple stole round his neck. Violet looked ill – and was kind.
I heard a little more of Charles's death, and how Lynn[15] is marrying

13 A mishearing of Anouilh.
14 An unfinished novel.
15 Lynn Prentice, Charles's common-law wife.

again – or married. I must be changed indeed, for Theo took such pains to tell me I was not. We came back past the corner where she wept . . . all the way I had a preoccupying sensation of how she felt that morning – how strange, how rapt, how in flight from the usual turns of the road, the familiar sights, and that gate, and the garage, and the house, and me asleep – and all her emotion turned like a river into a new bed.

I feel the hand of necessity again – and strongly. In the morning, for a few minutes, I felt extremely faint and dizzy: and the only thought I had was that I must not, *not* become ill, because that might delay their meeting and what must be learned after. It was the same last August, when I almost counted off the days still left me before Yeovil. But that evening there . . . it is foolish to think that one can experience a sorrow once and for all . . . it only delves the possibility of a deeper agony. October was worse than the last day of August, and the next time will be worse again, and my powers of concealing it even thinner. Last Thursday, I remember, I threw myself on the bed crying out, 'And once, I was so good!' It is true. Eleven years ago I was a much better being.

15. Up to a point one approaches a prospective suffering: every day one steps towards it, with fear, with defiance, with cunning, with blind woe. And then, at some given moment, the movement is interchanged: with a kind of idiot, weaseled-rabbit serenity, one stays quite still, and *IT* approaches. I did not know this when I wrote Elinor Barley, though I seemed to have known the psychology of the process. For the last four days I have sat quite still.

16. After lunch, she began to talk, and to ask me if I were not happy. Truth's cold finger for once lay on my lips, and I said I could not forget our unhappy circumstances. It was a windy night, I slept badly. She deceives herself about me far more than I deceive her. And came to say she had written to six travel agencies about a holiday. It is too late – it is too late. I told her there was more hope for her in vice with Eliz: than in virtue – and she agreed. And I said that this might be better for me, since Eliz: would then be giving her something I could not give. And she did [not] understand this at all, she thought I meant love, passionate love, and looked appeased.

17. On this day before she goes I will copy out what I wrote last summer. 7th June.

After a day of wind blowing, overcast, and alternate bouts of terror & aridity, I lay in bed trying to disentangle what could be mended and what is beyond my control. And the thought came to me that henceforth my life must be conducted as a – probably – very long process of dying. The death sentence has been said, I must accustom myself to being a dying person – not as we all are – but specially and consciously, and conductedly. What I have to expect are the common accompaniments of death: anguishes of terror and revolt, tedium, and loneliness, for all seem to agree that death is a completely lonely thing. Part of this thought came by her having said, the day before, that she would take out of the marriage vow the clause about till death us do part. I, rejecting all vows, have in me a kind of love that can only observe every word of that one. So I must consider, since this thing has parted us, that my process of death has already begun. I must shun all hope, all scheming, all ambition. Probably, I shall not write another book, for creation is no part of dying – though I can and must do some potboilers. Pleasures that come to me I can accept and enjoy, but only as things offered to the dying, like the sweetpeas in her poem. I can allow myself this, that to the last I can love her – and if she were to come back, my death sentence would be revoked. Meanwhile I begin to die.

That was nine months ago. How is the child then begotten? Twice, alas, I have allowed myself to hope. When I came back from Yeovil, and at the end of November. If anguish, and shame, and self-contempt, and repentence, can teach anything, I am not so likely to hope again. I have not schemed. I have had no ambitions. I have created nothing, for the poems that have broken out of me were no more creative than the sweat of anguish. I have done some pot-boilers – and now Nora's death has put by that need. (It is ironical to think that if I had had this inheritance five years, two years, even *one* year ago, my life might still have its real meaning – poor Nora, she would not have wished me this.) Pleasures – not very many – I have taken as dying to the dying. I have not ceased to love. Except for those two break-downs into hoping, I have been fairly consistent, and I think I am rather more than nine months nearer my death. What else? We live in the same house, we lie in the same bed. Yesterday, embracing me, she said she did it to comfort herself. Once or twice I have been more than that to her . . . or rather, she has needed more than that, and taken it.

Tomorrow she goes to London, and the next day they meet again. I will not write any more for a while. It is all written and re-written. Writing only leads me to hope. Teach me not to number my days.

23. She came back yesterday. 'I can't promise', she said 'that I won't fall into pits of depression. But it is at an end.' [. . .]

There is care ahead. Eliz: comes to Dorchester on April 11th and will be about probably during the rest of the month; and must be visited, seen to, allowed for. [. . .] But I believe the essential *No* has been said: the rest must be a bitter assorting of old circumstances to a new order. For yesterday my Love came back to where she has always wanted to be, only Fata Morgana, and then pity and chivalry and obstinacy and a will not to fail, not to give up, baffled the compass.

Now I must strangle all my imps.

Paul[16] wrote to say he was cold before The Sea-Change, and should he offer a revised Mr F. instead?[17] Cabled yes and encouragements.

28. Strange to hear the 12.14 go by, and think it carried that vexed and vexing spirit.[18] I was upstairs, lighting V.'s fire, when I heard it. And on an impulse I opened the east window, feeling that something was being borne out of the house . . . at the same time I think I counted every second of that pause at MN station, as consciously in pain for Eliz: as she could be. Afterwards I heard Thos. coming downstairs, very oddly, dragging his hind-legs. I went out, and found him sitting on the lowest step, waiting for me. I carried him out, and saw that he could not use his hind-legs. Remembering how I had found him yesterday afternoon sitting on his log in the river, bemused by the running water – for the last three weeks he has liked this place – I said to myself perhaps rheumatism. But by the evening there was no doubt he was paralysed. We sat up with him for a while – Valentine had suggested shooting him there and then – but I, thinking he might well die in the night – had said No, for I did not want this to be laid on her.

29. She carried him out, and sent me indoors. And I heard the first shot – that killed him – and two others, to make sure. She came in and lay down, I thought she would faint, or her heart break her in two. Then she shrouded him, and I dug his grave on the south side of the willow-wall, and she laid him in, and I covered him, and trod down the turves.

My dear, my true Thomas.

16 Paul Nordoff (1909–77), American composer and teacher of music. STW had met him on her trip to America in 1939.
17 Nordoff was writing an opera to a libretto by STW, 'The Sea-Change', on the subject of the death of Shelley. His previous works included an opera based on *Mr Fortune's Maggot*.
18 Elizabeth Wade White, returning to London by train.

April

7. [W]e drove past blackthorns, and the Maries like beaded bubbles on the horizon, & up the Green Valley, past Highland cattle & calves – and walked up Seagull Valley to the cliff-path, and lay in the sun beside a patch of minute forget-me-nots and the first cowslip, in love and refreshment; and I lost an earring, and she found it; and we lunched in the valley, watching a congregation of hares; and she said: 'I wonder if sheep ever get annoyed with their feet' – and we went on up to Chydyok, where Alyse was expecting Colleer[19] and already had a cold, but there was long enough to tell her, and show her, how things were with us. It was such intense happiness, and without a shadow of strain or uncertainty. Watching her walking towards me, the wind lifting her hair as caressingly as I do, and lying in the sun and being kissed: And rediscovering that in such a sky as today's seagulls look pink, as though transparent, and that in that landscape their voices are harmonious and pleasantly mewing, and that the wind in the brake along the hillside makes a noise like an inland wave.

May

28. Sometimes I wake early; and the thought of last year is borne to me on a rocket of cuckoo or the thrush or the blackbird that sings *going to leave here* – a seemingly blunted version of last year's sharpened phrase, but it was my pricked ears that sharpened it; and I look at her sleeping beside me, and take her sleeping hand – or she stirs, and we caress each other's sleep as animals do; and I cannot even now believe that it is I, saved from that extremity; but it is true, and in that truth I fall deep asleep again, as I did this morning, to wake again stretching myself for confidence and pleasure.

June

6. [London] In the morning to the Berthe Morisot show. How well *seated* her figures are; even the girl at the ball, who leaves off just below the waist is sitting below the frame. A lovely early group of mamma & two children under trees – her watchful tranquil face; the Mandoline girl; the quayside in the I.o. White with the pure grey angle of water in the middle of the composition; the piece of Manet's

19 Claude Colleer Abbott, (1889–1971) poet and translator.

daughter & her nurse, with the fleck of sunlight on the child's profile; a beautiful silvery nude (and a sketch of the stupid *open* face of the same model); and many beautiful drawings. I like her less well in her middle (Renoir) period when there is a great deal of tiresome peacock blue and *warm* flesh-tints. The Impressionists so true to Nature that they share Nature's badly expressed passages: for instance the pink waist-band and upper arm of the Mandoline girl.

14. We drove to Cauldron Barn Farm, at Swanage – a stone house on a hillside, with a plunging garden and a Guernsey bull, to look at Siamese kittens; and chose out one, and saw his father, who roared, and lay back languishing (but still roaring) to be tickled, showing a slit of leery squinting blue eye. His roaring boy came away with us, but soon slept, and woke to purr – and is to be called Niou[20] – and has been inscribed as mine by My Love. He slept in her bosom, and waking, I heard her crooning to him, her wood-dove note.

27. [T]he news has turned bad, with troops from North Korea invading the USA half. There must be a great deal we've not heard, for till yesterday's announcement of an advance over the 38th latitude, there'd been no whisker of the cat in the bag – except MacArthur[21] and The Times correspondent about ten days ago.

29. My back which had been painful, seems again rather smaller. The N. Yorker sent proofs of the Fire Alarm[22] and a check for $1031. The opening paragraph of the F.A. written a year ago in such dogged resolution to earn dollars for her in USA, strange reading now. Niou and Shan again met unconfined, and sat unconfined in her room. Colin gardened. I did the F.A. proofs, as they want it quick. 'Thrice toss these oaken ashes in the air'. The Times Washington correspondent – partizan of the Times Tokio correspondent, chastised by MacA. perhaps – says how USA newspapers say that Korea would be no real use to USA in a western war; in fact, that it is considered as outlying territory; Truman has ordered battleships, etc, to the fighting.

July

18. Stalin's agreement to Nehru's letter published in Moscow: his only

---

20 After The Perfumed Captain in *The Tale of Genji*.
21 General MacArthur, Supreme Commander of the Allied Powers.
22 'My Father, My Mother, the Butler, the Builder, the Poodle, and I', story, *SC*.

addition a suggestion that Korean representatives might be asked to take part in a settlement of the Korean dispute. Mild enough – but USA will have none of it.

19. USA will have none of it. They are bent on war. I realised with horrible clearness what Europe would be like when there is no more Europe. The Vatican, the industrialists, Monte Carlo and Spitzbuhel – and the Americans remaking everything so as to have more of what they want. Then Valentine came back from shopping in Dorchester where Mrs Florestine[23] said that all the people who came into the shop were wild for war – either because they had done well out of the last one, like the Colonel who grows her fruit, or because they hate communists – She spoke of not wanting another war, and was told, 'You ought to be shut up.' I think we may be.

26. I wrote to Nancy in the morning, and made a rissotto – but she [Valentine] came back in too much pain to eat. In spite of that, she went to Dorchester in the afternoon, because Mrs H.E.[24] must not be robbed a drive. A story rushed into my head – a theme, a situation rather, of last summer's brewing, the furniture falling back into its former place in a new London flat. She came back with a tortoise. We put it in the cage . . . She went to bed, and I finished the story.[25] I have not written like this, under such compulsion and persuasion, since those chapters of Emily[26] in early May.

27. It seemed pretty good the next morning, only its back was endangered by a shift of weight mid-way. In the afternoon we drove Niou to Chesil beach. It was the drive we took in May – but the news made it seem ghostly and farewelling, for all the heat of the day, the yellow flowers in the hedgerows, the brilliant immediate blue of the sea. I had been shaken by the vehemence of Sam's vanman, his usual spruce affable voice incoherent, almost incomprehensible as he burst into a speech about being shoved into a war that need not be – And when we are all killed, and everything is over and done for, the Americans will have won it! he cried out, furiously, looking back from the gate.

In the evening, Don Giovanni from Salzburg. Ljuba Welitsch[27] has a most exquisite slide and glide of legato in the first strain of *Non mi*

23 The greengrocer's wife.
24 Mrs Harley Edwards, an elderly neighbour.
25 'Farewell, My Love', retitled 'Winter in the Air' for publication in *WA*.
26 An unfinished novel.
27 The Bulgarian soprano.

dir; and listening to the Commander I thought that Valentine should arrive at dinner parties to the same air and sentiments.

August

13. The gladiolus just coming out, the phloxes in glory, a thousand apples on the trees . . . and a pair of earrings for me, like whelks, and a vase of mixed cornflowers and columbine leaves, and a piece of cold venison. And a letter from the N.Y. to say they might take *Farewell*, if I do this and that to it, including altering *all* the end. But the money is ʒo naice, and ʒo welcome, and ʒo warm, that I wrote to say I would do my best – (I think it is all that dear Mr Maxwell).[28] And a man at The British Council acknowledging J.A.[29]

26. A balance of £500 in my account, that N.Y. cheque for $1000 – so I sent Hilary & Janet a further £50 each. Revising Farewell My Love, according to William Maxwell's suggestions: I don't think I agree – but the revised Grandmother[30] *was* better in the end, and perhaps this will be too.

September

2. Though it is not the same ardent flawless weather of last year, the sun & the shadows and the birdsongs are the same; and I am haunted by the echoes of departure & Yeovil, they open in me like seasonal flowers. This morning a parcel of clothes & travelling presents, and a well-wishing cable, all came from Eliz: and there is a grey dress and I do not know what to do about it. That I should be here, and going to France with her – and in October going to Great Eye[31], as we had spoken of renting the Warren Farm for a winter – with four grey & white teacups she has bought for [me] – all this seems almost *illegitimate*: as if it could not be, only a year after the laceration of going to Yeovil, and the long anguish of that autumn. It is as if worms had eaten my body, and *yet* in my flesh I were arisen and going about. 'I

28 William Maxwell, the American novelist. His long friendship with STW began when she visited the office of the *New Yorker*, where he was a fiction editor from the 1930s to the 1970s. He edited STW's *Letters* (1982) and co-edited her *Selected Stories* (1988).
29 A short essay on Jane Austen for the British Council's 'Writers and Their Work' series.
30 'The Children's Grandmother', story, *WA*.
31 Great Eye Folly, a former coastguard station on the beach near Salthouse, Norfolk, which STW and Valentine were renting for five months.

am back for two months' I wrote last autumn, when I had made my compact to go away and Eliz: was coming in January for a year. And here I am [. . .]

Valentine's last day at Gaster's – I trimmed the gate with garlands of globe artichoke for her return.

October

27. Still cold – and still tired we drove to G.E.F.[Great Eye Folly] The fire was lit downstairs, there was tea ready for us, the table was covered with parcels and last thoughts from Mrs J.[32] Dreamily we read, unpacked, listened to the sea: it was the view from the upper room that suddenly woke us to a sense of place, and we knew we were here. We unpacked, put away, put out – it was almost dusk before we went out again, and picked up our first driftwood.

28. A cable from Paul to say he had finished *The Sea-Change* – it seems like a corroboration of pre-Eliz: when I wrote it. An intensely stormy day – we saw the sea darken and grow sullen, and an hour later it was rent with white horses. After waiting in for a baker called Jasper who did not come, we went off to the local stores, and bought staples like potatoes and toilet-paper, and then on to Holt, over a russet heath and through a violent hailstorm. Valentine bought nails at a shop resounding with anecdotes of cats, and everyone had Norfolk manners, and we much approve of Holt. In the evening, with the house practically settled, I sat writing, with the storm roaring outside, inside Niou sitting in his child's armchair, his little bell tinkling as he stirred.

November

1. *The newly caught skate* – still breathing – pink and ivory like a stormy sunrise, with pebbles still holding to its skin. The dusk, the sea coming out of the sky, no horizon, *the sky becoming sea*, rumpling, and breaking in very small cringing waves, and the boat being pushed ashore and up the shingle bank.

2. Shaw died early this morning – a comparable event to the death of Voltaire. I was very young when he was pointed out to me – that famous odious Mr Shaw – walking up Bond St in a pale homespun suit –

32 Their landlady, Mrs Jopling.

that seemed to annoy my mother even more than the beard or the man. And then I saw him at the dress rehearsal of Heartbreak House, springing onto the stage from the stalls to show the actress of Eileen how a young girl behaves, and becoming that young girl, and then modulating into Don Giovanni as he spoke to Edith Evans. [. . .]

In the morning of this fine calm day Niou was out playing among the fortifications – so stilly couched that we thought him a sea-white stone. Then I walked to the post, and heard about the flood of /47 and how a wave broke the shop-window and swept the wool off its shoulder-high shelf. The army, as usual, it appears. They dug into the sea wall and did not restore it. The flood in /43, at night, when no-one dared show a light. But the charming young man who came from Holt about the Calor gas said there had been a flood in the thirties. He could remember a bridge where the fishermen now stand, and his father could remember corn-fields under it – so much has the sea encroached. I read Supervielle's Colonel's Children – a poet's book, bird claw-marks on snow. We saw a school of porpoises near the shore, and the fishermen went on by lamplight, after seven in the evening: but now the wind is rising and blows fiercely.

3. And this morning a gale, north, with the sea very high, and the Cley coastguard not supercilious when I rang up to ask the time of high tide. It was 11.30, and at 12 we drove to Sheringham and registered, and shopped, and on the way back the car boiled – so we went back to S. to have a new poultice fastened to the side of the radiator. Now, as the sea is still high, the car sits on the front door mat. In the afternoon I worked a little, holding my breath, at Amy.[33] Spindrift like ghostly snow on the shingle, and flying everywhere around us.

6. In the afternoon we waited to buy a 2/6 poppy from a gentleman who rang – and this made our walk along the shore less glorious. I wrote ten thousand letters in the evening – and the news is very bad. McArthur detonating for war with China. He has been led up to the Korean border like a puppy after a gobbet on a string – and they have soundly enveloped and whacked him.

7. I awoke from a confused dream in which my mother was recently dead, but had not been senile – and she had sent a marlinspike iron object emmanchée in chocolate, and a remark – apparently in answer to something of mine – that bears were bad mothers. And on the fringe

33 See note 14 (11 March), page 160.

of this dream Eliz: was walking about, fingering little miniatures and bibelots, and unable to choose what she wanted. And by the post came a letter from Miss Castle, ready to buy Little Zeal for £3000 (I wrote to agree) – and for My Love an Elizabethiad which she showed me after lunch. It was full of reproaches, and grandeurs – and like some sort of salade russe in aspic, or fruits in ice, because of the long elaborately conducted and eloquent sentences, so much glaze that what was to be said seemed little more than the pretext of the sentence. In the evening I happened to read Proust's letters – they seem positively spontaneous in comparison.

14. My Love brought me breakfast while I was still in bed, and had cleaned and bowered my sitting-room. A letter from Kellock, rather peevish about Miss Castle, which I replied to with Nora's wishes and ashes. Still cold, windy, with brilliant colours on the marsh. Its dykes are now full of ruffled water – the curious look of the inland waterway flowing under the steep bank of sea-pebbles on our eastern beach. I darned a sheet – Niou killed two rats – and we drove in the afternoon round and about the Holt Heath. It would have been wholly happy if we had not met two gents and their keeper, the latter holding live pheasants upside-down: their wings fluttering and striving, and the gents awkwardly scrambling over a gate.

20. In the morning V.'s back was very bad – she had felt it give yesterday. And so I walked alone, by the sea's edge till I felt, like an animal – this is beyond any breathed air; and so it was, for climbing onto the shingle bank I found myself among the marrom tufts, and seeing a superb piece of marsh: the pale sharp poppy-horns standing above green frizzed cushions, marsh michaelmas daisy in thick grey thistledown mackerel-sky clouds, and the marsh water like blue lead above cushions of green moss and edged with rust-dark vegetation. I got a quantity of wood too, looking east to Salthouse church under a dark purple cloud.

22. To Sheringham & Holt in the morning. It was cold wet and windy. In the afternoon I pawked by the marrom tufts, and sat for a long while on my way back looking at the stern appearance of the smooth grey waves, and the tawny light in the northwest sky, and the band of dark slate blue of the eastern horizon between the grey of sea and the blueish violet of cloud; and then as I went on with my bundle I saw My Love, tall and slender, coming across the plateau to meet me. In the

evening worked on The Hostage – and read the life of A.J.A. Symons – a hero of our time; precious, mendacious, fertile in mind, futile in dealings with society, self-conscious as his calligraphy, and yet innocent and vulnerable. A sad story enough.

25. We have now most exquisite moonlight nights with foam as white as goatsmilk or Niou's bosom. The telephone restored. A reading entirely of Valentine's poems on Western Region – and, of all things, on the night when Ruth stays here.

30. A letter from Paul – at first about the composition of The Sea-Change – and then about the audition with Columbia:[34] they turned it down, killing it with expressions of esteem – and never did like that libretto. Alas, my poor Paul, my associations have done him no good, I fear. As a letter, it should be preserved, as Valentine said, in their own collection of mss about geniuses. He takes the murder valiantly, though it came at that moment when he was feeling all the lassitude of the emptied vessel.

December

15. Snow, hard frost, blizzards, icy roads, and the man cannot come from Walsingham. So we filled pails and buckets with snow, that sat in front of fires like large wet geese, refusing to thaw, and when at last they did were spotted with rabbits' dung. Meanwhile in a relenting interval the rainwater tank gave a trickle, and we got as far as Mrs Gray, who solved all our problems as usual, and has a father in law who is a rabbiteer. Paid 5/= to send Hostage to N.Y. In the afternoon a terrific blizzard: the wind round to the north, and at gale force ever since, so in addition to hoarding water we may be flooded. But a most happy day, for all that.

16. A slight let-up – but the landscape still mostly snow, and the wind icy: it blows to us from Yorkshire & Lincolnshire, which are deep in snow. Doris came in the morning, and so did the man from Walsingham – I found him with his lower half sunk in the well, like some Norfolk garden god with a scarlet face and a noble barrel. In the afternoon there was a blizzard. I worked on my pot-boiler, and read Donne, and in the evening my love read poetry aloud – Herbert, and Clare, and Fletcher, and the Afflictions of Richard, while I knitted on

34 Columbia University, New York.

Niou's rug. The man from Walsingham, who talked politics – anti-Soviet, alas! – and glumly resigned to war, with the resignation turning to resolution, said 'You don't mind the old waves, then?' They have been vast and sombre, but with explosions of spray that run westward, as though kindling along the wave. My Love be-bellied, and badly so, with a violent headache.

1951

January

6. Valentine drove to Holt & Sheringham. Doris[1] did not come, and in a flourish of duty I sat down and revived that story about the fog-horn in Cornwall,[2] suddenly seeing that the man was an artist, which would make it possible for him to be talked of to her instead of in answer to her. By the evening, 12.30 a.m. I had almost finished it. I also cleaned the kitchen floor and did some sawing and made a pie, and a partridge stew.

10. More pawking, more sawing, more chopping – for our wood supply runs low. A conversation with Mrs Gray – she still had no candles and no matches. They had been told there would be no [gas] cartridges for the next 3 months [. . .] On the same day, she had been told that price of knitting wool would go up from 1/8 oz to 2/8; and Mr Gray had learned at the garage that there would be very few small spare parts, as the factories were working – if at all – a 36 hour week because of the call-up of metal. She referred blastingly to the Festival of Britain (Oh! I forgot – they can expect very few tinned foods, no tin), and to the equality of sacrifice in which Europe equals USA. In that once sentence Eisenhower seems to have achieved a lead in unpopularity over MacArthur – mirabile dictu.

12. Today I part from Little Zeal – almost whole heartedly and quite whole headedly – though if it had not been for its dependence on poor Evans, whom I cannot decypher, but I am almost sure he would have hated me with undying hate – which would become extremely inconvenient – I should have been in two minds about the parting. But Miss Castle must certainly want it, and be pleased: to please two schoolmistresses is a satisfactory state to be in; and this evening my Love will read me 3 new chapters of the Norfolk story.

1 The local woman who was acting as char.
2 'Hee-Haw!', *WA*.

23. A misty morning. We set out for Brancaster, but in Wells on Sea the gears had a fit of impotence. [. . .] In Holt we learned with sorrow that taking down the gear-box, etc, would be a matter of 4 days – even if renewal parts could be got. Vauxhall Motors has now gone over entirely to armament vehicles. There had also been a distressing letter from E.W.W. which I read . . . the old insinuations about escaping from real life, and so forth, and a profusion of epitaphs. A very American way of life letter, with its desperate pursuit of the best and the biggest feelings. [. . .] But it saddened my Love, and dulled me. And, by God! – *such letters should not be written*. It is a base tyranny. Meanwhile, Robinson Crusoe is being a great pleasure.

25. I sat alone, making distracted notes a. for improvements to F.V. [Frome Vauchurch] b. for arranging it for another let. For this business of Ruth [her poor health] will make us Norfolk-bound, whether we buy or hire; and, alas! there is little hope of a holiday abroad. I have never before contemplated moving house without a spark of élan; if we were to get H.H.[3] I should enjoy its space and its cupboards; but I don't think we shall. I am afraid circumstances may crowd us into a hobgoblin. I'm afraid I want to go home, which is oddly pusillanimous of me. I want to go to something I am sure of, whose ways I know, whose demands I know are not beyond my strength. O Sylvia, can it be that you want to *Retire*? Meanwhile, the New Yorker pays $658 for Hee-Haw, and the Reredos story was posted today 3/=.

February

2. A frittering day – and one of the coldest I have ever known. A south wind, again: a steady stealthy boring wind; and no sign of it, on this clean-shaved landscape, except on the sea. As the waves – very small ones, approached the shore, the wind turned them backward, aborted them: instead of breaking, they faded out on the sea, one following another, like bars on a mackerel; and the rim of sea & shore was as inexpressive as the shore of a lake: By the evening this wind has intensified, and blew in multitudinous gusts.

4. Sunday. And a tearing gale. We drove to Winterton, taking Niou hot-water-bottled with us, because it seemed that we might well be

3 Hunworth Hall, near Holt, which they were considering to buy.

unable to get back. And at Walcott we had a puncture. It was opposite a kind house with a telephone, and a man who, when all garages proved to be sabbatical, came out in the storm, and helped my Love. [. . .] Valentine helped Ruth with her will, and I sat in the dining room with Niou. Then home, the gale still raging; and it took both of us all our strength to turn back the garage door against the wind. Early this morning a boat hoved to, or whatever it is, just outside our beach, twisting and turning for all its two anchors.

11. Tonight, in my bath, I noticed that the wind was rising. This morning there was a violent n.e. gale, a Craske sea of looped breakers running sidelong to the shore, and indoors, the kitchen a swamp, the larder a waterfall, and fountains of wind blown sink-water blowing up from the runaway. I noticed this aspect of it more, as I was feeling so ill, and let My Love do the outside jobs. But in flashes through the windows I saw how wildly lovely it was – and in the afternoon, the wind going down and the rain ceasing, I walked along the beach admiring the sea – sternly gay, destined and conscienceless. [. . .] I have felt ill all day – I am certainly re-infected; and only tomorrow to pull myself together in before another go of Ruth. I lack the superstition that could make me find her any more congenial because she may die within the twelvemonth.

21. A jet bomber has crossed the Atlantic in 4 hours. The BBC broke its news to say so. [. . .]

Mrs Gray has given up being a grocer, because there are so few groceries, so much paper work, and the margin of profit has been cut again. So wags the world. And Norway, though it will increase its army, will have no foreign troops sent there unless it first asks for them.

We were like this, once. Gide is dead.

24. Like a proud kangaroo the postwoman produced a large box from her pouch. It was beef, from Anne. Such kindness, and such beef, made us feel a great deal better. It was a misty-moisty day, and in the afternoon a rare sexless fisher, with hair like Monica [Ring]'s, and long narrow scarlet hands and wrists, and a long heron's stride. A beautiful being, with a severe inattentive regard, it went away on a motor-bicycle, and we supposed it finally to be male. How such an incertitude would have surprised our grandparents.

27. By the East Anglian to London. [. . .] Then to Chepstow Villas –

Stewart Wilson[4], his wife, the D.T.[5] critic, John Edmunds, & Ralph V.W.:[6] thick white hair, and a resemblance to T.F.P. Presently Cousin Edmund[7] & Mrs Fellowes came in. She scarcely changed at all, but shrunk like a withered apple – E.H.F. singularly thin, and looking ill (he had had influenza), but talking in exactly the same tune. He was very affectionate to me, reminded me of how the leaves fell off the chestnut tree in K. Gardens, and of the other meeting when I had to take him away & calm him. There was a nice birthday cake with a lute on it, and the presentation of the parchment I had signed in Holt P.O. and a speech from V.W. that instantly turned into general conversation. All this very affectionate, well-bred and of the old school. I felt touched, and came away rather sadly from this evocation of my old home.

March

8. A strong wind, and the sea roaring in with great plunging billows. So much so that with an eye on the p.m. tide, we took both animals in the car when we drove R. to East Dereham. [. . .]

On our return the sea was almost up to the gap, with nearly three hours to run. [. . .] I rang up the coast guards, who said Prevention was better than Cure. Not seeing how one can cure the state of being cut off from the mainland, we made a swift dusky get-away – and left for Winterton with the spindrift whirling after us and the wind dislodging the southern door post of the garage with one toss of the door.

20. We left [Great Eye Folly] at 8.30 and came a new detour by accident mostly, via Tring and Thame. It was a ravishingly fine day. Home about 6 – to find the garage locked and various incommodities – but the house very clean & orderly. And to me, very dear. She was extremely tired.

April

25. [Little Zeal] Woke, and went straight to work: labelling, listing: I tried to do the garage, but the dust, the heat, & Evans were too much. Being helped by Mr Evans is as exhausting as being helped by an

4 Steuart Wilson, the tenor.
5 *Daily Telegraph.*
6 Ralph Vaughan Williams.
7 E.H. Fellowes, who was celebrating his eighty-first birthday.

untrained elephant. Tattered with fatigue, I lunched in the sun outside
the porch. Mrs Hickey rang up, and was providentially kind and helpful with her impending sale. The wind moved doors, & I had an odd
impression that Nora was also packing (I seemed to hear her arranging
the dish-rack in the morning too). My Love, Ruth & Niou arrived at
4. In a last rush I discovered that the white cupboard wouldn't do, &
sank exhausted to drink scratch tea on the lawn. My last glance was at
the little dressing-room, mine so long ago, when I was young, sullen,
exalted, lay awake with toothache & La Cathédrale,[8] and dressed my
hair like a Velasquez infanta by candlelight. Very very tired. And my
Love the same, with her back bad. Near Newton Abbott we had the
narrowest possible escape, with a small Ford car overtaking on a hill
and a bend. I saw our deaths blazoned on the face of the overtaken
lorry-driver – we just scraped in between the idiot and the curb.

29. Waking, I thought: this[9] is the death-bed, and the love-bed is gone.
But it is a very comfortable bed, and does not hurt Valentine's back to
make. Sorting & arranging & washing china all day; the house oddly
full of Nora's noises; the drawers of her tallboy, & the little Swiss
cow-bell. A verse from Mellstock churchyard rings in my head – her
china, and all her industries & talents and enterprises. And in a commonplace book of hers O World, O Life, O Time copied out (with
Shelley carefully written below) – a strange aspect of her to me. My
Love, helping me sort the tallboy, said sadly how deprived of her
own past she is – next to nothing of Robert,[10] and nothing of her own
childhood: all her young possessions lost or charitably bestowed.

July

13. Made a blue & white nightgown, interrupted by Valentine coming
back with a coffee ice and a nosegay of pinks, Williams, and a central
pink rose: a portrait of her young self. Today I remembered that
though I had overseen everything else of my income tax return I had
not remembered to look at the balance. It was so large (swelled by
New Yorkers & that sale of Little Zeal) that I sat down feeling quite
faint. Nevertheless I spent some time mending one of my old linen
sheets.

8 J-K. Huysmans' novel.
9 STW had replaced her old bed with one from Little Zeal.
10 Her father.

August

8. A melancholy day, during which we gardened all the afternoon: and after dinner I read *We of Nagasaki*. Only the little girl really experienced it as a person – the others flutter in the burning blast, are paper-thin, charred, flesh & blood ashes hovering above ashes of flesh & blood. This absence of weight, of gravity, of form makes it more telling than Hiroshima, where art makes a glaze of verisimilitude out of an experience that could be like nothing previously true.

10. We began by a visit to the pathological laboratory, where a Dr Partington asked questions about [Valentine's] infective jaundice and tapped her chest. He was young, mild, and actually listened to what she had to say. His eyebrows, heavy as a charcoal drawing, made a Byzantine M over his eyes. The hushed cathedral tones in which he conversed with his assistant. The entry of the nurse with the chamber-pot draped in white like a coquettish confirmation candidate. After a serene – and dirty – lunch at the Antelope she went on and had X rays taken of her lungs. So home. We have decided to go to town next week, and to buy a refrigerator.

14. A stormy journey to London, thunder-like rain: and when we went into Joan's[11] flat the smell of cat mess almost drove us away again. Poor Niou was quitted & returned to, to give him confidence, and then left while we went off to the South Bank Exhibition.[12] The first impression that it is modestly small, spontaneously gay in colouring, and with a strong air of fortuity. First the Lion & Unicorn pavilion: the Beasts in plaited straw, the vast panoply of flowers on an Adams table, the roof trimmed with plaster doves and wicker dove-cage. Sounds of the Swan emerging from pretty little twopence-coloured paper theatres. The White Knight, not sufficiently equipped. The section of skill containing a great deal more (as we felt) of our green tea set, a most brilliant needlework picture – stitch & appliqué – of a spotted dog & game birds[.]

Then the shot-tower, extremely handsome, with silver spheres hanging from the upper darkness & below a kaleidoscope of London whose reflecting rim suddenly showed us side by side. A gay account of our coasts, including Prepare to Meet thy Doom, & children about to bring calamities on themselves & others with such seaside sports as

11 Joan Woollcombe, Valentine's elder sister, who had been widowed since 1935.
12 For the Festival of Britain.

beaching a depth charge: a small merry-go-round, *style* Rex Whistler, with Edith Sitwell jeune in it. A ravishing fountain, composed of metal scoops that filled & cascaded – the two larger ones most portentous & glorious in their overflow; a pink birdcage pavilion containing wax-works of the 1851 opening; ices, fountains, a great deal of space with-out any long walks: and in the L. & U. Gainsborough's Mr & Mrs Andrews, dear pets. We went home much pleased. A baddish dinner at the Charlotte St Bertorelli, but enlivened by six young Frenchmen, all sweetly performing – one cherub with great graces & development of the wood-dove note as he invoked the cash-girl.

21. Late last night I got out the revised close of Ullingthorpe,[13] wrote the last sentence on the telephone pad en route from bath to bed, and did the job today. To Weymouth, for haircuts. Genge's window at 10.a.m. was full of naked life-sized models, very white, very sleek, and all with their backs turned to the street. This is a very innocent prov-ince. A sultry, then cold, then raining day. There has been a hurricane in Jamaica. It blew down the prison, and seventy convicts were blown out into the storm. Most of the buildings are down. The hurricane lost force as it passed over a stretch of flat country, but regained power when it passed over the sea. It is now in Yucatan. My Love cooked a stately dinner for me. I read Denton Welch's unfinished Voice from a Cloud – as I finished it, its paternity, conscious or unconscious, blazed on me: de la Mare. And de la Mare is still alive, & Welch is dead at 31.

September

1. My Love spoke of going to visit Ruth between now & Christmas – by herself. And spent the afternoon typing labels for Barbara's[14] pic-ture show. I smell such desolation in such good deeds. If only she had been taught some selfish occupations, like embroidery ... A letter from Theo this morning; his handwriting blunted by age. It shook my heart.

5. A telephone from Ruth, still bawding, to Valentine last night, an-nounced that Eliz: comes to England next Monday. Valentine, mys-teriously, did not tell Ruth she knew it already: did, also mysteriously, report this to me. This morning, the thought of Eliz: so imminent (I had thought I could be at peace all this month) dejected and distracted

13 Story, not published under this title, if ever. (See 2 October 1951, page 181.)
14 Probably Barbara Whitaker, a friend of Valentine.

me. I wrote business letters, covered a chair-seat, pruned old wood from the Malmaison while My Love was in Dorchester. In the afternoon I thought I would clear my mind of cant by gardening – but I overdid it, and became extremely tired. A day ingloriously lost.

23. I continue to gallivant through profitless virtuous works. This morning I cleaned the fishing-room, and this afternoon, as the weather had cleared, I finished the raspberry section of the [fruit] cage, while Niou lay on my rosy coat, just behind me, the handle of the fork falling to right & left of his calm nose, like Sgt. Troy's sword. The King has had a rushed operation and a piece of lung taken out – poor creature! Small joy has he in being England's King. Presumably this was why the BBC dropped a Dillon piece[15] for a repetition of one of their national kedgerees – so My Love had lit a cigar in vain.

24. I was depressed by a melancholy night, and she thought I was ill. I explained my melancholy, the sense of autumn and our peace threatened. She admitted that it still works in her, has been working – but only mists & vapours, she said, as would rise from ground that is still damp; 'and partly because from time to time I enjoy it.' This was said exquisitely. My night was haunted by the absence of Tom; sweet Niou, who only knows me a fine-weather Tib, or Tib fastened to a sick-bed, knit to one purpose, lay against my side, and I felt how young and inexperienced he was, and that I did not want him to be made wise too soon, nor did I want him to feel slighted either. He has such force of love: it should be fostered, not strained. But ground still damp can call back the flood, suck it back. Floods are a frightening metaphor in this house.

25. A howling gale in which we drove to Weymouth, assignations with Gathergood & Matthews.[16] We drove back along the Wareham road, because the spray was dashing over the seawall. Remembering the burst of thornblossom there, I began to talk of seasons, and how one's strongest feelings spring from the first landscape – my suburban autumns, & my feeling for Middlesex cottages square & yellow-brick, against the winter sunset – and hers, she said, a muddy lane between brambles & thistles & beyond a great vacancy of sky – the Winterton shooting. The Traherne child that lives on into the grown-up artist who still keeps that brilliant eye. Not me, now, she said – with such

15 Matt Dillon, a detective serial on the radio.
16 The dentist and hairdresser.

weight of sorrow. The impulse to express these things has gone dead in me. But you still see them? No. I began to, at Great Eye, but after that influenza I lost it again through feeling so oppressed with sickness. I could not dispute it, for plainly she said it in truth. But I wish she had not said it, saying can become such a slab-stone.

October

2. *Absalom* followed *Ullingthorpe* as the night the day.[17] All day we dusted books & returned them to their shelves, and it was a *very* happy day.

3. As yesterday; and by the evening the room was finished, the dining room restored, and both of us in holy exhaustions of virtue. The Revd. Eliot read Ash-Wednesday on the wireless — a wiry twang in the voice is all that remains of his USA. It is a sour preaching voice, with fervour and without feeling. He sounds all the echo devices very markedly.

6. Yesterday evening, going into the l.s.p.[18] I felt *winter cold*. It is like a change in the specific gravity of air — no, not quite sp. gr. — but as if it had *jellied*; an analogous process to the formation of ice.
  [. . .]
  Reading Simone Weil's Attente de Dieu. A mind of dazzling darkness; some style of Lettres Provinciales, but from logic and mildness, not imitation, I think. Le meheur is bad for the soul, for it tears up its roots. I can understand all this.

13. A letter posted from Bedford[19] to say she [Valentine] had seen a quiet patch-coloured cat coming out of a church in Buckingham, and a young man who became an old labourer. I finished the Indian curtains, all but the rings (one always says that) and searched long & unavailingly for the Barnard sketch;[20] for lying in my bath it had suddenly quivered to life. I seem to have thrown it away, but for all [that] I made some notes & a beginning, and wrote till midnight.

14. A glowing autumnal day. I walked to post a letter to my Love, the empty street echoed the magnificent uproar of the church bells. No sign of a churchgoer, till I saw the schoolmaster come from his door, a

17 Both stories had been rejected by the *New Yorker*.
18 The long sun parlour down the side of the house.
19 Valentine was on her way to Winterton to see her mother, who required frequent visiting.
20 The story which was to become her novel *The Flint Anchor*.

dark grey suit, a raincoat over his arm, a great bunch of dahlias – he looked inexpressibly respectable, flamboyantly respectable – and I could not but feel a certain respect for him, so bravely dressing and doing his part. Then I came home, & sat down to write, and wrote with swanlike ease; and in the afternoon it was so fine that I went out to garden a little, and tore up the remaining thicket of ribbon border as far as the tree, and replanted it, and set some spare muscari bulbs in the first Robinson, and a knot of crocuses by the ribes; and it was dusky and cold when at last I came in – V. having telephoned me at 6.30, alone in the house . . . suffering a double twist, my poor Love. Norfolk so dear & Mr Pye[21] so insufferable. Then I wrote on, & got to Julia.

20. Today the weather broke, and it rained with violent sudden storms. Till now, it has been a long Indian summer (yesterday we picked ripe strawberries); and during this week I have done 12000 words of the Barnard story, writing with such impetus & direction of the story ahead as I have not known for years – perhaps never. If I can remain cool, & not too much gets in the way, I may even be able to do another 12000 before calamity sets in.

But My Love, when I went up to her room, was in utmost dejection & fatigue – having written a poem, the first, she says, for a twelve-month; and she spoke of how her mind has been useless to her ever since E.W.W., & that in that April, if she had ended it then – April, she said; and that confirmed me in saying that it wouldn't have done, that what had been latent & devouring for 10 years must have its way out if any sense were to come of it. We went for a drive after this, seeing a gold laced sunset, hedgerows brown, dun & purple, and cars saying Vote for Digby.

30. Page 63 of *Barnard*. The impetus wavers, & I fall into a pedantry of flat style, but that can be seen to later. What is so astonishing is that I still go on, and want to.

31. I made quince jelly – and introduced [into the story] Mr Theophilus Templeman, & everything curdled with his introduction, & I went to bed in despair; and Valentine has a stopped ear.

November

13. In the evening to The Merchant of Venice. She had got tickets on

21 Ruth Ackland's factotum.

our theory of always seeing Shakespeare – only in the hall did we realise it was a performance by the W.I. [Women's Institute] I pinned her down – and afterwards I was glad, for there was a good Portia, and an excellent neat lean Shylock – the virtuous aspect of Shylock's avarice comes out well in a woman-player. But the sweet music nearly finished the audience – squawking & squeaking recorders, probably the nearest we shall ever get to hearing the music at The Globe.

December

2. Valentine spent the day in bed, and I most of it in idling, and easing myself round p. 160 & what to do with Jemima. It hangs on me now a little, and re-reading it, I am pained to find it too skittish in gait. I must re-rhythm some parts of it, or it will become button-holing. I am like a stabled bean-fed horse. I am kicking up my heels too freely, and sweating at a mere mild trot.

3. The Frogs on the evening wireless. Odd to hear it in English, remembering all the Classic VI form business,[22] the lion-skin borrowed from the school-band, the frogs in flapping tail-coats & Sunday trousers, Xanthias in football shorts and Charon – what did Charon wear? – somebody's black mackintosh I suppose . . . and that ancient tongue clattering in their young voices.

23. Lunch glorified by roast duck: in the afternoon I forsook the new typewriter, which even Valentine finds difficult, and did a little to the Barnards – not well, though. And during this interval I have seen so much wrong with it – too much levity, if it is to end as it should. The wine-cellar, for instance, must be a much subtler hypocrisy – and Jemima & Debenham must not become *like characters in a novel*. He had better regret his impulses of kindness, & she must think him patronising, or mistrust him.

On the 21st the news of Cousin Edmund's death – aged 81. His red face, so English with its mixture of temper & debonairity – his hands in those cheap knitted black wool gloves – his lissome clerical singing of the less decorous lute-songs.

24. Christmas Eve. In the evening we presented: My Love's vulgarity turned out to be a pair of gazelle-coloured bedroom slippers – enchanting. There was also the Eluard-Picasso, a diminishing glass that

22 At Harrow School.

turned her shelf of folios to a shelf of pickerings, stockings, a pair of infinitely delicate blown-glass swallows for my ears, handkerchiefs – one depraved darling whose black lace butterfly wings lift and fall as if one's nose were Buddleia, a toy French taxi-horn, a particoloured pencil, a sugar mouse, bath salts, hand lotion, a bottle of *Jicky*, a small book of apothegms called The Moral Friend, a soap-purse, a file-folder, an emery strawberry, herbal cigarettes, eight plates of Wedge-wood Bramble – ravishing – and a lustre coffee-pot.

31. I made my sitting-room curtains; and in the evening we exchanged presents – Yeovil gloves & a charming mosaic brooch from my Love, & to her a passport wallet – she had seen it in Rothman's catalogue, wanted it, & refrained. Embarrassing to hear Ruth saying at the open midnight door – 'Throw it out! Send it away!' of the year in which she was supposed to have her death. Her intense hatred of everything – even the emptied stamp-book torn violently in two as though it were a denounced treaty. After hearing this, it was impressive to step on to the lawn & see – in air cleared by a hailstorm ten minutes before – a most brilliant, formidable & serene pattern of Orion above the laurels. And later, from the back door, the dark melancholy tree, & one glistening star. A year of threats & dangers, & sad [un]certainties of my Love's health – & yet a year full of solace & happiness, as we re-knit together, and 1949 withdraws & the wound heals.

January

26. A loud crash heard at 6 a.m. turned out to have been the larder rat hurling down jampots. So we cleared and cleaned all the larder, and found three enormous rat-holes. [. . .]

All the evening I was haunted by news of Charles Prentice, told [to Valentine] by Violet. [. . .] O poor Charles, so gentle, so very sensitive, so excelling in doing things right, taking such pains too, and with such insight and delicacy, poor Charles, who saved Oliver with such pains and kind concern, who was so scrupulous, and so modestly catlike-ly disdainful of vulgarity and clutter and indecorum. Dear kind Charles, of so many evenings in London, and days at Chaldon, so filial to Theodore & so brotherly to Violet, and so dear a companion; and so true a friend that I had that extraordinary impression, one bad evening in 49, that he would come for me in a taxi and take me away. I can't bear to think of such delicate goodness and integrity being kicked about by Lynn, and still loyal to his bad bargain.

February

6. Mr Samways' transplanted the Turkish roses on a milder morning; and Valentine came back from Dorchester like the Waterloo Coach, and came into the house saying The King is dead. His daughter, poor doomed wretch, spent the night in a tree in Kenya, watching wild animals from a naturalist's well-appointed hide, while he was dying alone, in his sleep. Unusually independent and unconstitutional nights for the pair of them.

7. In the evening Churchill spoke on the wireless – he has a cough which the nation can't afford just now – but did a magnificent close of being born in the *august* days of Victoria, & God Save the Queen.

1 Their part-time gardener.

William Rufus also died unattended: what a magnificent arc soars between these two deaths.

15. Slept abominably – but cheered by darling Niou taking possession of the back of my neck and ardently washing my hair. Valentine got up. We spent the morning listening to the King's funeral. Good things were – the muffled Westminster bells: the iron-chain noise of the feet of the ratings and the troops (just like Great Eye's beach after storm) and the ripple of the horse-hoofs. Big Ben tolling once a minute for each year (56) of the King's life; above all, at Paddington & at Windsor, the pipe-playing. I think I have never heard better, especially Macheidlhe – I don't know how to spell it – the Cameronian tune: strange how small, after the long piping and marching up to St George's, the actual church ceremony: a divine dolls-house after that timeless music. The Archbishop of Canterbury, belling like a ram, prayed that the King might be suffered not to fall into the torments of eternal *life* – shows how much he believes in it. I never say water when I mean wine, or Bach when I mean Handel. It all petered out very oddly.

17. It was curious to reflect that in my own life there was a time, & in other lives the time is still, when it was perfectly possible to spend a day reading Proust without a jaw abcess & a swelled face as ticket of admission.

19. N.B. Lying in bed, even in discomfort or pain, I find in myself a very definite compliance towards inactivity, retirement from life, a quiet sofa'd old age. I cannot say that these last five days have been agreeable; but my God, they have been congenial.

23. We drove Nancy [Cunard] to Eggardon to walk there, and afterwards revised the estimate of two miles home, and drove out again in the sunset to meet her – her slender silhouette oddly bagged with pocketsful of flints, which, on getting home, she washed and laid out on her bathtowel. Niou, serene little whoremonger, breakfasted in her bed. A gramophone evening – Cowards & Calypsos & South Pacific. Cousin Victor's[2] house in Venice – could we go there? Ah, if we could! Painted ceilings, high walls, a Maria & an Angelo care-taking.

24. Nancy & I, so drunk overnight, brisk as young green peas, & my drinkless love with a raging headache. My right cheek descending to

2 Victor Cunard, Nancy's cousin.

my right wrist. Sun by day, a freezing pale misted evening, spent in my room by Nancy & me, Bonnards of domesticity.

26. I struggled in a drowned-fly way back onto p. 223 of Barnard. [. . .] Dinner in bed again – delicious. But I must get out of this lotus-eating. I fall asleep like an old cat whenever I'm not keeping myself awake.

27. Ash-Wednesday – and waking early, & hearing the cocks crowing, I remembered this, & thought of Jesus setting out early in the morning, leaving the cockcrows and the villages behind, bound for temptation in the wilderness I daresay, but also the amplitude of self-sufficiency. This turned into a dream of notable colours, in which I first saw him in a desert of fired rock and sand, the rock a little crumbling, & both of the pigeon-breast colours of pale reddish lilac, pale grey, snuff brown; thence into another scene where he got into a small boat & floated down a very narrow salt stream, of the most brilliant emerald green, fringed with scarlet alder stakes and enamelled willows. The water had a saline brilliancy, sleekness & tranquillity.

March

11. She says she feels better[3] – but she looks ill, & worn, & speaking of a possible holiday, said she wanted to go into a hole. A Carthusian cell, I said, with dinners being handed in through a hole in the door, and otherwise nothing. She looked longingly. For myself, I want to see a new landscape, meet new people, go to theatres and operas in new clothes, and be told how delightful I am. However, I was happy enough finishing planting raspberries (5 rows in all) and cleaning some of the remaining [fruit] cage. Then she came out, clipped in the sun, & told me that E.W.W. is sending us 6 roses. Six roses is six roses, is a rose. I cannot feel reproach in a rose, or regret a rose.

17. The sun shone vehemently on a cloudy eastern sky, & I have never seen such brilliancy as the red willow mixing its scarlet with the silver catkins of the pussy willow. They were like *suspended hail*; glistening, and pearl-grey.

3 Valentine had been haemorrhaging.

May

12. I took heart enough to unpack Paul's parcel: *Lost Summer*[4] was in. The singer a Nan Merriman with an extremely wide, dark-coloured vigourous mezzo-soprano – an Amneris'[5] voice; and a very good serious method. The music I still cannot assess, for my heart is too much in it. But listening to the 2 river songs I could say, It is justified, I can accept that then, for this music that has come out of it. And then I fell into an agony of grief to think that for my Love, & that wretched Elizabeth, there is no such foison – that all was planted in a dead & killing soil. She was upstairs, still in bed, while I listened. Later, she got up, & we drove to Cauldron Barn[6] for Niou. He yelled all the way back, from emotion & impatience: the moment he set foot on his home ground he cast himself into garlands of love & joy, and then we all went early to bed, with Niou breaking into purrs every time either of us stirred or turned. [. . .] We also retrieved our two tortoises, less emotionally.

27. [Valentine] left at 8.45,[7] looking very elegant in her flat straw hat, her new shoes, a pleated grey skirt and a dark blue jacket. I cannot but admit it. It reclothes her in young looks and animation, for all she speaks, and quite truly, I believe, of not wishing to go. But what are wishes, compared with longings?

   All this hot afternoon of leisure and timelessness – for time does not begin again till she is back – I have been obsessed by E.W.W.'s voice, the timbre & rate of it, her smell, her pattern. I am saturated with it, can't escape it. It is not remembrance, I think. I don't remember her well enough for this reappearance after three years and before those few hours, ten years. It seems to me that I have become en rapport with Valentine, that her obsession & saturation and absorbed attention overflow into me. A hellish afternoon; and the morning tattered with dry anxiety.

30. In the evening I took, as calmly as I could, the hideous news that on June 25th – less than a month, there will be a visit to Holt & Winterton. Desperately striving to save my reason, I think perhaps a night at Cambridge could be contrived. I shall cut my throat if I see much more of Ruth.

4 Song-cycle by Nordoff to poems written by STW in the summer of 1949.
5 The mezzo role in *Aida*.
6 The home of Vera and Arthur Hickson, from whom STW and Valentine had bought Niou.
7 She was meeting Elizabeth Wade White in Salisbury.

Today the mistletoe gipsy's sister came to the house. I mentioned I had had shingles.[8] She told me an infallible cure. An ounce of the old black shag tobacco – it must be the strongest and blackest kind – soaked in a saucer of water, and the liquor dabbed on the spots. And our clever doctors knowing all about nicotinic acid. The people – the real low-to-ground people – really know everything; and in addition are too wise to bruit it.

June

3. This a.m. I took a load of books and papers to the Dorchester work-house – that used to be so kindly and homely, and like a superior farm-house. It is now a Geriatric Unit – painted hospital cream, the floor so polished you'd break your leg on it, no colour, no sound, no smell of life – and instead of that former kind matron, an insolent chit in a glass-box, occupied in trying to look like the Queen at her worst. Alas! Alas! – And all in the name of humanity. But it is really the medical profession's fear of death, and fear of [being] found out that leads to these heartless deserts of shiny anti-biosis.

22. I spent the afternoon playing Bach & Mozart – and got nearer than ever before to that enigmatical slow movement of A.mi. No one else is so *gratifying* to play. No other composer so *loves* his performers, even his bad ones.

July

3. Queen Elizabeth spent the night in a siding at Maiden Newton. Opinion is that she is overworked for a young breeding woman. Mrs Gould, who had seen her arriving cheerful last night, also saw her this morning, standing in her train's doorway to be observed by the children; and looking tired and stern. Facing another day – 'poor young person', as Mrs Gould calls her.

6. The day began with a superb thunderstorm. Valentine called me to look first from the passage window, where the sky was a dulled orange, and then from the river window, where a livid slate-coloured sky hung, *pressed* down on a slope of parched, pale, terrified-looking meadows. It came on slowly, majestically, and through the thunder we

8 In the preceding April.

heard the anxious hurried voice of the Hull boy calling the cows in Crocker's field. I did not think they would be willing to turn and walk towards that southern sky lit with long sideways arrows of lightning – and apparently they were not, for he went on hallooing, sounding more & more lost & human among the thunder, until the rain burst, & quenched him. It was a long storm; and the landscape wore in perfection that bright varnished look of being a quite unconvincing bad oil-painting or oleograph. Niou lay across my feet, looking soberly towards the window with slitted eyes.

August

3. During the afternoon Valentine took the idea to use the long sun-parlour as a semi-shop for own miscellaneous antiques & others bought at auctions. A good idea, and she would do it very well; but can we keep the local children out? Their any windfall apples policy might be a nuisance if carried on to any windfall silver spoons.

9. [W]e had a pleasant evening;[9] and strange to compare their outlook on Germans with Hicksons – they having both seen the DPs[10] immediately after the fall of Berlin. The girl (TB ward) suspected to be pregnant, and her abject terror when Meredith went to examine her. She was in a labour gang. Nothing was done to protect these children from rape, but pregnancy was a crime, as it spoilt their capacity to work – so as a punishment, abortions were carried out without anaesthetic; and if the pregnancy were too far advanced, the gas-chamber. Rose spoke with sombre fury about how the Germans will obliterate the physical Belsens & Buchenwalds under tillage – as they have already obliterated the thought of them. In all her journeyings she had only seen one German distressed at a c-camp: the number of dead – 5000 in this pit, 1000 in another, had hit him.

13. Valentine is now preparing her antique shop, encouraged by Elizabeth Warner.[11] We hunted old forgotten loves, and cleaned them: spoons, candlesticks from the hair-trunk, my old tortoiseshell fan, a vinaigrette, & so on. It did not look enough, however.

25. Barnard by my new course; and the new course swung the earlier

---

9 With the new junior doctor, Meredith Ross, and her companion Rosa.
10 Displaced Persons.
11 Oliver Warner's second wife.

river into a far better and speedier Euphemia–Marmaduke reach, which will cut out all that hovering between Christmas & Easter. I worked till I was shaking, then I sat in the long sun-parlour while Valentine read epitaphs, and the cats came in and out; then revived by Beaujolais, I got out the old willow-pattern curtains, & cut & machined them into curtains for the long book-shelves, full of our disgracefully childish & naughtily Left-ish books.

September

1. Today we began a diet: calories – and calculations before each meal. I shall feel very hungry on it. I feel hungry now.

17. Fetched in because it was beginning to rain, I said that I enjoyed digging so intensely I could hardly dissever myself from the feeling that digging was vice; some dear forbidden carnality. Did such notions never occur to those mat-making Desert Fathers?

November

18. I spent the evening tearing upstairs to hear Maria Kallas [sic] in Norma. *Casta diva* is everything he meant it to be, & so is the finale of the last act; and the two women (Ebe Stignani the Adelgiza) were lovely together, playing like race-horses. The bald straightforward classicism – peut-etre je l'ai senti, said Pasta; and Bellini felt it, though he made such comic druids & such excruciatingly inept modulations. Incidentally, the shindy of the chorus in the last scene is louder and more overwhelming than any recondite effects of clamour. It is just loud & threatening, like a cat-fight.

27. In a letter from Oliver [Warner], news of Ezra Pound in his lunatic asylum. 'Pointing to a television set at the end of one ward, he said "Look – they are even trying to undermine the sanity of the people *here*." '

1953

13. This evening, greatly daring, I took the last 100 pages of Barnard & read them through. It is worse and it is better than I thought. It is *bones*, sharp shining bones, *swaddled* in old woollen rags of psychology, motives, allusions, explainings. It must be purged, weeded, cleaned, straightened: there is six months work in it. But where it stands firm, it is good, it has teeth and they meet like a tiger's.

14. But I am not up to working on it yet. I sat for two hours doing nothing to page one, and developed a toothache from grinding my teeth in despair.

28. Katie [Powys] came in the afternoon, bringing the debated family teapot (v. ugly 1870) for inspection, filled with eggs: a match to Katten's[1] urn filled with quinces. I pinned one or two of her *fiorituti*. A doctor *diagonised* dropsy. Joan had quite *transferred* her cottage; and tomorrow she will consult her banker about a *disposit*. 'I get angry with inanimate objects,' she said, 'and with my hands.'

29. It was foggy when we started to take Katie to Somerset – but while we were waiting for her in Yeovil it began to clear, and as we drove on it became, as she said, a February landscape: pale earth, pale honey-coloured trees, an immense sun-lit purple cloud tattered with blue and wearing a rainbow. We took her to West Pennard, and went back to Glastonbury to lunch at The George: an excellent lunch, and the proprietor and the head waitress both of them beaming and tiddly: some over-night celebration, perhaps. Then we drove by a new road to Wells, almost to Wells, under a fine view of the Mendips, and gathered Katie. Littleton [Powys], scarcely able to move, yet politely getting to his feet, scarcely able to see, yet looking at books and

---

1 Katten Hallward was a friend of Ruth Ackland, and always generous towards Valentine and STW.

192

reading aloud from Matthew Arnold & Hardy, and swollen with dropsy, was a tragic sight: but family feeling held good, and Katie was perfectly unpitying, a rock-like antipathy, partly animal, partly childish. – No! *vegetable*, refusing to root in his soil.

February

1. On the 6 p.m. news, the news of the flood on the east coast – all Holderness under salt water, Yarmouth & Lynn innundated, and the seaward end of Sea Palling flooded, with people drowned. Ruth, rung up, told how two local men who had left their boats at Gurleston, wanted to see about them, & hired Ronnie from Hemsby. He was told there was no road through, but remembered a side-lane. Halfway along it, he saw a boat coming towards him. The floods go all down as far as Kent – and on t'other side of the North Sea, worse floods & breakings of dykes in Holland.

2. An aerial photograph in the Daily Mail seems to be Salthouse, though it was called Sheringham. Either way, ruin and desolation, with a great elbow of sea thrust inland. Essex too; and the wretched bungalow towns and caravan towns destroyed, and hundreds drowned on Canvey Island. We could not get through to Yarmouth when we tried to ring up Ruth for more news. The day began by Kaoru[2] bringing in a blackbird – its bright visceral blood spattered on the white wall and its feathers, its exquisite air & song feathers having to be swept up in a disgraceful tangle of Mrs Lambert's[3] dirt and flue from the rug.

5. A letter from Felix Young today tells of all the coast road houses in ruins or so badly damaged as to be uninhabitable. The poor old woman whom the sea killed in her kitchen – a tiger-kill, first it knocked her down, then when her old husband pulled her out of the water & set her on the kitchen table, another wave flowed in and carried her off in its mouth – was carried to the church, the only shelter: there she lay, while the wind raved in the high roof and shook the tall doors. The Patch, & the ugly villa next to it are unhurt – so is *G.E. Folly*. But the village, the true village, lost. The sea came in, not by the Folly Gap, but sweeping from Cley, and swept through the Dun Cow, and the Post-Office. Done up, 5 pairs of trousers, my tan leather

2 Their new Siamese kitten, more often called Kit.
3 The char.

waistcoat, woollen vests & scarves, the shawl & the gloves Vera knit for me last year. And £5 with a promise of more next month.

6. In the morning I began to pack.[4] In the afternoon, the postman came up the drive with a letter from Felix Young. The seaward wall of G.E.F. has fallen, the house stands open to the sea. Alas! And alas for my Love!

March

5. She woke me with bad news: Uncle Joe[5] has had a stroke and is dying. It was 'Uncle Joe' she said, turning back to the former affection & loyalty. [. . .] I have grieved and trembled. After him, there is only Churchill of the Europeans who feels Europe; and he cannot be relied on against the USA. Alas, alas, if Stevenson were President instead of stinking bragging Eisenhower . . . War & ruin stoop lower in twenty-four hours – and a world of patience, wisdom & experience is wasting in that demolished mind of the small man in the unbecoming grey uniform.

[. . .] Worsted, I said, in his 40 days campaign against Jesus, the Devil, being a Marxist, set himself to turn defeat into advantage; and invented the Christian Lent, when all the Christians become progressively crosser and more nervous as they unanimously and regimentedly fast. This apropos of Meredith[6] . . . who would be so much better fitted to keep the peace with Gaster & support the Kelseys[7] if she had not given up smoking in Lent.

6. News of Stalin's death; followed on the 9 a.m. BBC news broadcast by an account of such gross & vulgar malice that with all expectations of the vilest, I could hardly believe my ears. If it had been a large-scale swindler, or an American gangster, it could not have been more plainly designed to vilify; as an obituary of the head of a state it was incredible: either we mean to declare war within the next few months, or we are more basely sold to USA than we knew.

7. [. . .] in the afternoon Jean Larson[8] came to tea, bringing me *Memoirs of a Cat*, a child's book of the 1870s, that had come to her

4 For a holiday in Florence.
5 Stalin.
6 Dr Ross.
7 The family of a local vicar, who was on trial for fraud.
8 Monica Ring's cousin.

through her mother. Such a present is a true gift. We played the musical box, and the toy one. It was characteristic of her that she played the toy one *widdershins*, as she put it . . . naturally erring into discovery. I begin to like her very affectionately, she is like honeysuckle, her pale face & pale hair, & her wild twinings and loopings; and I am sure she would be one of the first plants to put out leaves in the winter wood.

13. Today I have cleaned kitchen details, cooked grey mullet in oil with tansy, wine, garlic & new potatoes (Good), written letters, knitted and performed two hours of ladylike gardening: cleaning and weeding the lavender border, distributing odd peonies, replanting lilies of the valley, and distributing that mat of long-leafed iris: which I may regret, as it is unearthlily large; but handsome, too. Such a day might normally seem well-spent and industrious: yet I am haunted by a guilty sensation of a life devoted to frivolity.

April

1. Meredith came to vaccinate Valentine, to tell us another Rampisham scandal (incest this time, and the offending father threatening to print a thousand handbills to avenge himself on Gaster for speaking so unkindly to him.) As one result of this, and t'others, the celebrated Inchbald wedding will be minus its organist (sodomy), the schoolmistress in the choir (victim & leaving for America) and officiating parson, the Rd. Kelsey, jailed for fraud. Now we must await Rampisham's third breakage – bestiality, probably; as my Love remarked, the inn is called The Tiger.

20. Preliminary tidyings and beautifications for the Maxwells,[9] whom we met at 6.50 for 6.48 (driving down the Herringston Avenue in between), and brought home by the high road on a ravishing spring evening. He looks exactly the same age as before, she is truly young, slender, a passionate small countenance & bluer whites to her eyes than even I had. Shy at first, they both flowered during dinner, opening first at the Craskes, his remark (apropos of the 30/= for the James Edward) that it was a mark, a destiny, of the real thing, if you gave your all for it, whatever the amount of the all. [. . .] We had a happy evening, Valentine likes them both extremely, and they

9 William Maxwell of the *New Yorker* and his wife Emmy.

are delighting in England, in books, in Covent Garden porters, in our cats.

21. Charming to hear the Maxwells walking up the drive & pointing out its beauties to each other; and charming to see their guilty faces when I asked if they had had porridge. They had, and it was terrible. William was put into his clean shirt, then we listened to the musical-box, and wandered about the house and garden, & drank coffee, and set out for Montacute. Not only was it closed, but the woman at the Lodge was odious. So then we went to the Church and admired Phelips tombs, & agreed that the Elizabethan pair looked much more in bed than in death; and pursued lunch as far as Somerton, and found it at The Unicorn, & drove to Muchelney which was entirely ravishing: a heraldic design newly-discovered in the Abbot's lodging, the sun pouring through the south window & stirring tortoiseshell butterflies on the stone mullions, and an aged soldierly one-eyed custodian, who knew a great deal about heraldry [. . .] Then we went rather mad, and drove to Bridport because their friend Urquart had been born there; and had tea, & cowslips, & Valentine bought nosegays for Emmy and me; and then to Dorchester, S. Peter's and Max Gate; and then back to Eggardon, where we let them walk their lane, while we sat in the car hearing larks, & the wind, & reading poetry. Home, to streaming cats, & dinner, & after dinner I read at request, the new story. They are perfect people to take about, they see everything, & *smell* everything. The only flaw in the day, that they must go tomorrow evening.

May

11. I meant to write today, but letters took up the morning, and in the afternoon and evening I gardened, weeding mostly, while V. cleared a path as neat as a 3d bit, & cut the verge of the l.s.p. bed. As an interlude we drove along the Crewkerne road to inspect Mr Hallet's hanging gallery[10] – as reported by Meredith. The daughter and the doctor hanging head-downward from a tree like Mussolini & Clara: they are made of sacking, very much foreshortened, roughly stuffed, the faces only painted. The woman effigy wearing a battered straw hat; her face and neck scarlet, very Roualt-like, the doctor heavily blacked, with some random wool hair; no likeness to his original except in the roundness of the head. Both have placards on their bosoms, the

10 Roadside effigies erected by a local farmer.

daughter's rather dully obscene, the doctor's in excellent bible language, A Defaulter on the Hipocratic (sic) code, Failing to Heal the Sick he torments the poor and needy. He's had it. R.I.P. And also to remember, the daughter's pulled out neck, enormously elongated by hanging head-downward. Altogether, a most stirring & reviving sight. [. . .] I never supposed I would see anything so savage, so racy, so fearless alike of law and of laughter.

12. Still hot & dry, with a wind on the uptake. The appleblossom falls, & is snow on the lawn and mosaic on the paths. Mended Shadwell[11] (the N.Y. want it, but want as usual more morticing of joins) and sent it off. Kicking off with Uncle Blair,[12] I now have £1300 odd earned this financial year, and Shadwell still to be paid for. I think I will do 3 more, get the quantity cup,[13] & be ruined for life.

June

2. The coronation day. Cold & wet, and wireless. Things I noticed: the rough *vivats*: the antiquity of the recognition, & the moving quality of the Queen's curtsey: so much more gracious and grand than a King's bow: V. Williams' setting of the Old Hundredth, with the flourish at the close of a line continuing over the melody of the next line, superposed instead of imperposed [sic]. Valentine spoke of the contest between Church and State; the Bishops dragging her to themselves like old spiders, the temporal peers rescuing her back again. We listened too long, and got tired; then we had lobster, and went for a reviving drive to see bonfires; burning like rubies in the Marshwood vale and along the coast, and in Abbotsbury, a trimmed-up lorry with a band on it, and couples dancing in the street. Our own village looked very glum after this.

19. It rained most of the day, & the wind blew, and I worked – and just before going to bed I went out onto the deck, into an embrace of rain & wind, and thought of Tushielaw.

20. The Rosenbergs were executed. The time of execution was put forward from 11.p.m. to 8. *because of the Sabbath day*.

24. Alyse came to lunch, with an elegant hat much improved by its

11 Story, *WA*.
12 Story, *WA*.
13 The *New Yorker* paid a bonus for six stories accepted within a twelvemonth.

rose being worn at the back contrary to nature; and flattered with discrimination: for after the usual outcries of 'How wonderfully peaceful' or 'How lucky you are!' it is very flattering to be praised for civilisation. She spoke of Beth Car, Violet exhausted, endlessly gallant, endlessly complaining, & Theodore's grey head in a sad cloud, and of the complete lack of rapport between them. She said several times how they live in different worlds; and it wrung my heart to think of what must have underlain this: she and Llewelyn who lived, for so brief a marriage, in one world. Then we had tea at the K's Arms,[14] and she bought the old mahogany table,[15] & we came home and cooked a chicken.

July

2–7. Every night I was too sleepy to put the day on paper. Much Barnard, many strawberries, raspberries in now. On Sunday Vera and Arthur [Hickson] spent a couple of hot hours with iced coffee. Vera was wearing the black silk shawl, and looked like a portrait. Arthur, with one of his dives into other worlds, supposed the fish were no more conscious of their flowing stream than we of ours. I had slight poisoning from the tooth of 1949, twinges and shoulder-aches. And I set pink cuttings; white for Janet round the shop-door rose; and opposite, fancies for myself in river-tree bed and necromancy bed. Two coloured photographs came from the Maxwells; I am fat, pale, *sturdy*, and have a cheerful expression. O my God! My raven locks, my medusa looks, all gone, gone.

17. A day of sad visits; first to Cauldron Barn Farm, where Vera and Arthur both looked unwell and were bitterly discouraged because they will not be able to raise enough money to buy the other farm, and must raise money to comply with the Council's persecution about main drains. Then, to Mappowder, where T.F. was alone. He looked very ill, his hand shook as Gertrude's had shaken, he looked down and marked for death; and though he talked with his old kind of enjoyment of finding his malady in old Burton, my dear, the bowel rumble, or perhaps the bowel flux, it was plain that he was terrified of falling into the hands of a hospital – where those *photographers* would get at me. We stayed a while, my Love prescribed and consoled; he suddenly

14 The Kings Arms in Dorchester, a favourite rendezvous.
15 From Valentine's antique shop, well established by this time.

looked tired, and propped himself against the door-post, waving us off with both hands, a sick man's exaggeration of a healthy man's gesture. In between, we drove through a wild windy day, hedges green and streaming, badges of sun on the moors, and going a new road from Bere to Ansty, saw a moment of Bingham's Melcombe, its yew hedge smooth and powerful as a wave. The wind blowing through the woods like water flowing, yellow bedstraw out.

22. Letter from Violet. Dr Smith had visited T.F. and told Violet – she doesn't say, but presumably, cancer of the bowel. The Powyses fall and die, last year Gertrude – Oh poor John! – and the elms of the Broad Walk are to be felled one by one.

31. Ian [Parsons] rang up early about T.F. and sending money, £50 to come, more in hand. Shades of kind Charles were in his voice – and missing Charles, as I often do, I was glad he was dead before this. In the afternoon we drove to Mappowder. Theo wore his guise of 17th cent. stoicism, Violet walked first with Valentine, then with me, pouring out her anxious heart, clinging, like a heavy butterfly, to my arm. Just as we left, having arranged to pick them up tomorrow for Sherborne,[16] Theo said – thrusting out his old bone – to Violet, Mind you don't drop down dead. A harsh joke – she is ready to drop down living – and it showed the torment of his mind, the fury of his soul.

August

1. To Mappowder. Violet had just begun to tell us the frightful night she had been through, Theo in agonies of fear, the first sedative not working, the second, given on her desperate initiative at 2.30 a.m. working so violently that she heard his breath labouring and thought he was dying – as he had wished to. Then enter Theo, in a decent black suit, silent, formidable, about 7ft high, in an austerity of despair. We got to Sherborne at 11 – after a usual pause for terror, and for examining the notice just inside the door, *To the Chapel*, he was taken in. [...] [W]e went up to see him in his room. He was in bed, wearing a wild knitted shawl, his room was pleasant, with a view of trees, gardens and red roofs. He was slightly relaxed, and comforted by the kindness of strangers. So are we all, when we realise that the kindness of kindred can do nothing for us.

16 Sherborne Hospital, where Theodore was going for tests.

8. Rachel[17] and Valentine fetched Theodore back from hospital. He was ready and waiting for her, looking very much the better for a week in bed – whatever else they have done or not done for him. He had been called on by a clerical Digby, and suspected him of stealing his orange scarf – 'which I knitted for myself' – however, it was under the bed, orange and yellow stripes, and the r. gentleman guiltless. 'Mappowder', he exclaimed with pleasure, seeing it on the sign-post. But Violet was unhappy – she had seen the doctors that morning. There was no time for confidences.

9. I spent a perfectly serene morning, sitting on the willow-garden bench, reading a novel called Mary Barnard.[18] Weeded with Rachel – a good weeder, a good hand at whatever she undertakes. It was very hot, we took her to Alec's pool, & she bathed. Pleasure of seeing a naked woman in the English landscape. She makes Valentine extremely happy, for that alone I would like her; but I can also like her for herself; and a pleasure to see her looking happy here.

September

4. It was on Sunday, after we had left [Mappowder], it all blew up. [Theo] came in, while Mrs Rose was there, and collapsed, weeping. Later, the whole (except that he has cancer – they call it an ulcer) was put before him, and he chose a year of life rather than two years perhaps with tubes in his belly. Today Violet was looking no better, she is relieved for his sake, but terrified on her own. He, in bed, did seem more serene, and looked physically quite different, and he was affectionate and as near demonstrative as he could ever be; yet I felt much amiss; for some reason he has turned against Violet; and he fished in talk for the nature of his illness; and at night, Violet reported, late at night, he tells her he will be dead in the morning. We shall be very silly if we do not expect a great deal more sorrow and torment, and I'm afraid it will be a Christian deathbed. Donne, Cowper, neolithic man, born in the shadow of a church. Poor darling Theo: as I write this, the word is written on my brain. *Ennui*: the ennui of a violent character constrained to a doctrine of non-offensiveness.

6. A fair fine Sunday, delightful for me, as the morning was Vera and Angus and Douglas Davidson came in the afternoon. How little a

17 Rachel Hickson, the daughter of Vera and Arthur.
18 Her own novel, *The Flint Anchor*.

regard changes! Angus became the Angus of the 1920s as soon as I saw him looking down at me. My Love had not such a good day, the morning was devoted to tidying the shop for Mrs Vestey – and when Mrs Vestey came, Bo[19] came with her, all noise and anecdote and affability to the poor. This impeded both pleasure and sales.

7. Vera left – looking so pretty that it broke my heart to see her go. Her grace, her fine carriage, her pure countenance, are half the ground of my love for her, I believe. There is also *the love of the eye*.

9. Nita Egerton drove me to lunch with her Debenhams, where I should meet two young men. Conversation on the way included a pious parishioner of Porksham, who was so much upset by the parson's sodomy – poor old Mr Cornish – that she had to be given injections. We explored the garden of the *very* well-contrived and seemly house and garden which the current Debenhams can't live in because of Sir Ernest's daughter-despising will: it shone in the sun with all its empty bow-windows, and two empty wicker chairs conversed on the lawn. Then on to the rather plain-headed house, whose notice Bell out of Order at once prepossessed me. Sir Piers let us in – a tall well-filled not fleshy man, with a leather voice. She was cooking, the footfall of one of the young men from London sounded, I turned, it was Douglas Davidson, and the other was Angus. Then Lady Debenham came – with a broad generous face and a silver stammer, very beguiling. It was a most agreeable merry easy meal, and I liked my hosts more and more; and somehow felt my hostess familiar – no wonder, for afterwards the name Paget came into my mind, and she is old Richard's daughter.[20] Other beauties were the village hall, with excellent oil portraits of local worthies by Aunt Alice, and a very false sham bright brisk Sir Ernest by W. Rothenstein, and a Gill war-memorial. Home to a solitude of cats, and then Jean [Larson] and her two daughters. My Love again had done less well than I. There had been a family fracas, and it was early closing in Beaminster.

11. This evening Furtwangler and the Vienna Philharmonic in Brahms no 1 from Edinburgh. The transmission not very good, and I am not naturally attuned to Furtwangler, he is the Thomas Aquinas of conductors; yet I am so profoundly impressed that I forget I am not profoundly moved. There is such searching honesty in his reading;

19 Bo Foster had settled in Dorset, and was prominent in the local Conservative Party.
20 Angela Debenham was the daughter of Sir Richard Paget, 2nd Baronet of Cranmore.

everything comes out – including the resemblance in the last movement not only to the theme which we all realise, but the key bugle orchestration of the 2nd Brahms appearance so reminiscent of the key bugle *tenor* variation of the 9th. And somehow he made the opening of the allegretto *approach*, like cheerful saints coming to meet a new one; and then how honest, how comprehending, his management of the close of that movement.

October

18. I have never heard the MN church bells lovelier than this morning – sounds are like fruits: a finger of frost, a warm midgy day will make or mar them; and this morning the climate was exactly right for the bells. I felt grateful to Slemeck[21] for whatever delayed him, and kept the De-um bell ringing on alone for over five minutes. I also admired the fine rubato of the ringer, always in measure, but never exactly to the dot. All this outside the coalshed, looking at the long slivers of fallen willow leaves on the dug ground.

November

19. On Tuesday morning she had a letter from the woman who runs the Hand & Flower Press. I had not known it – but she had got ready a volume of her poems which the H & F were, it seems, going to publish. It was chose entendu, but the woman had asked her to wait till the end of the year as she was so busy. The letter said she was giving up the press and going to sit on an Arts Council Committee to decide awards to publishers who publish poetry. [. . .]

I feel a speechless woe for her – everything goes wrong, and I am so little comfort to her, and go mooching about, talking to robins – it ran like a mouse while I was digging up artichokes – and wishing for Thomas who understood sorrows.

26. Valentine came down from a telephone call to say that T.F.P. is sinking. November, I thought. The fogs, and the fallen leaves, and the calm forgetful sunshine. That night – there was a wind – I woke many times thinking of Theo; and once, hearing him say [in] that familiar voice of quiet violence, 'A leaf has been blown away.' I knew it was part of a sentence about an autumn morning in Madder or Dodder, and

21 Canon Slemeck, the rector.

one morning seeming like unto another. But A Leaf has been Blown Away. After that, I slept; as I hope he does. [. . .]

Another dark spot on this day was to hear from Valentine that it was yesterday evening her story about the dead man was read on the wireless. She did not tell me. This is dreadful, it must grow from a most bitter root.

28. His death[22] announced on the BBC as novelist and poet. This is interesting, it would seem to indicate the following processes of official thought. A. as his novels did not sell in large figures, he must have been a poet. B. as he was a poet, no one would have read his poems, so their non-existence does not qualify the assumption. To what end are all the works wrought under the sun?

After rain and wind, this morning was intensely still, still as death, and air mild as forgetfulness.

December

1. Theodore's funeral. A mild day of winter slumbering in the open air – hollyhocks and ixias out in our garden, but the last sleepy leaves fallen from all but the beech trees. To remember, the coffin came out of the door upright. As though Theodore had sternly appeared on his threshold, terribly upright and contained as on the day he went to the hospital. Lucy[23], more like William Cowper than ever, her shaking hand holding a coral-coloured rose. The entrance to a churchyard full of crazy leaning tombs, preceded by old Mr Jackson singing the sentences in a wild warble, exactly like Billy Lucas going home from the inn. His admirable reading of the true lesson and of the right psalm. A young girl with the two remaining Aunts, she must be a daughter of one of Violet's sisters, small neat, bright-eyed, bright-ringleted, with a straight young back, exactly as if the Violet Theodore married had come to his funeral.

6. My birthday – my 60th. From today, I should be too senile to be a teaching master at Harrow, though I could still have ten years senility as a headmaster. How am I on my soixantaine? Fatter, alas! and heavier, and growing stiff in the knees and in the eyelids, and not so supple either in my wits. But cheerful in my spirits and in my guts still, my grey hairs strong-growing, my hearing, thank heaven, as good as ever.

22 Theodore died the previous evening.
23 Lucy Penny, youngest of the eleven Powys siblings.

I had feared Nora's deafness. And how much happier than ten years ago. Mostly by circumstances, I like to be not pressed with poverty, as I was then; and the shade of E.W.W., heavy on the house then, not heavy, scarcely a freckle, except that her letters twitch and tease Valentine. Poorer in friends, but with some new ones, and having performed two novels, and thinking I want to write another one. And with my love for my Love ten years deepened and patterned. Two sweet cats for my Thomas, the same house. Since Radnor Lodge 1895–1905, the first roof I have spent ten years under.

10. Nancy came on the 4 train, a slender support to her corals, and after dinner, out of a variety of handbags and paper bags and coloured handkerchiefs, she unpacked the treasures of Africa, quantities of amber, her Ladyship's pearls, and some very pretty Cartier jewels of his pre-USA period: an inch-long mat of turquoise matrix, rather rough, its natural outlines, clasped in minute bands of black enamel and small diamonds. The effect was very Nancy. She properly admired the shop, and Kaoru fell in love with her, patting her thighs as she sat on the floor, and squirming into the paper-carrier among the amber necklaces. His first affair – la femme mûre.

1954

January

7. O sad morning! for it brought the news that my dear queer friend Leonard Bacon[1] died on New Year's Day (my letter and a New Yorker story, I suppose Uncle Blair, had been read in time to please him). I feel profoundly bereaved. I have lost *a confidant*, a person to whom I could write quite freely, without reservations, without considerations, without any dross of personal circumstances. I recollect, in one of his letters, his simile of people meeting at a masked ball, who could speak with perfect intimacy and transgress nothing that should not be transgressed. 'Suddenly & peacefully' his daughter said, in a very good, brief, kind letter. And I miss his masculinity, deeply. My intellect was man-made, is still preponderantly masculine – and that part of me has lost a comrade. He loved life, he appreciated the dead, he was full of mental cordiality, and he is dead, while Ruth, abusing old years, and prattling of deaths and dinners, & dissatisfied with everything she cannot consume, lives on, already older than he. I have lost him, and to blinded Anne[2] I cannot long go on writing with the careless candour of for-your-eyes-alone. I seem to have no dispassionate unentangled relationships left, for since the Maxwells' visit, a spontaneity has gone out of William Maxwell's letters, and perhaps mine.

Besides, he found me charming, and delightful, and was content with only that. No-one to call me Charlie, Lamb lamented. I have plenty to call me Sylvia, but no one to call me Dear Miss Warner.

8. The day began with Ian ringing up in a fluster with the few little suggestions.[3] As I rather expected, C.D. Lewis had been helping with them. Ellen's remark during the allegro, and, if you please, the whole of the Crusoe conversation. I felt sorry for Ian, breathed on by all this

1 (1887–1954), American poet and Pulitzer Prize-winner. STW and he enjoyed a long correspondence, though they never met.
2 Anne Parrish's sight was failing rapidly. She died in 1957.
3 For the manuscript of *The Flint Anchor*.

howdydo about homosexuality (though my heart laughed him to scorn when he said so artlessly that no one could call it provocative, and it was a period story – like Forever Amber, no doubt). However, I said merely that if they liked they could hold up the English printing till the storm blew over, and that I could not take out the Crusoe conversation. Perhaps if it had not been for my real emotion of yesterday I might have felt more sham emotion – as it was I felt only a sort of embarrassment, and later, on a brilliant slippery iced morning posted the USA copy.

February

4. It has now been cold and colder since Jan 25. Frost every night, and during most of the days too: this week, frost all day. It is almost impossible now to scratch enough earth to fill the cats' trays, the ground is like iron with a little rust on it. All evergreens cut, even the yews, which droop and lose colour. All greens cut to pieces, only aconites – the flowers – partly survive. This will end my rosemary, I'm afraid – 4 good cherished bushes: and the hydrangeas, no doubt, though they are bushed over. All spare sacks are lagging, or in the car. Indoors everything freezes. Broth in the larder frozen into a block, and God knows what has happened to the eggs. All root vegetables frosted. The only place to keep food is in the refrigerator, where it doesn't freeze solid. Loops and bars of ice lie about for days on end. The birds get water from the river still, but are desperate for food, and harried by seagulls. Two days ago, when I opened the front door, a blackbird hopped to within a couple of feet of me, and stood clattering its bill – meaning plain enough. It was waiting when I came back with bread.

10. The Britten-Pears concert,[4] with Britten's new cycle of Hardy poems. All have power, and his particular forthrightness, and poetic reading of the words: those I was most impressed by were The Travelling Boy, with its reiterated figure in the accompaniment, a bouncing futile phrase with the frustration of To Lincolnshire to Lancashire to buy a pocket-handerkercher; and the last, Before Life and After, which is noble like a slow dance, a sarabande-like solemn climbing. Pears was singing very well, his Nacht & Traume superlative, and a Schubert I didn't know, Sprach der Liebe, most beautifully phrased. He began with a Mozart Masonic cantata, and there was the very same

4 In Dorchester.

emphasis in die Wahrheit that Alec pointed out in Zauberflöte. As for Britten, a head with no chin, a pounce like a weasel, and a total attentiveness and indentification with the music. He has a goblin look, like the child in the Carpaccio Annunciation who peeps down when she ought to have been at her lessons.

March

6. [Valentine] was no better, and had been better for nothing overnight. [. . .] Ruth rang up: the pills which Valentine had gone into Dorchester for were of course the wrong pills, 'the ones she gave me before which did me no good'; and when I said send them back and let me have an exact copy of what the label of the right pills says, Ruth said in triumph 'There is no label on the bottle.' 'But didn't she ask how I was?' said my Love. I explained that Ruth had done so, but at the beginning, when her mind was on the pills, so that it was like a piece of music in binary form, only she played it in the wrong order, half closing on the tonic and ending on the dominant. Afterwards, having got via egg-boilers to our childhoods, I supposed I had no small-talk now because I used it all up then. Valentine said I always had conversation with strangers, plenty to say to them; and I stopped just in time not to say, 'But I love strangers; they are so congenial.' Which is true, but only *in petto*, where it can't be misunderstood.

April

4. I spent much of the morning cleaning my nails and flattening my hair for Mr Pickering the hen-pecked & timid young photographer. He was a short elderly man, who rode roughshod over all my suggestions, said that ladies always tried to pose, and took a series of what seemed extremely uninspired views of me – but perhaps they will have something we can call quality. Unless he likes them, I shan't see one of them – and I shall only see the ones he likes. I looked wistfully back to that amiable, suggestible and complying young man, Cecil Beaton. I also mentioned him, but Mr P. only took me out of doors because I was interested in fishing, where the wind blew my hair sideways and reddened my hands.

7. Mr Pickering's photographs[5] came this morning, and dashed me.

5 One of them is used as a frontispiece to STW's *Letters* (1982).

Not only are they excellent truthful likenesses; not only do I look old and fat and plain – but I look so *tired* I could have wept over myself. But it was such a ravishing spring day that I forgot all this[.]

May

15. In spite of the Queen's return,[6] to which I listened from the Pool of London to Westminster, I spent a virtuous busy day, quickened by the news that Valentine may come back tomorrow.[7] I finished and sent off my USA proofs, and sent separately a painful letter of protest to Ben;[8] but it must be done, and my hand was stiffened by his pharisaical enclosure of a cutting about Roth's arrest for obscene publishing. [. . .]

Noted from the BBC reporters:

1. Of yacht Britannia; 'she now comes up to Tower Bridge looking really big.' – Anglo-Cat unction.

2. 'The finest view in all London, and indeed in all the Commonwealth' – of the view of the river procession obtained by lighters 50 yards from the yacht.

3. 'That famous smile of Her Majesty's that I have seen go all round the world.'

4. And a reflection in Whitehall. 'What a difference has grown up in the relationship between the throne and the people since 1649.'

No one will believe 2 and 4, but I wrote them instantly, and they are exact.

24. A note by Ben's 'own poor pen' to say that he agrees with my strictures, and will write at length presently. All day it has rained off and on, and a cold wind has blown, and the lane was speckled with appleblossom as I walked with Pompey[9] at my heel. Pompey has had a dull time of it since R[uth] came, and is sad in solitude, and touchingly demonstrative when I get a while with him. I have grown very fond of him, and full of esteem, and he has made himself handsome, licking and preening his thick coat. A tom cat's affection is sexually different: more innocently voluptuous, and with a kind of roguery which is charming; and in Pompey's case, much more dependent and trusting: but that may be his circumstances, not his sex.

6 From a 5½ month tour of the Commonwealth.
7 She was tending Ruth, who had fallen backwards down the stairs of the Great Eastern Hotel.
8 Ben Huebsch, of the Viking Press, about proposed cuts to *The Flint Anchor*.
9 A wounded cat they had nursed back to health.

Three days more, and tomorrow is Vera; and on Friday R. has to be driven to London. Even with tomorrow being Vera, I don't know how I shall hold out. It is not the work, though that is considerable: it is the gaping monotonous boredom, and the peculiar sense of being made worthless and disgraced: I daresay extreme debauchery might feel the same.

June

2. Began the day by cascading downstairs on my back – long enough for Valentine to reflect on broken thighs and how to get Meredith and avoid me being sent to Dorchester hospital to get bed-sores and eat boiled eggs with a dessert-spoon like Mrs Henning. However, nothing was broken. But by midday when she came back from Dorchester I was so bruised and so swelled that I most gratefully went to bed where I dined in noble contemplation off the New Yorker's providential beef and FitzGerald.

3. Up – with my left buttock from waist to volute a majestic awful purple – it was Van Gogh's pickle-cabbage that came to my mind. Mrs Lambert, Mr Samways, the Thursday wash, I dealt evenly with them all, and in the afternoon Bill[10] came to fetch away Pompey, whose hamper I arrayed in a Little Zeal cushion and Nora's old blue cotton kimono that I remember her wearing at Tushielaw.

July

4. Sorted the napery drawers, oiled Kaoru, picked our own straw-berries, wrote to Jean Untermeyer,[11] and cleaned my sitting-room. On such days one is mainly the servant of one's ideal self, who will spend a morrow better employed.

August

4. Colette is dead. I feel abandoned and unprotected. [. . .] while she was alive I never lost the assurance that came on me thirty years ago and more, walking miserably in the Queen's Road, Bayswater, on a

10 Bill Long was a friend (female) who was adopting the cat.
11 Wife of the poet Louis Untermeyer, and a friend of STW since her trip to New York in 1929.

wet winter evening, when I suddenly declared in my heart, I could go and tell Colette. What? Youth, unused love, the look of the chemist's window on the wet pavement, the *rustic* feel of rain on my bare hands: the condition of being alive. It was from the Davidsons in 1913 or so that I first heard of her, of her & Willy and the bulldog drinking milk at the English bar; and Andrew[12] lent me La Vagabonde, I read and was enclosed by her. There is nothing material, from the colour of a hollyhock to the colour of a pigeon's guts that she has not illuminated and established in my mental senses. Lady of Good Counsel, Notre Dames des Bêtes, farewell!

21. Together to Dorchester – she came into the car-park shaking with strain, because she was late, because Jean had delayed her, because, because – in fact, because yesterday she had obliged herself to read some of Russell of Liverpool's book about Nazi doings in concentration camps, and had lain awake with it most of the night. Jangled, and all out of tune. I have never seen this before, and it was very frightening – a *crise*.

26. Toothache still grumbling. In the afternoon I did a page one of the eunuch[13] – nervously. People came to the shop, then I got distracted into pruning roses, and then I listened to *Corona Spinea*, and then toothache got considerably worse. It was lovely to hear a finished production of Corona – though I daresay those scrambled performances under Terry were nearer the original truth. But this would have satisfied and interested Taverner – both. The brilliance of the counter-tenors, the groping low basses, the bagpipe opening of the Sanctus, and that majestic slow climb from the lowest to the highest voices in the 3rd Agnus. It was very strange to think, as I listened, that I had had a hand in its resurrection: and sad, in a way, that there is never on the BBC a flick of acknowledgement to T.C.M. [*Tudor Church Music*] As it can't be copyright, they are not obliged to; and I daresay by now it is a matter of faith that Collins and Cecil Stainer did everything, and R.R. Terry nothing. The triumph of the Mandarins. I knew then how much they hated him, and thought little or nothing of it. I was wrong. One cannot overestimate the power of a good rancorous hatred on the part of the *stupid*. The stupid have so much more industry and energy to expend on hating. They build it up like coral insects.

12 Unidentifiable.
13 A new novel, unfinished.

27. I did more of the Eunuch, and it takes root, But how intimidating it is to be at the beginning of a book. As it is of the birth of Mr F's M.[14] I am resolved not to sprawl, and *not to attach*. After the F.A. [*The Flint Anchor*], which lives likes a limpet, not to attach will be difficult. But what do I mean by attaching? Being more interested in the story than in the telling? Or trying to give it life instead of giving it art? Something like that. I shall have to read Burney and Hawkins and those people – what a bore.

October

30. Valentine's selected short stories came back from Pearns & P.[15] with an anonymous reader's report. She was better than the stories, was the gist of it. A downcasting appraisal, for no one wants to be praised for possibilities when one has submitted performances. Besides my personal grief I feel a professional remorse. I could, no doubt, have taught her some tricks – but she is so little monkey-minded that it would have been oddly infra dig. – and she would not in her heart want to pick up my tricks. Yet it might have *sold* one or two, and that would have refreshed her. A year ago she resolved to write no more short stories. She gets no pleasure from it, which seems a significantly good enough reason: yet she is uneasy about the resolve. And is this conscience, or is it creation?

One of the tangles, and an indissoluble one, is that there is no bodily exertion that can give her pleasure. Arthritis stops all that. A contented bodily fatigue is the best antidote to conscience; and she cannot take it.

November

17. [London] This day I gave to myself. First, the Diaghiliev exhibition. Vast, comprehensive, plainly laid out, successions of the best artists, russian & spanish inventions welded by French distinction. The Ballets of my youth, Jose Maria Sert, Derain, Joan Miro, Les Biches, Govenarova, and above all, Picassos. Drawings of Dancers Seated, 3 lines to a leg and everything said, and a design for the dress of the Miller's Wife in which the face is conveyed in a flawless oval – a hen herself could not do better. Then on my way down, after the

14 That is, like *Mr Fortune's Maggot*, conceived in a dream.
15 Publishers.

grand room of portraits (fine Sickert of Beecham conducting) a glassed-off dusky room, as it were the deserted wardrobe room, with a husk of a Sylphide lying here, a tunic of the Blue bird pinned there, Pavlova's little scuffed red slippers like mice in a corner – all worn, faded, shrivelled: husks. [. . .] Then to Nadia's,[16] who took me to see Violet Schiff;[17] an old woman, with remains of great beauty and distinction, in a shaded room. Then to Bea & Mark [Lubbock], and then to see Edith Evans in Fry's Dark is Light Enough. A poor thin play, silvered-paper Chekhov; but her acting, and especially her descent of a twirling staircase as a dying lady, clinging with both hands to the rail, a crablike descent, superlatively beautiful. Then back to find Norah[18] & Ian, and to conclude this indulged day with an offer of Proust's Contre Ste Beuve[19] to translate. Whew!

28. The weather cleared from storm to stormy, and we drove Alec [Robertson] to Long Critchel, driving towards a blue-black sky with a violent rainbow decking it. After 15 minutes polite conversation we came back alone, and she said something about the pleasure of being alone again, but I could not do more than a surface response. For tomorrow we drive to Minehead to bring back that poodle she has bought. She has wanted one for some months – to sit in the car beside her, she says; in fact, to be tried as a new medicine against her melancholy. But I feel with melancholy that tonight is the end of an epoch. Niou and Kaoru will be unchanged to each other, but every other relation will be changed. I have been so happy with them, it has seemed to me the perfect arrangement, and to them. But not to her. And alas, her woe, her void, can't be stuffed up with a poodle, and I know this. And little as I want the poor puppy, I wish it were going to a better situation, and not to a house where one expects too much from it and the other expects nothing to the purpose. But goodbye, dear years, that I am grateful for.

16 Nadia Gant, wife of the writer Roland Gant.
17 Proust's 'angel Violet', who with her husband Sydney had been a patron of literature, art and music since the 1920s. Under the pseudonym Stephen Hudson, Sydney Schiff completed the first English translation of *Le Temps Retrouvé* on the death of C.K. Scott-Moncrieff.
18 Norah Smallwood became a partner in Chatto & Windus in 1945, and was on the board of directors from 1953 to 1982.
19 Proust's book had been published for the first time in Paris that year.

1955

January

28. Finished revise of The Countess[1] – but still at a loss about that peculiar cathedral. Cooking dinner I turned on the wireless to an *intelligent* voice, talking very fast, his subject surging out of him. I could not believe my ears. It was the voice of scholastic, not genteel culture. It was Isaiah Berlin, talking about Russia of 1848. Thank heaven there are 3 more.

31. Today the fair-type of Sommeils[2] came back from Joan W,[3] and this evening I have just read it. Style is the oddest manifestation of man. It is almost word for word Pr: (he allowed it, there); and certainly I must have my mind stuffed with Scott Moncrieff; but this could only be mine – *it is so extremely rapid* – as rapid as the beginning of the Anchor. Rapid Proust . . . an odd thought. I hope he wouldn't mind.

March

5. In intervals of fatigue I have gone on with Proust, almost all the Methode chapter done – it is full of P's own hurries and lapses, unnoticed by his mandarin editors – and the article in *Figaro* and the Ray of Sunlight revised. In the revise of Figaro I restored the present tense, and thank God I did: the *moral* difference is astonishing: a remission of sins, for what in any other tense was hysterical. Let this be a *Warning* to me.

[. . .] [O]n March 1st Churchill made a criminal speech on the H. bomb; a froward wanton blaspheming speech, disgraceful at any age, abominable beyond all in a man of his years.

1 *Contre Sainte Beuve*, ch.4.
2 Ibid, ch.1.
3 Joan Wilkinson, STW's typist.

6. Finished the 1st draft of Methode.[4] I enjoyed the last bits of it very much, it is a schoolboy's job, with all the grown-up airs, patchy erudition and malice of adolescence. The *social* taunting of Ste Beuve is as though M. du Charlus had had a hand in it. Now that really tedious G. de Nerval confronts me. But before I attack I must set Figaro in order for typing, and get it away. Then de Nerval; then tidy *the sunbeam*; then Baudelaire, almost as unpromising as de Nerval; then I burst through to Balzac and pure joys.

7. How lightly one proposes! Setting *Figaro* in order almost cost me my life. But it was partly such extreme cold, and being somewhat becolded myself.

15. In bed this morning, thinking about Cocteau and his entre deux sommeils and his grand sommeil – for I had been reading about him overnight – and his sensitive desperately anxious performing poodle face and poet hands I conceived a *View of Death. We cannot live without it*, so in order to live, we have invented it. Life as far as we know is an indestructible form of matter – unlike Biro pens[5] –: the earliest forms of life and the least exploited, volvox and the virus etc, are almost immortal. These things could not feel themselves themselves, and feel their life in every limb unless they had an opposite, a sounding-board; that can only be death. We cannot live without it.

When I got as far as this I saw too a most entertaining speculation; for man is always inventing new varieties of death as fast as the individual men are inventing methods to overcome them. Death appears to move out of one disease into another, but more probably we move it, and with exquisite thrift and circumspection preserve our creation of death as though it were a kind of yeast, a culture. For just as the deadly diseases appear to be routed – they go away. Diphtheria has not been abolished, it has retreated: – with this too may connect the pareillement of forms of death to forms of fashion: the christian poetical chaste consumptions of the early 19th cent. in western Europe; the likeness between religious revivals and sweeping plagues; the killing disease of an epoch is part of that epoch's cultural life. And so we come to this interesting thought that in all probability we are on the brink of finding the cure for cancer *because* we have invented the nuclear bomb to replace it.

4 *CSB*, ch.8.
5 Hers had just died on the word 'indestructible'.

I write this in haste because I have a day of housework before me, and ten to one I shall mislay it in a dustpan if I don't put it down at once.

17. USA has published the text of the Yalta agreement. Rooseveldt and alas, Stalin, wanted to leave France out of the German occupation settlement.

25. 6 pages of de N.[6] achieved, and a large mixed vegetable soup. Half the soup was eaten tonight, more than half de N. remains to be overcome. It is MP at his most floating, least congenial, it is like translating a sweet soufflé when one's appetite prefers a cheese soufflé. Never mind! Balzac is ahead. It has rained most of the day, a warm rain, with birds and crocuses breaking into song. White crocuses with their alabaster curves.

April

2. Mrs King rang up to ask if she could bring Enid Starkie to see the shop. I pared my nails and flattened my hair and walked in on a backview, childishly short and bulky of bright blue trousers, very baggy, a baggy scarlet duffle-coat, a red beret, too large and some bunches of red-gold hair, falsely bright. It turned round, and the face was Rimbaud: the oddest mixture of thwarted childish brilliance & profound nervousness. If she has never acted a vice in her life, she is still vicious. Very shy; grunts like a guinea-pig; very ill, I surmise. Very much a don, though Valentine was not prepared to believe this, holding more subfusc views of dons.

22. I felt ill all the morning, in the afternoon I had a sore throat but felt better, and Prousted in the garden while V. went to Beaminster. After her return we went out again, so that I could see primroses. In the wild lane to Poorton we stopped and picked them as they grew up through last year's bracken litter. It was such innocence, such happiness that I felt as though it were Chaldon, twenty-five years ago. But I also know that Chaldon 25 years ago was not in the least like that. The sun's levelling rays stripe longer shadows; and light, but do not set on fire. And since last autumn I have come to feel ineluctably old.

26. Mrs Chubb[7] cleaned the bedroom as never was – but that silly child

6 The Gérard de Nerval chapter of *CSB*.
7 The char.

Maureen is not taking up her scholarship – instead she is learning to make cakes at Judge Jefferies[8] in Dorchester. Cakes! This country is rotted with cakes, and makes the worst cakes in Europe. Apparently Mr Chubb has had a hand in it. But it is very disappointing.

May

2. Katie brought Rose Powys to tea: tall, would be strapping if she had not a very agreeable demeanour; ravishing black hair, ancestral hair, a low quiet voice, talking the most dreadful RAF lingo. No pleasure in being a young woman of this grindingly emancipated into slavery epoch. Katie, on the stairs, turned suddenly & said 'I feel I have no ardour left.'

25. I have seldom felt more unwholesome – the same semi-myxamatosis [sic] swelled eyes and farces that I had a month ago. In the evening to the Eve of the Poll meeting in Dorchester, where Bo[9] spoke with professional arts & graces, far beyond the Dorchester guffaws, & Wingfield Digby[10] answered questions strikingly well, for he sounded both honest & wary.

26. Voted for him in the morning. Valentine gave me quinine with adjuvants. So I began to feel less afflicted – but she with such pain in her mastitis gland that I was shamed out of my own megrims. Polling-day. I lay in bed listening to the results and was awake for most of them till 4 a.m. The electric computator [sic], purring, and being fed with statistics, like a great cat. It is the size of a small bedroom.

June

27. Spruced by Norah Smallwood inviting me to spend what's left of the night of the party,[11] I tore on with Ste B. & B.[12] and almost finished its first draft. Prou misquotes like any one of us – the most interesting his Le *printempts* [sic] vaporeux a fui vers l'horizon – for Baudelaire could never, I think, have put that noun to that adjective – it is the difference between Manet & Renoir.

8 Restaurant and tea-shop.
9 See note 19 (1953), page 201.
10 The Conservative Party candidate.
11 Chatto & Windus were celebrating their centenary.
12 'Saint-Beuve and Baudelaire', *CSB*, ch.9.

1955

July

15. On June 30 when Valentine went to Wareham with Elizabeth it was fine. Candy[13] on heat was left with me, and invented a warbling howl – the first few genuine, and then art swept her away, and she went higher & higher up the scale with each fresh howl, stopping to take a good breath – like a singing pupil. When Valentine came back, the garden was beginning to smell of roses, we gathered a great many strawberries. It grew finer and slowly hotter. Mrs Goodchild came to clip Candy on the 31st, and talked of how she spent the winter of 40–41 in a basement flat in London, looking after some collies. Her husband had died, her home and all her belongings were occupied by Germans (the courage of her servant: the day she had to go, at the drop of a hat, the girl, that same evening, came with her father and a cart, and took away all they could to store it), London was being bombed, brilliant all night with fires, she saw no one, lived alone with the dogs. Odd to look at her – neat, cheerful, that English mixture of the genteel & the raffish, and see this cavernous period of loss & despair behind her.

17. Was it Josiah or Fanny[14] who throve so in Madras? Today of an Indian heat, for now the ground itself is hot; and on angel's wings I did an extraordinary quantity of domestic chores, and flew from one to the other as if they were parties of pleasure.

18. The morning was still hot, and walking in my Paradise I noticed a thirsty honeysuckle and told Mr S[amways] to give it a good souse. By midday it was beginning to rain in a vague way, with a mist. It rained harder, with a thunderstorm, and all our electricity went as usual, but this is so usual that I would not have given more than one damning thought to it, if it had not been for the 2 cats; who had come in earlier, and were sitting in my room, close together in a very nervous frame of mind. So I began to keep an eye on the river, and to notice that it was rising fast and running with a great force. It went on raining, and grew dark very early, so that it was like a winter evening, almost a Miss Green evening as we dined by lamplight. At 9.30 or so I noticed that the back yard was soggy, & the water beginning to rise over the steps. Less than an hour later I stepped into the back kitchen and was over my instep in water. So then in semi-darkness we cleared what we could out of the shop – not enough – with water splashing round us and

13 Candace ('Candy') was the poodle Valentine had bought. See 28 November 1954.
14 Hudleston, STW's maternal grandparents.

torrents of rain outside. We sat up till 1.30 but the cats still plaining in my room, and the kitchen in such a state of panic took me to bed, Valentine sat up longer. It rained all night. The river roared past on both sides of the house, and through the house too – odd to hear it sucking & gurgling underneath. At the first light I looked out – water everywhere, & some deboshed poppies rearing out of it. [. . .] After lunch I cleared the floor of the shop: about an inch of thick stinking black mud, rugs & carpets soaked, books & music too. Valentine woke up & helped me with the carpet, I could not have hauled [it] in single-handed; and by dinner time we had thrown away a great deal, and put more to dry out, and were over the worst of it. Luckily, the car had spent the night with Cousin Channon;[15] [. . .] as for our garage, it was a marsh, flavoured with paraffin.

19. This morning the full calamity of the garden impressed itself. While V. was in Dorchester I did what I could to rescue chrysanthemums & carnations in the tulip tree bed. The drive is in pits & gulleys, so are the paths, the gravel is either on beds, lawns, or in the house, but none left on the paths, and a thick grey mud is clamping down on everything under 3ft. Flies everywhere, and everywhere stink. Candy now chases the cats: excitement has put an edge on her passions.

August

18. Devoted to Roy[16] & the children – and illuminated by the arrival of Tiber-eyed Gerald Finzi & his wife,[17] just as I had covered my right hand with engine grease groping for the radiator cap which Valentine had dropped into the works with Freudian ingenuity while getting ready to meet Roy at the station. At 7, after tea in Beaminster, we returned them to their Weymouth Hotel. O heavens, he is so unpalatable.

19. Dorchester in the morning, buying myself stays, and Lady Spencer Smith[18] in the afternoon. The day before obliterated this day, but we

---

15 A local mechanic.
16 Roy Davis, whom Janet Machen had married in 1946.
17 Gerald Finzi, the composer (1901–56), and his wife Joy.
18 'Valentine with her sensitive pointer's nose for old ladies has found another one who could not be more appropriate; for she knew my mother, my aunts, my grandparents, even a great-aunt or two, saw them all with the attentive large clear eyes of a little girl in a provincial town.' STW to Alyse Gregory, February, 1955, *Letters*.

continued to look back on how charming Gerald Finzi was – and how Italian. His sturdy upright carriage, and his round green eyes.

September

18. Colin [House] came in the morning – unrecognisably stout and shortened by institutional diet; and his beauty gone, but his goodness and good manners just as ever. Then V & I undid the tropical trunk. The flood had got through its lead lining, all the bottom layers were ruined. Norah[19] was immeasurably, practically kind, and arranged our Faroe woollens to steep in the river: all the trees hung with less contaminated clothes. Another of our Sundays, in fact, watched with interest by M. Bungalow. She left before dinner – a guest full of graces.

November

6. Intensively re-revising P[roust] (*Noms*). It is disquieting that every improvement is so definitely an improvement – *not only in manner, but in comprehension of the original!*

8. By the 8.45 to London to the Pr[oust] Exhibition. They were to close last Saturday, have extended for a week – a feeling of living in boxes was already in the room. The tender waistcoat had the whole weight of Jean Santeuil on its stomach, pictures had moved about, more photographs had been thrust into the cases. I felt the same kind of confused acquiescent shocked pity that I do when I pick up comatose butterflies from our floors, see them stir their wings and fold them again and know that for all our care to put them in safe hibernations, hundred to one they will have been trodden on or dried to death before next spring. Only I shall never meet Pr. again. Things of this visit – a ravishing small watercolour portrait of Love-in-a-mist, *à gauche, une nigelle bleue*; a watercolour of Reveillon, with a moat & willows, an enchanting house. The inkstand a crystal rectangle – a sublime letter from Celeste thanking someone for a book he was too ill to read; his hair – dark brown, very heavy sombre hair, uncurling; the renewed beauty of Anna de N[oailles] in the Renoir bust; drawings (schoolboyish, elegant, a little under the influence of R. de M.) in C. Ste. B. I stayed for several hours, shopped a little, and came back on the evening train.

19 Norah Smallwood, on a visit.

23. A grim demand for surtax had the usual effect: my spirits instantly rose.

December

3. Continued to feel drooped, and weakly wrestled with Xmas p.s, till the afternoon, when I suddenly began to write a tirra-lirra little p. boiler for the N.Y.

4. The amiable Stones[20] came to the shop in the morning, and I carried out my intention, and gave them my great-grandfather's Flaxman.[21] The parting with its familiar flopping weight, and stained grey cover was harder than I thought (and it was a queer shock to see my bookplate in it: it has scarcely become *my* book even in the 45 years I've owned it). But Reynolds was really pleased, and it will have a good chance with an intelligent new generation.

Worked on the tirra-lirra. It is touching, poetical, and totally superficial.

20 Reynolds Stone (1909–79), the artist and engraver, and his wife Janet.
21 A collection of Flaxman engravings.

1956

January

7. It was the last day, and Ruth left by the 1.40. 30 minutes was allowed for catching the train, with the result that we got to the station before the porter came back from his lunch. This supplied an interesting chromatic harmonisation to the usual farewell speeches.

Jaded was the word. Valentine's midriff opening and shutting like a maw. I tidied here and there, and wrote a lot of cheques, always restorative in a fatalistic way, and after creamed scallops we fell into bed.

There has been another great fog in London & the Midlands, and Poujade has dominated the French elections. My dear France, you have never done more with a demagogue but experiment and discard him, so far; but which way does the wind blow now? — downwards through time and tradition, or sideways across the Rhine.

9. We shopped in Dorchester, and after lunch we drove to Yeovil, and went to Vincent's.[1] I saw the Charles I memorial locket, one of twelve, the cutting said. It is very small, about an inch long, heart-shaped, made of silver; very roughly and hastily made, and cheaply, almost a fair-ground piece. It gave me a strong impression of the man making it; hurriedly, in grief and anger and bewilderment. So little time, and so little silver too, and only the fine lettering and scrutched-work engraving of the caput mortis to grace it at all. And he with his delicate choice among splendours, so many jewels, so many great pictures, so much music of viols and organs, all summed up, clenched up, in a fair-ground locket. I have never felt so acutely, so nearly, the tragedy of that epoch. There was also a small enamel portrait of Charles II — very ugly, very Scottish, very formidable. A good likeness, I daresay.

12. Mr Samways in a plaid dressing-gown was duly driven to the Dorchester hospital — sent off with many my pets and kind apple-

1 An antique dealer.

dumpling endearments from Mrs S. Valentine called on Father Weelkes,[2] who spoke affectionately of Miss Florence & her meinie.[3] [. . .] Then we picked up Mr S., now dismissed to the charge of his local; and on the way back heard with awe his diet. 3 pieces of ryevita, 3 eggs (!), half a walnut of butter, a good helping of boiled greens, lean meat, dry or watered.

No wonder *we* fail to get thinner, even when we think we are trying.

We dined, according to my view of the date[4], on Dover soles, and tutti-frutti ice; and according to my view of the date I gave Valentine the étui, wrapped in a Jacqumard square (dear little gravestones of different sizes & perspectives) and received my grand, my formal, my much hesitated-over, my – first diamond. It is antique, and most beautiful, a silver openwork panel with a centre diamond, baguette, and four smaller heart-shaped stones at its corners, on a graceful but solid gold band. Calmly, I fell asleep wearing it.

14. Chardin practically finished.[5] Right at the end a superb passage about Rembrandt. In the evening the 2nd 3rd programme organ recital, this time Notre Dame de Valère at Sion. I long to go there. It is unbelievably brilliant, animated, forward in tone. The speaker said like bells, but in fact it is like birdsong pressed, magnified, against the ear. It is completely taken up with being a magnificent athletic *noise*, a heroic noise. The church stands on a rock, the wind howls round it. The organ is quite small. So are wrens.

The idiots of this world! Today I got a letter from an admiring reader, to ask if the monkey in At the M's breast[6] was a monkey, the man a lunatic, did either of them exist, etc. Presumably this is the result of other people reading Kafka. I categorically replied. V. said it would be a painful shock to them.

24. Such a hard frost that when we hunted through the garden for a birthday nosegay for Bo, the violets were iced, like crystalised violets, and I had to thaw aconites in my bare hand before I could sever one from another to pick them. Aconites, violets, white and crimson Xmas roses, a house jonquil, winter jessamine, a polyanthus and one daisy – which looked exceedingly sullen & stubborn, like a smacked child.

---

2 Fr. Weekes, the Roman Catholic priest in Dorchester.
3 Unidentifiable.
4 Of their marriage anniversary.
5 One of Proust's 'Portraits of Painters' in *CSB*.
6 'At a Monkey's Breast', a story about a man visiting his senile mother in a nursing home, *WA*.

28. Tonight, except for the first page, the page about the poems & some notes, *La Methode* is through, 26 pages of very hard work.

In the morning I received a cutting from La Gazettino – a Venetian paper – sent by Aldo Camerino who had written an extremely praising and glorifying and gratifying account of Winter in the Air,[7] and me in general. It is wonderful to begin a day by reading of oneself as *La Townsend Warner*. Such things occur but seldom, and I have been enjoying a compass of over two octaves, a flawless legato, complete control of all fioriture passages, great dramatic intensity and a commanding stage presence all day.

29. So when I had done the notes and the poems, I distracted myself, wrote letters, mended sheets, walked in the garden – it was a day like spring, and went early to bed. Valentine read me a poem she had suddenly written, almost been written by, about looking out of her window and seeing a swan.

February

17. Alas! There is to be an atomic plant built near West Stafford on the heath:[8] with what they call workers' dwellings, there, and in Dorchester. I think of those nauseous whited sepulchres at Harwell, the vilest building project I have ever set eyes on for smugness and pretentiousness: that *genteel* pretentiousness which is the blight of this epoch. And that lovely heath gone – and those poor Acklands at West Stafford & Framptons at Moreton, with the atomisers and their children dropping ice-cream cartons all over their meadows, breaking their trees, yelling away their peace. For how other can the rootless behave, planted down on [a] heath barren to them, and living in uneasiness about the nature of their work?

19. When I went into Valentine's room she was lying on her back with a face and attitude of extraordinary sternness and sadness. I was frightened, and asked, but she put me off, saying, A chain of thought.

20. Now Krushcheff, Mikoyan, Malenkov, have in turn said what a bad and ruinous individualist Stalin was. I remember his voice on the wireless in 43, and those broad serviceable shoulders that they were all

---

7 STW's collection of stories had been published that month.
8 Winfrith, about three miles north-east of Chaldon.

content should shoulder the burden, and I feel a deep distaste – a Tory distaste, I daresay, for my eminent comrades.

21. Valentine talked of becoming an R.C. again (Fr. Weelkes [sic] did not idly visit), but how can she, for she has not a hat to go to London in, her scruples would make her go to confession before she could with any satisfaction go to Mass, she could only confess in London, where these things are so comfortably anonymous – and she has not a hat. I hope it may rest there. I think it may, as in fact she has one very suitable hat.

28. I went into Valentine's room before she was up, and my eye fell on a small rosary by her bed, curled up and neat as a snake. The comparison was instant, it must have shown itself in my look, or in my prim removal of the gaze; for afterwards in her sitting-room she began to talk more about going back to that bosom; and her objections were the kind of objection that, I thought, she had already discounted, or slighted, and she talked without the smallest accent of dubiety or effort in her voice: she talked as though she had 'gone and done it'. I say to myself that it is no affair of mine, that people must go their own way, that if it makes her happier – all the suitable remarks. But it must have been a deep shock, for it is only now coming out. Looking back, I see that what really affronted and terrified me was that she said so serenely that of course she had always been a Catholic. She said it with perfect conviction; although in the next breath she was telling me that she had said to Father Weelkes [sic] that she lacked the gift of faith.

29. Last night she came to my room with extracts from a diary: what I read first was thoughts, invocations, musings, prayers – as it were crystallisations of an inner life. They were extremely beautiful, and pure as dew, and melancholy as the note of a thinking owl. These ran from 1951 onwards. From there I fell into an almost day-by-day analysis of how she has felt since this year's beginning: and it was different, so flustered, so full of stress and confusion & assertion and plain tragedies – a novena, even – that I could not believe it came out of the same mind. And when she came in later, I said this. She was sad, frustrated, so was I. And I woke with a load on my heart, and she came in & took the pages away, and said it was all over, and went to Dorchester to the sale. By then I realised where the difference lay – greater than the difference between poetry & prose, a different process – the one a completed thought, the other not even a record of thinking –

more like the first scrambled notes for a complicated novel. So I said this after lunch – whichever she chooses, I want her to choose, not to refuse – positive, I mean, not negative.

Still feeling rather dizzied, I cleaned all the walls of my sitting-room except the fireplace, and about one third of the ceiling. It was tranquil, and futile, & fatiguing. Not exactly futile. Fatuous, rather. A little before dusk she went to bed, staggering with a migraine. That too, is like the old wound. O my poor love, forever vexed!

March

6. I revised *La Methode de Ste B.*, *Balzac* and *de Nerval*, and did them all up for Violet [Schiff].

It has been a mild, mildly wet day and I have enjoyed every moment of it, but I can say no more – and really no better – of it than that it has had no history.

8. Finished Stendhal.

A letter from Peter Clarke of Bournemouth about the Heath – his in the B'mouth Echo, and to me, with all the people & organisations he had written to. It reminded [me] of early days in the Party, and made me feel dreadfully dry-hearted.

11. This morning Valentine drove to the Cat. church in Weymouth. A difficult matter to enquire into. I heard it was very full. I presume it may shortly be fuller. On the way home she heard two larks going up at once.

21. This visit[9] is going very badly. Nancy is rude about the shop and peevish about how she will go to Exeter. Meanwhile we took her to the Old Rectory[10] to see the Duff Cooper stone,[11] and the Pipers. Only Mrs P. appeared, alarming enough at first sight, with straight-combed milk-blonde locks hanging to her shoulders, no shape, upholstered in moss-patterns, walking noiselessly on no heels and giving a first impression of someone out of Charles Abbot. But at tea she improved a great deal, and told me about the Saintage which is full of small Romanesque churches, has an estuary and is like Suffolk – with convolvulus major, yuccas, oleanders, etc in its buttonhole.

9 Nancy Cunard's.
10 The Stones' house in Litton Cheney.
11 Duff Cooper's memorial stone, being cut by Reynolds.

(John Piper appeared just as we were leaving. He looked so very cold that I think he must have been hiding in a shrubbery or behind a gravestone. He is very thin, his face is white, bony, observant, censorious, and he looks like the Intellectual of a provincial Labour Party.)

28. So fine and warm that I spent the morning with Pr. in front of the house, with bumblebees burrowing in the crocuses under the lavender. Valentine came back from Hunt,[12] who had told one can get a building grant for restoring dead houses – and that Stratton M H.[13] had main water but no drains, or was it electric light and no drains? No drains, anyway; and that Hunt would meet us there after lunch.

We went in; and wherever we went, he and his surveyors seemed to be poking their fingers into rotted woodwork: all the beams are rotten, but worst at the north end of the house. And the west ground floor is damp: below ground level damp. £3000, said Mr H. all told. Then looking at this house, £3250 at the most, he said. This was sobering, though I still feel we should try to save it: it is so grave, so sad, and a very *good* house.

What is it? she said; Stratton or Catholicism? We talked then. No, it is not the Church, nor apparently its beliefs – at least she would be quite happy disbelieving them. It is the mass, and the wafer. *So pleasant*, she said: and the old spell snapped back and worked again, and I knew I could accept it, if it is pleasant to her. She's not in, would be, if it were not for Fr Weeks [sic] standing on the letter of the law, and demanding documents, and Mr Turpin.[14] All this is going on, and no doubt will end with all the doings, penance, contrition, reception back, I think is the order. One of the Peronista generals has just been down the dance, and I read the terms in the Times. So there we are. With great self-control I refrained from saying Une messe vaut bien Paris. Anyhow, for her that would be true. She swears it makes no difference to our relation – and a minute later I was saying I should undoubtedly settle down and get used to it. These two statements are incompatible, and both are sincere, and what happens with a sincere incompatibility I shall have to find out.

Then we arranged dinner, and at 7.45 both the kind Stones arrived, Janet clutching an earring (I put it on for her, and she sat looking sullen and patient and polite, like a child.) Their honeymoon. Janet

12 A land agent.
13 Stratton Manor House, which Valentine wanted to buy.
14 Valentine's husband. Valentine married Richard Turpin in July 1925, separated from him soon after and was granted an annulment early in 1927.

doing nothing but fall asleep, Reynolds reading aloud and longing to go home. I fancy it was a very happy successful evening – but I wasn't there.

April

1. [Easter Day] Last month is over, and I want to forget about it, and weave a fair mat of triviality and mesure – darling mesure! – and hope for the ground to heal beneath it.

She came back about 9.30, and I was up, and the house straight; and she gave me my presents [. . .] It was a fine day, but cold. I began the fair-copy of Le Balzac de M. de G.[15] – but it went badly, I was physically unable, couldn't spell, couldn't think what word came next. It is ridiculous to be so tethered to one's state of mind; and I am humbled when I remember how, at the same stage of Eliz. I sat down and wrote seven pages of flawless impartial nonsense for the N.Y.

W.S.B.[16] is going to be a great stand-by. I tried Clough, but I became too sorry for him.

7. I did La R. Maudite[17] all day, in great anonymity & solitude. A cold, windy day, fallacious brightness of flowers. Thinking of Pr. as I did that enormous tirade of the homosexuals, which is ardent, *but not eloquent*, and which is very difficult not to cool into eloquence, I thought how like he is to Racine: the same *paucity* of language, the same burr walnut patterns of motive and character.

8. I [. . .] woke with a raging sore throat, which I tied up in my black woollen scarf; but even so, I think I have a fever rising, so I shall take an aspirin.

It worked; and so did I. And now, with a feeling of being compassless, captainless and astray, I have finished the revise of *La Race Maudite*; and tomorrow I shall tidy the two typescripts and send them to Joan Wilkinson, and the fireworks will be over, and only a few little oddments left. But I had saved the great set piece for the last. It is indeed a masterpiece, raging with compassion and understanding, quivering with the delicacy of adjusting irony into the whole.

And as, even at my best, I could never write like that, for I have not got that stuff of genius, that steady furnace, only a few rockets and

15 'M. de Guermantes's Balzac', ch.12 of *CSB*.
16 Wilfred Scawen Blunt's poems.
17 The indictment of homosexuality in *CSB*.

Catherine wheels, I am grateful that I have had at least the experience of seeing, line by line, precept upon precept, how it is done.

Dear, dear Marcel, soul of tormented truth, how sorry I am to leave off cohabiting with your Muse!

20. Valentine went off for an afternoon with Father Weeks [sic], and I weeded in the garden. I thought, supposed, hoped in a way that it was now the final gallop down the straight – but NO: and she spent her return in writing to some bishop or other, and they want her birth certificate(!) and all the legal marriage and nullity certificates. As they do not recognise the validity of any marriage or nullity unless performed by them, it is odd that they should have this craving for Somerset House, or wherever such certificates are kept. Whether they recognise the birth of anyone born outside their fold I don't know. It seems a ticklish question, and I expect they will have to consult Rome about it. O God, how I resent their pettifoggeries.

However, Bulganin & Krushcheff are in London.

May

4. [S]till I have no idea whether I am really surfacing, or whether I am acclimatising, with my usual despicable hold on life, to a pis-aller. Since that crisis on the 23rd,[18] when the only thing I knew was a force of compassion that made me intolerant of any other consideration, I have set myself not to think, not to look back or forward, de ne jamais approfondir ni de se relâcher and to look at the spring with only the bare outward of my senses. There is the loveliest blackthorn blossom I have seen for a long time – but I dare not impale myself on it. It is a mean, poor-hearted, despicable way to live, and I reprobate it – and I suspect it is all going for nothing, too, and that she is as much aware as I am that it is a reach-me-down. But what else am I to do? And even to write this much has shaken my self-control, so I shall write no more.

14. In the evening, before the sky darkened, I saw the planet Jupiter as one rarely sees a star. Very small, round, and entire, a separate being poised in space – not clovés dans un drap noir. There was I, there was the echo of the set sun, there was Jupiter – held together by relative positions in space, like a triangle in Euclid. This gave me extraordinary pleasure – I tried to share it, but unavailingly.

18 Torn out of the diary.

15. Valentine signed (*out loud!*) – so help me God and these holy gospels which I touch with my hand – her sworn answer to the Bp.'s official interest in how she and Richard fell out of bed – for the moment, she supposes, the last hurdle in the Grand Ecclesiastical. This absurd Canossa has gone on for over a month, well over a month. If she has resented it, she is a better hypocrite than I suppose: there has been no trace of resentment, except for me.

16.   'Oh, there are wondrous heights to tread
             In every fearful place
             Where the poor timid heir of God
             Lies blindly on his face.'

So I read under May 16 in Valentine's *Holy Crumbs*; and laughed so uproariously that Mrs Chubb looked in to enquire.

[. . .] Ruth came by the 4.5, and I fell blindly on my face and have lain there ever since. I daresay it is the best expedient – if I can keep up enough strength to remain lying, and shun treading those heights.

June

6. Finished *Conversations*. On and off it rains, and the wind blows continually. Suddenly in myself I have begun to feel better; lighter, not reconciled, nothing so feeling, but a sort of carpe diem acceptance. But how much of this is integrated, and how much mere technical improvement, disciplined dodging of awkward subjects & painful remembrances, occasions for sin, I don't know – and won't enquire. She, my poor love, puts more faith in it than I, so much is plain. Yet I sense that she in her world is as much removed and as prosaically thankful for a growth in detachment as I. But again she has spoken of her enjoyment in the bosom.

9. At Valentine's suggestion I spent an afternoon making two dolls to sit in the deckchairs she had bought for Phillida & Emma.[19]

Personality is queer – when one of these dolls is entamé something happens, it develops a character and after that I have no more say in it. It is what the psalm means when it says, Go on, & thy right hand shall teach thee terrible things.

The physical repulsion I feel at the thought that she sticks out her tongue & has a wafer planted on it came up in a dream where I found

19 The young daughters of Reynolds and Janet Stone.

I had a limp white disk in the palm of my hand and said to it – But I wouldn't harm you –

which indeed is true. I don't want to harm anything – only to escape uncompromised, uninvolved.

July

20. Began La Race Maudite: for once, I felt reasonably satisfied, and in the 5 page sentence, even pleased with myself.

Now my mind begins the rope-twist of water that begins to run out. The familiar pleasure & exhilaration of working *towards an end* contests with something almost like terror at the thought of where shall I be when I no longer have this regular and tried preoccupation.

August

4. Alyse to lunch. The moment she got me alone, it was to ask if I too had become a Catholic. I reassured her. Why indeed? But afterwards I saw the train of thought, Valentine & I have always done the same things. Later she began again, did Valentine go to mass, to confession to a great fat priest. A small thin one with a stomach ulcer, I said. Curious, here was my opportunity to confide my feelings in a wholly sympathetic and *not* silly bosom. Yet I never said a word.

27. Stricken with renewed shock & melancholy – a remark of hers had pierced me as being so despairingly *silly* – but walking back from the pillarbox I had a minute of rational perception. All my life I have been dutiful, probably too dutiful, dangerously dutiful anyhow; and tolerably sincere. And a religion that is centred on sacraments, and makes all its position and authority on a claim of being their sole dispenser, outrages me in both my besetting qualities.

Flippancy is the only armour, the only remedy. In the drive, waiting for me with concern, was my remarkable Niou; and in a voice shaken with tears I said to him that henceforward I would be flippant.

29. To Bettescombe[20] [sic] for tea; and with prompt civility we were asked if we would like to see the skull.[21] It came out of a handsome cardboard box in a china cabinet. It is very small, polished, a remarkable

---

20 Bettiscombe Manor near Bridport, the home of Michael and Betty Pinney.

21 The Screaming Skull, in the possession of the Pinney family, is a notable curiosity, said to warn of the approach of enemies.

beautiful feuille-mort colour; no lower jaw, and unusually small narrow upper-jaw, more like that of a child.

Then we saw the house, which is entrancing, with panelling and powder-closets everywhere, and a most agreeable balance of decoration – a sumptuous golden bed, for instance, all lions and cherubim, and quantities of books, and no self-consciousness at all. A well-bred house. After tea, it occured to me, since Mrs Pinney's brother-in-law was a tarot hand, to suggest a tarot reading of the skull. It was fetched out again, laid on the floor, twelve cards dealt round it. Interesting, this: the first card, which by his method sets the key of the reading, was the ace of the material suit; a skull with no soul left in it. The two nadir & t'other thing cards *both* representing servitude (he is by legend a slave). All this may have seemed a fine example of les Anglais chez eux to the French girl who was of the party.

September

5. It rained almost all day, and very hard. The floods are out. O poor cornfields, that grew up so good and true! And poor ploughers and sowers – like my father in the 14–18, seeing his pupils break & die.

All day I have been sad, discouraged, apprehensive – and a poor little mouse gave me my only foothold to life; for it squeaked in Niou's jaws, and Valentine, who had just come back from Dorchester, having got it out, it was broken though alive, and she had to kill it, and it screamed in extremity. I saw her face, ravaged with despairing compassion, and went out into the wet garden to condole, and this suddenly changed her, or unloosed her, for she spoke out of her heart, thanking me for what was so natural, so spontaneous, so nothing at all, as if it were a great deal.

I have worked hard, really with effort; and *La Contemplation* is still not finished.

But I think I have demolished those *valves* in Sommeils. An impulse took me to Larousse, and it is also a term for the discarded periscarpic part of dehiescent fruits – whatever they may be. Husk, perhaps. Better than valve, anyhow.

October

21. I went to the Goulds to see bits of Swan Lake on their television. I had forgotten the feeling of Paradise. I had forgotten that the kind

of body I see, the kind of body I wear, could be lovelier than words, than painting, as lovely as music and more moving than music since the music is visible to one's eyes and refers back to one's limbs. Ulanova is of all the dancers I have seen, Pavlova, Kavsarina, Tchernicheva at her best in the Donne adagio, the slowest: as slow as a sun rising, as a tree falling, as leisurely as a yawn. Her arabesques, her approaches, abolish time. She dances with intense ardour, intense nobility, an *Ariane, ma soeur* dancer, there was a moment when she stood motionless beside a group of swan-dancers, before she melted into their ranks that was Holds all perfection in a little moment. And though it is hard to see in that little box, there was a most exquisite corps de ballet counterpointing her movements and making their bends adornings. I can't write it. I am still in a trance.

November

<u>27</u>. I woke into melancholy, hearing Valentine's footsteps, early massing, and tossed into thinking how like it was to the return from the USA and I heard her typing, typing those letters to a dearest she away. And unfortunately, she came in, and I couldn't disguise.

But I was smartly tossed into more courage by a disconcerting set of pass-sheets, with a balance of exactly 50% less than I presumed. So I sat down and began a story for the N.Y. about gluttony.[22] And Mrs Chubb was restored to us.

28. The story, still no name, but the characters come along – and whatever its like, its not like my loved Marcel, as blessed and tactful in his withdrawings as in his presence. Cleaned the sitting-room from head to foot, and cooked a dinner for Jean Larson. Her hair was in the utmost beauty, and I hope the lace mantilla will not be too thick to hide it from the Pope. It is the soul, the spiritual essence, of honey, and if he notices that it should give him a foretaste of what he no doubt expects. For she hopes to get an audience, not just the usual huggermugger, with two monsignori to invoke. One of them she had to write to, and couldn't think how. It amused me to dictate such a letter, and find all the right phrases under my tongue.

29. Cold, fine, sharp. The story extends, one very spirited conversation. [. . .] Tomorrow I hope to finish the 1st draft, and get to typing. If it don't

22 'Barnby Robinson', *SR*.

pay, I can still get an advance from kind Ch. & W. so I shan't sink. But it is plain that if I don't earn, we live beyond our means. Otium cum dignitate is not for S.T.W.

And really I don't know what I should do with it if I had it. I began when I was twenty-four and have been at it ever since, and it has never been disagreeable to me, and very seldom alarming.

December

23. [A] group of elderly carol-singers came round – their voices were sweet and tuneable, their conductor conducted with his electric torch, its light flashing over wet spectacles and wet faces. It was pretty; and kind of them to come so far, and in Mrs Slemeck's teeth. Perhaps they are Chapel carollers. Anyhow, they were friendly in their merry Christmasses. By dint of long residing, and never interfering, perhaps we are mellowing into popularity.

1957

January

8. The morning at the Winfrith Heath Inquiry,[1] where Sir John Cockcroft was first examinee – a squat, heavy man, with a dislikeable smile, sly & complacent. It seemed odd that science – any science – should so obviously have bred ineffable conceit like his. The Welsh alternative was in the air – and Cock: blandly went on insisting – *a* that Harwell scientists would need to do some of their work at Winfrith, go there for the day to do so; b. that this would be compatible with 90 miles, and 90 miles back, $2\frac{1}{2}$ hours drive – but that it wouldn't do if they had to go further and spend a night away from home. When hard-pressed, he relaxed on his underlings, who knew everything. The counsel, a young man, was very deft with him. They were there in rows, and a shabby scurvy-looking lot. It seemed a far cry from the 20s, when I alternatively wrote astronomical sonnets and dined out on the quantum.

10. All day at the Enquiry. Most of the morning spent on Mr Abbot, Town & Country planner, a man of singularly sturdy stupidity. Then Pinney – no better. Then – withered, and looking like Gilbert Murray, Vera's Sir Theo, Education Committee. A gentleman, an old-fashioned idealist, and alas! – sure that it would be a good thing. Then lunch with Bill & Sybil[2] and my Love – then back for our part. Mrs Rawlinson not as good as in organisation, and hampered by the silly misapprehensions of what makes an association a committee, but quick-witted. Mr Tommy Hooper's 18th cent deeds – with rights of pasture and turbary made a strange irruption. I spoke briefly on the letters after our *Times* letter,[3] and came home on a cold frosty night. It is all no use, the heath is doomed.
   I liked both the Assessors very much, shades of R.T.W.[4]

1 The public enquiry being held preliminary to the building of an atomic energy establishment at Winfrith.
2 Bill Long and Sybil Mason, friends of STW and Valentine.
3 STW and Reynolds Stone had written jointly to the paper on 3 March 1956.
4 STW's uncle Robert had worked for the Ministry of Education.

234

11. I went on feeling melancholy, remembering the beauty of the heath by Tadnol, the nightjars and the sweetgale and the adders and the honeysuckle tangling the little brakes, the peat-water pools that were the colour of William's eyes, and the ash-tree my love prayed to – all to go, all to be trampled on by genteel conveniences. But there was Marcel to attend to, and decisions to make: I think I will translate all the quotations from Bau[delaire]: not merely those entangled in sentences; and then I found charming accounts of Brighton in Dame Blackstick; and finished the little white brocade box for the cornelian ring; and went to bed companioned in commemoration;[5] and so forgetfulness and industry and philosophy pulled me along, as the maenads pulled along Silenus.

March

8. A sad moist day, yet the willows thrive in it. Bill [Long], who now wishes to be called Jane (thank heaven not Chantal) is at the Frampton guest-house, having her Anglicanism removed by a priest in Yeovil – dangerously much at a time, I feel, like teeth.

15. Katie & Alyse came in the afternoon. It is tragic to see Katie bent and shabbied by her stiff back. Yet the fire is there. Alyse, enquiring on about to what purpose does one strive against mobs, officials and atom bombs, asked how I should feel about such vain strivings when I come to die. I said, 'When I die, I hope to think I have annoyed a great many people.' And Katie, suddenly breaking back into the old Katie, rubbed her hands on her knees and shouted out 'That's it. That's it. I *like* to hear that.' I liked to hear that.

26. Bed-rid. But less severely, for my aches were better, and my temperature coming down. So I lay in bed with all the animals disposed about me and heavenly sun outside, and two red roses, and extra pillows, and champagne, and lordly meals on trays.

28. Doing the thing thoroughly – and by now loving every moment of it – I spent another day in bed, and read Shakespeare. O Lord – how lovely. The aged angel coming down the hill; and the queer blandly grim social irony of the speech where the gentleman has drunken Xtopher Sly put to bed, to wake in a gent's heaven. So good, too, the realisation that a gent's heaven is not a tinker's heaven. He wants to

5 Of their anniversary.

go to bed with his lady wife, he thinks the first act of the play is the end.

Then I read *The Winter's Tale*, and *wept* for joy. *Breed* coming out in Perdita the moment she's threatened.

April

26. Duty bid, and I did Valentine's bedroom, and the upstairs passage, and thought of the story of the servant doing the same rooms, only the nature of the objects change, but whether pill-boxes or reliquaries, they are all the same to her, things to be dusted & put back.

In the afternoon Vera, Rachel & Lister [Hickson] came to tea, Rachel holding a baby lamb on her swelling womb, and looking like a slightly inattentive mother of God who had picked up the wrong symbol from the property box. It had a broken fore-leg in a bandage, and sinus trouble which made it snore. Valentine gave it snuff. But played gaily on three legs and pursued the sheep-dogs round the garden. P[roust] preface in the evening. Now coming to the boil.

Vera brought cream & veal.

27. So I spent the morning in cooking, and had fo[u]r meals ready by lunchtime. Too soon must fade the ro-ho-ho-hoses of summer, as I used to sing with Dorothy Wadham. Now there are only two. In the p.m. I washed & worked, and before dinner we drove up past serene bands of bluebells to feed Skimper. Mamma not there.[6]

That evening, late, Valentine tapped on my window. 'Tibby, the comet.' The north-west sky was clear, and there it was, a lance stuck through a constellation. I really did not think back to Halley & my youth at all, I gazed at this lovely remarkable being – a virgin, since it has not been seen, or is it identified, before? Happy fellows who found & forecast it, and now it has come, trusting as a tame bird.

May

7. Out of the blue Reynolds rang up to say that Stanley Morison *likes* our book[7] – so much so that he wants to produce a limited edition of it to distribute as an example of what can be done – and that my poor poems are part of the charm. At the same moment I looked out of the

6 Skimper and Mamma were two of the 'hill cats' who lived rough nearby.

7 *Boxwood*, a collection of woodcuts by Reynolds with 'illustrations in verse' by STW.

telephone window, and saw the first rain breaking the drought, and knew just how the plants & the ground felt. For a blessed stranger called Beatrice Ward had found them moving; and after so long, to rouse an uncompromised emotion –

Jane[8] was baptised a Roman Catholic at Yeovil and Valentine was her godmother. I had refused to go. Sybil went. She is both kinder and braver than I (My courage is quite as far out as Macheath's). They all came in about 5, Jane looking very wet still, and Valentine with a raging headache as well as her bad thumb. Except that I thought Sybil was glad to be here, I would have called on Hell to get them away. It is cold, and intermittently a little rain – but not enough to do more than wash the plants.

8. O, if I could write again – really write, not *FOOL*, how much better I should be.

16. Oh, what a noble mind is here o'erthrown . . . If only I could bring myself to lie, how happy I could make her; but with everything else lost or in hazard of losing, I hold on to my truth as if it were something of importance, though I don't know what for, or who to. I suppose I should feel more desolate without it. As I was thinking this, I had a sudden overwhelming recollection of *exactly* how the water arched over the fall in the Upper Ettrick burn whose name I forget. Grangecleuch, I think.[9] I felt it on my hand, its cold, sleek impetuous, unsizeable force.

Ruth came in the afternoon. And in the evening told me how, eventually, in grave tones, Mr Pye & the policeman told her that 3 copulating couples had been surprised in front of her garage; and how in the morning, the ground was 'a *mass* of contraceptics'.

I did not say three times three.

24. Both of us singularly exhausted. I managed to do a little Mado,[10] & a little gardening – and read Stevenson–Baxter letters. I wish, how I wish, I had a Baxter. But I think only men have such friendships; and Stevenson, with all his friends, had only one Baxter. Baxter's letter at the time of the Henley row, pleading for Henley, is one of the most absolutely *good* and magnamimous expressions I have ever read – a just man, made perfect by the occasion.

---

8 Bill Long had changed her name as well as her religion, see 8 March, p. 235.
9 In the margin she has amended this to 'Rangecleuch'.
10 Story, rejected by the *New Yorker*.

31. After Dorchester & lunching in Weymouth we drove to Chaldon, pausing just beyond Winfrith – where the contours are suddenly so much smaller & milder than love and recollection remember them. The place is as magic to me as ever – it is only from me that the magic has gone. I stand a heathen in the holy place, And question with the gods that I embrace.

Then Mr Webb, grown old, plump, & fatherly, drove us up to Chydyok, jolting in the Landrover. Katie, bowed & grey (only at a *distance*, still startlingly masculine & handsome) and cumbered with cares, Alyse scarcely aged at all, & her sitting room with its Chardin quality & casual eclecticism unchanged. She asked me how I did – there would not have been time to say, so I lied, & she knew I lied. But she has often lied too. We came back over the doomed heath.

July

24. Into Newbury in the morning, and drove to make sure of Ashmansworth.[11] It was very hot, we stayed about in the afternoon, and set out at 6 for the Finzi party, Valentine wearing a new silk dress like a blue fish. It is a beautiful small modern house that already looks mature. We sat on a terrace, then went into the music room, 2 groups of songs, his last, and a Hardy group. In the first group, O Fair to See, a Blunden poem (very beautiful) of a dead baby, and the Bridges, Since first we met, especially. In the Hardy group, Beeny – a rapid lyric like a fall of rain, and a most stately setting of the eclipse sonnet. Then we had a grand supper in the hand with champagne (the Finzi boy persuading Valentine: Have you quite given up drinking'[)] and the songs again. Valentine talked to and liked Edmund Blunden, I remet Navarro of that distant book-sale of Vera's, Robin Milford, Laurence Whistler, and met an amiable Mrs Sumpshion [sic] of Gloucester. Dr S. played, the singer was William Brown. It was one of the best, the most amiable & well-knit parties I have ever known. Candles all over, 21?[12] I asked Joy. 'I bought six pounds' she said. Cascades of swallows, & pears ripening on the wall. Alas, poor Gerald![13]

August

9. It stormed all night. The morning garden a ruin, a bough off the tulip-

11 The Finzi family's home.
12 Nigel Finzi had recently celebrated his 21st birthday.
13 Gerald Finzi had died the previous year.

tree, and the leader sagging. I wrote a page & a half of a childhood piece, enjoyed it, but did not root. I feel that if I had the money to retire on, I would not write – so little is left, so little impetus and conviction.

10. In the evening I sat listening to *Norma* (on records) with Kallas & Stignani. Kallas's fine-drawn pianissimo – like a fiddler's rather than a singer's. I thought of first times – the time when Pasta waited to sing *Casta Diva* for the first time. These are indeed unique occasions. The gale was so intimidating that I asked my Love to sleep with me. She did, and I felt assured, though it was a queer facer to be told she must say her prayers first. It seems as if one said, I must raise the draw-bridge first. In spite of poor Candy's fleas, a happy night.

15. We drove, on a sad grey morning with violent gales and cold as winter, to Wells, and then back to lunch with Steven.[14] A Bible of 1802 with a stamped motto on the title-page, *Spes Manet*. We can still hope, I said as a construe, & Steven laughed in a way that warmed my withered self-esteem. His plain house, which he has made so hand-some, and now his portico is to go up in the field with a walnut avenue – and poplars in between, he thought, wistfully, so that he could enjoy some of the fin in his life-time. He was looking exceedingly handsome, & I begged him to have his portrait painted. Pausing on the way back where Gertrude heard the chiff-chaff, I looked across a half-cut field of pale corn. Dark trees, clouded sky, a line of horizon cobalt, it was as though I were looking at one of my mother's early watercolours, the landscapes of my young childhood.

In the evening we unstopped the kitchen sink – a reviving mud-lark, and like old days.

16. To Dorchester, for hair to be cut. Met Betty Muntz, who said she was a great deal better from her rheumatism, but looked ill – and so much shorter. I *see* the shrinkage of age. This morning, lying in bed, I happened to raise my arm, and saw the wrinkled, withering skin, the unmistakeable skin of the aging. It was as though I looked into such fine wrinkles as into my own grave. Yet I looked with strange ser-enity, and the sense of Baudelaire beside me, looking too.

It cleared, and in the afternoon I gardened. And Valentine gave me a ridiculous pair of earrings from Woolworth's, premising I was not to wear them – but rescinding this.

14 Steven Clark had been a close friend of STW and Valentine since 1936, when they met in Barcelona. He ran his family's shoe-retailing business.

18. It was a fine blowing morning, and suddenly she said Let us go for a drive, and I added, Let us lunch out; and in a short flash we were off, wobbling by Sutton Bingham & W. Coker (such a pretty village) and Stoke under Hamdon & Muchelney, to have lunch at Langport; and on the way home, by Odcombe & Gibbesius Gollop, turned off for the Barwick St John beech-trees, and conversation on that month,[15] of which I seem to have retained so much more, alas! than she. But I drew on my own resources, she on another's – that is why. What one gets from oneself is germane, and memorable. Fed both little cats[16] – dear creatures.

A little rusty meadow, with a mere, off the Yeovil road, where we picked blackberries, very sour, and mushrooms, very good. All this was mutual & delightful.

20. Interval for Metaphysics[17] – and it suddenly took a new ending to itself and became considerably better – though it is a kind of ending I must not employ too often.

21. Finished *Interval*.

My Love brought me a haystack of all manner of sumptuous *gentle* dahlias. Against the sense of doing & duty that now eats her, I persuaded her to sit in the garden for an hour. Afterwards Mr & Mrs Samways came and sat there, much more naturally.

That night, Valentine was wakened by screams and thrashings about. For five minutes she watched, in a beam of her torch, two otters desperately fighting in the pool below. The screaming one held back its head like a woman in an orgasm. Finally, she was able to shout them apart, and they disappeared like bubbles.

22. A conversation that almost approximates to the former estate, so nearly that it gives an illusion of being the real thing, though on a post-earthquake site, or more exactly, taking place in a dream that is almost like life only the view out of the window is Africa – that concludes as a conclusion, not as an intermission, rather solemnly – and later on the revived warmth is gone, and a feeling of even greater hopelessness & frustration whelms one: I thought of this, watching Valentine trying to make a fancy clock go; and the strike rang out, and there was that little chirp & mutter of machinery, and the pendulum

15 September 1949.
16 The hill cats. See note 6, p. 236.
17 Story, *SC*.

wagged & the clock ticked; and while we were talking, the pendulum wobbled, weakened, and the clock was ticking no longer.

28. My final list of poems for the book of Valentine[18] – and after so many readings & indecisions it suddenly became easy for me to know my mind. And to a surprising extent, it turned out to be her mind, too, though she rejected the Landscape with Girl, which I am sorry for.

[. . .] A wholly pleasant deed today, sending £10.10. to UFAW[19] because my good balance warrants it.

29. I gardened most of the morning, & all the afternoon, and finished my damson cheese in the evening – 9lbs, or a little over. Reflecting on mercies & mitigations, I realised how fortunate I have been that I have never for a moment hoped that the old state of things would return. Thinking how I was scorched & shrivelled with misplaced hopes over E.W.W. this is a matter for thankfulness. (The poems have been heaped in my room & no further word said of them. Now, if I had had a hope, how painful this would have been.)

September

4. From time to time, when I happen to be in a vein to talk naturally, openly, and not just about food or plans, I am aware – not that I have run on a rock & torn to pieces, but that the rock lies underneath, & that with the ebbing tide there is much less water to carry me over than I thought. Yet, if only out of good manners towards the past, I cannot hold my tongue & say nothing except practical grunts, pig-comments. Besides, the rock is under the silence, too. I handed over the chosen poems, & came downstairs. And it was an extraordinary comfort when I turned on the wireless & heard Jean-Louis Barrault lecturing about Claudel & the Total Theatre. He was so warm, so passionate, so fanatic, so devoted to what he was saying: it was as if he had come into the room, & with his ardent Latin inattentiveness, had begun to talk to me, regardless of whether or no I was in a state to be interested. Well, I was, too.

22. Fed the little cats on a cold misty evening. But early next morning, when I woke feeling old & melancholy and clumsy with age, and grimly *feeling* the resemblance between my aging body & poor senile Nora, I

18 *Twenty-Eight Poems*, privately printed.
19 Universities Federation for Animal Welfare.

looked out of the window onto such a glory of stars, solitary, unfrequented, secure, *& yet transient*, that I cried out In wisdom hast thou made them all, and slept again, comforted by that enormous transience.

30. After I was in bed Valentine roused me for an inexplicable light in the sky: Aurora Borealis, I said. Strange comment on space wars, space saucers, red skies, etc, that she had not thought of this.

[. . .] In the evening I had to review my will. It must be a life interest, for Janet's sake – though I don't like life interests, they seem so uncivil. But I can't risk Arthur's daughter, and to stipulate would be equally, no, more, uncivil. It is not that she [Valentine] would consciously damage Jan's inheritance; but she is so innocent about money that it might happen through a sudden impulse to build a church, or something like that: and the Wolf of Rome has a keen nose.

October

13. [W]oke sad. G.M.[20] & the cats supported me. I baked good bread. But the house oppresses me, so full of black missals – a dead yet unctuous black – and everywhere some holy artillery pointed at my poor tattered natural levity.

December

9. Horrible news, more of this unhappy island is to be made over to USA. Guided missiles this time; and *we* are to pay for the launching sites!

13. I must have caught a chill on the liver or something, for I felt tired and depressed all day; and then, suddenly, a Light Surprised. At dinner we were discussing the need to do Ruth in the true Xmas spirit. 'We shall have to go about in fancy hats,' I said. My tone was so negligent, so resigned, that the words caught her quite on the hop. She sat up – all in her native Taurus; every vestige of her Roman Catholic demeanour & expression blown away. And I laughed – so wildly, so easily, that from that moment I have felt quite well again, and still feel fresh as the lark mounting at break of day – and have festively put forth on some of the Dorset stichery stitches. They are uncommonly easy. I never thought to laugh like that again – without a vestige of caution, fear, or time-serving.

20 An unspecified author.

1958

20. All day haunted with snow. Forecast in the wireless report, present in the coldness of the air, visible in the few flakes that hung before us as we drove to Dorchester, enforced by the tarpaulined Plymouth lorry we saw there, with snow hard frozen, encrusted on it.

In the afternoon I visited Mrs Chubb. Talk about the child in Holland who will die because a radium needle, snapped off, was left in its nose. House, garden, family, all cordoned off. The daughter Eileen, a rather good-looking, dashing slut, with the fashionable couldn't-care-less manner, suddenly leaped up, like a Theroigne de Mericort, saying, 'And now they have no idea what to do for the child. They can't do anything about it, they don't know anything about it. Why do they do what they don't know how to deal with?' And it was very impressive.

[. . .] And now [Valentine] is going early to bed. I too. As I went out with the ashes, a childish joy swept over me. The ground was white. Snow had fallen. Why does one feel this acknowledging joy?

21. A Swiss morning, said my Love, bringing me my warm imbedded breakfast. Sure enough, there was a sharp blue sky, and the boughs and branches so motionless that each leaf carried its coping of snow as tidily as an eggcup holds its egg.

28. [L]istening to the Wreck of the Deutschland read by Gielgud, I trotted ahead with my second blue-stitchery towel. The W. of the D. was preceded by newspaper reports of the wreck. Curious to read them, and to think of Hopkins. But thinking it over, I wondered if he *did* read them, or got the news through some licensed R.C. paper. Some of it was there. *The tall nun* was described as 'tall and gaunt', and when she spoke with a lion's tongue, she was standing on a table in the ladies' saloon with her head and shoulders coming out of a skylight. H. certainly appears to place her on deck, but the truth is — as usual — a great deal more striking and unexpected.

31. After lunch, and tying a final ribbon to my bouquet, I went to Mrs Lambert's[1] funeral, where for some time Mr Squires and I had to make conversation. Then a lean mousetrap sort of woman came in. Then entered Mrs Lambert, wearing the lightest oak and brassiest conceivable coffin, with six mourners: a daughter with a defiant hat, a great likeness to Mrs L. and an even greater likeness to something by Manet. Mr S. and I again conversationally blended our replies in the 39th psalm. Then the procession on the bier up the road, the daffodils and anemones and brass yelling in the overcast pale day, the Idiot and Hilda in slate-grey stockings, to the cemetery, where the mute put down his top-hat – O so black! – among the snowdrops, and a train snorted and chafed in the station, as though it were Elijah's chariot with steam up to carry Mrs L. to London.

Janet [Stone] stayed to tea, and to see our grand pasts, V.'s Gill drawings, and my Beaton photographs. As she left, she begged us not to see her off. 'Stay here drinking tea'. Valentine, who an instant before had been sitting naked to Gill, remarked 'That would be too much like Cranford'.

March

3. Valentine brought me as a present an avocado pear. Its smooth cool hide, too freckled for obsidian, too cool and with too much play of surface for leather – what is like? The look of a stone *under water, perhaps*. And perhaps that was why I thought so intensely of Tushie-law in the evening.

15. Still at Helen Logie,[2] and in the morning a letter from a solemn ass of Boulder Colorado, who is doing a Ph D. dissertation on Arthur Machen. The A.M. Club is primarily composed of book collectors. O God! O Boulder!

In the afternoon we drove to Abbotsbury to see about bamboos (not till mid-May) and walked a little, seeing peacocks. There were at least a noble dozen of them, the first posed in noble melancholy on a corner of the wall, as complete as a perfect Alexandrine; others scratching & turning their jewelled heads in a border, a young one proudly raising his preliminary tail, yet another walking over the lawn with that inimitable strut, each fine step expressing the length of tail balanced on

1 Mrs Lambert was a former charwoman of STW.
2 Story, 'One Thing Leading to Another', *OTL*.

it; finally, one walking circumspectly on the greenhouse roof, first on the ridge, then descending the slope, with all its rippling canvas of tail blown sideways by the wind.

18. By Way of Ste-Beuve[3] came, an advance copy. I felt the usual jolt into common day, and made no better by a dust-jacket I don't like. But I went & had a bath, and when Valentine came back from her church I gave her the copy – and a little later she appeared with a charming silver heart-shaped urn – I had seen it when she brought it back for the shop, and said it reminded me, as it did, of a similar toy at my grandmother's – Tennie[4] gave it to her I think. And then we shook ourselves, and drove off to Ilchester.

April

2. A brilliant sunny day – cold wind, though – made me feel so well that Mrs Samways remarked I looked younger than ever. All the way back I laughed over this mystical statement – for when was *ever*? Another pleasant event was that the Moir clock was no sooner placed in the larder than it began to go, and has gone ever since. This however is equilibrium, not mystique.

5. Janet [Stone] came in the morning, having done some shopping for us in D. & looking, in an old weatherproof jacket, a fisherman's jersey, black watch trews of much hard wearing, & a pair of short rubber boots, more elegant, more nymphlike and better dressed than I have ever seen her look before. It is odd how English breeding blazes as soon as it is wrapped in clothes of this kind.

May

30. To Bournemouth, on the invitation of Bob & Isa.[5] They met me at the station, Isa with a stately port, and handsomely dressed, Bob quiet & warm & gentle as ever. They were very kind, and full of loving enquiries, and remembered my old cat. They wanted me to stay the night as their guest. Not for a moment was there the least tinge of cutlet for cutlet, of scoring off an obligation. I felt the *nobility* of their manners; yet these old Communists have almost an old-world charm

3 Her translation of *Contre Saint Beuve*.
4 STW's great-aunt Anne, Countess of Drogheda.
5 Old comrades from the Communist Party.

now; social Arcadians, dwelling in a former world of trust in the future & in mankind.

June

6. Jane [Long] & Sybil [Mason]. A torrential rain in the late afternoon. They had come through it this morning. Russian scientists in the South Pacific have been forced to leave their ground because of the strontium density in a rainfall there.

Apropos of Sybil's conversion,[6] V. made the strange remark that S. Augustine was a manichee *before he became a Christian*.[7] When I queried this, it developed that Christians were Catholics from the beginning, that one is the same as t'other. I had not the energy to murmur about the Greek Church. If this sort of thing goes on, this missionising of history, it will be doctrine before long that Jesus worshipped the Virgin Mary – like any other good Catholic.

> Whilst afar off the vessel sails away
> Whereon the treasure of my soul's embarked.

And at times it strikes hard on me that the treasure of my soul is sailing boxed-up with a lot of very deplorable animals.

29. USA has let off an atomic bomb which damaged seismographs in Tokio, 3000 – more, perhaps – miles away. BBC announced this at 6 – said nothing of it at 9.

July

15. Frightful news: USA Marines & what-not have gone into Lebanon. And yesterday Iraq blew up in an army revolution.

I clipped the ivy, Valentine cut back brambles. Janet & Emma came to tea.

16. [W]e drove in late afternoon to Crewkerne where there was a preview V. wanted to see. [. . .] a happy drive – till we hurried indoors to hear the news. Bad. With a sense of carpe diem I picked pears & strawberries. The air was clear, & sweet, and everything I looked at looked back with innocence.

6 She had followed Jane into the Roman Catholic church.
7 From the sense of the following sentence presumably STW meant 'Catholic' here rather than 'Christian'.

This evening dying, innocent of care – so I wrote in 1937 – even then.

17. We have landed troops in Jordan – officially on the request of King Hussein. USSR is having manoeuvres on the Turkish-Caucasian frontier.

Valentine off early to Crewkerne. I picked lavender, & tried to work on the Bell Sturrock story,[8] and hung out the washing in the sun. Poor Janet S. when I rang up about Sunday suddenly said, in a voice I have never heard her use before, Had I heard anything more? Mrs Chubb, equally frightened, and harking back to old tracks, spoke of sending out 'these young boys who don't know anything about atomic warfare,' Neither, poor wretch, does she.

Valentine came back, not very successfully, & with a raging head-ache. She looked so yellow under her skin that I am alarmed and think of another return of her infective jaundice. It wrung my heart when she tried to comfort my misery. Even as she spoke I was saying to myself that we hung on the Soviet self-control. If that is superhuman, this too may pass over. But this is such deliberate provocation – and the American Government is so crassly abjectly stupid (they are now turning on Hammarsjold & the U.N.) – that it will be now or next time.

The N.Y. has taken Shadows of Death:[9] pleasant news on any other morning.

21. The Geneva meeting uncivilly & indefinitely put off.

Wrote various buggle-letters in the morning, in a room where yesterday's honeysuckle is so sweet; and in the p.m. in my little house[10] I set myself to copy out the few things I didn't want to lose from the /49 diary, and burned the remainder. Shut up in that domestic little donkey-boiler, it flared and roared as loud as if those days were still alive in it, and I stood by with an oddly empty heart at the obsequies. But better gone, I think; and now, irrevocably, gone.

28. In the evening we drove to Wareham through a modified version of the morning's gale, but just as much rain; miserable holiday cars were foundering at the sides of the road, with their doomed passengers striving for picnics: one was even cooking on an oil-stove, which he had protected

---

8 'A Question of Disposal', *SR*. The character in the published story is called Bell Kirby.
9 Story, *SC*.
10 A small summer-house in the garden.

with 3 saucepans. At the Black Bear Rachel & Marc[11] dined with us. And were the better for doing so, I think. Chablis flew to Marc's head & left Rachel sober as a Dresden china judge.

One of their bulls pulled its stake, frightened itself into a frenzy, & charged her. She nipped behind a fence, on a bank. While the bull was tearing up the bank with its horns she looked round, saw the gate across the field was open, went off & shut it, & only then went to find Marc. And she is seven months gone with child.

We drove back in the late dusk, very stormy, pale, vexed, & romantic; & paused for a wet interval near the Moreton brook, while Candy wandered. I smelt this year's fleabane. Curiously pungent, a sort of rural curry smell.

August

6. A noble piece of colouring out of my bedroom window this afternoon. The whole sky loaded with a violet-purple thunder-cloud, like a ripe fruit in the sun; the trees very green & foaming, the phloxes in the garden white & crimson, with yellow splashes of gladiolus & evening primrose – & in the centre of this splendid reverberating composition, the bleached thatch of the old barn – a skeleton colour in this parade of the pomps of the flesh.

13. It was the day – I had almost forgotten – when Joy Finzi was bringing the Vaughan Williamses. They would come early in the afternoon, she said; but we were just beginning lunch when she stood on the doorstep with her Saracen nose, saying they could not picnic in the rain, could they sit on our doorstep. So we set them in the diningroom. Ralph refused all offers of hot food. It was his bread he wanted: he is only allowed to eat bread on holidays (apropos, Ursula's story: Ralph only dreams music, but the other morning he said, I've been dreaming about a yellow cake with sultanas in it; and we went out to tea, & there *was* a yellow cake with sultanas in it). By [the] time we descended with coffee they were feeling their well-buttered paws, & a delightful afternoon began. I had a long talk with V.W. who asked why I had given up composing. I found I was doing nothing of my own. Originality! pooh, stuff & nonsense. The essential thing is to go on composing, never mind who it's like. Authenticity, I said, not

11 Rachel Hickson had married Marc Helfer the previous year, and now lived at Knitson Farm, Swanage.

originality. He gave me a long look, & said, against the grain, Well, you showed unusual strength of mind. But in my next incarnation I think I shall be a painter. What about you? Music, said he, music. But in that world I shan't be doing it, I shall be being it. All the Druid came out in him as he spoke. Still about composing, he told me that after Brahms's death, pious musical executors found a notebook with a good many entries, inscribed *Good Second Subjects*. Meanwhile Joy & Ursula were buying quantities, with loud cries, in the shop. But before then an enquiry about the American, reported by Howard Ferguson as going to write an opera on *The Flint Anchor*, introduced Paul. His grand opera, his lovely slighted chamber opera. U.V.W. was off at once: the new opera company, insolvent of course, but television has been tapped. This made me very happy. Joy came in, laid her hand on Ralph's shoulder, & said, We really must be going, Gerry. She read it off my face, alas! Departing, she gave me a long, groping, almost demanding glance, as if to say, Does this one understand? – and then stooped down & kissed me goodbye.

R. reminded me so much of Arthur Machen, that cross between an old woman & an old mountain. Its the mountain of their Welsh blood coming out, I suppose.

Valentine went to bed for dinner. I wrote to Paul & to Joy.

25. Valentine's knee no better.[12] I drove into Dorchester with her. It was blowing, & cloudy. But as I walked towards the Bank I became suddenly aware that I was in Heaven. Heaven was a perfectly clear blue sky, a rainwashed air, & the light falling on St. Peter's greenish grey stone. A small thing, & very brief. So might heaven be – no longer than the surprise of finding oneself happy & unblamed.

Janet [Machen] & the children came after lunch, en route for Chaldon. Valentine had brought back innocuous foils & masks for them, they fenced on the lawn, where Matthew[13] ocasionally had to stand on his hands for pleasure. He was in heaven too – but more accustomed to it.

[. . .] The children were discussing our ages. Matthew said with decision, Sylvia is about thirty-five. Janet, faintly voicing reason, asked him why he thought so. I know she is. She laughs so much, said he. *Ex ore infantis* – but I am certainly surprised, at the statement and at its basis.

12 She had hurt it on a visit to her sister.
13 Matthew Davis, Janet Machen's younger child.

September

5. An invitation to give the Peter le Neve Foster lecture on *Women as Writers* to the Royal Society of Arts. February 11th. I felt pleased, & competent. Agnes Paston, saying in vehement Norfolk What about ME? sprang into my mind. Other emergences were Murasaki & Mme. de la Fayette; question of why women aren't composers germane; Sévigné. Court society servile, at best pug's parlour. Jane Austen & Flaubert. *J'attends le coit de ces beaux volatiles.* J.A. under no such compulsion. Her simple theme. Boy meets girl. Girl gets Boy. George Sand. George Eliot. Odd she should have been taken as a man – except that at that date so many male writers could have been taken as old women – but AM I SURE?

Mrs Radclyffe, Mrs Browning, Ctina Rossetti.

Colette. Virginia Woolf.

Womanly qualities: nice calculation, neat stitches, industry. But also a particular freedom and intensity. Julian of Norwich: Colette & the champagne bottle.

After all this I retired serenely to Norah's hat-box.[14]

N.B. Should I – yes, I must – read Selma Lagerlov?

Language was given us in order to conceal our thoughts. Look up exact text. NOT a feminine outlook.

We jointly cleaned the refrigerator.

19. In the morning I listened to the Vaughan Williams ceremony in the Abbey.[15] First, his Dives & Lazarus variants. I had never heard them – they are echt V.W., with that power of imaginative invention, phrase growing from phrase like rose-wands. Then the Bach Con. for 2 fiddles. The slow movement at the slowest tempo I have ever heard, ripe for eternity. Then the Sons of the Morning pavane.

Then the funeral itself, Croft, Ps. 104 (bless it!) and Greene's extraordinarily moving & accomplished (better than accomplished – *coherent*) Lord, let me know my end. V.W.'s choice. His ravishing O taste & see before the ashes were taken to the North cloister, and finally his Coronation All People – sung soberly, almost sotto voce, till the last verse with those exploding trumpets with their air of going off in the wrong key. Valentine came back from Dorch. in time to hear the last half. And the BBC delayed the weather & news. Almost as grand as an Abbey burial itself.

14 A *découpage* intended for Norah Smallwood.
15 Vaughan Williams had died on 26 August.

[. . .] Gerald Finzi's Hardy songs were sung – not well – in the evening. A *jour des morts*.

28. Janet S. rang up to cry off, nevertheless Phillida & John Nash came in the rain. He is short, spare, dry, detached – the type that is called shy & is not shy at all, but self-possessedly wary. He gardens on a bottomless alluvial loam, on the Essex-Suffolk border, & belladonna lilies are a commonplace to him. I imagine he is a good practical botanist, apart from his *Poisonous Flowers*.

Then I began to sew a small brown brocade pill-box, & then Ruth & Tony Scott[16] arrived. My first sight only showed me the unlikenesses: a ridiculous snub & snubbed up nose instead of that tranquil little aquiline beak, and a height slightly below mine instead [of] slightly above – then, as she glanced and the same airy wrinkles displayed themselves round her eyes & mouth, I saw only the likeness. She *is* like Maud. She has the same outlook, alert and demure, the same tune of voice, the same regard: she gives the same impression of a person who succours, who shelters, who comprehends, & who is incapable of trespass or exploitation.

October

14. In the evening the Amadeus played opus 132; and I danced to the last movement, I rose up & danced, among the cats, & their saucers, and only when I was too far carried away to stop did I realise that I was behaving very oddly for my age – and that perhaps it was the last time I should dance for joy.

24. Between Horning & Winterton, we drove to Sheringham: & as we neared Smallburgh, & passed signposts saying Sloley I felt the same sort of hapless disturbance that the muddy ditchwater in the Essex marsh must feel, rising with [the] rising tide beyond the sea-wall, the salt sea from which it has so long been cut off, differentiated, alienated – *not estranged*. It was as though some part of me, some separate me inside myself, were going back to Frankfort with Valentine, quite naturally, quite normally, from some ordinary expedition.

December

7. The last of the Reith lectures by the radio-physicist, Lovell: the

16 Ruth was the daughter of Maud and Constantine Moorsom, of Harrow School, and STW had not seen her since her youth. Anthony Scott, the composer, was educated at Harrow.

galaxies receding; a minute ago they were 100,000 miles nearer. The Abbé Lemaître's theory of a primitive cosmic atom, intensely concentrated, set centrifuging by some cosmic impulsion or explosion. But why? Why not the gravitational pull of space? Nature abhors a vacuum.

1959

January

14. Typed, revised & finished *The Quality of Mercy*.¹ Surprised, as usual, to find that it is the sort of story I write; I never feel, when I am making, that there is anything typical or characteristic about what is in hand – but the brand is there. I hope not too much there, that's all.

19. To Dorchester. There we saw Monica [Ring], looking so ill, so withered, so lifeless, that my heart staggered. V. was talking to her, I went on to finish the shopping; afterwards, as we drove on to Wimborne, I said something must be done to rescue her. One cannot see anyone so drowning and just sigh on the brim. And, as I said, she has everything, husband, child, home, that is supposed to constitute a woman's happiness. Pooh!

20. High flood, & rising. Mrs Chubb, deathly pale, asked me to ring up the hospital to enquire for Maureen who had been taken in for an operation – 'something to do with her womb'. Desolately, when I came down from this, she was standing by the sink, talking to Valentine of Maureen's resolve to marry this shabby young man, of decayed heredity, who already beats her. Of marriage, as opposed to courtship, she said 'Its very different when you've got that plain gold band round you.'

After lunch I looked out & saw the river in the garden. Then out to my little house, water on three sides, a fresh cold air, as if I were sailing down a river. Valentine stayed awhile, took some snapshots, left me with a cup of coffee – leaning out of the back window with coffee cup in my hand, like Frau Noah. Then I saw two exquisite very small birds, coloured silver & pink, the plumage of puss-willow buds, long black tails, & went in to enquire what they were. Long-tailed tits.

Later on, desperately dredging, I found (I think) a story to write,

1 Story, *IG*.

253

also a Q. of M.[2] The vulgar illicit transcended lovers asleep on the four-poster bed. A couple called Pilligrew, a rector, a swarm of bees all settled on the body of this theme, & a long quietened coda.

26. Drawing freely on Caleb Simper, I went on with that story[3] and the same thing happened that happens: a puppet character turned round & bit me. It is where the vulgar-minded woman says the fake lacks sincerity. This surprised me so much that I went meekly to bed.

February

11. [Ash Wednesday, London] V. was ashed early. Then to Whiteley's & Art & Book. I could find her no suitable shirt in the A & N. Then we separated, & I set forth to drop the hat-box at Ch. & W. & then to Boulestins. I was there first, early. Strange to sit there, & think of kind Charles, who wouldn't come in. What did come in was Leonard [Woolf], Ian & Tr[ekkie],[4] Norah, & a Betty Crichton-Jones – or something. Would women prefer to mate by the luck of the winner, as female animals mate? or by ballot? Talk ran on green things: Leonard's Hellebore, our Balkan butterfly. Leonard was three years in the Ceylon jungle, with a leopard so harmless that it played with his spotted deer, riding on its back. Only the monkey disliked it: but one day he found it hanged in a tree. On to R.S.A.[5] where there was a splendid rotund marble gentleman, Dr Ward, in the entrance, & a horrid microphone, which daunted me through my speech, & a kind audience, which applauded much more than I had conceivably expected. David [Garnett] was there; & Betty Pinney, Roland & Nadia [Gant], Bea & Mark [Lubbock], Ursula [Vaughan Williams], Joy [Finzi], Victor [Butler], the Day Lewises. David's proprietory air. I suppose one never loses the sense of a woman possessed.

28. Daring all things, & obeying John Nash, I attacked the nerine hill, & took down ⅓rd of it. Replanted it, planted a colony of about two dozen at the hollyhock corner, and put by 12 for Bo, who has been so kind about Candy.[6] John Nash was right about overcrowding, but I only hope he was equally right about replanting. Meanwhile Valentine

2 'Quality of Mercy', the title of another story, see 14 January, p. 253.
3 'On Living for Others', *SR*.
4 Trekkie Parsons, Ian's wife.
5 Royal Society of Arts, where she was giving the Peter le Neve Foster lecture.
6 Recently ill.

was in church. Bo on the telephone was uneasy about her resolve to go
in to early mass tomorrow. Needs must when the Devil drives, I said,
calmingly.

March

2. A book of Breton Calvaries from dear kind William; the R.C.M.
Vaughan Williams number from Ursula, [. . ,] a sad note from poor
Nancy who is being driven into a hospital for tests & examinations.
And earlier, the sound of rain, a lovely sound, & rare, after this very
dry February. But Valentine was melancholy & abstracted; & when I
had done some washing, & ordained the 3rd row of peas, & the
rhubarb covered, & the lawn-mower cleaned, & cooked pigeon &
pommes lyonnaises for lunch, I felt uncommonly done myself.

However, in the afternoon I made a Victorian cover for the spare-
room stool (its blue brocade finally shredded by Candace), & in the
evening finished the curtains, & hung them. Valentine depressed,
reading all those letters of Ruth's that Katten bequeathed her.[7] Indeed
they are melancholy enough: R.C.A.[8] perpetually ill & tired, Joan
perpetually cross, 'my Molly' perpetually ill & angelic: & nothing said
that is her, no deed, nor word. There is, however, a great deal about
Mr Green & his spiritual harem, among whom Ruth seems to have
been a spiritual Mme de Pompadour, always providing new Souls for
his jaded palate.

Extraordinary to set them against R.V.W.'s span, so fruitful &
hard-working & *practical*. It is the *practical* nature of the creative artist
that in the upshot stands out. They are the plain hard-headed men in a
scurry of dreamers.

10. (A week ago – and it seems interminably far away and long ago.)
When I got to London I went to Whiteley's (coming from the
underground I saw in succession, a negro, a chinese, a white man
reading a book) and ordered that suitcase for Valentine. Then to
Nancy, wan & worn in her handsome flat overlooking the Regent's
Canal; but not liking it, & feeling drained with 'nervous asthma' and
anaemia, & aches. We talked about Africa, & mysterious Spain, &
Roma's return. I was sad for her, she looked drained – and Lord knows
what that hospital won't do to her. Then to Norah's, where Rose

---

7 i.e. letters from Ruth Ackland to Katten Hallward in Valentine's possession.
8 Valentine's father.

brought me tea, & I dunked a gingernut in it, & looked at *Lolita*: a dreary piece of lubricity, an extemporisation on a harmonium, pump, pump; & a shocking case for the battle to be fought about. In came Norah, & she too is again anaemic; but Lord, she looked so pretty, appearing in a black lace petticoat with my grandmother's pendant sparkling on her white rose skin. Then Ian, & then we trooped off in Norah's new Jaguar – yours? Both ends of it? – to Victor's. There we dined at length & leisure, with smoked salmon, & *new* potatoes; and after dinner Ian spoke of his anthology of the up to datest scientists, *none* of whom could write plain English, & how everything must be translated. My Father, I began, wrote a book about ... Norah intervened, we were all talking our heads off. Later, Victor said, Sylvia's father wrote a good book about how to write English;[9] & pulled it from a shelf, & handed it to Ian. O my darling Russie, after all these years, you live. Ian began to read, began to read aloud, was entranced, wanted to reissue it. We stayed, talking & talking till nearly two in the morning. A heavenly party, no affectation, & no claptrap, & NOT A WORD ABOUT THE NEIGHBOURS.

12. [Jugg's Corner, Kingston][10] Birds, several delightful wakings, then down to walk in their garden, a quick breakfast, & away. 'I cannot understand homosexuality, can you?' remarked Trekkie as the Lewes grammar school boys decanted onto the platform. We went via London Bridge, where I suddenly recalled Lucia having doubts about Boileau.

Then on an impulse, I drove to Devonshire Close. No one there, no car, but a charwoman offering tea, & saying they[11] would be back soon. They weren't – after a while she produced a note to her from J.W. saying that R. had had a heart attack. I rang up; & listened for hours on a disquisition from which emerged that R. was coming by a later train; that V. had heard overnight that Candy must have her womb out; that V. was waiting for me at Whiteley's. At last I broke through, rang Whiteley's. She [Valentine] had left a note to say she was gone to see me off at Pad.S. 12.30. I caught a taxi, got there just after 12. I saw her, waiting, tall & sternly composed. As she saw me, as I waved my hand, a current of love arched between us. Let me never forget this, for it trampled on years.

9 George Townsend Warner, *On the Writing of English*, Blackie & Co., 1914.
10 The home of Ian and Trekkie Parsons.
11 Joan Woollcombe and Ruth Ackland. Devonshire Close was Joan's flat.

<u>22</u>. Palm is out, & the wind & the rain-storms whirl it away. Anemones are out, too, & the early daffodils, and blue primroses & the frilly white one V. gave me last year.

In the afternoon to the last Music Society concert:[12] Gioconda de Vito, a solid, grave, embattled woman, with a superb large bullneck – pleasure to see her sternly settling the pad on her shoulder, a privy smile vouchsafed when she had got it right. She played that dull Leclair sonata, then Brahms in A. I could have yelled for joy as she swept along the first entry of the theme. Then La Folia: the cadenza most enthralling, for she managed to make it sound extemporised, & it almost flagged, & then rose with whirls of wings to the close. By now she was looking rather pleased with herself. Then the Kreutzer Sonata – in which Ernest Lush played with great brio, & Beethoven substantiality.

Then on to Stinsford, where I remet Henrietta Bingham,[13] each assuring the other with the warmest hypocrisy that neither had changed in the slightest. Her eyes are the same colour, her voice the same rich low bellow, and something of the pear quality hangs about her; but it is a pear no teeth could sink into. Indeed, it is a pear with teeth, for she instantly seized on Valentine, con amore.

<u>27</u>. This morning, by some adjustment of spring light & moist air, the Schalken picture[14] suddenly came out of its den of varnish, & smiled on me as it had done when I was a child – for about 30 minutes or so: then it retreated again. It was curiously moving – as if, after so many years, a face had looked out of a window, its hand shielding the lamp, & a voice had said, Come in, child; it is too dark to play any longer.

April

<u>17</u>. Last minutes. Packed. A sad interview with Mrs Chubb, who has been courted by that doomed child, Maureen. Her charming swain, to express his little pique, jerked up her arm & punched her in the armpit. Strange that such behaviour should exert an irresistible charm: but when I told Valentine, she said as a matter of course that it would re-rivet Maureen's determination to marry, & bring forth monstrous births in Rural Lane.

12 In Dorchester.
13 A noted American beauty in the 1920s, who had been part of the set surrounding the sculptor Frank Dobson, and a friend of Stephen Tomlin.
14 An oil painting attributed to Godfrey Schalken, now in the Dorset County Museum, and the subject of a story by STW, 'The Listening Woman', *NY* (May 1972).

July

3. V. out all day with Miss Buller.[15] Her headache was better, 'almost gone', but came on again when she got home, & after dinner turned to a dizzy attack. Eye-strain, liver, or a vitamin deficiency – the deficiency of pleasure? In this serene summer weather she is never pleased; & the only interest she expresses is in the shop; which for the moment goes well, though it needs incessant letters, lists, & packing.

27. Despatched *A Dressmaker*[16] to N.Y. A good theme, but the writing is laboured because I found it a labour to write. My Mrs Jelks rising to sing He was Despised, & a flash about empty milk-bottles rang true to me. It took three weeks, too.

August

3. A cool Bank Holiday.

After lunch Valentine told me about M[eredith] R[oss]'s soi-disant vocation. Her wisdom & diagnosis were extremely impressive. [. . .]

I admire thoroughness, grasp, professionalism. She has all these, professionalism of faith. I ought, therefore, to feel reconciled. But I don't. Like the devils, I admire, & tremble at this enormous & growing distance between us.

15 A co-religionist.
16 Story, *SR*.

1960

January

2. Valentine took Ruth away at 11 a.m. It was just beginning to be a mild spring day – and we had a brief moment of looking at the Goya book together, the stiff, good, stupid little boy in scarlet, with his birds and the two cats: an epitome of Spain.

Then in a stupor I cleaned R's room, in which her last act had been to press on me a drawful of crumpled paper-bags which might be useful; and make a clean bed for my poor love; and to clean [sic] the sitting-room floor. In spite of all our precautions, the carpets are considerably the worse. With mild thankfulness I ate a speechless lunch of two sardines, the remains of the Brie, and a bottle of lager. Then I sorted the larder, and made a curry. And threw away my Proust proofs, for what silly sentiment to keep them. And when I rang up Apsley Farm' the line was out of order, so I do not know how the journey went. But the invoked Alec undertook to let her know that I had rung up and was alive.

I am so tired I can scarcely creep; and the house is still full of unresolved messes, relics, and confusions.

7. Still cold. But Mr True² came, and painted the old garden seat. It lies upside down, looking foolishly, decrepidly summerlike; but not so funny as the three white chairs on the lawn, that lean forward over the white table like three surrealist spinsters in ardent destruction of someone's character.

10. And shakes this withered heart at eve

With throbbings of noontide –   So I thought this morning. But also the analogy of the old shrub, cut down to the root; the new growth that straggles up is *young* growth, weak, vehement, & sensitive. So, one's feelings emerging from mutilation when one is old; an inappropriate, *inexperienced* intensity & surprise.

1 Apsley Farm, in Sussex, where Valentine's cousins lived.
2 The new gardener.

23. [. . .] I came in, and went on with A.L.R.[3] When I look at the extent of work before me, the reading, and revising, and then the copying, I feel rather as if TCM were before me again: however, Sco-Mo translated all those pages, and what one monkey can do, another monkey *bis*.

It would be less laborious if I could speak of it to anyone. However, if that collaborator turns up, this may mend.

V. came home having had a vehement conversation with Ernest Hardy.[4] She had begun by asking if he approved of Adenauer's fisticuffs proposal: he exploded against it. Then, whitening, he let out; against the sheepish submission of Austria, and against the H. Roman Ch. 'He could have murdered me,' she said. Very natural, said I. When you see someone patently good, intelligent, respectable, and converting, and think they are ranked with your enemy, your esteem for their good qualities intensifies disagreement to hate and fury. They parted friends, she said (she had spoken of Spain, and had, of course, to correct his natural misapprehension: odd, if this didn't rock her); but to be on the safe side, I rang up later about a Phaidon Rembrandt – and his voice was calm & defensive, so I am glad I did. Little by little, I have come to have some understanding of what one feels, living in a strange land.

[. . .] Now I am listening to some calming Indian classical music, with all the charm of a reasoning one can follow about a subject one cannot grasp.

February

12. Snow in the morning, enough to blanch the ground, but not lying, and turning to a fine rain later, varied with melting feathers. Extremely cold. Shopped in Dorchester & had a word with Mr Florestine about his righteous mercy to poor Roy,[5] who was flitting about in the back of the shop like paper-ash, so grey and weightless. The other man is that wretched creature on the way to Frampton who lives with a devoted domineering mother & can't call his soul his own, and tries to go to concerts. The only comfort is the change in public opinion since

3 Proust's *À la Recherche du temps perdu*. The new Pléiade edition of 1954 established a text which had no accurate English translation. Chatto & Windus were planning a complete revision of the famous Scott-Moncrieff translation, and had approached STW.
4 A bookseller in Dorchester.
5 An employee, accused of homosexual acts.

I was young: but that won't be much comfort to Roy, and change in public opinion may not be very evident in juries – anyhow, it is a plain flagrante delicto case.

17. Brilliant sun, snow still lying. I think I have a cold in my head. But while I walked to the butcher & the post-office I thought no such thing, for the bright cold air was such rapture to breathe; and then, for pleasure's sake, I went on beside the smoothly glittering, rapidly flowing river, to inspect the snowdrops in the churchyard. They are really no better than snowdrops anywhere else. I suspect visiting snowdrops in churchyards as part of English folklore. I remarked how the course of time had embellished our churchyard by adding so many people I know to it. In the afternoon while Valentine swept the car I pruned lilacs of their own superfluities, and of encroaching pink roses. That was the last of my well-doings, for presently I began to feel hopelessly becolded and went to bed after dinner on the coldest night of the year. Candy was clipped, poor inappropriate luxury article.

18. Snorting cold, so I shan't see *The Cranes are Flying*,[6] alas! And it has got into the south-west corner of my jaw.

But I saw the heron fly past, above the river, so close that I could see every feather in its banded wings, every detail of its sagging flight. It was going very slowly, cold and hungry, I expect. Feathers are more cheating than fur even. Only man exposes his woe.

I was put to bed for dinner by my Love, and gave way with disgraceful expeditiousness. Indeed, I felt singularly chewed.

March

15. [W]e lunched with great courage & detachment, and drove to Dr Jarrett – where I sat for nearly an hour screwing myself up for the worst.

What she has is temporal arteriosis; a rare disease, an inflammation of the artery; and if it spreads, the pain spreads and is extreme. But the area affected is small, and he could find no other signs of it, and said that it was remediable, since she had gone in time, and that he hoped to get the better of it. The treatment is cortizone, not very auspicious since she may have cortizone sensitivity along with all the others. [. . .] So here we are. She liked him, believed him, and will I hope observe him.

6 Film.

16. How soon one accustoms! I woke with the feeling of being already on terms with this new anxiety.

28. I worked on Miriam,[7] and got her over the switch from passé défini. And this morning came a long, plain, perhaps slightly lay-down-the-law letter from Andreas Mayor.[8] But at this stage, I am glad if he lays down the law; it shows he means work.

He does, too. He wants to revise S.M's punctuation.

This evening, coming on Valentine with unexpecting eyes, I saw that she is definitely thinner – a thing to be thankful for, provided it does not stem merely from sleeping uneasily – as she does, with vivid dreams. This last, though, might be hunger quite as much as cortizone. I gauge this by being hungry myself, though I eat more bulk than she.

May

9. C. 49.[9]

Summer-blue – a momentary change of pressure, when the air became full of swallows; and just enough rain for Niou to draw my attention to his wet back.

I weeded the necromancy bed, under a canopy of bees, and washed with the scent from the oleagnus. All the apple trees now, instead of the pear: the cage-tree glowing like a sunrise, the river-tree and the old tree crowded with a paler blossom; the little tree almost white.

That tiresome Joan [Woollcombe] rang up, and harangued Valentine about all the trouble she has taken to find out about t.a; and how she should duly gratefully go to London.

She went to bed assuring me she was drenched in Eau de Lourdes. Whatever it is – and why not E. de L.? – she again assured me [the pain] was less extensive; and I saw her pass her hand over that side of her brow and remain sure of it. The hand was calm & fluid in its gesture, that is to say: *not forced*.

June

2. And this morning I had an invitation from Leonard Woolf to talk to his Literary Society about French Literature. And instantly my mind began to dance and invent, and see the red-haired scabby shabby youth

7 Presumably STW's story 'In a Shaken House', *SR*.
8 Her collaborator on the Proust project.
9 Forty-ninth day of Valentine's cortisone treatment.

in his provincial boots entering the Salon Bleu to have some of the Seneca shaken out of him. I accepted it as instantly as I instantly refused a Foyle lunch – C. Day Lewis, poor wretch – in an interminable telegraph invitation for June 25th. Wicked waste, silly ostentation. Oddly, Valentine wanted me to go: half-really wanted, I believe.

9. The Mayors came to lunch, and were introduced & paw-buttered by our cats, tactfully arranged on the jessamine wall. He is tall, brown, thin, an air of the former Angus about him – very bright filbert-coloured eyes – shy, a slight stammer. [. . .] Lunch was singularly good, sweetbreads, florentines, hors d'oeuvres with superlative asparagus salad in cream – and Vouvray, but neither of them drank it. Pretty, too, the coffee and florentine air of the table, with the large cut-glass bowl to rinse our fingers in.

After lunch, he & I went off to Pr. He is going to be a comfortable collaborator, for he is careful, acute, scholarly – & not bee-bonnetted, I think. Various small points we mostly agreed about. He hates the Julien illustrations – he would include the pl[ot] résumés – end of each vol. & index. He accepts *que je butine*.

17. C 88.

She came in; looking scornful, set, and yet ravaged. A letter in her hand. Hollins cum Jarrett[10] felt that there should be a 'very minor operation', to take out a bit of artery for examination. It would not entail more than two days in hospital – and might stop the pain altogether. And if it didn't they must set about a new diagnosis. I could see how she felt. She felt SOLD.

Late in the afternoon we went to see Katie. Her grey cat sat among the sweet-williams. She goes to the Weymouth Eye Hospital on Friday. I sat in the garden with Lucy while Valentine went in with Katie. Presently we saw them through the kitchen window, shadowed. Don't they look strange? said Lucy. As if they were behind a veil. True goblin daughter of that goblin race: it was as blood-curdling as anything of T.F.P.'s.

23. Joy during the night was moved to advise, to persuade V. to try the witches at Oxford. I listened, while she drew.[11] Gerald, not good at operations, was boxed through the removal of his spleen, and the next

---

10 Doctors.
11 Joy Finzi was drawing a portrait of STW.

day sat up and dictated to her for several hours in perfect possession of himself & his faculties. This swayed me. Feeling that I should muff it, I asked her to speak to V. Going to & fro, I heard Joy urging, & Valentine – beginning to agree.

25. I fell on the story that will be called *A Work of Art*. And proof of Hugh Whiting[12] came, with a letter from William to say that *The Children's Grandmother* has been chosen for the 1950–60 anthology.

Seeing my abstracted looks, my Love roasted the chicken.

We visited Katie in the Eye Hospital. For a few minutes, while she inveighed about the noise in the men's ward next door – which reminded her of sermons & hated hymns in her youth – she was very near madness.

She also looks extremely ill – more so, perhaps, being out of her own home.

While I was talking to Lucy, she made a passionate avowal of her former love, distraction, all night wanderings, to V.

26. That night, as she was going to bed, she suddenly remarked, in a rather taken-by-surprise voice: It has just struck me that I am feeling very well.

It might be the diminution of her Cortizone – but –

27. In the morning we heard from Joy that she was on the box.[13] Kind dear Joy had acted immediately, & got everything going that could go.

I finished the story, did the proofs – and walked to the church in a Sabbatical hat to examine the harmonium's stops. Its lid came away in my hand, and it has no stops. On my way I admired the Anglo-Saxon's[14] rose – a Hiawatha, I think, No one prunes it, no one sprays it, no one attends to it – it grows & rambles all over the mound of the ruined house, the lost house – and I have never seen a rose in more glorious beauty or more perfect condition.

But when I came home, full of roses and harmoniums, V. was listening to the 6 o'clock news. And USSR has walked out of the Disarmament Conference.

---

12 'On Living for Others'.
13 Joy Finzi had contacted the witches in Oxford – See 23 June 1960, page 263. The box was part of their equipment.
14 A cottage in Maiden Newton.

July

4. A very suitable date on which to get a letter from Nancy to say that she is in an asylum, having been certified insane, after having been arrested on a drunkenness charge, with police evidence against her & the magistrate accepting it. If she had had a house in London she said, this might not have happened. But why certified, instead of being sent to jail. We each wrote to her. I wrote also to Roger Senhouse, Anthony Thorne, & Diana Cooper: waistcoats & diamonds seem the best allies to invoke.

23. [T]oday she said that she was finding it difficult to focus with her right eye: and she has now been off cortisone for a week.

And nothing happens.

And Joan on the telephone did one of her most earnestly sadistic flesh-creepers.

Listening to Parry's De Profundis as I roasted pork, and as if to something unknown, the first solo entry came at once out of the performance and out of my memory. I knew it as well as though I were the singer. I breathed & phrased it. And recalling, I found it was at High St[15] I knew it: 1913, perhaps. One preserves a time so completely intact – for I hadn't given it a thought since – that one feels like an airtight jar when it comes out again.

Prou'd.

And this morning as I came along the passage, I met a baby bluetit on the top step of the stairs, as on a peak in Darien. The *coarse* perspective of our human stairs.

August

2. We got to the hospital at 2.30,[16] & the room at first sight seemed charming, shady, with a huge window & a door opening on a roofed terrace with untidy flowerbeds & a walk beyond.

In fact it was not so perfect. It soon became small & overcrowded, & then a MOTH[17] appeared. I went out to shop for her, & when I got back, a further blow. The operation will not be till Thursday. Ross Steen's[18] preference: possibly sound for the body, but ruinous to the

---

15 The house at Harrow School (now called Bradby's) where her father was housemaster.
16 Valentine was having a piece of artery removed from her temple.
17 Valentine had a physical aversion to moths and butterflies.
18 The consultant.

state of mind. I came home very sad, wrote various letters for her, telephoned the change of plans; then telephoned King to be taken in again that evening. I got there at 7.30. She turned a resigned face to the door (people incessantly go in & out). I knew how right I had been to go.

10. In the afternoon, having set out to clean the glass of her shop cupboard, I was fired to go on and clean all the windows. I had cleaned all but three when she came in. She was not as pleased as I was. Indeed, it is seldom that the pleasure of those who are ministered to equals the pleasure of those who minister: *vide* my latest short story.[19]

I rang up Janet, to remind her that if she ran out of money I could provide by telegram. She has a grace of accepting – a sort of filial grace which I find very easing. Valentine did accounts, but thank God decided not to do parcels.

[. . .] BUT she should not have got up so much; and she is talking of dressing tomorrow. What is it I do wrong, why won't she stay in bed and let me look after her?

25. Dr Hollins came. He came into the house like a ship, so bulky and so smooth-moving. Impossible not to feel confidence in a man like a ship. He told Valentine that the block[ed] artery was probably arteritis – though sedimentation rate & the absence of enlarged cells also make a clot a possible explanation. And that she need have no more fears for her eyesight. So I wrote in the evening to take her off the Box: which she didn't believe in, though she urged me to go on it.

September

5. Today to see Nancy. We lunched at the Cricketers [. . .] a notice in the ladies W.C. above a cluster of little paper bags: Please make use of these receptacles in order to avoid choking the drains. Baffling if one were a foreigner well-versed in the English language.

Then to Nancy. An enormous Victorian pile, blistering in the sun: a long walk through corridors, then let into the ward, & locked in, & shown to a more social corridor where we sat at one of a row of little tables, while Nancy was told. I was, I suppose, so surprised to see her still alive in this hygenic limbo that my heart rushed to her & was momentarily warmed. She was very affectionate, asked anxiously after

19 'A Work of Art', *SR*.

Valentine's health, looked at us lovingly; but she is *ill, ill*. Something has died in her, perhaps her objective has died in her. Meanwhile she may be getting out on Thursday, to stay with Louise Morgan. She must stay under someone's roof, that is the terms of release.

It was too long a drive for Valentine, & when we got back she was exhausted.

October

4. Still feeling rather lack-lustre, & deafened with quinine, I set off for London – where at dinner – poor Ian, poor Norah, poor George Painter,[20] who had arrived full of kind pleasantness & looking even *more* youthful because he has grown a *bacca* beard – at the Garrick it was made plain that Scomo & Miss Scomo[21] are prepared to throw everything to the wolves rather than allow a single revision to their uncle's text. Against stupidity the gods themselves fight in vain, but I'm conscious that stupidity is too simple & charitable a conclusion – there was such patent malice too.

5. I came home, feeling ill as well as discouraged. When I walked into my room & saw the black & silver box with all my work in it, & and all Andreas Mayor's work on my work, I felt as if there were a corpse in the house.

My kind love, herself staggering with aftermath of entertaining Bill AND Sybil, put me early to bed, & lay beside me listening to Alan Lomax folk-song recordings till I fell asleep.

13. Valentine went off to Wareham, to lunch with Vera & Arthur, to spend the night as E.W.W.'s guest at the Black Bear. I finished the proofs, & began a new light story *Hattie*. I spent the day at it, in great pleasure, & went to bed laughing like a jackass at a silly joke of my own. But it damped my flourish to remember that my Love never laughs like this, so foolishly, so light-heartedly. Though I told myself she has other pleasures which I do not feel, I went sobered to bed.

November

9. The fog had cleared. Driving north of Oxford we saw the first rumple of the Midland contours, large & unemphatic, like mid-ocean

---

22 George D. Painter, the biographer of Caxton, Proust and Chateaubriand.
23 C. K. Scott-Moncrieff's nephew and neice, who were his executors.

waves. Near Luton we also saw M.1.[22] We lunched at Hertingford-bury, and at Dunmow she delivered her things for Mrs Chiswell with smooth speed. Then we drove on into lovely Suffolk, how it combines amplitude with modesty, a model to the English mind; and settled in Long Melford at The Bull. We walked up to the church. It was a great deal further than it used to be. Too dark in the church to see much. And I failed to find the heraldic windows.

During the night I felt so close to Mrs Parker that once I felt myself flying along the dusky road where the wild roses had been so tall on my way to join her. It was her last kindness, of so many, to give some part of me burial in that dear earth.[23]

10. Through Lavenham (we stopped in the church and heard a quarter struck) and then out by Brent Eleigh. It was a road neither of us knew, & exceedingly beautiful, plastered houses & rich timber. At Heigham we stopped because of a church on a rise of ground. Inside it was pale, clean, sweet as linen, clear windows, an east window patterned with trees beyond (I had forgotten how very annoyingly that Long Melford east window is interrupted by the lady chapel roof line beyond). It was an exact expression of what I had said the day before, that the empti-ness of a church is its holiness for me.

11. To Mr Fokes, who abounded; then to Bartrams; finally up Hamlets Street, where she found two more shops, affable & profitable, and where we bought brown shrimps.

These, overfed though we were, we took out in the afternoon on a drive to Burgh Castle. We did not find Burgh Castle, though I think it may have been the village where we drove round and again round, regreeting the piebald horse and Mr Kelf's stationary van. So giving it up we drove to Fritton; & again failed to find lake or church, but did find Waveney Forest where, looking down on watery flats, we ate the shrimps, and listened to the wind.

It was strange & reviving to me to be in Norfolk without all my pleasure being tattered into care & dissatisfaction; & as she said, Not to have to go back to Mr Pye.

22 The new motorway.
23 Mrs Parker had asked to have a photograph of STW buried with her.

1961

18. I was sweeping the stairs, and as I did so, I was asking myself what difference did it make to such an act that my Love was a Roman Cat. Just then a very pretty light soprano singing came to the door. It was Mrs Candler, bringing groceries, and singing to herself on this wet yet rather springlike morning. My silence, I thought, must seem to her morose. Morose perhaps was the word. It is the lack of a former impetus that I felt as I swept the stairs. The thing that made the action fine has gone. The small things, though, keep their old validity, *provided I have no hand in them*. For going into the kitchen I was immediately refreshed because the robin was eating the Dundee cake in the string bag. Dear Bobbin, with his ruffled plume & faded breast. And perhaps a like pleasure sometimes visits her from some thing or other she sees me do.

Andreas Mayor sent me some more green sheets – his translation of Le Temps Retrouvé.

But thou, sail on . . . I feel sincerely glad that he can sail on;¹ and for my own share in the general frustration, I really would not give a paper-fastener, except that it is a frustration to the others, & that I am so much afraid that it will impair my easy relationship with Ian & Norah.

Six swans brimmed up the river, & stayed to feed, looking demandingly at the house with narrow severe faces. After a while, the male swan tilted his head & listened. We could hear nothing. But a minute or so later a seventh swan like a seventh seal flew overhead, & down river, and instantly they turned & swam down river at his bidding, his warning, his – what?

---

1 Because Scott-Moncrieff's executors would not give permission for his text to be revised, the project had been cancelled. Chatto & Windus had to content themselves with a new version of the part of Proust's novel previously untranslated by Scott-Moncrieff, *Le Temps Retrouvé*, and Andreas Mayor was undertaking it.

26. Posted the 13 stories,[2] & then on to have tea with the Stones. It isn't as it used to be. I felt Janet straining to seem pleased, to *be* pleased; & Phillida has had her hair permed, & it has ruined all her nymph looks; & Reynolds was morose, gently morose, but like a large quiet animal that has been hard-driven. [. . .]

Driving back from the Stones, on the hilltop we were stopped by two gipsies, a man & a woman. A baby was ill, if we were going near M.N. would we ask the doctor. There were two caravans, rocking in the wind, shaggy half-seen ponies feeding about, & between the two caravans a fire and figures huddled round it. There was a strange contrast, yet an alleviating one, between these people & the rich Stones' sitting-room. The man, as V. said, looked friendlily – which Tom-gipsies seldom do. When we stopped, relief *flared* on their faces.

February

1. A strange day – for I worked on the Swan's Nest,[3] & even, for ten minutes or so, *wrote*. This unusual animation may have been caused by the double dose of anti-Asiatic flu I inadvertently took this morning.

Parson's new van-man routed out an entirely new Miss Warner at Cruxton & left the coffee there. Advised, we drove out to fetch it, & I met Miss Warner's handsome cat – a massive dark tabby, very affable with black velvet breeches like Parson Woodforde. Odd to look into these old cob cottages and see them all sparkling with electricity & modern contraptions. A mercy if this saves them, for they are solid & home-like.

But the muddied lane was appalling – sad cows standing hopeless, up to their knees in wet mud. The child driving them had disappeared – swallowed up by the mud, I suppose.

8. Candy brought home by Mr King – very sorrowful. Poor Kit appeared to be lost all the morning, in fact he was in the coal cellar. It was a horrid morning, but I don't think the coal cellar would be any mitigation. He yelled, hearing me pass, and came out plump, smooth, unreproachful – just a trifle surprised. I have not got influenza, but I do not feel well. I am de-illuminated.

Days alone are not what they were. This was a quietly wet one, a kind of poetry in it but of a trivial grieving kind.

2 Of *A Spirit Rises*. There were fourteen stories in the published book.
3 Presumably her story, 'A Spirit Rises', in which the poem features.

10. The Universe: Cambridge scientists announce that it was probably caused by one immense explosion, and is gradually thinning out and away; but again, after expanding, it may begin to contract.

A breathing out, a breathing in. For a wild moment, I could conceive it.

20. Mr True not coming, we supposed he had influenza. I hoped to garden, but got no further than juggling sweet peas, since the morning was curtailed by an early lunch. To Dorchester – on our way we saw a very healthy Mr T. sweeping his doorstep; but no time for unkind enquiries – to have our neglected hairs done. An hour & a half of blissful repose for me, hearing about Mr Martin's jackdaw which slept with the cat & followed Mrs M. mère when she went into Weymouth to shop.

Then in full hair fig we had tea at J.J.[4] And on our return found Mrs Batten's kindissime, richissime ray lamp on our doorstep. With care & diffidence & trepidation we consulted the oracles, & prepared to use it. Just as Valentine switched the ultra violet on my naked form, Candy made her way in – not wearing dark glasses. All to begin again. I was vainly saying Shoo when Valentine majestically walked out & returned with the carpet-sweeper. Exit Candy.

Afterwards, this exhibition of ready resource struck us as funny – at least what could have struck others as dementia.

27. Valentine bringing a catnip mouse from Dorchester dropped it between Niou & Kit who lay in more than oriental slumbers before the kitchen stove. It was like a dropping a new idea into the Athenaeum. They became conscious of, while still not stirring, a joint growing consciousness. Then Kit seized on it, rolled and rolled in an ecstasy, lay stretched out with wild glazed eyes, not like the Athenaeum any longer.

March

5. Waking at 3. And feeling a blank of desolation I got up and walked about for a little, to walk off my depression and the pain in my side. When I went back to bed the cats took sweet care of me – as though they had planned, arranging themselves round me with politely flattering purrs. Waking as usual, I had the strangest impression of this month of March, a glittering narrow crescent along which I must walk

4 Judge Jefferies' tea shop, in Dorchester.

towards my father's birthday on the 31st; and that he stood poised there, on the extreme tip. Going to fetch clothes from the airing cupboard I saw Valentine's table loaded with oblateries. So I was right. Alas, alas! But it is her life, and I am twelve years older than she – and it must seem very sad & hard to her that I cannot listen and rejoice.

A most beautiful serene day, with a very faint north east wind. We sat drinking after lunch coffee before the house. Then I trimmed the jessamine, and did a little gardening – but felt too dispirited to do much. Thinking of places I could hie me to – after all, other people go blamelessly away for visits – I found there was really nowhere; [. . .] there is the rosy visit to Trekkie & Ian. But how shabby and displumed I have let myself become, I have *consented* to becoming.

June

18. Bridget Vaughan,[5] her husband, her daughter Juliet, came in the afternoon. We had tea on the lawn. I was strangely confused, and kept on thinking that Juliet was the little girl at 113 Inverness Terrace. She, Juliet, just as they were going away, leant out of the car with her toy of composition pansies for me to smell; and Dorothy's eyes looked at me out of her face. A pretty child, with pretty ways.

That evening I sat for a long time thinking back to the Warnerium, and the disasters that blew it to bits. My going to Dorset, I'm afraid, weakened that cheerful fortuitous structure. But Dorothy spoke: 'Let there be no remorse'.

19. Let it be set down, and marked with a white stone. This afternoon I pulled the long rattan chair onto the lawn and sat there for over an hour, Niou companioning me. I heard the baler going round and round the hayfield, its regular outburst of sound as it reached our corner being like a strong beat in a bar. I looked at the willow-trees, and the birches, and listened to the rainy poplar, and snuffed up the rose that is not Ippolite. At intervals, as my knee goes on hurting me, and I hirple[6] in my walk like Amy Mearns,[7] I feel a desolate responsibility about what will happen to the garden without me, what will happen to me without the garden. I have mislaid so many cares in it, so many indoor cares.

5 The baby from 113 Inverness Terrace, Bridget Warner.
6 Presumably a dialect rendering of 'hobble'.
7 A local woman.

Then Valentine came back from Mr Vincent, and I did some gardening.

28. The piano tuner came – just when I needed him for purposes of study. After he had gone, I began to play some Chopin – and Valentine returning from Dorch., insisted that I use the empty afternoon to play on. So I wallowed like an old hulk through the Pastoral Sonata, and the first Sonata alla Fantasia. Odd, but true. My hands are less out of practice than my eyes. I have almost forgotten how to read a chord.

July

1. Very hot, still, sultry. Valentine packed, against Monday, I sorted against leaving her: we were lying down in virtuous repose when Janet came to take me to Chydyok[8] in her van.

The water-splash at Winfrith is gone, otherwise the village seems unchanged. Mr M[ackintosh]'s hideous bungalow mars the old lime-kiln approach, but from there on the twin-ash valley, and the snake-shaped valley were exactly the same: only the track up to Chydyok is stonier, & rougher, from more traffic on the farm. Janet drove with dauntless discretion. Alyse's parlour, so dusky & mothy, is now a cool uncluttered room, and there is a good new kitchen. The garden a waste of wild grass; Katie's roses still blooming amid it. We sat, we saw two loads of rye go down the valley, we dined, talking of Arthur & Purefoy, and the clothes 'to match' that Nora bought the little Janet. After dinner we sat out, watching the storm gather. Because it would not be possible for Janet to sleep out, and her bedroom smelled of new paint, I remembered hay in a bucket. The air was heavy with the enormous crop in the barn, ten foot deep of it and warm as an animal in the main part, a great wall to roof beams on one side. We hurried out in the sudden blackness & whiteness of the storm, the lightning repatterned in the blackness & whiteness of the chalk and broken slates underfoot, and snatched hay, and were just going to bed when the light went out. Janet cried 'I've put my hand in a mug of milk', and I answered with 'I've found my teeth by lightning'.

Violent rain – and the queer unreality of rain noises in a house of unknown gutters.

3. Looking back on Chaldon, it seemed so rich, so richly pastoral,

8 Janet Machen had taken over the lease of the house in 1959.

though it is poor country, thistles and flints. But richness of colouring, amplitude – amplitude of days, richness of feeling.

And that *city* of hay packed into the Chydyok barn.

5. I sat for a while listening to a *No*[h] play; [. . .] extraordinarily slow, belching, hideous declamation and arioso, both solo and chorus, the very antithesis of the delicacy & poignancy of the text: like Papal Bulls and Papal Pigs roaring, squealing & grunting: and very beautiful snatches of a mad-scene flute; and those wooden hammers urging it on. It is almost unassimilable, would be quite, if it had not an authority of extreme technique & tradition. Then in the dusk, I blooded all my gentle roses; & finally wrote to Ludwig[9] – an honest letter, since at last he knew about Valentine.

7. Contre mon gré, I have agreed to be absent when Joan comes here – I don't know when, but it is to be for four days.

I do not want to stay with anyone, except Trekkie, for four days. Trekkie would leave me alone. No one could want me for four days, anyhow.

9. A great burst of Côte Sauvage.[10]

And a great tract of Hope Muntz,[11] talking like a grass-cutter. Some of her stuff is interesting. She isn't. She brought the comfortable Betty, sad, and bored, and looking an old woman. Arterio-sceloris [sic].

Strange that Valentine, whose health is so much worse than all these, should look so young, so stately, so elegant, with scarcely a grey hair or a wrinkle. One would say that pain is a preservative.

14. Rain and wind and a great deal more Côte Sauvage.

Valentine all loveliness and grace with her hair freshly clustered by Mr Martin – who will be leaving next year, Heaven help us – came in to say goodnight, and said as well that she loved, that she loved me; and looked scarcely a day older than when she said it first. O felix culpa – for this had been provoked by a rather painfully cautious discussion about East Germany.

26. Everything is going to be much more expensive. 6d more on every parcel & 3d on each gallon. So helpful to the shop.

9 Ludwig Renn, the left-wing German novelist, whom STW and Valentine had met in Madrid in 1937.
10 *La Côte Sauvage*, a novel by Jean Huguenin, which STW was translating for Chatto & Windus.
11 Sister of Betty Muntz, and a painter.

And the Western Allies seem bent on buggering the Berlin negotiations before they start, with slam-down speeches & moving troops. Oh God! Why can't they leave it to the U.N.? That misbegotten veto, I suppose.

August

2. A fine fair morning, darkened by the looming approach of Katie, Susie, & Count Potocki de Montalk[12] – for a while it seemed there might be Lucy too, to add her witch's cat terrors to an awful party. It *was* an awful party. He is combative, loathsome, pitiable, and trailed his drawers continually. We were tired out with snubbing, batting down, coldly ignoring, by the time he went. And Katie is grown so old, so broken, only a noble childishness remains, and staggeringly behaves so well.

6. I heard a motorbike stop at the gate, Candy begin to bark. Visitors, I thought, and heard my Love say, Here's a bull. She appeared clasping the yelling rescued Candy, & we whisked into the house. The bull went quietly down past the phloxes, followed by Mrs Eyre & the policeman. Cooing noises from Mrs Eyre, silence from the bull & the policeman; then they went away. It was the Eyre bull – a pretty young Hereford.

Meanwhile a Soviet astronaut is circling the earth, and will probably continue to do it for twenty-four hours. He is called Titov. 110 miles up, & weightless, he eats, does exercises, observes, reports, & radio'd down to his dear Moscow citizens that he wished them goodnight, as he was now going to sleep.

23. This evening, unprovoked by me, I hope – except that I am inevitably I – a lacerating conversation. She would give her eyes, she said, her very eyes, to have me of a changed mind.

27. While I was in my bath, the next story, which I had despaired of, miscarriage having followed miscarriage ever since June. I leaped out, to write quickly what had arrived: precious little, a precarious cobweb. And during a morning of this & that, I thought it would die.

But hooking & crooking, and sternly holding my nose in the narrow

12 Count Potocki of Montalk published a derogatory pamphlet about the Powys family, *Dogs Eggs*, in 1972. Susie Powys, christened Theodora Gay Powys, was adopted by Theodore and Violet Powys in 1933.

path, I got enough of it to know Lavinia Fenton & Mr Naylor, & the house, and the woman, and the pear-tree, the pear-tree.'[13]

And crawled out, reeling with fatigue, to cook grouse for dinner.

Niou is much improved by grouse; he still looks wasted, and walks distortedly, and saves his leg. But he now supposes he can do it.

28. Worked on *Happiness* – fatal fluency. This story will contain several harsh digs at myself. Knowing it is myself, I shall no doubt soften the digs.

September

15. Wandering round the shop, I chose this and that for Christmas presents: the soldier for Joy F., the ivory hand for Norah, the loveliest jug with roses for Ian & Trekkie; and so began to make a list. Then we went to Dorchester for my hair; and I bought some pipe cleaners & pulled out the old wool box, & began to pad a shape for a ploughboy. I had intended him to be stumpy, rustic, *a clown*; but the accident of a knot of wool supplying an elegant neat little behind, & the pleasure of breeching it, overcame all my intentions; & he stands half finished before me, a gay limber young man; a character on his own. Character is the most astonishing thing. Whenever I set to to make a doll, and think only of technical problems, what to cover its legs with, piecing roses in old cretonne for a rosy face, suddenly, & quite without my knowing, it turns into a Person, it comes to its own life. Now I have to make a pair of boots, a pair of hands, a raffia wig and a smock-frock; but the person is made already.

16. His smock-frock transformed him into an oaf. This was very Marxian: the garment expresses the grade of labour, we then judge by the garment. A great many gay limber young men must have gone this road. [. . .]

Shakespeare, I thought too, was typically provincial town; his countrymen are extremely well done, he is conversant with them, & even more conversant with their work & functions; but he is urban, & despises them; except in the lyrics, where poetry gets the better of him, or in moments of pure creative genius, when he does the old shepherd in Winter's Tale: yet there is despising even here.

13 Story, 'Happiness', *SB*.

October

30. All [shoulder pain] gone but the haunt. A much colder night. Mr T. displayed a solemn jubilee over the new roller; and cut down the willow which was smothering the ash; and forked in preparation for the Murrell roses which were announced this morning.

I have spent most of the day twiddling over Christmas presents; and [as] usual, find dozens for Vera. Meanwhile, USSR has loosed off its 50 megaton bomb; and Stalin is to be removed from the Lenin tomb. I wish neither decision had been made. I remember that snatch of voice I heard twenty years ago, when he was addressing the October revolution meeting. It was so substantial & so calm – an instrumental voice, like old Friedrich Schorr's singing Wotan. Then, at any rate, he was neither mad nor bad.

November

23. I have a large balance. 6 N.Y. stories, added to a prosperous last year. I am almost a wealthy woman, though I continue to behave as a poor one. I noted with amusement that I paid bills in old Leonardian[14] envelopes, on the heels of this discovery.

14 Re-used from Leonard Bacon's letters.

1962

January

19. Snowdrops have come up with a rush, they are in the stage of holding their noses straight up in air, & looking like cherubim badgers.

24. It was wet, & not a day to see Bath at its best; so I settled down to a story which may be called *The Beggar's Wedding*; or may not; and after a stagger or two, since I have written nothing since Cornwall, a long spell of nothing for me as I am now, found myself trotting on not too badly; though I am still on the outside of Cedric, though I know Ottilie as though she were my old stays. The moment I called her Ottilie she whisked into life. I propose this to become rather a long story.

29. A silver frost, the first orange crocuses. The air so still with cold that earlier I had woken to the noise of an engine shunting, and snorting, as imminent as if it were in the garden; and the old phrase, the iron horse, rushed into my mind, I saw its height, its blackness, its steaming streaming mane, as though I were my father as a boy. He loved trains all his short life long. [. . .]

When Valentine referred to Elsie Yetts, who has now become part of the background, as wonderful for 80, I said with feeling that I hoped I would never be wonderful for 80. This distressed her. It led to embraces (my God it is embraces I still want) and to the animals' food tray being arrayed, and an early bed. But I should not have said [it], though it was not ill-meant.

February

13. Another windy night, and Valentine went off early to Mass, Ruth's birthday,' and I felt sure the car would be blown over. Even though I

1 Ruth Ackland died in June 1961.

think dates have little hold over me. Strange, too, to think of Ruth in her timeless Aquarian year. I think of these things, I never succeed in saying them. [. . .]

Beggar's Wedding suddenly rushed forward, telescoping two days into one; & I am so near the end that I tremble; and then calm myself by recollecting it will all have to be written again, because of the different tempi of beginning & continuing. It can't be less than 12,000 – probably nearer 15,000.

Almost certainly a piece of total unprofit. But writing it I have, after so many short stories, tasted the queer excitement of giving my characters enough rope to hang themselves. And of course, of course, industry has redeemed Ottilie. I expect it is all a form of self-glorification.

18. In the evening I finished & did up La Côte Sauvage.

And now *The Beggars* lies on my table – and how *nice* it would be to be settled down with it. No doubt of it, even now, I love my profession.

20. Colonel Glenn finally got off & into orbit during the afternoon. There was a final delay when his liquid oxygen flowed in the wrong direction. I listened, it was extremely painful – a modern auto da fe, with damp faggots.

March

4. She told me she would start at 11,[2] to match the midmorning thaw. By 11.40 she was standing in the hall, a carton under her arm & Kit on her shoulders.

But this evening, while we were talking, I was suddenly reft out of myself, and was in the post-Yeovil evening waiting for her return from London. Everything was there; the mist in Cornum,[3] the misty round moon, the feel of the logs I stacked to get them out of her eye, Thomas on the windowsill watching me . . . the whole rigour of hope.

There I sat, the same woman in the same house, talking quite placidly about Buckfast Abbey goings-on; and there I was in the autumn dusk & chill. It was appalling – not a pain, but almost an

2 Valentine had been on retreat at Buckfast Abbey.
3 The field which lay between their house and the village of Maiden Newton, and which they owned.

abolition. I waited to hear myself fall in half, as a cleft log does, suddenly, & in surprise.

15. In the kitchen I looked out & saw a glittering French grey span: & it was the heron, who settled in the river, his long legs in the water, his wings carefully raised like a paddling woman's skirt. There he stood leaning his long neck down stream; then with a heave of his wings, his back, his neck, he rose & flew after his gaze.

21. The sun shines, but the air blows cold, & I hung out the washing with hands going blue.

The evening was pure bliss, for Valentine put me to bed before dinner, & there I reposed listening to the 32 variations – *very* heartlessly played – and feeling warmer & warmer, & righteously idle. Idleness is righteous if it is comfortable. Uncomfortable idleness is sin & sinful waste.

25. Virtuous acts – I am too drained for anything else. Washing in the morning – and while I was hanging it out I noticed that the holly tree is now about 4 ft above the level of the eaves. In the afternoon I sorted drawers, & mended my Newton Abbot shirt to go to Italy. And listened to Messiaen's Catalogue des Oiseaux. The first time I had liked him. He has worked out a genuine piano resonance for the bird songs that are so nearly cries; a very fine Oriol in an oak tree; its sharp bitter-sweet summer voice. A passage of choral curlews that nearly undid me & perhaps most impressive of all, an Alpine chough flying alone up a snowy pass. The birds are realist-formulae; the backgrounds are landscapes – very much as in old bird pictures, the landscape suitable, picturesque, & entirely detached & background. This indeed I enjoyed.

May

10. I woke up *knowing* that I wanted to write, and knowing what I wanted to write about. And began the Waxham picnic.[4]

It is odd that after this long and agonising interim of fret and complete drought, I scarcely even feel relieved. I just feel confident and forward-going. And I have not the slightest notion what set me going again. I was not. Suddenly, I am.

4 Story, 'Heathy Landscape with Dormouse', *SB*.

July

6. Valentine dined with Meredith. In the dusk after intensive cooking, I wandered in the dusky garden. Cats & roses – and this morning darling Niou coming to sit at my feet as I stood talking to Valentine; and now sitting on my book, purring and rubbing against my lips with his head, his wild-silk head. Cats & roses – it should be enough.

But I sometimes pine to be found worth eliciting, to be found enjoyable.

9. A sultry day, with tempest gusts of wind, and promise of thunder, & of rain – and performance of neither.

And the USA have let off their hydrogen high altitude bomb, to coincide with the first day of the Peace Conference in Moscow. However, Mr Churchill's leg appears to attract more concern.

December

20. Suddenly fine, sunny, sparkling: astonishing beauty of the very few yellow leaves left on the ironwork of bare boughs. They look placed, not left. Jean Lathorn and her mother (Keith Henderson's sister) came bringing a dolls' house to the shop, and staying for lunch, and enjoying everything and being delightful.

And when their car bore them away I basely left all the washing up to Valentine and tore out and got all but one of those Murrell roses in that had arrived a week ago and been sheltering from the rain ever since.

Frost this evening. The sound of the bell practice would have told me so, even if I had not looked at the fire-opal clear sky.

January

6. A thaw so slow as to be imperceptible – except for a few lumps of it falling off the roof. Still a grey lid, half-starved birds; and now another wind howling. And Valentine still in bed,[1] and the drive still blocked.

7. It goes on. I feed the birds every morning & afternoon, I feed the animals, I feed Valentine, I do the fire (bless it) and the cats' trays; and little enough – but by the evening I am so tired I can hardly put one foot in front of another. The snow has not yielded at all.

9. A scouring east wind. The coldest day yet. And no hope of a let up.
   Valentine insisted that she must move about. She got me breakfast. She was up till 10.30. In bed she felt cold and tired; but not for long. Because of the wind we gave up all hope of Dorchester. It would be death to her.
   The gale is so bad that no food could be dropped to the starving animals on Dartmoor. Foxes devour the frozen sheep.
   One rose: the Hazidim book from Helen[2] arrived. I realised it will make something for the 12th. No chance of getting anything for it while we are housebound.
   We have not been out since Dec. 24th – first frost, then the snow.

12. Another night of hideous frost. Blinded windows, deathly silence; and Alyse rang up to say that Katie died at 10.30 last night.
    A fire has gone out. I am glad for her proud sake, but I shall miss her irreparably. Who shall I find to speak out loud & clear as she did? Music, though.

22. We drove out into the village. It is like a foreign town, something from the Switzerland of my youth: frozen, *scentless*, deadly pretty-pretty in its colouring of painted houses and white ground and background.

---

1 Her back had been injured slipping on ice.
2 Helen Thomas, widow of the poet Edward Thomas.

In the afternoon Valentine, who had been bird-feeding, called me out to see the lynchets in the western sunlight. A French impressionist's canvas; rosy pink, yellow gleams, mauve shadows, and a pale turquoise sky above. But stranger still, the wind-smoothed, frost-ironed field behind the village: a pure strong unmitigated French grey: the very colour of cold. This put on by *a house-painter's brush.*

23. We drove to Dorchester – with one slow majestic skid near Wrackleford – like a dowager waltzing. Valentine said of meeting approaching cars – very few of them – that it was like Thomas and his orange friend crawling threateningly on their bellies towards each other; and smoothly avoiding and swerving onward.

We shopped; and I recovered from my fears, for I had been considerably frightened, when she gave me a rich rewarding lunch at the Antelope. She drove with the utmost skill and said she enjoyed it; but afterwards, and walking in Dorchester, she felt extremely tired.

Relays of little Chases[3] bathed. Their main is frozen, their cottage full of plumbers who can't discover where.

I did a page, my God! a page of Machen.[4] I also suffered a spell of agony, as Kit got out after dark; and not long ago a local cat was killed by a fox. It was my fault, my negligence, that he got out. He came and cried on my window-sill, enormous with cold. I carried him on my shoulder to the warm kitchen, and said how thankful I had been to hear his angel-voice; as I uttered the foolish words he yelled Waa-ow! in my ear.

26. Listening to Schubert 9th, and the first sfz[5] in the second movement I was suddenly back at 113, with Purefoy beside me at the old Broadwood, and as we brought off a remarkably unanimous & precise sfz she muttered 'That'll wake 'em!' The fellowly vulgarity of artists who give of their noblest & best.

28. The thaw goes on, piano piano. We still feed the birds. Kit thought he'd assist, but the slush offended his delicate feet: so I came back up the drive like a figure of English Charity, supporting that enormous cat under one arm and scattering my bowlful of chopped apple with the other hand.

---

3 The children of Sibyl Chase, a local woman who at various times gardened and cleaned for STW and Valentine.

4 An article for a centenary celebration.

5 Sforzando.

But today began, when we were getting the food ready, by Valentine seeing a dead heron in the river. It was lodged under the brake; as we watched, it detached and floated slowly downstream: as if, she said, it had paused with a message to us. It looked extraordinarily flat in its rigid pattern: like a squashed iris. How one death fills up a river, I thought, as it floated out of our sight.

February

11. Finished Bathrooms Remembered, *Leg after leg*, indeed . . . I have heaved such tired legs forward; and put it in an envelope; and though I can't blame them if they send it back again, I shall be both peevish and fractious.

26. Anonyma[6] sent on a letter from George,[7] writ to her in his own hand – but very shaky, she said. And a parcel turned out to be a book of poems by T. H. White, inscribed with immodesty 'from an unknown worshipper.' But modest withal, for there was no address beyond a post-mark of Alderney. Some of them I liked very much: partly no doubt because they are of my own way of writing.

The sun shone, more aconites emerge, more snowdrops, all stiff upright as if they were frozen; and Blanc de Coubert & Roseraie de l'Hay have small red buds on them. But the cold is intense, and sheets of ice preserve the original snowdrifts.

March

4. Valentine brought back the first narcissus. 'Shut your eyes. Smell.' A slightly mouldy smell, increasing in pungency, then in sweetness as my breath warmed it. Provence, that field with the cherry trees, was round me, and I opened my eyes on that clear rust scarlet and white muslin white.

[. . .] Valentine uneasy about Hollins' prescription of a stilboestrol pill, and tried and troubled with her waterlogged feet. 'Like walking on hot water bottles' she said.

Both of us early to bed, separately dispirited.

6 Anonyma Bingham, a friend of George Plank.
7 George Plank (1892–1962), the American artist and designer. He lived most of his life in England, and had many influential friends, including Lady Cunard, Edwin Lutyens and Henry James. STW had been introduced to him by Anne Parrish. They met only once, but conducted a long correspondence.

7. Mild, moist, gentle; the garden full of snowdrops, and the soil so freed that Sibyl[8] was able to work it, and get in shallots & broad beans.

And I finished, revised & enveloped *An Aging Head*.[9]

But Valentine is no better. This morning, when I mentioned to her the possibility that the snow was radio-active, a reason for everyone feeling so unwell, I found she thought so too. Our radio-active electricity bill was £30 – and that merely an estimate, since the man couldn't get here to read the meter.

My own ailments thin out: I scarcely notice them now. And this is very useful and convenient. But sincerely I would prefer an easy heart.

20. [W]e drove to Beaminster and lunched and slightly shopped there. Mr Cox with more news of Hardy.[10] He whistled always on the same note as he went about; & every evening went round the house with an oil-lamp locating cobwebs, & calling the servants' attention to them.

April

4. It turned cold & grey in the morning, and by the time we got to Coventry the sun was out, to show the Cathedral glass. Her first impression was Selfridge; but it is not Selfridge, it is a strange phoenix. The phoenix with its flashing unfolding wings of glass *has a voice*: the loveliest echo I have ever heard, a gentle continuous cooing & murmuring. The Sutherland tapestry does come off: the crucified Xt the finest thing in it, a bleached broken tree. But what I admired most, after the echo was the engraved west glass wall, with the view of people coming & going, and up and down the steps in the roofless remains of the old building – counterpointed by those etched glass angels, as though one looked out on the world one had died from. I thought it deeply moving; the roof too, and the arrangement of the organ are admirable. I thought it a really religious building – she could not. We sat debating this while in front of us two women were on their knees. I felt that echo solved & reconciled all.

6. She was no better – and varied it with dizziness, feeling sick, loathing her food; and went early to bed. I went dejectedly to my room, turned on the wireless. It was Monteux conducting the 9th. The applause is still tempesting on as I write. Never have I heard such infallible tempi, nor singers inspired to such fire. Never have I heard

8 Sibyl Chase. See note 3, page 283.
9 Story, *NY* (December 1963).
10 The poet.

such applause, breaking in like a finale to the final chords. Freude, Schöner Götterfunken . . . Oh, it is true! In his 89th year, Monteux proves it. He gave such life, such fluency to his singers that even in the barking passage they didn't bark, they clamoured.

June

3. The fine weather broke with a gentle rain.

John XXIII died this evening: wading out towards his death, it seemed to me, slowly and with step by step patience against the incoming surge of all those prayers for his survival, all that regret and clinging to keep him in the world.

16. I wrote a little.

17. I wrote a little more. Mr Macmillan survived the Profumo debate. But all his horrid back-biting back-benchers implied that he will presently think best to retire.

A very disagreeable example of our occasional fits of morality.

September

7. To Brighton from Yeovil Junction – the quality still persisting in that flat south coast country – the rich muddy flow of the Arun & the Sussex Ouse. At Brighton I caught sight of Ian, feeling sure I had missed the train. The V.S. Pritchetts the other weekend guests; she large, rather alarming, with splendid devils' hook eyebrows; he like a Midlands business man – as his father was; but a talker of great pith and brio. Mr Shaw wearing a green tweed waistcoat; his father, resigned to V.S. becoming a writer, buying quantities of current books: 'Your friend Galsworthy.'

We drove back through Peacehaven. It is a California. Trekkie's heavenly welcome, all warmth & outgoing. A new bedroom, with two contrived cupboards, just large enough for a skeleton apiece.

8. To Monks House, where Leonard [Woolf] proffered me a flourishing green branch of what I did not recognise: it was my cutting of spicebush which he had grown into a far finer plant than its parent. [. . .]

An overcast afternoon. A gay dinner with Leonard and the Humphreys,[11] who are very affectionate to me. They are off to Virginia, en

11 The American novelist William Humphrey and his wife Dorothy.

route to return to England. Leonard & I after dinner fell into a conversation, apropos of taking part in village life (my only contribution being the funerals of mauvais sujets), about St Paul, & what anyone is to make of him: type, I said, might be helpful: a break to italic when he goes off into to rhapsodies, and perhaps Gothic for his saws and axioms. We were interrupted by Ian & Bill H[umphrey] trying to tell me that Marshall Best was enquiring about film & musical rights of Lolly Willowes. Leonard was emphatic that I should take all the money I could get & not fidget over the rest. 'You've had the writing; now take the dollars.' This austere common-sense was as ordering as a roman pavement. It was a path, and I was prepared to walk in it.

11. A misty-moisty day. But I contrived to do some gardening, and the midges contrived to get some nourishment.

Valentine lunched with Elizabeth W.W. I remarked to Kit how oddly things turn out, and how surprised he'd be if he could see what a state I might have been in once over what I now take so calmly. He purred politely, and said, Indeed.

18. In a fit of desperation at my own incompetence, I pulled out various beginnings, & could make nothing of them. And then, set out, almost blind, on a Mr Edom[12] story, seeing only his discomfort at a temporary assistant called Know-All. Then a mosaic drainpipe rolled in, and somehow there was some sense of a story. But God knows. I potted bulbs for the spring. And thought of the cold that would intervene between now & their blooming.

20. I suddenly felt *active* to write, and tore on with the Edom story. So it was like an unanswer to prayer when the second post brought a return of Moodie.[13] I felt a deep, subterranean, and as it were forgotten woe, though it is not forgotten, heaven knows! It is clear as the autumn crocuses now coming out round Niou's grave.

So I went out and did some sensible satisfactory gardening, & then came back to the new story.

21. And finished it. Lively, not very good. And did 3 sets of N.Y. proofs; and thought how much better and more substantial *Consequences of a Hat*[14] was than the two written after it. I must acclimatise myself

---

12 Mr. Edom was a character in a series of stories by STW about the antiques trade.
13 Her story 'Total Loss', based on the death of Niou in July. It was rejected by the *New Yorker* but published in *SB*.
14 Story, 'Some Effects of a Hat', *OTL*.

to Decline & Fall, and try not – if I do still write – to become a gay grandam, frisking beneath the burden of fourscore. I must study to be plain.

November

15. Shopped on [in London], various needs, and a great clod of celeriac. Caught the 3.30, and the damn thing was half an hour late. Leaving outer London, seeing the dusk, the clusters of houses lighting-up, the rambling lines of street lamps, I thought how evening descends like a tea-cosy over Southern England.

Dined at the Ant[elope] with Valentine, who was exhausted by a whole day at the Cat. Womens (venit omen) Bazaar. As usual, I had godlessly won a raffle. A tray, quite inedible.

Kit in a solemn rapture to see me; and wearing a neat white dog-collar bandage like a late vocation. Quiddity[15] knew me, and was pleased too. But Kit sat in my room all the evening, praising my eyes.

A little thunder at night.

22. Fine. To Weymouth, where departing Gathergood, alas! stopped a tooth & x-rayed the stump he will take out – and replace with a garniture de la machoire – and introduced me to his successor. His story of the bone-merchant from Hamburg who produced, like black-birds in a pie, 20 skulls with 32 teeth in place. I saw one of them: the elegance – the *mechanical* elegance, like a car engine – of the teeth rooting in the lower jar; with a slant, and a bias.

Home, to plant Ian's two roses and my own R. le Diable off-shoot; and to mislay Quiddity, who was traced by his cries, up the river-tree and unable to come down. [. . .] Then, an announcement on the wireless of an announcement; the news that Kennedy has been assassi-nated: shot in the head, his unhappy wife beside him when it happened.

23. Kennedy's killer was a young man, pro Cuba, and announced he was a Communist. He had tried to settle in USSR and had been refused.

So it works out: Kennedy's good valuable life cut short because there was no recognition of the Cuban revolution; and Battista [sic], received and cherished, lives on.

15 Their new Siamese kitten.

December

6. My happy though slightly betoothed birthday:[16] another cat brooch, 'a white cat with a charming expression' in relief on a white ground – in fact a rather peevish expression, une chatte incomprise; and my birthday Quiddity bounding; and a book my father would have liked about mediaeval technology (the stirrup began the feudal system), and a scarlet nightdress. And we dined on smoked salmon and marrons glacés in Vera's cream: as it was a fast day; and listened together to Tchekov's Platonov: a rich dark mixture, early: impressed but slightly confused.

And in the afternoon Vera & Arthur came with a beautiful basket of blue primrose roots, an Irish loaf, roses and sweet viburnum, and clotted cream. And in the morning a coffee & walnut cake and a mixed posy from Sibyl.

16 Her seventieth.

1964

January

17. We drove to Wells in the new car: a winter Caldecott landscape.

The Kit and Quiddity relation, which had been so good, suddenly went awry on our return – and Kit privately in my room roared his complaints to me.

I finished Johnnie B.[1] It is blacker than I meant; it got very black yesterday evening in the bedroom passage.

T.H. White is dead, alas! – a friend I never managed to have. He sent me his poems, I wrote out of my heart to thank him. That was all.

February

4. A brilliant morning, a strong cold wind. Beauty of the Low Knap purple willow in full puss against the dark northern sky.

I felt unwell, be-stomachered – and got out G.T.W.'s Little Zeal diaries for companionship. I was abashed at his gaiety, his energy – till I recollected that this was a man 20 years younger than I am. So many tricks and turns in common – such a resemblance in timbre of mind, that I felt like his ghost.

March

17. A letter from Michael Howard of Jonathan Cape invited me to consider being the biographer of T.H. White. [. . .]

I wrote provisionally agreeing to T.H. White – too romantic to be discounted, and there are diaries and letters, and living friends; but proviso'ed David [Garnett]'s prior claim.

April

3. [M]irabile dictu, I am with another story: short, this time; *A Jump*

1 Story, 'Johnnie Brewer', *SB*.

Ahead.[2] The couple occurred to me earlier this week, and today I could sit down knowing all about them.

But T.H. White may be off. Michael Howard wrote to tell that the local Bank is the executor, that they are led by the nose by his agent, that the agent has another client in mind. Only the bequeathed diaries and some letters are safe left to M.H. I wrote saying that something might yet be made out of them.

4. *A Jump Ahead* is finished – about 2,000, or a little less, and seems to me good. Even more does it seem to me astonishing. For I said to myself that with luck I might get something shaped before we go away. And before we go away it may even have reached William.

This morning it snowed. And Valentine in gloom and elegance went to lunch with that persistent husband, sposo in aeternum, and came back ditto and dittissimo.

7. Sun. I gardened. V. posted Jump Ahead. I felt a queer pleasure of an *earned* truancy. I was at once virtuous and defiant.

It is not N.Y. who are the task masters: but age and failing powers, and rising expenses.

For all that, I blissfully gardened, and Kit sat in the sun.

25. Still fending off J.B.[3] I spent the morning in washing, and concocting an elaborate entrée of brains, not worth it. [. . .] Not till 3.30 did I dare open that envelope.

However if William thinks he has 'headed off sexual implications' he is wrong. They look out like the rock at Hartland Point did through its wedding veils of foam. And with a little re-insertion, I shall conscience-calm send it off to make number 5.

And then set out on the nice calm story about incest[4] which for the last 3 days has been brewing.

26. P.D. o' the left side.[5] But it did not prevent me from some joyful gardening, nor roasting a very good chicken. Nor beginning the nice calm story about incest. Which must be flat as flat, and dry as dry – and WITH NO FRISKS OR QUIPS, my old girl.

29. The nice calm story begins to take shape, 5 pages should settle them in Hallowby: then back to the night in 1917.

2 *SB*.
3 'Johnnie Brewer' had been sent back by the *New Yorker* for adjustments.
4 'A Love Match', *SB*.
5 Pleurodynia was the name STW gave to a variety of pains in the thorax.

[. . .] Janet Stone visiting V. related how her *Dean brother* took her into St George's Chapel by moonlight. A small flitting shape pursued them, and stopped abashed at their number. It was Prince Charles, who had escaped in order to beg the Dean to beg him off Gordonstoun and a bracing Navy camp. Poor child, he hates Gordonstoun and its rough play. But the D. of Edinburgh is set on keeping him there, and is not amenable to any reasoning, persuading, or pleading. Presumably Ma'am does not plead.

May

14. Valentine drove to Bournemouth, and exactly at 11 Michael Howard came up the drive in a car like the great bed of Ware and in at the gate like a modest human being. Not tall, well-knit, cat-headed, with grey eyes like Ronald's.

The agent is David Higham, the literary rights were given, shortly before his death, to International Authors. The legal position is complicated; and Ian's friendly acquiescence [to] a joint ownership of S.T.W. between Chatto & Cape[6] had led to violent opposition in the firm (I gather, Peter Calvo[coressi]). I never thought to become a Helen of Troy in my old age.

He left letters to Mrs H[oward], Sidney Cockerel, extracts from his diary, and a list of mss – enormous. I am to go to Alderney.

17. [Whit Sunday] Another day of heavenly *fresh* heat. Eleagnus in perfection, lilies the same, Lent roses, the Corsicus, glorious in decay with their seed vessels, tulips everywhere, roses showing buds, *lilac out*, and the rainy tree spangled. There could not have been a better day for the Holy Ghost – who appeared in the form of two buzzards.

This evening I got Justin & Celia[7] into bed: now only calm daily life lies before me.

A tramp appeared, a neat, trim, upright figure with a curly beard. His smooth small hands. In an honourable manner, he said he wanted a cigarette. I gave him beer as well, Valentine gave him Teilhard de Chardin & a pocket *Hamlet*.

21. Rain, mist, wind: and so cold that Kit bemoans. Morning & afternoon I went on with Justin & Celia; and the last section grows under

6 T.H. White had been published by Jonathan Cape since 1947. STW's biography of White was to be published jointly by Jonathan Cape and Chatto & Windus.
7 In 'A Love Match'.

my hand, and the delphiniums have fitted beautifully into the little girl.

By six I was so exhausted that I had to go and rearrange my jewellery to unbend my mind.

I aim at the end of the month – but quail at the thought of how much retyping will be needed. However, the stretch of sun has left me feeling strong & disciplined. From all this flow and satisfaction I auger that *Between Two Wars*,[8] even apart from its theme, will turn out to be another The Beggars.[9]

30. I finished B.T.W. today – composing up to the last, even when I supposed all I had to do was to copy. And wandered out into the sultry garden not knowing who or where I was.

And came enough to my senses to say I would dine in bed. Rapture. And Valentine cooked the trout she caught for me yesterday. And it began to thunder in the distance. It had thundered earlier, she said. It might have been the Last Day, I wouldn't have known the difference between it and the Last Page.

31. Woke to an early morning thunderstorm, with cuckoo obligato. Valentine up, in her room, by lamplight (the electric as usual had fainted) in her silk dressing-gown, with her long legs up, just like a Cruikshank debauchee.

So I went to sleep again, and dreamed a whole extra chapter to Vanity Fair. So lifelike that when I woke I still half believed in it.

I feel totally relieved and frivolous; and string beads, mend earrings; turn up hems – and listen to Verdi's Macbeth.

June

5. Flew to Alderney. Much too small to land on, however, we landed and met Carol[10] who sent off my telegram to V.

Tim's tall house, half-gutted: his bookroom at the top. I felt it intensely haunted, his angry, suspicious furtive stare directed at my back, gone when I turned round.

Met a great many talkative people. I liked his Harry.[11]

6. More people: a drive round the island, its steep southern cliffs

---

8 Her original title for 'A Love Match'.
9 'The Beggar's Wedding' had been rejected by the *New Yorker*.
10 Carol Walton, a friend of T.H. White.
11 Harry Griffiths, another friend of White.

falling into a tormented sea. Lady Sherwill's house, overlooking France. That evening, alone at my request in Tim's bookroom I decided to do the book.

7. A last sort of books at Tim's house; for annotated copies; and I set aside 3 shelves of his working 18th cent. books, and perhaps they will go to the Alderney library. Reeling, we had drinks and our farewell lunch – graced by lobsters, and off in the 2 p.m. plane with 8 enormous cartons £12.10 freight on them, poor Michael. [. . .]

Home by the 6.20. Everything loving met me, but no interest; and again I realised that I should not come home having got drunk at the party.

July

18. I suddenly saw how to open the T.H. White book – a poem in the 1938 diary gave me the clue. So I tore in at it, *selon ma guise. Selon ma guise* it must be, or dead as door nails.

1965

January

17. A gale rages on all over the country. Trees down, 101 m.p.h. gusts at Portland, 5 wildfowlers drowned by the incoming tides at Southport; and in the middle of all this old Churchill lies dying, slowly, with his usual obstinacy, from cerebral thrombosis. It is like the death of the Lord Protector – except that in real fact, the storm was before his death by three days. This storm death must be a very old belief: & this will give it a new lease of life.

24. Churchill died at 8 this morning. He is to lie in state in Westminster Hall, have his funeral at St Paul's, and be buried at Blenheim.

After a great spurt, I got to the last page of White-before-war last night. And the break between that & Sheskin-alone I now think is the place for White and Warfare. David is back; and again wondering if he should do the correspondence.[1]

30. Churchill's funeral. He had lain in Westminster Hall for three days, in icy weather, and four-hour long queues had filed past his coffin. Crowds all along the route – even on the wireless one could *hear their silence*. For the service in St Paul's he had chosen the hymns. With his usual mastery, the first was 'Who would true valour see, Let him come hither.' But I think the R. Navy's (unless he chose the post-funeral route) usual tradition produced Rule Brittania [sic] as the launch moved off from Tower Pier. It was as brisk & gay as a wren's song and perfectly expressed the sense of changing from earth to water beneath. Stories go on abounding. I liked the story of the Colonial Governor who remarked to him on the regrettable increase in venereal disease among the natives – 'Ah! Pox Brittanica'.

February

9. David wrote vehemently denying that White had anything in common

1 David Garnett was contemplating editing his letters to and from T.H. White.

with Turgenev – and that White was a swashbuckler & like Falstaff.
No one will believe my book, because it is drawn from his diaries not
from what is called life.

March

18. Nancy Cunard's death in The Times. She died in a Paris hospital.

It was in mid-war we first met her – 42, 43? She walked into the
tank-like lounge of the King's Arms holding a Spanish onion: inestim-
able treasure, 'your marvellous Dorch.' She was a harsh breath of life,
an embodied Resistance. Her light gait and mincing walk – like the La
Fontaine crane: her ivory bracelets, that hid in our stair cupboard for
so long, slipping rigidly over her narrow hands; her leopard-skin
bonnet, her pale sea-water eyes, her flat sheep's nose in that pale
predatory face. Our romantic frontier meetings on the Evershot platform before D. Day:[2] and all the provincial hotel bedrooms she perched
in and spattered with her bright strange belongings. Her passion for
cleaning & polishing, and the abstract way she cleaned her nails. Her
courage, her invincible courage, walking lightly to the Regents Park
Tube with me, the last time we met, when every step was pain to her
bad toe. Her quarrels and her urbanity, talking to Mme la Voisine at
La Motte, and the golden house on the hot hillside where she slashed
at brambles with her serpette. Her instant phrase. What is de Gaulle
like? I asked, during the war. In a flash, 'Froid, sec, et cassant.'

And now, lightly, she has gone – et je reste dans la basse-cour.

And again her courage, her invincible suavity as she walked towards
us when we visited her in that intolerable place of detention. Oh! – as
proud and detached as Lucifer, and with us – gently gay.

April

5. George is dying.[3]

[. . .] At intervals during the day of re-arranging, de-arranging, I
found myself meeting George picking his daffodils, noticing how well
his tarragon is coming up.

And I shall have to part with his letters – with his serene refusal of
sentiment & sacrament.

A sudden wave of energy in the late afternoon: and I thought of

2 Because of the wartime ban on travel in and out of the area.
3 George Plank died on 4 May.

such: they are like the wave that picks one up and carries one towards the beach on its shoulders: and each of these carries one on with energy towards death.

May

11. Today I re-wrote the end of *Total Loss*, with struggles, and with no struggle at all jettisoned *One Thing Leading to Another*. One day perhaps I will write a story called Anything for a Quiet Life. When T.L. comes back there will be only the pen-pen-ultimate of the book.[4]

The weather is suddenly warm, windless, benign. Everything stands dressed in living green.

June

3. A day like summer, no wind blowing and the grass growing. And though the drear business of a move has blown up again and I lie awake thinking where, hating the thought of anywhere, grieving over the garden, the river, the fritillaries over Niou & Quiddity, George's daffodils, the grateful thriving garden we have made – even so, because of the first windless warm day I have suddenly begun to feel well again; as I have not since Ireland and did not before. And to see my way forward in White though only this morning I wrote to David White was killing me. The remaining White–Garnett letters are abstracted, done up and ready to go.

A possible story of the charwoman with a bad son who worked for an elder employer whose son had cut off from her, reappears after his mother's death to inherit, has inherited so much of her look & manner that the charwoman against all her views goes on working for him. Then *her* bad son must turn up – steal – his clothes? In a confusion of rancour against bad sons, she abets him.

This would be a TEASER.

14. For Valentine I rang a light-voiced woman in a possible house at Stourpayne which we shall look at this afternoon – this lovely summer afternoon. Looking out of my window I saw Pericles[5] prancing with a mole. It was still alive, and headed back to the long grass above Niou's grave; and he caught it again and dropped it, and it ran on. I thought

4 *A Stranger with a Bag.*
5 The replacement for Quiddity, who died falling into the river.

how desperately I too wanted to shelter and die in my familiar place – and my grief overwhelmed me, and instead of going down to find it and kill it I sat crying on my bed.

November

2. Ireland was finished, and now I am cutting it down, trimming it like a butcher. Today I posted *A Watery Gleam*[6] to the N.Y. The first since July. Not having written a story for so long, I was astonished to find how like myself I wrote: probably *too* like myself.

21. Yesterday I finished the Stowe Ridings section:[7] so either I underestimated my powers of application or overestimated my powers of dawdling. About 12,000 words, I dare say. Encore le vaguemestre ne dit rien: and a fortnight even by deferred air should have got Ireland to William by now. I begin to think William must be ill – or Emmy ill. And then I think it must be that I write ill: yet Ireland is not ill-written, I know that. The likelier truth, that I am passée.

Listening last night to the new Rome production of Don Carlos; a quick soft purr of clapping at the beginning, at the curtain-rising, of the dungeon scene. The new set, of course. How agreeable for the designer to get this instant approval.

29. Proof of *Item an Empty House*[8] posted. Ireland no go to N.Y. but an upholding letter of comprehension from William. It is rude winter. Blowing & snowing and the river in flood.

6 Story, 'A Visionary Gleam', *IG*.
7 Of *THW*.
8 Story, *NY* (March 1966).

1966

January

4. Posted Oxenhope.[1]

Dorchester was cold, wet in a dispirited wetness, yellow. I suddenly *liked* it, it was what London had been on similar mornings when I was recovering from similar colds. [. . .] The USA Swans on an A.R.[2] arrived. The jacket shows a cross swan on some dark red linoleum.

7. Heaped groceries in a carrier for Bozanko[3] – which Valentine now doesn't believe in. Old Walter, waiting for the bank to open, told me that the Town Clock is attended to by 'a man from the North'. He is incarnate Hardy Wessex: the man almost had snow on his boots.

Walking along South St. among all those spiritless shopping women, the thought came into my mind: why did all these poor creatures take so much trouble to get on their hind-legs?

8. I packed. And after dinner, to the last act of Figaro, I brushed the cats. Mozart's Almaviva was not da Ponte's emotional adaptable *perdona* latin, but a much more impressionable, wrong-headed, ultimately more right-headed person. This came out noticeably with an English cast. All the same, the total change of ethos is now overdone. Mozart does it all in his music, there is no need for the conductor to draw red lines and pointing NB.s all round it.

But how lovely, how eternally lovely!

11. [Bozanko, Cornwall] We ran about admiring our very pretty well-found domain: 2 deep cupboards and a kindly fireplace in the sitting-room, an admirable kitchen, charming bedrooms, all essentials and no flummery, constant hot water and a shining bathroom. And waiting us were flowers from Peg,[4] daffodils, carnations & freezias, and William

1 Story, *IG*.
2 *Swans on an Autumn River*, the American title for *A Stranger with a Bag*.
3 In Cornwall, where they were going for a holiday.
4 Peg Mannisty was a senior civil servant who had met Valentine through a correspondence in the *Tablet* and became a close friend to Sylvia.

seizing the chance to cable to this interesting address, to acknowledge with praises my 6th story, Oxenhope.

13. Still bitterly cold, but clear and handsome as we drove to Come to Good and then to the Falmouth Garage: seeing V. through the window of the paper-shop, moving like a ship when all the rest were bobbing like hand-carts and perambulators.

I spent a happy afternoon painting the trees opposite: very falsely & badly: but so earnestly that I have given myself a muscular cramp in my back. Early to bed – rather ashamed of myself.

14. My poor love went off early to Truro to see Rachel-Canada.[5] I was happy & busy with the bright fire, re-arranging beds, making a mushroom soup, doing some washing and hanging it on a blue shiny line to sweeten in the frost. They came in about 1.30 while I was consuming my virtuous hard-boiled egg. I went to Truro with them: the extraordinary beauty of the latening afternoon, the winter turf umbered and gilded and the kaolin hills like snow-mountains on the horizon.

V & I back in time to do a little private wooding in Lilley's Wood. Back with joy on the cold clear evening to our private pleasure: I reading *Illustrious Friends*, my 12th day present. A tiresome telegram from the London *Time* Office asking me to ring them up about a piece on Swans.[6] I wanted to telegraph No: but she gradually dissuaded me, saying I must do my duty by the Vikings.

Then at dusk we went out behind the house on the estuary she wants, and saw the laid-up boats all lit, looking like cities, and the last ferry going across.

Going indoors I realised that Bozanko smelled of us: coffee, garlic, woodsmoke and Fougère soap.

20. Very much a day of return.[7] The same icy wind. Kit alarmingly low and declining all food except half a mouthful of chicken liver, and thin as a rake. V. and I both coughing. And the drawer of my chest a mouse banqueting-hall. They had eaten all the cigarettes except the herbal ones. I was glad I had refused V's offer to bring back White. I turned it out and sorted and rearranged. All the time my toe hurt more and more; and a relay of Tannhauser from Bayreuth produced the most out-of-tune Elizabeth man has ever endured. The pilgerzug were

---

5 Rachel Braden, a friend of Valentine since the 1920s, who had married and emigrated to Canada.

6 Her book. See note 2, page 299.

7 They were forced to return early from Bozanko when all the pipes there froze.

schnellzug. This depressed day opened with a kind letter from Leonard about *Swans*. [. . .]

Sad to put away all the Bozanko preparations for domestic art – with only that soggy water-colour to speak for our blissful beginning.

29. V. off early to Lucy [Penny].

Thinking how much more useful those useless diaries[8] would be if they had dates on their backs, I took them all out again, and spent the morning checking and labelling them.

Results 1. An aching shoulder
          2. A sore spleen
          3. A renewed conviction that soon I must burn the lot. I did burn some E.W.W. weeds.

Valentine brought back *real* daffodils.

February

10. Scribble-scrabble round Duke Mary's[9] – but writing *too well* for a biographer – as though I were creating it.

20. Re-writing and re-writing, I have got White away from Duke Mary's in some sort of marching order. But what this book needs is a baggage-wagon of sources trundling after.

By the evening I was so tired that I packed up and went to bed after dinner, leaving all the chores to her. But I really *was* tired. I couldn't shut my mouth.

March

7. It was a fine morning and we made a neat start and sat like ladies in the tall train surveying the country. Spring arriving round London, weeping willows and hawthorns in leaf, damsons in bloom. It was nourishing to get Bonnard straight: he had three periods; the first Paris-coloured, the paint seeming to flow onto the canvas and trickle into every corner of the composition; the 2nd decorative, rather garish, the paint thinner (*in appearance*), the manner touched by poster work, & experimental. In the middle of this, a series of bath tub pictures, wonderfully expressive of the abandoned uncomfortableness

8 Her own.
9 In the T.H. White book.

of lying in a bath: then some dreadful seascapes with blue plush seas; then a turn to much more composed and *stated* designs: the Gods-eye view of the bath-tub lady's legs going up the canvas balanced by half the man walking in: he on his feet, she head foremost quasi head downwards. A number of people at meals feeding their animals (one young man with English hair and a red sentimental face); wonderful early house-fronts: the old bootlace seller on his folding stool in front of one: a ravishing (late) housefront view in beige, olive-grey, slate grey 4 clear red chimney-pots; a lithograph of winter, an old tramp and two alley-dogs in an enclosure of brilliant poster hoardings and a bitter white & grey waste-lot hill beyond; a marvellous family group of Bonnards & Terrasses and their dogs and cats sprawling in garden seats with short stout black M. Prudhomme weighing down the right-hand corner of the composition balanced by an elegant dog reclining on a step and gazing out of the composition to the left. [. . .]

His odd liking for hot-yellow nudes; just the colour of MacFisheries crumbed fish-cakes and very remorseless & ugly – but a colour he uses all through the œuvre. Finally the power of painting a person or persons in a room and somehow conveying their relative fleetingness and fortuity. I don't know how this was done: it is quite special.

26. A full gale, marvellous speed of clouds, and the strange emotion of watching a clouded sky, grey and shapeless, beginning, as it were to boil, to thin, to tatter, till the blue sky brimmed into it.

Worked myself rather sick on the 1928 diary. Earlier the electric coffee-pot gave me an electric shock which for a minute staggered me considerably. It is such an *alarming* pain: a kind of abstract snake-bite, perhaps.

April

9. [Holy Saturday] Waking to remember the day I suddenly saw how the sabbatum sanctum doings can't mask the contours of the original Sabbath below them. I saw Mary in the house of John lighting the Sabbath candles, and how the flames burned blue under the salt of her tears and then straightened into a steady light, and how the stern repose of the Sabbath embraced them and how they yielded to it; I saw how Jesus in the tomb stretched, subsided, entered into the twenty four [hour] rest that was laid up for him. I saw the faces of the women coming to the sepulchre, and that they were tranquilised. The Sabbath dominates all the Christian after-thoughts and obliterations: lovely as

they were at Orta and all that they are like the garment of silk petti-coats on the gipsy saint at Les Saintes Maries.

21. A relenting day: and all the morning after I'd torn through wash-ing, I gardened in bliss and forgetfulness. [. . .]

The trial of the sadist couple who killed the children[10] now being held. It hangs over my mind. It was this, exactly this sort of thing, the raped girl & boy, the *tape recording* of their cries so up to date that waited round every corner for White. This I must both grasp *and STATE*.

Such a vice would account for his queer infantilism: under such a burden one cannot wholly grow up.

24. Alderney: with a long delay of research in which I ascertained that the waterlogged book came to Alderney in 1948: (his letter to Mary [Potts][11]). I think this must go into the A. Section, though it would be easier to fix it in Cambridge: but last night's scheme of the sequence of books works out well.

Sometimes as I handle these mss, note-books, letters the sense of his existence – that he handled them, knew the look of them – almost overwhelms me, and I think, I shall die when these are withdrawn: *they are mine, he bequeathed them to me.*

June

21. At 11 the telephone rang. It was Lucy, trembling like Larry the Lamb, bleating to me that V. had had a car accident. While my heart said DEAD, L. the L. got out that she was in Dorchester Hospital with shock. Clive[12] drove me in. I was there just as they brought her in from the ambulance, streaming with blood, her left eye like a toadstool, her nose torn. Fougère[13] trembling under her arm. She was laid on a trolley – and left, though a nurse or two flipped in and out. [. . .] It had been a head-on crash, *slow* going, in a lane near Mappowder, about 9.20. She drew in to let the approaching car pass, braked, & found herself up against it: a skid? a steering failure? All the front of the car is in tatters. It was an hour or over before the ambulance arrived.

---

10 The Moors Murderers, Myra Hindley and Ian Brady.
11 A friend of T.H. White who became a friend of Sylvia.
12 Who worked for the Kings' garage and was a reliable driver.
13 Fougère was a miniature poodle, successor to Candace.

24. Fr. Flanagan came. He is one of these up-to-date with the Pope persons, she told me. But he also went.

I picked a great many strawberries. The pugilist's pride[14] has reduced the swelling of her eyes. But her headache goes on and on, and she feels waves of sickness, and the whole of her left leg, not just the knee is fearfully bruised. She is too active. Up and down with Fougère and to spare me stairs. I can't stop her, even though she has White to keep her in bed. She likes it, and spotted several things to mend. Divers don't dive, only dabchicks & coots [. . .].

I settled my income tax papers – which shows the rigour and efficiency of a distraught mind.

July

2. As she was late night walking Fou in the garden she called me to look at a fire. It was a brilliant steady flame, down the river. We debated it, then walked on to the bridge to enquire. It was the full moon rising, plumb opposite the western sunset glow. All was still, serene, timeless as we stood on the bridge together.

18. To Dorch. museum, to open White's box. Read all the morning, part of the p.m. his dream diary in red, and his readings of it from Good and Evil.

This is going to be very painful.

19. To Dorch. It was, increasingly. I went for sandwiches to the K.A. – the one place where I could be sure not to run into V. and Eliz.[15] And there they were; however, I was fended off.

August

1. Calm bliss, sitting in the Museum Library, reading & copying poor Tim's tormented mind. I dive deeper into the yellow tin box ¬ but comfort myself with the thought that I must yet re-read & check.

9. In Dorchester. Such rain and wind that as I walked up the street I was as wet and carefree, predestined wet, as if I were walking up Ettrick.

14 A treatment for black eyes.
15 Elizabeth Wade White owned a house in Oxford, and visited.

I go deeper into the tin trunk as if I went deeper into dungeons. It is the attentive childishness of the private fancy volumes: the care with which the photographs of endless buttocks bare or scarred are stuck onto the page, that frightens me. Perversions like his are like a goblin child that will not quit the grown man's being.

I would like to present the whole series to Cheltenham College.

24. Suddenly sickening of Alderney I began a piece of nonsense for the N.Y.[16] wrote delightfully for about a page & a half, and then staggered into irrelevancy and archness & the grin of death.

September

16. Like a winter evening – indeed, it is slightly freezing outside – I sit here with my 2 fine cats beside me, having this day got back to the Museum, scoured the yellow tin box, read the flagellating fancies, tidied all and locked it up for Michael to collect tomorrow – also, a box full of ph. albums which he didn't expect, poor Michael.

Then I came home and DID the Naples section *as* I intended it to be.

I wish I could live on Cortisone: my 2nd day of its smallest dose: and I am a transformed being.

29. Left White at the Dorchester Museum. (The yellow sarcophagus was hopefully out, on the vain assumption I was going to take it away.)

In the p.m. I packed Charity et alia for putting away. I was still at it when John Arlott, even at that distance an unmistakable plain clothes policeman, was on the doorstep. He is tall, thick, prosy, self-esteeming. He arrived all ready to browbeat me.[17] I got him away in about an hour & a half in a state of tolerable civility and acceptance. Indeed, as a parting douceur, he told me that *Lolly Willowes* was one of White's favourite books. He also instantly identified the big Craske as a Wallis. Such lips, such lettuce. Oh, poor Tim: what awful friends you made.

NB, however; the anguish, dull to searing, of persons who from their desire for higher things, make friends with Tims.

If I come back from Scotland able to write again, this, dear gentle Sylvia, so understanding and compassionate, might be a pretty story to unfold.

---

16 'A Brief Ownership', *NY* (October 1967).
17 John Arlott, the cricket commentator, had been a neighbour of T.H. White on Alderney and was anxious not to appear in the biography.

December

16. Envoi.

Goodbye, my poor Timothy!

Valentine was out churching. The house so cold and silent, and I longed to rush into a congenial debauchery, to boast, moan, be praised and pitied.

So I fed the animals and cooked smoked haddock & drank a little solitary whiskey. Then Kit saw my state and said with large clear eyes that life had a lot of partings. I don't think he will live much longer. He is becoming profoundly wise.

1967

February

13. I prepared her Valentine parcel – with a ridiculous hassock pincushion, and quelled a back-ache and found a second copy of *After the Death*[1] for Mary Potts, whose original copy is lost, and fell to reading it.

And this evening is the news that the Pentagon has begun bombing Vietnam again: just when for four days there had been a tremble of hope.

Incidentally – but a midge among bombs – it is a slap in the face for us.

15. Rain and wind. And I assembled the last parcel of T.H.W. mss, copied out the Brownie[2] sonnet as a leavetaking, assembled all the odd bits with notes as to whence I had drawn them, did it all up and wrote to Carol [Walton].

And then with Finis staring me in the face, sat down to the acknowledgements and groaned out its first paragraph.

I have never been at a lower, longer ebb. I positively look forward to tomorrow because I shall have the washing to do.

16. It rained heavily. I washed heavily. The kitchen sink leaks and Mr Palmer did not come though he most obligingly vowed to. I wooed Kit with Epicure prawns. I renounced that groaned-out first paragraph. It was too well-written. Valentine visited Lucy.

The disappeared wife, the charwoman who stays on longer because it is the day she is paid. This vaguely glimmered in my mind as I fell asleep.

20. I feel as costive as W.B. Yeats; but livelier, livelier. It poured with rain and poor Sibyl had to work indoors. The hall is much the better for it, and a Valentine neckerchief found in the umbrella stand went off to the cleaners. The wind as high as ever: lovely to feel, lovely to hear.

1 STW's novel, *After the Death of Don Juan*, published in 1938.
2 Brownie was T.H.White's dog, to whom he had been devoted.

21. The lights are going out all over Sylvia. The last preliminaries are in an envelope for Michael. Cockerell, Wren & Carol[3] are in a bale of a parcel. White to L.J. [Potts] is sombrely wrapped in London Library brown paper, ornamented with red sealing-wax. I read them through again, and wrote to Mary. Valentine was out at Wells, and as I walked to the kitchen to eat after finishing off the preliminaries I said to the air, O Tim, I don't like to lose you; and could have sworn that a large shape – much too tall & too broad for the passage – was following me. It has been a strange love-story between an old woman and a dead man. I deliberately say love, not friendship nor intimacy. One cannot have friendship or intimacy without some foothold on living memory.

A windy dusk, just enough light to see the pushing growth of the daffodils – a smell of the past – of Little Zeal, away to the south-west. And this morning a turquoise sky and pale fields and black tossing trees in the light before sunrise.

27. I felt tired, what with making over the dining-room into a dining-room again, and madly doing Thursday washing; and I was worried about Kit, so thin and listless – too listless to come along to meet Vera though he heard her voice, I found him sitting up with his faithful ears pricked. So she came to visit him in the kitchen, and helped us do his jaws. And later, after lunch I found her lying on the kitchen floor beside him, talking and talking; I stood on the edge of tears, listening to the unconscious Vera and hoping desperately that no damned S. Africa or Rhodesia[4] will rob me of this darling creature. It was a happy serene visit, while the gale yelled outside.

April

3. All energy spent, I lay blissfully all the morning while my Love posted White, chap 13, 14.

La plus belle fille du monde ne peut donner plus qu'elle a.

This, since decency demands, is almost true. I could say more about his aberrations – so puny in fact, so overwhelming in feeling – but there is a kind of ill manners about such discussions *with strangers*: and that is what the printed page means.

So I paid bills and wrote long-neglected letters, and one to Michael Howard about the illustrations – for that still remains – and flourished off to bed at 10.15.

3 Correspondence and papers connected with the T.H. White book.
4 Over which they disagreed.

4. And woke deliciously, stretching among my sleeping cats and falling asleep again, all as undutiful as when I was young. And I have spent this fine day sometimes gardening, sometimes getting on with Lucy Aurelia.[5] If I am very clever and God very willing I shall get it off to William before we go to Wales. That is to say, I must finish it on Sunday.

May

2. A letter from Bunny – who was depressed . . . and leaves it at that but I am afraid it is a recurrence of last year.[6] He sent me a Japanese volume of his short stories with one I didn't know: *The Lost Arrow*. Of great beauty, his *everyday* manner transmuted into a light that never was. And Kenneth Hopkins[7] returned my Powys papers. How gay I was – too gay, it became nearly arch – but how flowing and fertile.

I have filled a large carton with my past. Lenzerheide, Tushielaw, Harrow. My executors won't realise what a lot they have been spared. It was easier since my mind is so distracted with my present, and what Valentine forecasts Hollins may say.

3. He did not say it. What he did say was serious enough: an extra or compensatory systolic beat: he had earlier thought it a fibrillation. But no word of that radio-active iodine treatment we had been dreading.

Sibyl burned the large carton. This morning came a long, exquisitely calligraphied letter from Fr. Morrin,[8] urging me with great kindness and a queer simple materialism to turn into the church and make my peace with my neglected God. The fine cold weather has changed to wet cold weather and a gale rages round the house. Kit ate a great deal of mackerel unsolicited.

Downhill all the Way[9] came & lay on [the] bed with Fr. Morrin – a queer pair. I felt like the world's child in the middle, since neither of them altogether convinces me. Prophete rechts, prophete links. O, brave old world that has [such] prophets in it, both so convinced, so sincere, one an intellect, the other a schooled simple faith; and not so long ago the priest would have been burning the intellectual, the intellectual burning the nest to see the rooks fly.

5 Story, 'But at the Stroke of Midnight', *IG*, begun on 16 February 1967.
6 That is, problems concerning his second marriage, to Angelica Bell.
7 Kenneth Hopkins was preparing a biography of the Powys brothers.
8 One of Valentine's priests.
9 Volume 4 of Leonard Woolf's autobiography.

Handel's concerto in A no. 8 transports me with that language so explicit, so consecutive, so perfectly at home in its other world of sound, as I fumble with these words.

13. Re-reading *Mr Tasker's Gods*:[10] much better than I remembered, substantial and observant and unmannerismed. The chapter called *The Visitation* up to Balzac in real imagination of details. And of course it is Montacute: we were all too polite to say so.

Valentine baked & caked for Norah, *and* mowed the lawn. N. came looking singularly Scotch, the sculpting hand of cortisone – and *by herself*. Though it was so long since a tête à tête we were soon at it. Strange effect of cortisone: she told me of her horrifying nose-dive towards death, the sudden stiffening, the nights alone wondering if she would be able to move by the morning; and all without a line or wrinkle in her face. [. . .]

Leonard, apropos of [Bertrand] Russell's book, in answer to her earnest enquiry as to what the high mathematics really meant: 'Nothing whatever.'

28. The compositions of Solomon's Seal & peonies are gone. The loveliest thing now is hawthorn branches stuck in the chinese soup-bowl – and the smell of hawthorn bloom all through the garden & house.

Tits squeak in the letter box, *two* parents feed them. My fears were mistaken, would my other fears were so.[11]

I meant to do much more to Gilbert & Bruno[12] but Pericles came in and fell asleep against the typewriter. I went on by hand – but it was difficult to concentrate on old age & villainies with that guileless repose beside me.

June

4. Proof.[13] I have finished up to Alderney. Then broke off to reflect on the Middle-East, the loggerheaded Security Council, the rational abhorrence of war, the horrible after-taste still lingering in me of my greasy sense of relief when the Foreign Sec. said we were to be neutral.

10 By T.F. Powys.
11 Fears for Valentine's health.
12 Characters in her story 'Bruno', *IG*.
13 Of *THW*.

6. I left early for my lunch on David's Moby Dick.[14] The posters when I got to London said 'Israel 40 miles into Egypt'. When I got to Moby D. I heard that Egypt says we and USA gave air-support yesterday. The sweep of strike should sufficiently disprove this.

The boat was joggling on Thames mud when I arrived. During lunch the tide turned. I had no idea the tidal Thames was so vehement.

I came home to the news that the oil supplies will be cut off; and, from Joy, that Jacqueline du Pré, in Jerusalem, has cancelled Norwich, cancelled Bath, and is with the army, she & Daniel Barenboim already giving concerts in the front line. Happy happy creatures.

10. I began properly collating & have got to galley 41.

Nasser has unresigned.

Syria has accepted the cease fire. The six days' war is over – fighting war, that is.

16. Valentine came back from Dorchester with reports of how everyone was either saying that USSR was nicely taken aback or that it had everything planned – without expecting it of myself I let off all my guns at the ignoble states of mind where the Israeli miracle is only seen as a pretext for puny ill-informed surmises & grudges. It is so long since I have exploded I could hardly believe my ears.

17. Waking into the depth of such a midsummer morning: scented, serene, immeasurable. And in the heart of this vast container a cuckoo was singing.

July

5. I saw a cat chewing and devouring a vole on the lawn, another cat looking on. The devourer was Kit, marvel of marvels.

The arena of these scenes of carnage is all roses, the tall and the Stourhead syringas, delphiniums, crimson single pinks, Valentine's sweet-peas, Canterbury bells. I sat on the old stump dangling a coffee-cup and opened my senses to this small earthly paradise.

After this it was sad to come in and go on with that bleak story of Bruno & Gibbie.

20. A letter from William [Maxwell] about the White book – in which he says almost word for word what Pat Howard[15] said about the book

14 David Garnett's boat, moored on the Thames in London.
15 Michael Howard's wife, and a friend of T.H. White.

releasing him. But says, what no one else has said, that White was an animal 'one of Them'. And that the trap I released him from was 'the clue to everything.'

And today I finished finishing Bruno – as in myself I contain millions. But it has its parallel in the satyr-play after the Greek tragedies.

Today is a little autumn: a cool wind, skies overcasting, the first harvesting of peppermint bunched & dangling by the door, the rose-petals gathering on their white cloth, earwigs coming indoors, seagulls coming inland. At any moment it may be summer again, but every year sometime in late July, there are these little Autumns, just as there are little Springs in the New Year.

August

5. Post White, by hook or crook.

Did so: but by the morning tray came a letter from Michael with a staircase consideration of: there had been no sodomy. White *said* so; but how am I to substantiate this? It was a sensible objection & I spent a hideous hour tailoring an alternative – for they hope to go to press on the 7th, though they won't, of course. I had gone to bed too late, too tired, to sleep; this last fence almost did for me.

28. A telephone call, Lucy's bleat, I put her through to Valentine. Alyse was found dead in her bed this morning. I can scarcely believe it. People so seldom get the end to crown the work. She has, dying as unvexed and solitary as a blade of grass. Not a familiar voice nor a familiarised fuss round her deathbed. Her eyes closed on [the] man whom she studied with such attention, scrupulosity, tolerance, entertainment and independence.[16]

As for me, I think sadly that my store of congenial minds is running very low. Never mind, so am I. And she is safe at least. Sleep and his brother Death have seen to that.

September

4. In the p.m. Valentine drove to Mappowder – an agitated letter from Janet this morning told of Oliver Stonor telling her Alyse committed

16 Alyse Gregory died with a photograph of Llewelyn Powys at her side.

suicide. On the agreement of a drive only, for I don't like three's none, I went with her, & sat in the churchyard visiting Theo & Violet – always kind hosts to me – and ridding the ivy off James Gillard aged 53 departed this life March 8th 1909 – a tall headstone sulking in the hedge with nettles around it.

Apparently Alyse did kill herself: farewell letters of sorts, but the clinching evidence poor Mr Parkes ringing up on Sunday evening, his usual custom of enquiry, and to his usual 'See you tomorrow' her reply 'Perhaps'. My own feeling, considering how she never did a thing foolishly though often daringly, is that death is swallowed up in victory. A Roman end, foreseeing the ignominy of dying of old age in a hospital, beleaguered with wireless, chat, women's magazines, and choosing to die after her own selection.

October

24. Lucy, with kindly baited breath, had broken it to her that the County Library had commented on her request for *A Stranger With a Bag*, 'Not acceptable'. Presumably the incest story, anyway Valentine took it to be so. A belated & *very* dowdy accolade at the end of a long career, but I was endeavouring to be pleased when Valentine went on to tell how she had assured Lucy that there was nothing in the story but what would lead to moral betterment, nice feeling all round, etc.

And Alyse, who would have enjoyed this joke, is dead.

November

8. Irises among wallflowers: ornithogalums among violas: 12 iris reti-culata – hopefully – along the s.e. edge of the winter jessamine bed. It was a bland golden morning, but deceitful. As I was hanging out the washing and listening to the talk of the river a mist fell between me and the brilliant young red willow and in a minute I went indoors chilled to the bone.

Sent off Peg's pink cranesbill and David's copy of T.H.W. Helped V. list Mr McKay's enormous consignment,[17] then to Monteverdi made a lettuce soup and sat on listening to Gabrieli's sinfonias while a sombre cosy melancholy gathered round & Pericles slept in my lap. It

17 An order from Valentine's antique shop.

is now a thick fog. The sombre cosy melancholy was like a turn-back to my past youth; only then one enjoyed such dusks frankly and without suspicion they might darken with age.

1968

January

1. There is a high & rising wind, a fitful sky. Rising prices, too. A characteristic petty cheat that yeast, that renowned import, is 4d an ounce from 3d. Workers are volunteering to work longer for the same money. Purveyors and company directors see otherwise.

8. Some pretty trifles of snow this morning have changed to a steady drizzle. A letter from William brings the news that Mr Shawn[1] wants no more Edom stories[2] – all with great kindness, & taking the Hoopoe, but preferring my others 'which are wonderful' says he; though he doesn't often take 'em.

I feel routed out of my easy chair, off my gout-stool. I enjoyed writing them and wrote them pretty well; and could manage them under distractions and difficulties, where t'others miscarry.

9. Valentine was better, up and soon away to Ringwood, plus Lucy & Mary.[3] And against my grain and with my eyes foiling me & my wits failing me, I sat down to that Crickhellow story[4] – since stories it is now to be.

Brief & black – but life crept into it, and I was engaged enough to be faint and famishing before Perry came to fetch me for lunch.

18. I try vainly to convince V. that I am well and spry again. This is one of the two hundred things she worries about. They are partly fever worries, partly habitual: Ruth coming out. I realise that it is as one ages and loses one's natural force that one is at the mercy of heredity. The young are themselves: the aging, their parents' children.

There was an interval of pure repose when we enjoyed a photograph of a cheetah at Whipsnade & her three round-headed speckled

1 William Shawn, editor of the *New Yorker*.
2 See note 12, p. 287.
3 The poet Mary Casey, Lucy Penny's daughter.
4 'Truth in the Cup', *IG*.

kittens. They have all got mamma's jaw & brow pattern to a T. Such heredity is only admirable.

27. A robin on the windowsill below Valentine's feeding-contraption sang a loud grace *before* he began to feed. According to the bird sociologists he was staking an imperious claim and threatening rivals; but it sounded like a grace.

31. She rang me up after seeing H. to say – all right. This was rather qualified later. Hollins said it had no sign of being cancer – too painful, and moveable. But he can't be sure what it is: a cyst, a buried bruise. He saw a slight discoloration. This made her remember back over an impression that there had been a blow – a self-inflicted blow because something she was pulling or holding gave way.

February

2. I finished Mr F'sM [*Mr Fortune's Maggot*]. It is an astonishing book. I don't wonder that Charles and David were astonished by it. The emotion is so oddly mature. Only the opening is weakened by too much T.F.P.

And it is sad to think that if it is read now it will be read in this edition,[5] *deformed* with idiot misprints.

But White read it in its blue frogspawn cover, undeformed, unsullied. In a queer way, it is our book; a child I bore him. His style remained totally uninfluenced by it; it caught him lower down, a below the belt impact.

A letter from Alyse's solicitors brought us each a legacy of £25. For a moment I could not think who 'Mrs A.G. Powys' could be.

7. She stayed in bed, & Hollins came out before midday to visit her. Talking to me over coffee he said she was in a very nervous state and that tension accounted for the pain in her breast, though not perhaps for the lump. He said if it were cut out it might be a relief; but that it would *not* be an operation for cancer, which he discounts.

After he had gone she called me up. It had just occurred to her to relate this lump & pain to what she had in 1949 under Elizabeth; she went on to tell me that she has been, ever since Vatican II, in a state of increasing fret & misery over the new goings-on: as bad, she said (and I could say, as obsessive) as anything in 1949.

5 The Viking Press, 1967.

[. . .] Listening to V. it almost seemed as though she were pinched in half on her way out. Twelve years ago, how my heart would have welcomed this. But now I can only hope she will somehow reconcile herself & stay in. She would be desolate without it; and I no longer feel for my heart.

14. Valentine was out almost all day, taking Fou to be clipped. Tomorrow thank God the car will be out all day, at King's.

I wish I did not feel so bloody defeated & useless to her. And also listless & base in myself. Only the old viper sometimes rears its head, as when remembering a drive in 1948 I said to myself 'Ruth's one-legged friends all so ideally happy' and laughed as at the wit of a stranger.

Still raining. The river fast & high, the garden sodden. No day for Saint Valentine. And the freezias I ordered for her did not arrive. And she gave me a most elegant milk-glass flower font, daffodils, and a carved bird which Mrs Powys always had beside her bed, mysterious woman, with a beautiful musing poem about it & her. Lucy had given it to her with other reliques for the shop.

16. Valentine back from Dorchester, tactlessly greeted by me & Sibyl with prate of the coffee disk[6] vanishing below the horizon, flew into a controlled fury while looking for its duplicate in her workshop. 'Everything out of place'. I said my usual about longing to clean & tidy it. 'You can when I'm in hospital – or somewhere.'

I went out later to prune roses (the hind-garden though not all the Old Sailor) and the Caroline border. It was a pretty afternoon, I heard her out & commending the pale crocuses; but though I left pruning & went to join her, nothing came of it. She is in near despair and has no more faith in me. And since I can't help, I don't wonder at it. I age daily. Lene Moder, lat mee in.

Titus[7] has been ours for a week. He has grown, is loving & lovely, will walk with a collar and lead; but will not so far come when he is called.

23. The belated sun streams through my window but the wind howls on against t'other side of the house.

Her sickly life, her menaced health, her cheek by jowl with death so often, have robbed death of all substance for her. It is too familiar to

6 Part of the coffee pot.
7 A Siamese kitten.

hold out comfort or repose. It is the wind howling against t'other side of the house. I realise that this is Yet Another unfair advantage of my good health.

Today I opened the Clare poems by her bedside; my inscription of 1931, my addition of 1932. They fluttered on the page like bewintered fading tortoise-shell butterflies in their hide-outs.

26. We left the house at 7.30 and were away before the contemporary sun rose on a pale frosted landscape. By car to Farnham, then to Waterloo by train: her design, though she did not design that forbidden right-turn up to the station, with consequent pursuit by two policemen. They were, however, amiable, no ill came of it.

She entertained me to lunch at Solange. By this time I had regained all my old confidence qu'elle si bien conduiser that all would be well. And she was looking so handsome & duchessy in her new black coat that perhaps the two policemen were similarly impressed.

The Gwen John pictures. At first, deeply impressive: the smiling young woman with black buttons curling under her breast & her locket falling straight; the two young Dorelias, a self-portrait in a scarlet blouse, a picture with red roughened hands, toilworn, marvellously conveyed; but eventually, too many, though it was such a small exhibition, and too many sad-looking youngish seated women turned to the right. But in the large room a *ravishing* small interior, in dirty whites & greys, cold weather colours, centred round a brown teapot; and a fine shaggy black cat sitting upright on a seated woman: seated, not held. A narrow talent, sharpened as a pencil: one unsuccessful dash into John bravura with Augustus en famille, a few landscapes – *no* epanchement, no sensuality. Her woman naked & clothed: the naked one lean and repellant as a larva mortis.

28. [Ash Wednesday] She was no better. I got at the business of her bodices & took away the one I had already enlarged, & remade the whole left side. Trying it on in its tacks, she noticed that the pink discoloration she had seen that morning was much larger and deeper. I was allowed to look at it – previously adjured to remember Florence Nightingale, as if I needed that! – it looked like the purplish cloud above a coming boil. I rang up & reported this to Hollins – her incentive: he humphed & said it might mean anything. This was very disappointing. I realised how apprehensive she was by her downcasting over it. And worse still, she now declares that Hollins now dislikes her. I finished the bodice at a canter & she went off to be ashed in it.

Ashes, indeed. I ended the day by writing to explain to Trekkie why I had wired to put off my weekend.

There was one interval of release from our stoicism when she came in on me sewing this deformed garment, embraced me & said How beautiful we were. True for her, still part-true . . . and told me of her reply to Fr. Hazlehurst's kind assurances that she must not grieve for my station outside the fold. 'We are so much one that anything I do in the way of sacraments is shared with her.' This was merrily imparted. It eased my bosom of those regrets over her regretting which were an irk, almost a torment when this business began and she still had those pathetic hopes of me.

March

1. She went.[8] And came back tall & stately, to say that he *does* want a surgeon's opinion. The discoloration had alarmed him, contrary to our hopes. He thought it might be a cancer about to suppurate. The discoloration has completely gone, he thought the lump might even be rather smaller; but the pain, he said, might, since it now darted, be neuralgic from pressure on a nerve. The surgeon is called Hanna, in Weymouth. She goes to him on Wednesday, at 5. Hollins, she said, was extremely kind.

So we looked at each other and made no moan. Now it has snapped down, she says, she has no more fear. Her fear was the anticipatory fear of fear.

2. I try to acclimatise & try not to think. Crocuses are in bloom everywhere. Birds tear off moss for their nests. She is braver than I, which is as usual & doesn't surprise me.

On a letter from David this morning (I read the sad brief passage about socialities keeping him from knocking his head on the wall), she asked me if I would set up a ménage à deux with David if she should die. I assured her that quite apart from David's views, nothing would induce me. Solitude was the only other ménage à deux I could manage. This is so. It would do *pro tem* though I could no longer thrive on it as I did in my twenties.

5. A life without her seems inconceivable: *physically* inconceivable, like trying to conceive walking without a sense of direction, a flow without a bed to flow in to, an aimless plenitude of time.

8 To see Hollins.

6. We started on a beautiful clear pale afternoon. Weymouth with pale bare sands, an aquamarine sea, one stout man muffled against the wind.

I sat in the car reading Johnson till about 5.30. He saw her to the car, smiling & looking so friendly – he is hideous, Irish, coarse-made – that for a moment my heart leaped up.

As we drove she told me that he had considered the lump might be carcinoma, that he must have a biopsy to be sure; but if the biopsy showed malignancy he would prefer to go to straight on to the amputation; and again saying he could not pronounce without the biopsy added that in the case of breasts one expected malignancy.

[. . .] I was in bed, the cats playing, when she came in, saying she had stood outside my door wondering if I were grieving. How did I answer? I can't remember, except that I said I grieved for her. Lying on the bed, staring close at me, she said 'Don't grieve. I have had a very happy life.' If I had thought this, my own would have been more secured. But certainly, when she spoke, she meant it.

16. She was away early, scented & elegant, to ask Hollins about Hedley Atkins & Pullan.[9] And came back discouraged. He looked up H.A. and found him all qualifications etc, but was not co-operative. Then we spent a long time trying to find Guy's Hospital on the map, being perversely convinced it must be on the right bank. This, and the scent & elegance suddenly brought back Angela Debenham to my mind, looking & smelling so roseal beside Piers's grave; a year before she died herself. She came back with a sweep, sweeping & inconsequent, and bore me through the afternoon. But before dinner there was a Pit. She overheard me saying to the cats, The days are gone. And applied it to herself with reproaches, whereas it was merely a lament to myself.

[. . .] I abscond into sleep. A kind asile de nuit; but about 4.30 the ropes are loosed & I fall into wakefulness.

A strong gale – and the country, Sir, is meanwhile going to the dogs and my cheerful reliance on the N.Y. is not quite so relying, since the dollar is taking a wobble.

April

11. Her operation. Her voice in the evening.

21. From Guys to Mayfield.[10]

9 Consultants.
10 The home of their friend Peg Manisty.

June

28. Horas non numerat.

Revisions for a pinch-patch.

The nerines away from the white lavender, to continue the frontispiece. Plant them forward on the path. Bluebells & greenbells in a circle round the lawn syringa. And the pinkbells from beside the laurestinus, and under cherry tree.

2 Southernwoods, blue rue, piebald sage, thyme.

Rue, Jackman's blue $1\frac{1}{2}$ft.

Thymus serpyllum, Doerfieri, and lanuginosus.

Lemon thyme (bush).

Leave *in* crocuses, g.hyacinths (group them).

1969

January

6. This day from Guy's to Goring Hotel.[1]

10. *We* came home.
We came home: Joy with Juliet[2] as far as Marlborough, then Clive with Fougère. Sibyl had arranged puss-willow, yellow jessamine, winter honeysuckle, one standing snowdrop in a purple glass tub. We had tea politely, like strangers, then she went to bed. Began to unpack.

15. She drove to the post-office, then on as far as the Toller Porcorum turning, then to Kings Garage. Dear Mr King's face – amazement, pride, tenderness, compassion.
But by the afternoon she was the worse for it.

20. On a very wet morning we drove to Dorchester to have our desolate hairs washed & cut and civilised. Valentine had a comforting encounter with the talkative Friend,[3] who, having said they had held her in their prayers, went on to explain that this was no effort; 'since you are in the light.'

23. We noticed in flower: snowdrops, aconites, polyanthus, violets, white lungwort, wintersweet, winter honeysuckle, violets, lawn daisies. She picked me a little bouquet of these. The thrushes in the evening singing from the hoary apple trees and the air so mild and pensive and the sky so clearly yet deeply blue . . . I thought as I stood on the lawn, if one were to die now, one would not die bereft of this year's spring. She dined in bed. I have an exasperating cough.

---

1 Valentine had undergone a mastectomy in late December 1968.
2 Juliet Shirley Smith, wife of the artist Richard Shirley Smith.
3 Quaker. Valentine had become disillusioned with the R.C. Church.

February

4. We set out in darkness, with iced roads. My mechanised eye, seeing a glow far off, took the sunrise to be the headlights of cars.

Time killed in Westminster Abbey: the painted, far too painted, royal chapels. Then to Keats House. She came back, seeking my eyes. He [Hedley Atkins] had found no harm and told her not to come back for three months. Inattentively we caught the 12.30 by its flying locks, and were in time to shop in Dorch. for a celebratory cassoulet.

22. The river in spate: the air sweet & alive with birds & water voices. V. set off to visit Lucy: and could not get there because the road from Haselbury Bryan was impassable, with white cats of waterfall leaping out of the hedge. So she came home & fetched me to drive with her & admire: twirling patterns of flood, leaping freshets, brooks being rivers: the Stourminster Mill in its violent skein of flood. [. . .]

Fou jumped against V's breast: *and did not hurt*.

25. Came to life & more or less finished the CHEESE.[4] An elegant frippery, but at least 'twill serve to show William I am not dead.

March

1. She slept badly, her arms swelled, bogeys & discomfort. 'I want to be cared for' she said. Alas, who by? Janet [Machen], a dove with healing in her wings, came to lunch. When for a minute we were alone together she said unprompted how much better V. looked than she had expected. When I demurred she said 'I wouldn't lie to you'. And I knew she was not lying. I would like to be cared for [by] Janet.

2. Meeting:[5] two murmurs from Winifred & Alma, otherwise heavenly healing silence.

5. Valentine was cheered by a morning with Winifred & Alma. Interrogated (in case they asked, they didn't) whether I professed or called myself Christian I was categorical that I don't. Odd, after all these years.

April

24. I went on gardening: polyanthus plot extended.

4 Story, 'The Cheese', *SC*.
5 Valentine had begun to attend Quaker meetings, and Sylvia accompanied her.

[. . .] Then, in the evening, Valentine suddenly flamed against Hollins, who had not answered her letter – nor had I, I gathered, done much but said I would go and ask him. This time I said it overridingly, though she said it was useless.

25. So after lunch, I did. An unpleasant interview. He knew he was in the wrong at having ignored the letter & produced various shabby miscellaneous reasons to be justified. Large strong men cornered are à regretter. But I didn't wish I hadn't gone.

May

12. Mr Ball's man washed the tin-ware.[6] There was a thunderstorm while he washed on a ladder from the deck, so we old-maidishly bade him down.

Struggled with my pass-sheets & so forth.

13. Mr Ball & his man & their machine finished painting the tinware by 1.30. Mr Ball also rescued a bat, as pretty as Mozart.

The Pope has ordered a pair of trousers – this will be another blow to Christendom.

20. Another taxi-wait at Waterloo, after leaving our luggage. This did even less good. She was away for 30 minutes, my heart beat on. But he found no more cancer. Her shoulder & arm must be dealt with: Dr Madden of Yeovil, an orthopaedist. Possible thrombosis. By catching the 12.30 (I had mistaken the time of her appointment by an hour) we waited till 5 in Dorch. as the garage telephone was out of order. She drove like a fierce wind to Low Knap[7], where Perry saw us from afar & bellowed. Home seemed distanced by weeks & years.

June

1. She had a vile night, it hurt her all day. 'I was not here. I am here. I shall not be here' I thought at meeting, triangulating on that mathematical carpet. Thoughts of Ettrick where I was, am not, shall never be. Then a close thought of my father.

---

6 The corrugated metal panels which covered the river-wall of the house, and were supposed to prevent damp.
7 The cattery.

9. Dorchester in the morning. Do you like setting hair? I asked the silent Miss Maureen. Her face flushed. 'Yes' said she with intensity & went on setting mine. Met Winifred. Met my love, who asked 'Why are you looking so sad?' In fact, I was trying to follow Winifred's advice about transferring one's thoughts to the nature of God – and had fixed on his inscrutability.

July

1. She left for Yeovil, by Clive. And I came back with him, all in a K̄ing rattletrap because just as we set out, Clive saw a puncture in the R[enault]. At 4 I rang up, to hear the Sister say with genuine feeling 'She's in a very poor state. She's taken a battering; in great pain after being so pulled about.' A kind of grim comfort in these accents of truth – the first I have ever heard from a hospital person.

So I turned out the lower half of the boxroom. No Shakespeare. All animals slept *on* me. A hot night – with an aching heart.

8. Bad portents: [Madden] thinks her shoulder more compatible with cancer of the lungs than any other stiffening. Which is why all those X-rays were taken. She told me as we drove back. [. . .] I feel so *shallow*, so inadequate, to receive this grief. Black on black. She had foreboded it, ever since the X-raying last week.

9. It was a day. She rang up Paquita[8] whose magic could find nothing; but it found nothing before.

I felt oddly unwell, supposed it was shock. But by the evening I was rambling in fever & off early to bed.

29. She left at 6. in the tempest – with her 17th cent. seemliness outraged because she had to revise all her clothes. Perry, Titus, Moth,[9] played in my bedroom. I was busy, got through the morning, sat waiting for Peg [Manisty]'s telephone. 'Not to worry. No operation or radio-therapy. Pills.' She came back at 6, exhausted, but not intimidated. If there is a spread to the lungs, as Madden thought, it can be contained by hormone treatment. He was very nice to her, and didn't make her feel she'd made a fuss. Cosa rara. She went to bed. 'Only a sweet & virtuous soul like seasoned timber never gives'. This rang in my head all the morning.

8 Paquita Morshead, a friend who practised healing arts.
9 A grey kitten.

August

2. A letter from H.A.[Hedley Atkins] The X-ray has indications: tiresome man doesn't specify what of: but she is to begin Stilboestrol.

14. And summer has a shortening stay
    And steps slow to decay – So now, the rare raspberries, couchant marrows, beans, wormy or shrivelled peas and myself gathering; the cats waiting on my steps.
    Valentine thinks herself the better for the change of sedative pill. She helped me with both Thursday beds & in the afternoon we drove to visit Dr Smith in his spare hermitage on the heath. Books & boots, otherwise *very* spare. But she overtyped & went off to bed jaded. An irony. I am so much more ready for death than she.

15. Janet rang up with her device for Hilary and his singers[10] to sing for me in the F[rome] V[auchurch] church. And at 6 I was fetched in her van, & they grouped themselves under the arch and set out with *The Silver Swan*. I almost wept for ecstasy to hear singing in the flesh again. The concert ended with *When David heard*, twice over. Meanwhile Valentine had been to Dorch. in the a.m. & made bread & to visit Lucy in the p.m. This [sic] things seem wondrous. I sit with my hand on my heart.

22. She called me to look at the morning star. Blake's infallible statement. In *weary* night's decline. The fading darkness was exactly that.

30. The coffee-machine failed; she put it right (3 times) and between us we rectified the syphon. This was too much standing for her. By the evening she was too tired to eat the pâté she had helped me pound. I see with horror how *reconciled* I am growing to all this.

31. Sorted letters of /30 & /31 . Rose out of my glittering trance, combed my grey hair, went to meeting.

September

1. She felt ill after lunch, went to lie down. I gardened. While I was cleaning up she came out, and gave me a perfect skeleton leaf off the rainy tree; then picked some raspberries, saying she could only

---

10 Hilary Machen, his wife Marion, children and friends – all on holiday in Dorset.

totter – it is true – and went to bed. Walking in the autumnal garden, past the tattering sweet-pea row I realised how totally lost I shall be without her. For she is my only Love, has been for thirty years, and my only care, and I can endure no protection, no solicitude but hers.

15. We got to London. She had Joan to tea, I went out to look at French artists since 1900 – [. . .] Peg called. Then she took me out to dine at Overtons: oysters & champagne. And she looked so handsome, so grandly a host that I forgot the present, and was back in our glorious glorified beginnings – almost.

She stooped like a loving hawk & put a half-crown in the tray of the blind old match-seller on the steps of [the] arcade. All her life was in the gesture. And am I to lose this?

16. I was sent up to meet H.A. He told me plainly that things were going badly: the lump in her neck another growth, and her general condition bad – bedevilled by plurality of drugs, he said. He wants her into Nuffield for a series of tests: then, with a clearer picture, to begin at Square One, stilboestrol & as little as possible else.

So we came home, feeding the Waterloo pigeons & putting a good face on it. I felt as if we had been away for months.

17. The good faces hardened, & cracked. After a morning start of pleasure at an account of Longleat, where giraffes forget their long legs of flight & lie down in peace, she began to realise that she had been cheated: That nothing was done or suggested to help her oedema, that the series of tests is to ease the medical mind, not her. And she raged. And I could do nothing. Yet late this afternoon I saw the Sun dance, as it's said to do on Easter morning. A thin variable cloud moved over it. It shone, it broke through the cloud, whirling, dilating, contracting – a shimmy dance: with a cold black rim to its brilliance. There had been a violent rainstorm just before. Now I can hardly believe it. But I saw it.

18. This morning she felt so ill I was to ask Hollins to come. When he walked in, his whole countenance changed, acknowledged. He promised her that when the time came he would see her out of it. [. . .] He was kind & serious. She told me all this after he had gone. It is a weight off your mind? she said. It is; for both of us. It is like the lifting of a mist. He will undertake for us; she has for so long had to undertake for herself, or trust to me, and I am a shaken reed.

October

1. She came back from Dorchester (after a bad night, unreported) with a cherry red M&S jacket for me, and muscat grapes, & diaries for 1970; and the news that in Dorch. she had been taken with such inability to draw breath that she thought she could not survive. Yet by resolution and contrivance, did. This put a terrible irony on the diaries, as she admitted. She feels the growths in her lung gaining fast on her. Yet after dinner we sat on, feeding Moth on shrimps and zabaglione and talking about the London of when we were young.

And now, as I wrote, she came downstairs, tall in her pyjamas to tell me not to grieve, to run away as the wise do, to Trust. And I could say unwaveringly, I *do* trust.

23. 'It is sad' she said this evening, holding her hand between mine, a farewell to hope, for the vaginal bleeding has come back.

Dr Wyatt came this afternoon, spoke of 'a set-back', but was honestly without jollying or belittling.

She still walks along the passage & sometimes down to me in the kitchen; but bent, crouched under her pain, with how slow steps. Her lovely gait, her proud carriage. I had to tell Jean [Larson], who had come back from Lourdes.

25. A melancholy morning: for there had been another bad night & she had been violently sick and was hiccuping. But having read Alyse's diary of 39/43 I ran to her room and said whatever my sorrow, I would not have to spend years & years lashing myself into an infidelity, a widowed infidelity. And I sat on the floor by her bed & she stroked my head and told me all would be well.

26. Fou was taken away by Mr King. Sibyl came to do the night-watch – for now Valentine is too weak to go from bed to bathroom. I knew I had given up all hope. Panic descended on me at the thought of watching her die, then living half-dead without her. I read my diary of 1966. They glinted by when I was wi' my dearie.

November

2. Janet rang up – and wept. To weep in a public call-box. There's desolation.

6. I rang up Hollins, who came, and going away spoke of an injection tonight, and brought the syringe & two morphia ampoules. She was

drowsy, wretched, head-ached all day – sipped lemonade, no more.
[. . .] Now Mrs Mitchell[11] is talking to H. on the telephone about
whether or no to give the injection. *Dies illa.*

7. For a while I walked in the cold open-air, up & down the drive
under her tall trees, and to look at the meadow where she carried Niou
back & forth, for he was drawn to running water, the noise, she said,
made dying easier. Now she lies dying above the same river. A great
raining gale in the night, and now it is rising again. I hear her cough,
though an hour ago H. was here giving her a reinforced injection. She
is, he says, extremely strong – clear in her head, for all its ache.

8. Under morphia all day, emerging & submerging. I turned to her
poetry. H. had said another 24 hours. That was 26 hours ago. In the
late afternoon she was restless, plucked at the sheets. I stayed alone
with her, talking gently[.]

9. The stormy morning: the flash of sunrising, the tall rainbow so
upright. Breathing like a tree creaking. I held her hand, wiped her lips.
At 10.15 she died. S[ibyl] & I laid her out: her beautiful long body, the
pliability of the newly dead, lending itself to our hands. The dead
Christ at Orta: to think of such beauty lost to me, I rang up Joy Finzi,
who will come tomorrow & draw her.

[The following entry was written in a separate book]
November 9th
[. . .] When the first light sifted into the room I knew she was beginning to die. A gale raged round the house: a torn cloud let through the
low sun. I saw a tall rainbow standing there. Hollins came. By now her
breathing had changed – slow, harsh, like a tree creaking. His part was
over, he went away. Sibyl & I stayed by her, wiping her lips, I still
holding her hand. The intervals between her creaking breaths grew
longer, longer. Then, no more. The silence seemed to solidify, like
hardening wax. We cleaned her face & Sibyl took away the soiled
towels. Sibyl spoke of calling old Mrs Stewart to lay her out. I said at
once that we would do that. So between us, we cut away her red silk
pyjamas, & washed her beautiful beautiful long body, so smooth, so
white, & re-dressed her. The pliability, the compliance of her dead
limbs – the last token of her grace and obligingness. And we bound up
her jaw.

11 The night-watcher.

Soon after her death, I saw all her young beauty flooding back into her face. It was the Valentine of forty years [ago], the Valentine I first loved. Binding her jaw slightly changed this. She had the tragic calm beauty of the dead Christ we saw carried in the Good Friday procession at Orta.

I put her wooden cross & rosary in her stiffening hand, and some sprays of wet rosemary and the remaining white cyclamen from the garden.

Later that day I rang up Joy Finzi & asked her to come & do a drawing of my dead beautiful love.

10. And in the morning I went to my room, where the window was only a chink open because of the gale and there, on the floor by my writing chair was a feather, a brown & white pinion, a flight feather. And it could only have come from her. My heart soared up, I KNEW she was up to her old ploys, surprising, delighting me with feathers.

Then Joy, tall & brave walked in. And spent the rest of the day in a trance, drawing that lovely reclining head.

Telephones & arrangements all day. And Bungles.

11. And [Joy] went this morning, taking my wave & seaweed picture which Valentine had promised her. Went to register the death with a pretty young man, an underling. I felt it was his first. Pouring rain. Now she has gone, in a raining dusk, carried away in a *blue* van, which made us laugh together. For today, to follow the feather, was a love & parting letter, assuring me of what the feather had already told. We always rejoiced when people went and left us alone together. So we are now.

12. The feather; the letter; and today when I went out in a gale to take down her sheet such a gust encompassed me that I knew where it came from and ran upstairs to Dove & Seagull, the winter storm *Salutation* poem. 'Lathered & loved' I stood there, reading it with my whole heart.

14. A day of savage beauty. Wet beechtrees smouldering under slate-purple skies. The maple opposite the kitchen window casting its yellow leaves to the wind, yet looking at me with a steadfast crystal eye of undislodged rain. Followed by a plaining Pericles I went through the wet garden picking beech boughs, rosemary, lads love, fern, bay — and finished it with a breast knot of thyme. Georgia[12] drove me to

---

12 Georgia Wordsworth, of Baglake, Litton Cheney.

Dorchester to leave this, and her breast pocket, and those hateful drugs to Hollins. The electricity failed. Candlelight.

15. The Kings & Sibyl to the cremation. She had suborned a large white cat to repose in the chapel porch as we arrived. The smooth progress of the coffin through the doors was like her own untrammelled gait. Driving back along the esplanade, one whiteness of a wave broke from the flat stone-coloured sea, and was a signal. Schubert's B♭ sonata in the evening. But in such loneliness.

17. Her diary for this year: pain, sleeplessness, *timor mortis*, set-backs, threat, sentence . . . and her cry 'She looks so tired!'

I sorted things all the morning, and rang up about probate & casket.

In the afternoon I began to read & order our letters of 1930. I was back, in our blazing love & joy. I read on – her stamping handwriting, my sliding one. I was swept back to then, and called back by starving cats, I got up in such a riot of joy I forgot the present: but KNEW, KNEW, she had been standing behind me, reading them too. *Vincit omnia.*

19. To Chaldon – with her ashes in my lap.

The place, near Katie & Mrs Lucas, lies under a tall holly, close to the wall, with the smell of field beyond. An air blew from the sea as I stood talking to the parson. A newcomer, he has fallen in love with Chaldon, in a serious unaffected way. The sun shone on the Five Maries. My heart exploded into joy and recognition. I am to lie beside her. Came home, to sort papers & read her lamenting furious diary. O my falcon!

20. I unmake the death-bed I remake the marriage bed I said. And as I lay thinking of all the beds we had lain in, she came and pulled aside the sheets & leaped in beside me. And so I slept all night, with her ashes in a respectable little fumed oak tabernacle beside me.

Requiem Mass in Dorchester. Jean [Larson] *supporting* grief. Then home, to go on sorting and writing. And found another heart-rending little horde of pain-killers in the recesses of the Caskae desk.

22. When I woke, it was a pearl-coloured morning, pale colours through a watery mist, a pearled morning such as she loved. Strange interval to fill up between waking and burying the ash-remains of the treasure of my soul. A kindness from Janet's Robert[13] broke it for a

---

13 Robert Shrubsal, Janet Machen's lodger and friend.

little while: a bunch of dark red roses & a card saying 'Sweet rois of vertew and of gentilnes.' Gentilnes was exactly her: that well-bred kindness, duty & goodwill.

Janet Stone, Sibyl & the car at 1.30. By now it was clear, fine, arrayed in light. [. . .] The wooden box lay on my knee. At Chaldon Steven was in the road, looking at 24 [West Chaldon]. 24 is empty, gutted, staring black windows. We were too early. People came up the road like deformed ghosts, Betty shrunken, André[14] limping on two sticks. At last, without any stage fright, I followed Mr Tate up the steep path into the church, holding my Love and my mate in my arms. In the darkish church, Betty Pinney's face, dead-white & small. I put the box on a little table. He took off his long black cloak, & read the two funeral psalms, verse about with the congregation. The first wrung my heart: it was as though her sadder self had written it, 'Let my young grow up'. He read the epistle extremely well; as if it were meaning something to him as he read it. Then the prayers and the blessing; and he came out of the chancel & I picked up the box and followed him into the brilliant green world, and to the pit. There was a hassock beside it. I knelt, & laid the box in the pit (such good earth) and settled it, and put the knot of rosemary and married myrtle on top. And the sexton threw the first handful of earth. I turned my eyes to High Chaldon above the low stone wall, and knew she was there beside me, looking the same way. Not comfort – but acceptance. I was loth to come away. But I drove back with Janet D [Janet Machen], who looked so young with grief; and near Owermoigne we stopped for old old Dr Smith on his bicycle.

Our queer impromptu tea of crumpets & red wine & prawns. She stayed till dusk had fallen, & went away again in tears. [. . .]

And so I began my widowed estate, with three cats & a book about Scotland by a man called Smout.

23. Lay in bed till mid-day. Accepted, rather unwillingly, a lift in to meeting. And there I sat, thinking of her beside [me], so constantly in pain; and suddenly she turned me toward her, and I lay against her, & rubbed my head against her with the sensual freedom of the days before calamity. O my Love!

So I went home & began to copy out our letters of 1930.

25. Copying her letters I was transported again: the sun through Miss

14 André Bonnamy, Betty Muntz's companion.

Green's window fell on me too. Outside, it suddenly darkened. I looked, and saw snow falling. Winter – but she wears the turning globe.

Whiskey did not avail. My eyes are arid with unshed tears.

28. Remade my bedroom. At intervals I am checked by a cold amazement. WHY am I doing this, that, going on as usual when there is no sense or significance in it. But I remember the feather; and she dominates my room like the moon.[15]

December

3. She had left £10 to the burly broken-nosed stall-keeper in South St who had known about her operations & had always encouraged her & kept his fingers crossed for her. He was there today, looking detached & philosophical and reprobate, drinking out of a large white mug. I stopped. Did he remember the lady with the poodle? At first, not. I coloured the poodle. Yes, of course he remembered her. I told him she was dead, and had left him a parting present with her love. He stared at me, all woe & incredulity.

'She was a lovely lady', he said. 'We shall never see her like again' said I. His eyes filled with tears. The reality of his words and mine broke into my composure. I began to cry. With tears on our old cheeks we patted each other sadly, while a woman who wanted to buy a cabbage stared at us. Here was the truly feeling heart and the beautiful folk English of the ballad. My sorrow felt *at home with him*.

8. I cleared the car. In a way, it is more her than even her bookroom is: so much her that I laughed as I wept.

In the afternoon Sue Pinney[16] bravely came to visit me, to tell her story, her perplexities. She is loving and candid, an honourable character. Once or twice, especially when she said she didn't seem able to love, I was carried back to the viola voice at Miss Green. The voice, alas! not a viola voice, and says *Gosh* & *Super*, but she raised my head because I felt I could help her.

9. And I slept late & Sibyl brought my breakfast. And I sorted the small drawers of Cascae. And then to be happy with the letters: Hers was the walk on Winterton beach. So living, so young, so rejoicing in

15 Joy Finzi's portrait of Valentine was hung on the wall facing Sylvia's bed.
16 The daughter of Betty and Michael Pinney.

her youthful sap that I held her again, saw her in her solitary joy, this young creature who loved me & was vowed to shelter me: and my riches, & my loss (Oh, but brief loss!) bowed me like a spring wind bowing a tree. But this is in immortality. *It was. It is.*

11. Past russet trees & grey downs to Sarsen Cottage.[17] There, after a while, the telephone rang. Like a snakebite the thought darted into me, I shall never be rung up by her again. Total grief is like a minefield. No knowing when one will touch the tripwire. I put it off, or Ruth kindly ignored it. I slept badly and in woe.

21. Paquita came in the morning 'But you were always a person alone', she said. 'Never' I cried out. 'I was always companioned.' The loss of that company weighed on me all through this weeping day. Use & wont took me out to clean the cats' tray. The soft wind, the wet air, the trees gently stirring pinned me. I went in, weeping, and wrote a poem *Tall, yourself*. I rang up Janet, who was instantly kind, but kindness evaporates in a moment.

31. Here ends the year in which she was still alive. It is a formality of time; but it rends my heart.

Peg came through the snow, through the snow of my heart, too. But she has a thawing sweetness.

Oh, farewell, farewell! After Peg was off to bed and I had washed up and came into my room to the music of Aeterna Christi munera, there on my desk was next year's diary, inscribed by her; and a very small feather.

17 Ruth and Tony Scott's home in Wiltshire.

1970—8

Bereavement and age sapped Sylvia's interest in keeping a diary. Friendships sustained her, especially the newer ones with young people, such as Susanna Pinney and Antonia Trauttmansdorff. She continued to write poetry and stories, though she had tired of the conventional kind, and turned to the fantastic and supernatural in her stories of elfindom. By 1975 her diary had become little more than an engagement book, though she was still writing letters with her usual wit and energy. She weakened considerably in the latter half of 1977 and took to her bed in January 1978, dying on 1 May of that year, aged eighty-four.

1970

[Sylvia kept two diaries in 1970; one in the printed diary which Valentine had bought her the previous autumn, the other in a lined notebook. Extracts from the former are printed in roman, the latter in italics.]

January

2. With Peg to the Dawes, with Edward's[1] picture; on to West Bay. Winter had cleansed it. I walked onto the fox-coloured shingle beach, saw the deep cornflower blue of the sealine, felt the cold air; felt an agony of remorse that she & I had never stood there together, because there had always been holiday-makers in between.

Lunched by Peg at the Bridport Hotel, a simple mutton lunch, drove then to Mappowder, taking the Plush road since that is now set free. Gave Lucy her keepsakes, had tea, talked of Africa & Henry James. Came home over Nag's Head, thinking of My Love & her slender hand on the wheel. A rent of sunset like a scarlet wave breaking.

8. In the afternoon it began to snow as I sat writing my woe to the Chutes.[2] Casting about for comfort I sought out old diaries: I found 1930 and 1933. Like a return to Eden.

9. And the bureau in the L.S.P. [long sun parlour] yielded two more envelopes: a disproportion of me, but a picture of our resettlement in domesticity – and a proof, being only *two* envelopes, of how very seldom we were – unwillingly – apart.

9. For the last two days I have lived in two worlds. For yesterday I found my diary of Chaldon 1930 on to Winterton, Lavenham. It is the ground our letters traversed. All yesterday evening I read: and such happiness burned in me, such reality and such confident love that I was sure she was

1 Edward Stone, son of Reynolds and Janet.
2 Marchette Chute and her sister Joy.

with me, followed me out of my room, watched me do the evening routine, followed me to bed (but was there already, waiting for me). I fell asleep in this amazing euphoric reality of the past, of a past surpassing, far surpassing the reality of the present. It is like a resurrection of the body – as if body had itself its own soul.

And today, looking for the spillikins I found two large envelopes of our letters: of the forties, the fifties: the upheaval of 1949 which almost destroyed us, only our love held out and held on; and later, the restored domesticities of home and garden and the animals, the conversation letters of a long happy marriage. And when I leave off reading I believe she will come in, will come back, as in those letters I waited for her return from Winterton or mine from Little Zeal.

I believe. I believe. I feel the elation of expecting her.

12. I woke in her bed, having celebrated the night of 11–12 x: 1930.

A dark rainy day. I turned to the gramophone chest of drawers; found the Frankfort spy-glass, & a packet of p.c.s marked 'Places where we have been happy'. But the not-happy of her last years appalled & reproached me.

At last I was reduced to ringing up Janet S. – who is better. She told me to turn to whiskey & writing. Obediently, I did, & set off on the N[orthanger] Abbey introduction.[3]

12. *Last night I commemorated Oct 11th 1930 and went to her bed and remembered her forlorn voice and the impulse which shattered all our respectful behaviour & swept me in to her bedside, where I knelt, whence she drew me up to lie beside her; and the calm valley between her breasts; & how in the morning I saw her stalk into [the] room, tall, slender, severe, to ask if I regretted it; and how there was no need to answer. I was there. All was once and for all.*

And today, a dark raining day, I am drowned in misery; haunted by her sad ghost of the last years, the sad diaries, the remorse that I only served her, did not match her sadness with my own sadness, did not show my dependence on her.

And though there were tokens today, for I found the little spyglass in its leather sheath I gave her at Frankfort, and a pack of postcards labelled 'places where we have been happy' (and one of them here) I am lost, I am lost without her. And tonight is the anniversary of January 12th 1931.

15. I finished the N. Abbey thing: and felt myself dangled over the

---

3 I have been unable to trace publication of this introduction.

abyss when I'd done so. But I managed to swing clear by sorting Loebs for Mary Casey, doing up Rachel Canada's[4] guignol doll, and so forth.

I felt no heart in writing; but at least it seemed a natural occupation. Nothing else is.

18. I resolved to rid her room of death: it involved clearing files, reading part of a diary, reading her letters to me during Aug–Sep. 1949. To unriddle my heart I did a last tidying of the 1930 letters. And through the long stair window saw the moon & the mermaid[5] and the two birch-trees like a vision from her.

18. I set out to restore her sitting-room to look inhabited: it seemed an insult to leave it so scattered with files & boxes and parcels, and legacies to be parcelled. I spent the morning at it, and cleared a couple of files & threw away those hard-working painstaking ledgers of the shop. One file holding various letters of praise, of approbation; kept against that old cry of being utterly unloved, ignored, slighted. It was a slant of her character; the northern face of her diversity. The room looked no better & I felt guilty & appalled that I had not been of much succour to her. Then I found the autobiography to Sylvia – of 1949. Then, to pull myself out of this perplexed straying of the past, I re-read & checked the first letters, and then it was time to go upstairs & draw the curtains round this empty house. On the stairs, in the narrow window, she halted me to look at the two birch-trees in their lacework, the moon shining over them, a mist, a mermaid mist rising through them. I felt her, then: her compassion. So I went out & walked the drive and came in chilled & drank whiskey and caressed the cats. I know nothing, nothing.

22. A day like spring: birds singing, snowdrops opening, rosemary in bloom. I realised that spring will be the cruel season, the thorniest ascent to climb.

23. To Dorch. with guns for Jefferies, then to Coombs, to talk probate with Miss Francis, to tear open [Valentine's] seals and flawless packaging at the Bank. Vulgarity, formality, blasphemy. I came home cross and sad. Worked a little on that story.[6]

26. Today Wort came and took away the Bonheur, her great grandfather,

---

4 Rachel Braden. See note 5, p. 300.
5 A mermaid mist. See following entry.
6 Story, 'Distant Mountains', either lost or re-named.

her table clock, the clay tortoise, the oval mirror which saw her oval face. After the van had gone, I walked down the drive, remembering with what queer exalted calm I watched the undertaker's blue van carry away her coffin – in which she still had a bodily existence. *Then I came back & looked at the empty places: the rooms looked raped. I had no heart to rearrange anything. Soon I must set about dismantling the shop. Impiety! It is I who should be carted away, not these innocent insentient familiars.* Ultima necat. *It has not pierced me yet. Strange.*

27. Dream or vision, I don't know. But this morning I had a complete recall of the Frankfort meteor. It was a foggy November night, we were walking back from Scottow, had passed our first gate when a brilliant light darted down on us. Our roadside trees were suddenly blackened, defined, like shaggy iron. There we stood. There we still stand. In my dream I had an intense consciousness of our relative heights: hers, tall, erect, sheltering; mine, an ordinary height ('ordinary common pink') yet exactly fitted into hers. I have felt this amazement, yet this security, ever since. It has flashed, like the meteor, out of my dull woe of yesterday. O my Love, my bestowing Love!

February

1. 'Sweetheart, this is the First of February'. But that changed in my mind to an intense recollection of the disaster of Bozanko; and how, as we were departing she embraced me & said 'Goodbye!' An omen. For Bozanko was a recall of Miss Green.

2. Joy here. A lovely wild soft blowing dawn – cats flitting in the garden. Drove to Dor., deposited the .22.[7] Posted the letters to Carol. Then to Chaldon.

2. *We drove to Chaldon: a smoky cloudy day: snowdrops, not enough, in the churchyard. Joy talked. I could scarcely know where I was, except for the s.w. wind, blowing fresh out of the old quarter; and no sense of her burial remained, for all the way back by West Chaldon I was answering questions & telling the past and feeling unutterably VULGAR.*

5. Shoulder-ache, virtue and inertia took the morning. In the afternoon I went on with Distant Mountains. I can't quite think why: there is so much else I ought to do.

7 Valentine's gun.

But it helps me to keep her dear commandment.[8] Executing does not. I still have: Chutes, Maxwells, Mackays; and then the cameras and the god-children.

24. A most strange day. I took the beginning of the Winterton story[9] and worked on it all day and now have finished it. It came out as though it were a physical symptom – a rash coming out. I felt no excitement, no felicity, no impulse to write again.

27. Shadows cast – cooked again for Peg. Shopped in Dorchester. Posted the N.Y. *Two Children*. Considered re-hashing Mr Dalrymple; but it is just an itch, a psoriasis; and while I scratch, absorbing; and when the scratching is over I come back to my solid widowhood.

March

3. A long happy night, wrapped in her love – a night out of the past. So I woke with life, and found a letter from Rachel [Hickson] who had got the tortoise; and wrote to her & to Janet, and was busy and content till the wireless tuned in with *I would give my Love an apple*. And that cast me into an anguish of bodily craving and grieving: so for the rest of the day I dryly did up the photograph French albums for Janet and so forth; but after dinner I sorted letters of the /50s, and was soothed. Sorted in her room a little. Her sad passioned poems of /49 – alas!

4. There was a great blizzard in the Midlands last night, and this after-noon a wind swooped on the house, the sky darkened; and I knew another aspect of widowhood – for I was afraid. But comforted, when I remem-bered another gale, in the sixties, when I was afraid and asked her to sleep with me. And this must have pleased her. I cling to remembrances of when I must have pleased. For I am wandering in the thicket of her poems of /39 & /49; and those which came after. What was I to do? In /38 – /39 I took what seemed the right path. I stood aside, I opposed no obstacle, I hoped all things, all good for her, believed it might be so. Grau, teure Freund, ist alle Theorie; but I was no longer a golden tree of life.

I WAS WRONG. *I traduced my own unwavering love. I sullied our marriage. I hid my sacred distress from her when I should have been open & honoured it. Even in ghastly Warren, where I lay awake saying that Frost poem about going down when new leaves came up; and hearing E's*

8 Against remorse.
9 'Two Children', *IG*.

ranting forensic voice and the dog scratching & my Love's wearied tones, I went on; it was not till we were in N.Y.C. that she called me back; and in mid-Atlantic I threw away my sorrow.

So in /49 I was honest; I showed my misery, my disapproval of complicities; and went to Yeovil. What followed? Months of craving and laceration for her, and a wound which left her maimed. Last night, I thought; I should have gone away, stayed away, till the affair had worked itself out, the poison been enjoyed, digested, naturally discarded?

But I don't think she would have consented. She only half-consented, consented in desire but not in heart, to my month at Yeovil, when we wrote every day and stole clandestine meetings.

Either way it seems I was to wrong her, whom I loved with my whole heart, having made that primal mistake in /38/39. And yet I did it to please, or thought so; and to succour her renewal of life by lust: or thought so.

But not for a moment do I doubt the truth of our love, it shed the dear pleasures of the flesh; it carried heavy burdens of doubt, care, calamity, disappointment. It never failed. It does not fail now. My true love has my heart and I have his.

6. *Grief, my sole comfort, do not go.*

8. Snow again, but not so much, and this evening, thaw. Janet D. came in the afternoon. I have the book about Arthur Waley to review for the Spec[tator]. On the whole, harness is supporting wear.

28. *I heard the postman, but did not get up, for the cats were so prettily composed beside me. I lay thinking tomorrow was Easter, that this was mysterious Holy Saturday, when all lies hid; I recollected many Easters: Easter at Orta, Easter of 1931 with the egg-hunt in the garden, Easter presents of airy summer clothes, books, herself in ceremonials of our life. And as I lay, I became conscious of a deep indwelling happiness, peace, security. Beyond even the sense, the remembrance of lying beside her. I lay within her. [. . .]*

It lasted long; and when Edward [Stone] came to lunch and immediately spoke of her and of my state, & followed me into the kitchen to ask if I believed in another life, & said, musingly, if there were another life, it would be so wonderful one would be dead to it, my heart demurred. One would not be dead to it, I said, since one is at one's most living at its intimations. So there we left it.

'And I bless you', she said. It was her blessing that enveloped me.

29. [Easter Day] Such a clear morning I got up and walked in the garden. And there was the first celandine. Sibyl & Rob [Chase] came with presents, I gave Rob the camera. Copied her Free Poem. Wept for pure loneliness at white violets and the Winterton teacup of our last tidying there. Then Janet [Stone], saffron as Hymen in a fantastic hat drove me to the O.R.[10] – a family lunch. [. . .] At intervals today I have felt *blank* incredulity that I can go on enduring.

30. A *normal* (!) day. I cleaned the frig and tidied much miscellaneous food, & ate some of it.

And in the afternoon after breaking my heart in the garden, I copied more of her poetry.

April

2 . *It is as if she were showing the responsive power of a saint. Yesterday I was most melancholy, inert with loneliness. And fell asleep invoking her love, invoking myself to do better & to avoid this brooding and mistrust. This morning I woke resolved to look forward, to take something in hand. And when I found myself craving back to diaries I resolved against it. And felt a compulsion. The diary I took out was the one for April–September 1950; the summer of the processional hawthorns, it was full of our happiness, our re-establishment, her assurances. As real, as cogent today as ever. One cannot revoke a true happiness.* She was glad to be back. *Perhaps saints are begotten between the love of the departed, and the love of the invoker, the invoker's need and trust.*

4. Jean translated *sciolta* for me.
   And I listened to Brigg Fair.
   But, having been filled with pure emotion, an essential, I waned and went early to bed.

4. [. . .] *I listened to Brigg Fair: the first hearing since, another cuckoo. It did not need to come back, it is as fresh as ever, that morning when I came back from walking on the drove, & stood at the gate of Miss Green hearing her playing it, sharing her listening unbeknown, and realising the intensity of what she was to me. It was as fresh as ever, fresher than my sense of loss. My emotion was so pure that it was like a pure alcohol: not a trance for it did not remove me; not a heightening for there was no acceptance on my part; I was* inside *acceptance.*

10 The Old Rectory, Litton Cheney.

'There I stood, leaning against you, listening –
I have never been away' is the nearest I can come to it. It still encloses
me. It was physical, too, for I had that penetrated feeling in my heart.

6. The Italian lesson on the radio: Florence. It flooded back – our
happiness, our abundance: the little balcony, the trees, the smoke beyond the Arno, the Etruscan monument in San Miniato, the wind in the
loggia of the Palazzo Ve[c]chio, buying her shoes, flowers, nonsenses; &
the Arno. Beauty shakes off those who loved it, discards them, flows on.

8. At intervals it snowed violently. I was inattentive to all except a
poem copied this morning – This [is] the world exactly as Adam had it
– which awoke me into an idea of how to write a preface to the first
letters.

9. Tore up & tore up – but wrote on.
   The search for truth. It MUST not be dichtung.
   Reynolds came to tea – so kind, that I did not fidget though I had
my Love on blue paper before me.

10. Shopped & haired – and got caught in literature. A lifetime of
deceit is hard to overcome – but es müss sein.

11. Got us down to Miss Green in September. I bleed from every limb
from cutting my way out of thickets. But I live – and can bleed.

15. I retyped and pruned; and am arrived at Love amazes but it does
not surprise. This, scrabbled on an envelope, was the beginning word.
   Did up a large miscellany for Mrs Bakewell in Leicester, wrote to
Joy, to Peg, to Steven, to Reynolds about Miss Florence's wood-
blocks. [. . .] And made a pâté for Janet. Surprising how much one can
do in one's sleep.

*17. Coming back from Low Knap to the lifeless house I ran upstairs to her
portrait; and remembered myself for comfort that she did not have to know
this. But there is no equity. She didn't want to die. I do.*

May

5. I woke – I came to myself – in a blessed quiescence & serenity – as
though it were the first morning at Miss Green. I knew I had been
loved – when? It doesn't matter. I woke from a love-night.

10. Peter Pears (with sister) came to see the Craskes. And in five minutes SAW them; and in fifteen had conceived a Craske exhibition for 1971. I liked him a great deal: he has the ardour of his singing. So then we went on to a festal lunch at the Old Rectory.

11. Dies mirabilis. Peter Pears, deposited by R[eynolds] till his sister picked him up in ¼ an hour, stayed, ungathered, for two; and sat talking about Mozart productions, et al. & singing folktunes mezza voce. And after a belated lunch I wandered into V's workshop, in pursuit of flat candlesticks, began, sans savoir comment, to unpick the further corner, found forks, buttons, all manner – and at the back a damp cardboard box. And in it, her letters to me of 1932–39 – filling gaps, restoring those years; and as well a folder of our letters to Llewelyn. The house is full of her. I cannot *believe* in this sunset glow.

12. Began the new batch of letters – to /37.

Vera & Arthur took me out to lunch at Piddlehinton where we ate fish & chips (scampi) out of a basket. To save washing-machines, I suppose.

Home at 4.45 to loving cats.

A most beautiful May day: bluebells, Queen Anne's Lace. Arthur drove over the Cerne-Piddletrenthide at 30 m.p.h. in his poor admirable Rover. O my hawking Love!

16. To the Old Rectory for supper (a most heavenly evening, the beechtrees fire-new). Leslie Hartley,[11] that American neighbour with whom I praised Jefferson, and Frances Partridge,[12] dinted and channelled with grief. We agreed the hardest thing was to preserve enjoyment or appreciation.

20. [Valentine had written 'Non omnis moriar' under this date, her birthday.]

O my Love! The steady hand that wrote this, the faithful foreseeing heart. And today, having seen Brother Laurence in her dressing-room, hidden till now, I took him down to check casks[13] for a note to Letters. And there, written firm and black on the fly-leaf, the same words. And

11 The novelist L.P. Hartley, who had been one of George Townsend Warner's pupils at Harrow.
12 Frances Partridge, the writer, was the sister of STW's friend Ray Garnett.
13 'Rolling on casks' was a metaphor for overcoming adversity, taken from Nicholas Herman (Brother Laurence) in *The Practice of the Presence of God* (1692). Being lame, he had to roll on casks to get from one side of a boat full of Burgundy to the other.

a loving letter from Vera, assuring me that I am not for a moment lost. And a cable conversation from the Chutes.

A beautiful day – so far as I could see. Lilies, and a letter to Chutes, and for the rest, meekly washing the monkey, trying not to recall the dreadful birthday of 1969. Yet even that she sweetened to me.

22. *A Return.*
In my dream I was in widowhood and sluttish industry, with some woman, showing how to clean a piece of marble in the dining-room. Dusk.

The bell rang fiercely. I jumped up to open the front door. It stood open, and Candy was prancing on the doorstep. Half-fainting, I stood on the doorstep and shut my eyes to call in my scattered senses. Then I heard her calling, 'I'm sorry to be back unexpectedly. But I couldn't wait.' It was her voice. And then I was in her embrace, and my arms clasped her, the smooth strength of her body: her actual bodily presence. She had brought the whole of herself back to me, all our years of bodily love and worship. 'With my body I thee worship.' Then I woke, still clasped in this dream.

This is the practice of the presence of Valentine: non omnis moriar, as she wrote on the 20th May with a steady hand, a steady courage, in my 1970 diary.

23. Peg & I did the books for P[oor] Clares, Peg handing & I packing. And in the p.m. we sat in the garden, where the shabbiest apple is covered with bloom, and two long spindles on its unpruned leaders. The thrush sang.

25. *Still this heavenly elation, ever since the 22nd's dream – though snatched from the dailyness of Peg's visit. Now she has gone & I have it untrammelled. Last night brought me two returns: how she came to tea at 113, in the winter of 29–30, very slender and composed in her wood-brown velvet dress and pigskin shoes (faun's feet) and sat in the large chair by the fire. And again, the moment when Bo broke in on us at 2: I tousled on the floor, no doubt about it, and serene. And she sprang up and stood defensively between us. And in the slender visitor and the defender the same long exquisite body I embraced in my dream and Gill drew.*

But it seems to me on this May morning that she is coming back because she can't bear to wait.

You always outdid your promises, my Love. You gave, and then gave an after-gift. And you promised to stand by me, and I took it to apply to adversity and found it so; but now you are with me in joy and felicity.

June

15. Cooler, but dry as ever. I woke with an unusual kind of lightness &
gaiety, exhilaration, even, as if drawn from the air, from Valentine,
from yesterday's completion of the /49 letters. [. . .] In the p.m. I began
to consider the notes for this section, then I began to write its Introduction, trying to be honest, which is hard, and accurate: which is
chancy. For instance, in my preface I had totally omitted the room at
Florrie's and left us walking in the autumn lanes.

19. Soo[14] brought the ts of /30 to 54. And will come here to type YEOVIL
– most gravely and gracefully, too. She took off Paradise Walk.
Strawberries, roses. Mr Heath is P.M.

23. Re-lay from Aldeborough – B.B. [Benjamin Britten] conducting
the Unfinished. It was a *transfiguration*.

Gloomily I set about the Grimm review. I suppose I can write until
I try to. Then my ink turns to curds and whey.

30. *I spent the morning sorting her poems. Afterwards, I went downstairs
feeling very cold and* translated. *And then she gave me an* assurance of
my death, *as I listened to the last variation of op. 109: the gathering
ripples coldly pulsing round me, like wading into the sea, swelling, rising,
encompassing,* irresistible; *and the theme emerging, bare & naked in its
original being: the old metaphor, I see now, of crossing the river, standing
on the yonder shore.*

*And after that, I felt a profound thankfulness for all I had given her:
whether she availed herself of it or no, it was there, I had given it.*

July

1. I took the nine parcels from the shop. Clive carried them out to the
car. I did not think it would upset me, but it did. They were so many
coffins of her enterprise, hopes, skill. Dorch (hair done) was not
improved by the sour-Alyse old woman at Parsons asking what had
become of the tall lady. Nor Mrs Wallis harping on my feelings to tune
them with hers.

I thought long, and more mercifully, on May /49. But set myself to
write a N.Y. piece about Guy Stoat, which had woken up with me.[15]

14 Susanna Pinney had begun typing up the letters.
15 Guy Stoat was a character in STW's story 'The View of Rome' (*SB*). The fate of this new
story concerning him is unclear.

And cooking a fresh chicken, the smell of aforetime called back all our happy domesticity, her pleasure and boast of my skill. A strange, tender, trivial recall, very brief.

2. I fell to work on the notes for 30–31, and described the first journey to Winterton. That, and the nights at 2, flowed over me. Exhausted, in a happy dream, I sat down for my supper, leaned back; she was standing behind me, I thrust my head against her and felt her hands plunge down and take hold of my breasts. But which of us is remembering?

12. Soo came to type. She is grave and kind. A fact which is in fact mercy. She was also firm about restoring my cuts in the Yeovil letters. Strange to think of Valentine now real to her, a degree of possession, even: an intimate, without intermedia[c]y of acquaintance. It pleases me, so.

August

7. Peg drove me to Wells to leave the poems at Clare.[16] At moments I thought I could not endure the drive. A harvest field bared: all since her death; the beech-hangar, the familiar roads turning off, the place of that melancholy pause in June 1949, coming back from lunching with Steven, the nightingale woodland. Peg *talking*. Passing the house with the medieval mask I happened to glance up and saw, unbelievably, a stone swan on its roof-line: and it was as though she were beside me, smiling her secret smile at having got the better of me with a kindness. The young man at Clare sensible, & soon over, and I went to look at the moat: pigeons cooing, two swans & their slender cygnet; and among the sweet-papers & debris, a pigeon-feather.

And in the tall afternoon, the word *Relict* came into my head: and put me into my category. I am a part of her she left behind. So in the evening I was able to break into terms of affection to Peg.

8. Who left this morning, sad to be going.
Now I resume my colloquy with my Love[.]

13. *I approach May 1949. I endlessly question myself as to whether I should have left her then; looking at the Gill drawing, remembering 'I was young, silken & made for love', I wrung my hands to think I frustrated any movement of that body: then I said: 'We all want to be guiltless.' And the*

16 The printer in Wells. STW was arranging a private edition of Valentine's *Later Poems*.

universality of this touched me to the heart. For we do: we all crave back to Paradise.

September

6. Out of the kitchen window I saw a long white neck, it was the parent swans and three well-grown cygnets, their white plumage *powdering* through their first ash-coat. I fed them: they stayed for a long while. I watched with her eyes, in a trance of joy.

11. Fine. I came back from Mrs House across the field, and stood on the bank saying: That is the house where I lived with Valentine. Then I glanced up river, and there were the swans. They waited for me till I was back and on the deck with some mouldy Mothers Pride for them.

18. In my bath, looking at my arm, remembering how often she kissed it, I bethought me that I inhabit my body like a grumbling caretaker in a forsaken house. Fine goings-on here in the old days: such scampers up and down stairs, such singing and dancing. All over now: and the *mortality* of my body suddenly pierced my heart. For of that, there is *no* question: no marrying or giving in marriage.

30. The wind had risen: a westerly wind, the wind of Miss Green. I half slept, half woke, listening to it, seeing her again in her triumphal gleam and beauty; and remembering her *shirts*, their colours: the scarlet silk, the grey & silver brocade, the cobalt blue canvas-cloth, the willow green silk.

Then to sleep, to a dream of meeting her in Dorch – now and so domestically that I bethought me of the cats' rabbit and how she could drive me back with it: and the dark brown topcoat she was wearing. And waking from that, I felt a kiss, the long imprint of a kiss above my right cheek. And the wind blew and blew and the house was full of her presence. Too full to write of then: So I did useful works and read some of my own poems for a change, and began a story which came this morning about the dispossessed owners listening to music in their former house.

October

1. The story about the dispossessed owners[17] suddenly began to wag its tail, and lured me into attending to it.

17 'The Music at Long Verney', *NY* (August 1971).

I see how it all springs from that visit to Knole with her in 1930, and Lionel Sackville walking – a thin man with a thin dog. My Love, everything I have flows from you.

12. And as I sat with mist outside and exhaustion inside, dully writing cheques, I suddenly knew that our 12th October 1930 was real and abiding: far beyond any reality of today. It is still there. We are still lying on the Maries in sun and wind.

I finished the proofs of Later Poems. As I sat breaking my heart over the last galley, I heard her praising me because I was truthful.

I also did up the Introduction and letters of 1930 for William to read & keep.

November

2. Proofs of Innocent Warner.[18] I sat at them, increasingly aware that I was alone, that she would never hold the book – and remembering the circumstances when they were written, more carefree, for all are of that decade; some, like the *Green Torso*, embodying our sad lot. And the Norfolk Children, began long ago, finished after her death.

3. And I was so melancholy this morning that I uncovered my grief to Soo. The first time I have wept on any shoulder.

It was a windy, after-gale day. I was in the passage when the wind burst the front door open: that familiar noise of return. I looked: there was light, sun, colour – and *nothing*: only the recollection, the exact recollection, of her height and presence.

6. Peg sent me freezias – which tore my heart. It is a year since I smelled them. Clare sent the *Later Poems*[19] – without end-papers – which crushed my expectations. Between the two, I was denuded. But since one must be going-on, keeping about, etc, I sent off 16 copies, and went on with Adam & Tiffany:[20] though by now it has turned into a story like any other – and a story she will never read, as all the others now must be.

9. I go to my sad bed thinking that if I have spared her the sorrow of the survivor, she has spared me the anguish of leaving the loved one

18 *The Innocent and the Guilty.*
19 See note 16, p. 347.
20 STW's first story about elfindom, 'Something Entirely Different'. It was re-named 'The One and the Other' for publication in *KE*.

alone. A parting kiss between us: of many thousand. A last mutual comfort of our wedded lives.

My Love!

Janet S. came to tea. Kind letters from Bea, Joy F., Rob, Janet.

15. Soo — in her winter plumage of black velveteen trousers, black jersey, shiny black boots. Questions about the Powyses. Observed that Alyse was the only one who knew what V & I 'were about'. To my statement that before V. I was exceedingly sophisticated & world-ly. 'A good thing you loved each other. Otherwise you'd be intoler-able by now' — for which I was loving & grateful. Finished typing Tiffany; and was desolate, she not there to read it. Her poems to Soo.

18–19. Last night I went to bed in despair, having found the melancholy letters from her & then read in the forbidden diaries. [. . .] I woke in my comforting cats; but still stained with melancholy & unavailingness. Then came the photographs of Joy's drawing. So I sent off 6 of them, with letters. After lunch, to strains of Siegfried (the 1st act, & how good it is, allowing for the fact it is by Wagner) I prepared a boeuf en daube, did up the last photograph for Chutes, knew I must pull myself together. So I remembered the tree-feather piece for Janet S. And nearly desisted, from fatigue; but went to her cold workshop, to glue the feather base. Then began vaguely tidying the base of the old Frankfort table: left off; began again, from mere perseverence, with the battered tin pavese box which was among other boxes holding bits. Opened it; and there were my missing letters of 33–37; mine, not hers; but completing the run of hers. And I read them, and I was flooded by a conviction that all these letters which hasten to a meeting DO Hasten to a Meeting. That they are another case of the Feather.

27. In the dark before dawn I woke & lay thinking of how to answer Alec [Robertson]'s letter — leaving church, etc — a kind letter — and thinking of her, and her sad spring-cleanings of her character, of that date, the mid-fifties; and so fell asleep again, warmed with Perry & Titus. And in a dream we stood side-by-side at her sitting-room window, watching a star appear & disappear in a web of cloud. And I said to her: I do love you so. And in a moment she clasped me in [a] living, solid *embrace, her very arms about me. And I heard myself cry out, 'Valentine! Valentine! You are* alive!' *It was like a sudden change of key & molto animando. Life was there. We were alive again. And then her presence ebbed, moved, bending a little, towards the mirror wall. As light floods a shadowed air, then dies out again: the star appearing & disappearing. But it was so real, so actual, that I lay with my body resounding with joy & felicity, warmed and kindled with the sensual reality of that embrace.*

Valentine! Valentine! You are alive!

27. See t'other book for my morning dream. It trembled through me all day.

I wrote a letter to Alec, who is hurt because it was left to Apsley[21] to tell him V 'had lost her faith'. This took much of the morning. In the p.m. I copied a letter of /36 but couldn't settle to it. So I tried to settle to a parcel for C.P.L.[22] This took me to my bedroom. Then into her room, where we stood, where she embraced me, in my dream. In what I knew was a foolish hope, I got the serpentine box from under the sofa. Nothing in it. Yet hope held on to me – tighter. In the furthest corner was the papier-maché desk. I tore it open. Inside were all her letters to me of March 1931. I have walked in a daze ever since.

December

17. Sorted some poems & packed all in the light suitcase. And read, alas & alas! her diary notes of becoming a Catholic again. My Love, my Love, I did my best; but my truth would out: the very truth you loved me for, saying My true one.

19. Janet [Machen] called for me earlier to drive to Chaldon. It was a mild clear morning. We went over the Five Maries. How steep the Drove. Potter wasn't there, so we waited. Janet walked, & reported 24 [West Chaldon] razed. Sure enough, not a stone left. Harrowed ground & the grass just covering it. Then Mr Potter cum filius drove up; there was the stone[23] on a little trolley. He & his son & Janet pushing got it up the path & to the place. They began cutting the turf. Then Mr House arrived, all sextonly, and was much better at bedding slabs than they. All wooden posts, [he] said, apropos of leaning Katie,[24] go at ground level, 'between wind & water'. He liked this phrase & used it several times. The wind blew cold from the old quarter. The rooks cawed. I felt like a revisiting ghost, so much less living than she. Janet drove me to D. and was in tears when she left

21 Apsley Farm, in Sussex, see note 1, p. 259.
22 The Cats' Protection League.
23 Valentine's gravestone, which was also inscribed with STW's name and birth date.
24 Katie Powys's grave, just in front of Valentine's, is marked with a wooden cross.

me. I visited Jean, her charming young cat, her beautiful intelligent daughter. Then home to my own cats and to letters. 'My dear, dear Love'.

1971

10. Soo came when I was still a pale hag, and tried to send me back to
bed. But I painted my face to decency, and revived myself looking at
her beautiful silken hair and her solemn round spectacles. [. . .] She
left me a renewed being, and I walked smelling spring in the garden.
What she bestows is *trust*. And the house was full of my Love all that
afternoon, gentle, approving, encompassing: a rosemary scent.

11. Lunch with Nita Egerton, who read aloud the Anne Donne poem[1]
with amazing power and understanding, and a nasal ring of the -ings
that swelled like bell-noises. Kind, how naturally she accepts me
among the widows.

And in the late evening I went to lie in our marriage bed, & fell
calmly asleep to the sound of my voice talking to her. – Forty years
ago, my Love, my constant Love, my kind cherishing Love.

20. Kind Janet bksted [sic] me in bed and left me there to sleep. Which
I did till 1 – then recollection of the hare got me up. Fasting, I cooked
it. Sickness partly, weakness, emptiness? – I have never in all these
months felt so lonely, so desolate, so childishly lost. When I had her,
I *enjoyed* being unwell, hearing the car come up the drive from shopping, turning to the door of my room, seeing her come in, answering
her – 'Much better – and so *luxurious*'. My mind, my consciousness,
safe in her arms.

The wind blows, rain falls, sometimes spurts of hail clatter. Chaldon
weather, my Love.

But GLORY. Glory in the knowledge that even at that time of devastation[2] I was *myself* to her, and her Love.

29. Sibyl brought me the first daffodils. They smelled of the first
daffodils of all our wedded years. They come up, unacquainted with

1 STW's poem 'Anne Donne', *KD*.
2 1938–9, in America. STW had been reading the letters of that period.

any grief, Herrick's to see them fade, or hers, who knew she was fading; or mine.

March

8. Mrs King rang up to say they are leaving, first for her hip operation, later perhaps for Malta, having ascertained Fougère will be safe of quarantine.

I realised that I must call on her – and then, that I must see Fou, whom I lifted from my Love's dying bed. And suddenly I was drowned in real, unhinderable, *free* weeping.

10. It was as I foreboded. Clive drove me to Frampton. The moment she saw me Fougère cast herself on me in delight & recognition – and les beaux jours passés, helas! – her hard little feet, her rumpled *dull-* feeling coat, her beady eyes, and the *actuality* of this. Then she jumped on my lap and sat there while I gave Mrs King Catherine Farmer's address in Malta, and some books; and we talked. Then she got off my lap and wagged round Mrs King and it was time to go.

So I came back from a real contact with the past; and that is over.

16. I sat upstairs, with fire & forsythia, because the room had begun to look forsaken: and sorted another carton of poetry books;[3] and then began, knowing what lay in it, the diary of /52 onward. But I had not realised how *soon* she began to lose hope of our love, to be ravaged about her poetry in silence, to *feel the cold*: when Janet came, I was in a trance of despair; and stayed so, all the evening. And crept to bed, saying to myself, reiterating as her diary did: My Love came, My Love came.

April

7. The bulldozer in the field across the river; the earth groped for, gathered, thrown aside with a very bull-like swing of the neck.

Another thing she is spared.

8. William got 2 envelopes. And can't make out why my mother didn't cherish me. For my first seven years she did, though doing her duty by me impeded the cherishing. Doing one's duty by hardens the heart against. Insensibly, we repudiate our good deeds, our filthy rags of righteousness.

3 For the Arts Council Poetry Library.

19. Finished 1st batch of annotations & posted to Mrs Cannell.[4] All the spring flowers in the garden speak of her: the Cashmere primrose she was fond of: and the spring nosegays she arranged for me.

Meanwhile, they tear up the hill across the river: *noise is a pollution*. And Mr Palmer is compressed in the downstairs loo, & it is a ravishing day & I have done nothing in it except read William Allingham's Diary.

21. Sibyl brought me a bunch of cowslips.
The field is quiet again.
The cuckoo.

Stooping down to tidy a cat's dish I was suddenly full of the awareness that she knew I would die and be welcomed. It was brief, nothing to do with my thoughts; and like a deep breath of the smell of the sea *inland*, landlocked inland.

May

10. The Craskes have gone, taken away by Peter[5] after a comfortable not very well *established* lunch. O my Love, these are piecemeal partings. Before then, in a green-mist morning, a Chaldon morning, I fetched the cats. Perry heard the horn, & was instantly in his window, exclaiming to me. Moth's legs are longer with inaction. He will end as a stately cat. He will end as a heart's cat. For when I rose, cold, shaken, dimmed, dazed, after sorting that very dense wallet of her early poems, he was sitting in the Earicker chair, silently keeping me company.
And I needed it. For a cold young ghost, burning-hot, clammy-cold, rose out of the wallet & intimidated me with all that force of woe — even then.

11. Sorted, sifted, ordered the Juvenilia Wallet, to the end of /34, a day's work. An interval of sitting in the garden, but the flourish of May overcame me, and I cowered in again. Then, talking to Pericles, I said a truth: Only two things are real to me: my love and my death. In between them, I merely exist as a scatter of senses.

12. Apprehension? It is the nearest word. The blackbirds sang, I was picking lilies, the first this year, my thoughts full of her poems I had

4 Typist.
5 Peter Pears was putting on an exhibition of Craske's work at the Aldeburgh Festival.

been sorting, of her diary of 1930 I had fled to for comfort, the poem about Browning's love-death-wish. And I began to shake and tremble at the thought that she was imminent – or death? Can I have called her? A little before, when I went for comfort to 1930 I had said aloud, with all my sad heart, It is not that I shun you, that I shun the you of this house – it is your grief I shun. I spoke with my whole heart & voice to her, suddenly. Can I have called her? She said she would never leave me. At Miss G. we were both pressing our hearts to the blade of our believed-in disbelief.

Another flawless May-day. A sparrow-hawk flew into the garden, through the yew-tree.

21. [T]his morning I remembered the poem I sent her in a letter from Little Zeal, a poem about all my pleasures in the spring being her, aspects of her I hoarded up to give her: and the thought, certainly not my own, flowered in my head: How lucky she was to have me. A thought, since I am in the midst of the link of 49, which certainly would not have occurred to me. Her pink May just coming out – and the white-thorn.

And I daringly believe it. She was lucky to be loved by someone who so delighted in loving her.

June

1. So many signs & wonders on the way to Aldeburgh:[6] a scarlet poppy, *true* carpets of shade under trees, Marks Tey of Lavenham memory, at Ipswich (!) a sudden recollection of waiting for the breakfast car to be attached, a silver swan – and coronet opus, a cock-pheasant with his silent hen. I needed them. For landed in my comfortable bedroom looking out on the sea, with a note from Peter, a card from Joy – I felt a sort of animal panic. How was I to unpack, how was I to settle in and know what to do?

But she had another trick up her sleeve, for after dinner when I was morosely reading about Staunitz, in came Imogen Holst and welcomed me.

And now I sit quite quietly, hearing the sea & having overcome a struggle with a too steep-sided bath.

[undated, 2 or 3 June]

Lunch at the Red House[7] – sherry in the sun; then Ben: with hooded

6 STW was going to the Festival.
7 The home of Peter Pears and Benjamin Britten.

watchful eyes; an ear for conversation as if it were an orchestra. The mysterious *outer* life of the creative artist.

[...]

Hoisting my mishapen fat clumsy body with constipation & sore toes out of my bath this morning, I thought of past love & pleasure and wished it dead, so that I could escape it.

But all the wings of my spirit, love & beauty & the sea and music & art & all knowledge & enlightenment and sorrow & pleasure & joy ALL came to it via the body I was wishing dead. *My body was the hostess*. And even now my sight totters to my eyes to see the wind and the sunlight on the sea.

4. Of many Suffolk churches the sad last. [...] I sat, & she came & sat beside me; and I went out into the sight [and] sound of the sea, & she came with me, & I came back & wept to remember how she longed for the sea in her last years – and then remembered our first stay at Lavenham, & the churches & churches we explored and the winkles we ate against the cold – and our new-wedded happiness.

By dying I shall lose my *loss*.

The final bereavement? The reconciliation?

14. It is the body which grieves, grieves for the body of the lost one. I realised this as I was sorting clothes for Nita's Bengali sale, and took up her gloves – her paws, her little paws – and looked at her bedroom slippers. I do think her soul survives; but my body grieves and grieves for hers. My courage at the time has shredded away. I have none left. I am an old woman, and crave for comfort and protection like a child.

August

19. Soo came. I was jaded because my beautiful reviving night of no ache was taken over by a violent thunderstorm; but she calmed me. There are not many more letters now.

In the afternoon Steven [Clark]: virtue and moderation eat him. He is so handsome, so charming – and so *deprived of himself*.

Dutch elm disease is in Somerset. All those golden towers along the Fosse Way will perish.

20. He drove me in his MG (O my Love! – not a patch on ours) to the Wild Life Park at Cricket St Thomas. *Far* too many children; and cages in the walled garden, though the monkeys look healthy. But the

lake-sides ravishing, with uncaged birds, herons, long-legged waders seeming to float on air, and deer. I stroked the velvet on the antlers presented to me under a rail: warm, voluptuous.

Then we drove home & stroked cats. Pericles & Titus both full of trust & possession over Steven. I wished he could stroke me. He does in his goodwill; but I want actual stroking, alas!

September

14. Sorted poems for Chinese box: to Mrs Hare.[8] It is putting away one's heart – and hers, and hers, my sad, saddened Love. Finished rubbing lavender to the slow movement of the 3rd Beethoven concerto; and as I did so, in the long room which is so much hers, I suddenly felt that if I could sit down beside her that would be all the immortality I would need: to sit down beside her & flow back into her keeping.

Hilary, Marion & the children to tea. Hilary very kind and affectionate.

15. I woke to a regular . . . knock, knock. My first thought was the tradition of knocking for death, and instantly a tranquil delight of believing it: it changed its rhythm, knocked faster, ceased. I lay in a calm ecstasy – without a thread of fear. I looked at my watch. It was 3 a.m. – a suitable hour, I thought & fell asleep again, clasping warm Perry.

But it was illusion – the knocking. By daylight Titus marauded on the bed-table & I recognised the knocking.

Took them early to Low Knap, left the Chinese box with Mrs Hare; sorted the garage packet. My ecstasy of believing still hovers round me like a mist.

But by the end of the day only the real mist, cold & quelling, hung round me.

October

24. Sunday evening. United Nations concert. Peace Medal given to Pau Casals – aet 91. His speech of thanks went true as a bird to Catalonia, was all in praise of Catalonia. O true and faithful servant.

8 Constance Hare, a neighbour in Frome Vauchurch. The poems were being sent to her for safe-keeping while STW visited the Parsons.

He, & U Thant, who spoke plainly: the sense of single vertical *men* on this chaotic horizon of masses.

26. In the evening listened frozen with shame to the broadcast on Kurt Geisen, whom no one believed: the Swedish Government suppressed the story the believing Swedish consular office had passed on, the Dutch resistance advised him not to exaggerate, the papal Nuncio listened unmoved, then told him to get out; and the French, to whom he escaped in /45, put him in jail as a Nazi genocide official; & in the end he hanged himself. I listened with *shame*, remembering how Valentine had bade me believe against my loyalty to the USSR. Alas! Alas!

November

11. Still cold. Still rheumatic, so I rang up for Paquita; and with my melancholy washing forsaken on the line, I spent the afternoon in bed. And in the evening, dourly wrestled with a short story, for the N.Y. to reject so that I can offer it to Arnold Rat & Edgell.[9] I fly from my hideous old age, my wrinkled sallow monkey-mother to look at the Gill drawing of her weasel grace, her long arms & thighs which held me so strongly. And she overcomes my present with her past.

(My hair washed.)

December

23. In my drowse, I remembered walking beside her to the burning Anglo-Saxon cottage; vividly, her exact height above mine, step. Then Pericles stirred beside me. I woke with a passionate wish to write the story now written & called Love.[10] I tore through everything or neglected it. And wrote. And by the late afternoon it was finished. My feeling she had been with me, here, *in this house*, was overwhelming; and slowly it thinned out, very slowly, *as if she were loth to go*. It was as if by some action, the turn of a door-knob, adjusting a flower, I could call her visibly to me, cast myself into her arms.

Since then I have mended the seaweed plate and now I must write thank-letters.

24. In the morning the story ('Love') was still there, and needed little except pulling together. Not much remained of me, however.

9 Arnold Rattenbury and Edgell Rickword were planning a new periodical.
10 *NY* (September 1972).

28. I set out on the link of /49, but it roused up too much woe – her own writings in the note-book – I couldn't go on. I dread my wounds: and I thank God I destroyed the diary of those months, Alyse's letters, every fragment which might smite her if I died first.

I began a letter to Joy Chute, implementing my plan that they should read the letters and pronounce on what to do. And *Love* was posted to William. And Nita rang up, 'Look after yourself. I couldn't do without you.'

It stirred my ghost-heart, my incredulous ghost's heart.

1972

January

19. A letter from Norah Smallwood [. . .] asking what if anything had been mooted by Eric White[1] about Valentine's [poems]. And this evening I have answered it, & this afternoon I began to consider a selection.

25. A letter from Norah. I hope against hope as I hoped. So I began to put a choice together.

29. Snow travelling on the wind, snow *a thing in the house*. And I woke with a strong sense [of] her love about me. [. . .] I bless my fidelity; which she gave me. We often enjoyed being snowed in. These things no man taketh from you.

31. 13 civilians, Civil Rights marchers, shot in Londonderry yesterday: a demonstration got out of hand, then paratroops were ordered in full blast.

February

2. Soo, pale as death and limping like Nemesis. Her reaction to Londonderry – seen on television – the atrocity of discipline. Told to be inoffensive, the troops endured nailbombs, stoning, spittings & revilings. Orders changed: obediently they went in to attack; and as no one gave a new order, were powerless to leave off killing.

After much swerving and changing my mind, I wrote to Paul to say Nenni, because the return journey may be at the mercy of total power-cuts.[2]

---

1 Eric Walter White was at that time in charge of the Arts Council Poetry Library.
2 Paul Nordoff and Clive Robbins had invited STW to visit them in Denmark. More swerving and changing of mind resulted in a short visit about six weeks later.

361

March

1. Norah rang up to say they will do a book of Valentine's poems. I don't know my breast without a stone in it.

April

11. To the American Embassy.[3] The vast defensive curtain-wall. The Ambassador a rosy cosy man, very easy to encounter. Graham Sutherland, his story of Swanage where every evening there walked a man swathed in bandages with a coloured attendant. Rebecca West, looking oddly virginal: she lifted me to Waterloo and I knew why. Her husband newly dead after a long illness.

And so home.

16. Soo complained that I had not shown what a bitch E. was. Soo will see.

And I wrote the kind partizan a reference for a post in Italy.

17. To lunch at the Old Factory,[4] and afterwards to Baglake, to a relaxed Robin,[5] a calm house, a gentle concubine, called Antonia.[6] She drove me home & stayed to talk. She has eyes rather like Pat Howard's: a truthful, slightly anxious, trustful regard.

21. The day our happiness began, when the large key turned in the lock and I suggested & she agreed and we walked up the Drove talking of how to keep out strangers. And mainly, my Love, we did.

And today I finished Narrative Seven: true as I can make it.

29. [I] felt *her Solitude* walking in the house; & then realised my own. Two solitudes move about the house, in this cellular prison of time.

May

3. A letter from Paul, who has to pay 4000 Krone for new recorders, the 10-year old ones past even Clive's mending. Ennobled by the N.Y. cheque for Scent of the Roses,[7] I told the Bank to send him £100. Miss Galton of Compton Valence came to tea. Her face a heavier version

3 STW was being made an Honorary Member of the American Academy of Arts and Letters.
4 An alternative name for The Old Rectory, Litton Cheney.
5 Robin Wordsworth.
6 Gräfin Antonia von und zu Trauttmansdorff was living at Baglake. Georgia Wordsworth was not.
7 Story, *NY* (November 1972).

of Norah Smallwood's, and her tailor-made as calamitous as any of Norah's. Affable, conversational, but nothing came of her.

In the dusk I sat in the porch listening to a blackbird, who assured me that when I have finished the poems I can die with an easy fulfilled mind.

Yet to Miss Galton I must have seemed as superficial as she did to me.

June

3. [Marchette and Joy Chute] arrived: as I went forward to greet them, their faces were contorted with grief. Marchette's hair is iron-grey, her eyebrows black & iritabile semper as ever. For their arriving presents I had taken the two very small *May* books of birds and animals which my Love gave me on Valentine's day in 1950 – the year the Chutes first came here with their stately mother she liked at sight. [. . .] I raised the Letters.[8] Marchette was impressively against storing them: declared they were for now, now was when they were needed; and instanced W.S. converting Bardello's morality of obeying parents into *Romeo & Juliet*. She *lectured* me. And I attended.

5. Full of love & insistence they cleaned my shabby windows – and with even more love do not attempt to clean me. They love, & caress, & allow my grief. So it is possible to talk to them without falsity or constraint.

6. In the morning they went to see Constance Hare. And in the after-noon to Baglake. Alas, the first elder is in bloom. We were shown round the house (where Robin had been polishing brass all that morn-ing): Wordsworth portraits, a remarkable silk panel with a phoenix of trailing plumes. They talked and were listened to at tea, and Robin's cows went past in a classical procession. It was a successful party. In the evening, the poems again.[9] Marchette resolved, too much resolved even to persuade me. Finally I said, Perhaps a limited edition at my own cost. Names muffled, no diminution, said she. Joy added that there is no monotony in love's testament.

11. Soo's voice, talking to Pericles. She has agreed to the Rome job & is already 'working in' to it. She feels, said so, regret at leaving me: 'the only thing', she said. I praised Italy and she recovered her spirits.

8 Which both sisters had read.
9 STW presumably means letters here, not poems.

I may see her once again before she goes. But she twice begged me to take care of myself. I shall miss her trust and her solicitude, and her integrity of mind: also the sense that she has established herself in the house, in my life, in my dependence on her. But seeing her go, I turned back to my Love, the sun which cast this kind shadow across my limbo, the voice which echoed from my 'more than music'.

27. To Oxford with Ruth [Scott] – the car so familiar with its paces.[10] I wandered in the Ashmolean, entranced again by the Piero di Cosimo Burning forest: I had forgotten its setting of a tranquil green downland landscape. The two forest deities with human faces, mild & bewildered at being routed out of their kingdom. Among drawings, a self-portrait by Bernini: a *scholar's* face. It rained. The classical beauty of the Thames valley landscape with its massive walls of midsummer trees. And pale elder blossom everywhere: and my Love who called it flat-headed not there to enjoy. All enjoyments are wormed by that.

July

9. Sunday. I was working on the last section of the poems, absorbed. I became aware that there had been footsteps overhead, I so far absorbed that I had taken them for granted. They were light, intermittent. It isn't her, yet they may be hers. With some such thought, I ran upstairs. They had ceased: looking round the empty room, I saw Moth in a corner, with a dead vole.

Weeping for my foolishness, my childish old age foolishness, my loneliness's credulity, I came down and went on with the poems.

14. We [Sylvia and Peter Pears] drove to Apple-Tree Cottage[11] to see Betty's Craske. Strange to be in that room, where Valentine had looked as elegant as a water-wagtail in Mrs Wallis's décor, & Llewelyn had sucked a raw egg. And now so lettuce-eaten, & poor André like an Invalide on his crutches, & Betty *melting* into senility; part slug, part heated jelly. 'Valentine used to kick this ceiling' I said untactfully as Peter cracked his head on it. We had to drive past the church to be in time for Janet's lunch. A single magpie crossed the [illegible] road. 'One for sorrow', I said, to myself rather than to Peter. He has a very compassionate heart: for as we drove home, & another

10 STW had given Ruth and Tony Scott Valentine's last Renault.
11 The home of Betty Muntz and André Bonnamy in Chaldon.

magpie flew, he commented that this made two. Which it didn't. But it was said very gently & kindly. I was sorry to see him go.

18. Antonia came with eggs in the afternoon; and told me her story: a story of selfless practical mercy, told without a vestige of self-dramatisation or gratulation, or astonishment at her calm career from one dauntless mercy to another, neurotic Max, starving Robin.

25. A Tennysonian interlude. I was near the cherry tree of 1963 when I saw a paddle whirl past. Two boys in a canoe were going up & down the garden reach. I filled the Winterton shrimping net with straw-berries & lowered it down to them.

When I told Jean of this, later, she said they would remember it all their lives.

August

8. Parcelled them [Valentine's poems]. It is as though she had left the house – but would come back. I had the familiar sense of making out in her absence and thinking it a feat of technique, uncongenial experi-ment. But it is a stage, a milestone in my long journey towards my dear death.

26. Laid out rose leaves, violets, crystalised cherries for the trebles, & made them a cup with wild strawberries, and set out cider & claret for the others; and was just into my paisley dress when Hilary collected me, having left Jean & the rest at the church.[12] Janet there, just ar-rived. 'Dear Sylvia' said he, turning his back on the altar. A new bass, a very good one; a new discovery by the counter-tenor of a Marian hymn to the B.V. (extremely beautiful, possible White); the Purcell 2nd service where P. forgets he is addressing divinity & repeats his ever, ever, ever shall be as though he were addressing his profane mistresses. Then home to the secular half in the garden: Oh Robin, gentle Robin, where Marian's treble pierced my heart, where Felicity, straight as her recorder, played twiddles on Greensleeves to a bourdon of three male voices, where finally they sang a bawdy catch of Mr Eccles, while Ronald[13] crouched behind the lavender, taping it to take

12 The Machens and their friends were going to sing for STW at the chapel in Frome Vauchurch.
13 Leonard Bacon's daughter, Marnie, and her husband Ronald Ballinger were visiting from the United States.

back to Providence. I was proud of my party – prouder still of such honest love and goodwill.

September

6. Mrs Cleale's first morning.[14] A Londoner, a cat-lover; brisk mover, brisk brown eyes, works like a refiner's fire; and appears to like me.

Tea with Mrs Hare – whose reaction to my cold was to say that the next time I'm ill I must go to her to be nursed. And the kind practical heart meant it.

20. Conversation [with Mrs Cleall]: how she used to enjoy Empire Day; and no loyalty left, since the Abdication. Then I went out to continue the ribbon border; and overdid it, for when I capsized on it I couldn't for the life of me get up. Only the sight of Parsons's van galvanised me on to my feet.

No doubt if I had prayed more often my legs would not be so ineffective.

23/24/25. [O]n Saturday Peg arrived with pictures of the State of Washington – very solemn & secret mountains, gorges, untrodden plains.

And went on Sunday afternoon.

And I felt suddenly tired & cold and went to bed for my supper and thanked her for my padded quilt for winter nights.

And somewhere about 3 a.m. I woke in my sleep and there she was beside me in actuality of being: not remembered, not evoked, not a sense of presence. *Actual*.

I was sitting in the kitchen & she standing beside me, in a cotton shirt & grey trousers, looking down on me, with love, intimately, ordinarily, with her look of tantalising a little, her easy amorous look. She was within touch of my hand. I looked at her, & felt the whole force of my love for her, its amazement, a delighted awe, entrancement, rapture. We were familiar, ourselves to ourselves. I was witheld from speaking. I looked, I gave myself. I loved with my whole being. No words occurred to me. I knew I must not try to touch her and I was wholly an embrace of her. And then without ending it was at an end, I was conveyed into another layer of sleep.

Sibyl came back – and mowed the lawn. I arranged the china cats for

14 As char.

the National Trust person and wrote a long letter to William. All day I felt serenely sure of my death.

October

11. A heavy dew, a stealthy morning. The garden drooping. I picked roses for my Love; and was grateful for Mrs Cleal's kind presence.

This anniversary & Jan 13th are unknown. Only her death-day is for the world, to be remembered and then forgotten. The other two are mine alone and safe in my memory till I am back in Chaldon with her.

This evening the wind rises. As I rubbed the last lavender the boughs of the bay-tree walked on the sun-parlour roof.

November

6. [W]hen I woke this morning it was so strange to be without pain that I thought I must be dead.

I began to look at the C & W proofs.[15] Norah has cheated by re-paging; & has inserted a horrible little floret. *This*, at any rate, I must deal with.

8/9. *The Threshold Dream*
I went to sleep, remembering that night, thinking that I should have an uncompanioned death but not unsupervised; for she would filch me away. 'Filch' I said to the cats, remembering our joint departures from L. Cheney; and fell asleep.

This morning, a little before the light, I dreamed with total distinctness that I was standing in a passage between one room and another, face to face with her. She wore a long straight dress of brilliant rose-red, the colour of our love, of my love-locket. She was looking down on me – I always remember our relative heights exactly – with commanding desire, with triumph. She had filched me. I cast myself on her breast, and as I buried my eyes I saw hers brighten with tears. I woke, and saw her still, and fell asleep again.

Later that morning Norah Smallwood rang up. The re-paging was a mistake. I had my 64 pages.

A cold wintry day, the beech leaves thick-fallen. All made happy for me by its beginning.

15 Of Valentine's poems, *The Nature of the Moment.*

1973

15. Antonia suggested a drive. I asked to be taken to Chaldon.

16. It was a clearing morning, a fine afternoon. We drove by her invention: over the ridge, past Little Bredy, through Martinstown; then Broadmayne. And we went by West Chaldon. The snowdrops are up, not as many as I want; the rooks were cawing: our stone was washed pale by the frost. And she called over the wall to walk with her, she with her long easy stride, both of us light-footed. And back over the Maries, with a long pause to look at High Chaldon.

Antonia was tactful from the heart: mousing about, sometimes questioning, sometimes silent; so furious about Katie's defrauded death[1] that she wrenched at the cross & would have had it out. And she had brought brandy against the cold.

18. Soo came, & drove me to Chaldon. It was a gossamer-veiled day: the rooks were cawing. Soo was already bewitched by High Chaldon: we listened & heard the travelling noise of the sea. It was the same spell. And where the thorn had been she stopped & stared and stared. And she knew it so well, she had known it through our letters – and did not need to proclaim it.

Late at night I finished cleaning, combed the cats & fell exhausted to sleep.

---

[1] Katie Powys had specifically requested not to be buried in a churchyard.

1974

6. Worked on the poems of 69. By the end I was in state of desolate loneliness, craving and craving for her to appear to me. I went out to stand at [the] half-door of my little house; and there, looking down on me, never seen before, her head of Aknaton, where she had put it on the beam. Non omnis moriar.

27. My back hellish. A white night, when I dreaded the cats moving – they caught my state of mind & moved. Lying on Eldon[1] I read ballads, & realised how early I was blooded to Elfin.[2] In the p.m. slept under my Love's blue ceiling, where the light of the river quickened & faded.

28. With awe & disbelief, found myself without a back. And the weather has changed. Rain all night, everything, even Sibyl, gentled and calm.

---

1 A chaise-longue.
2 STW had by this time written some eight or ten stories about elfindom for the *New Yorker*.

1975

March

29. Soo – who will look after the letters. And we shook hands on our affectionate regards.

May

26. Back in Scotland, suddenly, & back in a *realised* elfin story: A Fortified Enclosure.[1] Maureen [Chubb] telephoned. I said Wednesday, but not the night. I daren't risk breaking the spell, & have Joy on Friday. But I think the spell will hold.

June

4. Becolded; but Fortified Enclosure. Up the stairs to the saloon.

5. Referendum.[2] Antonia came in the morning with lemons, honey, orange jellied: and a view of Strix being professionally visited by God with a little black bag.[3] This followed a truly Addisonian morning earlier. We ate strawberries & discussed her illustrations to Crabbe.

July

7. Proof of Castor & Pollux[4] posted. Back restored. At dusk, the cows in the river, thick as water-lilies. They came roaring. Titus out late. I looked for him by sheet lightning, finally sat up for him. About 11. he sat on the doorsill, looking pensive. Rumbles & flickers suddenly turned into a vehement thunderstorm, with hails & crash & flash so constant one could not tell which belonged to which. A sudden re-

1 Retitled 'Foxcastle' for publication in *KE*.
2 The referendum on whether or not Britain should join the EEC.
3 One of Antonia's pen-and-ink drawings, depicting Sylvia in the guise of an owl.
4 Story, *KE*.

membrance, *presence*, of Valentine sitting up reading by candlelight, stern and nervous.

21. Dug up dandelions & daffodils: hurt my back.

23. My back ff. sfz. Telegraphed Paul to postpone.

25. Paul. Very hot. I felt ill, but Soo noiselessly washed up, & talked to Paul for me.

26. All this glorious weather, & all the use I can make of it is to creep out & put my back in the sun.

29. Soo, lunch. Sylvia revived. Soo picked lavender. I feel as if I had been rolled on by passing cart-horses; but they have passed.

August

4. Soo – lunch. Grün, alles grün. Dragon bowl, plates, olive-bordered side plates, large green dish, green St Mawes pots. Lettuce soup, salad: green beans. Angelica cream. My one orange lemonade much praised. My pigeon-coloured dress. 90°!

1976

January

4. A near-inundation of East Anglia – same pattern (Holland, Scandinavia) as last time. This time they put it down to the gale. Cold-damp here; and corpse-feet all day. Sat at seed-lists, Unwins & Suttons, & planned this year's layout of the vegetable garden. Corpse feet led to indigestion. A Valentine nudge said Brandy. So I obey, & shall early to bed.

14. Began sorting *Kingdoms of Elfin*.[1] Picked snowdrops. *7 years* in November.

19. Made a vinegar loaf, & overcooked it, listening to Peter P. & Dowland. Climate of Exile[2] finished, bar the last paragraph.

Where is my enamel colander? Where is my wooden soup-ladle?

30. Bitterly cold, north wind. Wandered with vague projects of tidying.

During the night, it fell, and snow by the morning. Yet two starlings quarrelled & *mated*.

February

4. Cold as ever. Some more snow, but melting. Sat at Entirely Different.[3] Titled it. Tearsheets got ready. Antonia, waterless, washes her face with snow.

14. A cold Valentine. The entry in my diary for 2:ii:69 – our dishevelled days, her suffering, Fortune's malice. A false thought, 'I am happier now'. False, and flimsy, and soon dismissed.

---

1 The collection of her elfin stories, published January 1977.
2 Story, *KE*.
3 Story, 'Something Entirely Different', which she was re-titling 'The One and the Other', *KE*.

23. Posted Viking contract, emended Enright blurb,[4] permission of copyright to N.Y. & a surprised acceptance to Michael Schmidt[5] for my collected poems. Antonia with the wireless.

March

1. All the crocuses out in the sun, bees flying over the frosted lawn to loll in them. A letter from Peter Pears about an S.T.W. day at Aldeburgh. My first dishevellment was abated when I realised it would be 1977, & I might well be dead by then. Letter to Viking, counterordering Queen Mousie;[6] *Carcanet*; and to Dennis Enright, and to Priscilla Napier. Picked first daffodils. Worked on V.A.[7] in the p.m.

April

26. The Duke of Orkney[8] taken. But Mr S[hawn] will have no more Elfins. Vieux singe ne plait à personne.
    Rising again, I got out Hamlet.

July

4. On the 7 a.m. News the news of the rescue from Entebbe. O my Falcons! 2500 miles, & landed on the runway, neat as cats.
    Antonia in the evening, with rabbit. She hadn't heard the news. I had the glory of telling her.

19. Antonia.
    The thrushes on the wall looking at the sunset. My Love.

October

3. Great rain, river in full flood, violently flowing towards me breasthigh as I walked in the squelching garden. Flood water all round the house.

4. Still there in the morning, and cold. But cleared in the afternoon.

4 For *KE*. The poet D.J. Enright worked for Chatto & Windus at this time.
5 Poet and publisher, of Carcanet Press.
6 Story, *OTL*. STW decided not to include it in *KE*.
7 STW was preparing a selection of Valentine's poems for Julius Lipton's Welmont Press. The book appeared in 1978 under the title *Further Poems of Valentine Ackland*.
8 Story, 'The Duke of Orkney's Leonardo', *OTL*.

Brought in marrows, white beans, etc. The last Honorine de B. Sat at Epilogue, saw the end in sight.[9] Long stint of shortening.

November

9. *rainbows* an inherent possibility: the sun so – the cloud – so. The rainwashed transparency of air in between. So *apparitions*.

Sea-Symphony. My love in the doorway. Her exact height.

December

3. Telephone from Rosemary Manning[10] – Paul [Nordoff] alive, & less in torment. Rang him in his Krankenhaus – his voice a mezza-voce of before, but his laugh – he laughed – the same.

4. 8 o'clock news. Ben [Britten] died this morning. Peter beside him. Hard stiff frost, Morning fog.

25. I opened my window, and it was an Ox & Ass landscape. Silent, unhuman, innocent. And all day, sun, and cleanness: and at dusk the childish moon.

9 See note 7 above.
10 Alyse Gregory's friend and executor.

1977

14. [T]elephoned Herdecke. Paul's familiar kind voice, and even bronchitis hasn't taken the life out of it – though it may out of him.

18. Rosemary Manning telephoned. Paul is dead. He died last night, in his sleep. 'I hope to die before my patience gives out' he said. Between a dying man, & the dead, there is a total difference.

19. Sybil Beresford Peirce asked me to do an obituary bit about Paul for The Times. I was just going to bed, but I did it, wrenching my vitals; and had it finished by 1.30 a.m.

20. Tired and cast down all day. Mrs Cleall very kind to me.

February

26. Arise 7.15 for that parcel. It was the xeroxes of all her letters to the kind Chutes, and recalls of our kind days. The girl¹ came & gardened. I seem to have a kick-back of that influenza. But her letters encompass me. Frost in the air.

27. – a sad embrace, really. I was then a crop of weedy cares – till 63 – that is. I read no further, but wrote to the Chutes to thank them for all they meant to her. An icy east wind, cold as bright reason. I was worrying at Verdigris² when Antonia came, with hare soup and a hand-plucked pigeon – and a tactful non-attention to my scorched throat, whatever has caused it. Could be laryngitis.

28. A clear cold day, and I am no longer a baritone with asthma, and well & brisk. More of her letters; then the opening of a story about Miss Lucretia Vaisey. Silent frost. The harpsichordist's sigh of relief at the end of the cadenza in Brandenburg 5.

---

1 Her name was Janet Wareham.
2 An unidentifiable work.

March

3. Another April morning – with a wind. Flowers out everywhere, hyacinths in bloom. But I sat up too late, & carelessly slipped on the bathroom mat, & fell in a heap – unharmed but shocked.

4. And for some reason, felt much the better for it. Antonia came with eggs & a card of condolence. Suddenly a cold evening, with a shining sunset-lit moon in the eastern sky.

28. Brilliant with cold & north-east wind. Antonia revitalised me, so that I fed the birds, & dug up a pink violet, all in Nora's grand fur coat.

29. Antonia with coffee 5 a.m. My dream of being on an embattled warship, c. 1915, longing for an apple. Antonia the apple. Later Dr Dewhurst in his goblin's hat, who went over me, praised my circulation & will deal with my legs.

30. Janet and Antonia in the a.m. both kindly shopping. Then a cable from Vikpres[3] to say K. of E. going into a paperback. Adieu, panniers. Vendages sont faits.

May

5. A tit's nest in the letter-box – exquisitely soft, I wished I could lie in it.

10. Dr Dewhurst. SWALLOWS. Asparagus ready, irises in flower. My legs pronounced much better. In the p.m. tripped on the river-path, fell on all fours, grazed my improving right knee. Letter to David.

17. Antonia-Aurora woke me & Pericles about 6.30 with hot coffee. Seen from below her face is libertine, in Gemini contrast to her thoughtful, tranquil observant face at a level. The Zodiac justified.

<u>19</u>. Wash, washing, weeding, cooking: on my feet all day, and woken at night by alarming cramps & pains.

[Week of] 30. [in margin]
    Note on fatigue. Things remembered, one by one & at intervals: like the basin at the Lloret:[4] regurgitations. Each involving a gymnas-

---

3 The Viking Press.
4 Presumably a hotel.

tic of going off to do, to make a note of it: Continuity has to be powered by working-order battery.

June

2. [A] bad night. Leg-ache, sleeplessness. Tottered into life at 10 a.m. Recovered later, & planned and cooked forward for the week-end.[5] But pauvre de ma tête.

October

<u>14</u>. An atrocious night. Combatted legs with cigarettes & Wordsworth. Then a spiritless foggy morning, & duties. Sun in the p.m. I gardened vigorously, outed dandelions etc. Violets out, & the first Hellebore orientalis. Mrs C. shopped for me. Insurance posted.

17. I fell against the toolshed with a loud clang. Little the worse. Revived by a fine performance of the Pastoral Symphony.

18. Asleep with both cats when Aurora came – coffee & two last figs. She fetched a fragment of meteorite from her pocket – dating aetatis suae 7. I proposed the house,[6] she accepted it as a thing of course. Now the sun shines, cats bask, I bask.

20. Improved an aching small hour by a cigarette & Dryden's *Annus Mirabilis*. Then slept balmily with Titus as a bolster.

21. George Painter's Chateaubriand (1) – with me a dedicatee. Antonia in the p.m. with Partridge's Dict. of Catch Phrases. A golden beginning, legs in the evening.

25. Deboshed all day, routine just kept me on my feet. A flawless blue sky, but myself all flawed & spotted. Why? Food-poisoning? Too much social life?

November

<u>21</u>. Here is your warm dress, said the cleaner's man, with chattering teeth. Snow blocks the northern roads, the wind is spiked with it. But the late Schubert 4t looked after me. It is remarkable how his music encompasses one, in its youth & outgoing.

5 Peg Manisty was coming to stay.
6 STW was proposing that Antonia live at Frome Vauchurch after her death.

24. Day of efficiency flaring into fidget. Assembled Maxwells' parcel, planned others, DID UP nothing. My will fixed by plump Mr Wylde. Feverish p.m., raging thirst.

December

19. In the morning she [Antonia] was by me – with breakfast. I spent the day in bed, sleeping mostly. The D[istrict] Nurse came & bandaged my right foot. Bladder wrack.

21. Rose late & shabby. ?How does one bathe with one leg? Did things badly, & read serenely – another B. Pym – all day. It rained all day.

23. Rain all day. Exhaustion & insignificance all day. And fruit from Marnie & daffodils from Pat & Brian,[7] and manzanilla from Ian – and myself as undriable as my wet washing.

25. Baglake. Taxi 12.15.
  [. . .] Paused at the Old Rectory. In a flash the whole lawn covered with rejoicing young persons. Edward alone serious. He had his portrait with him for me to see tomorrow.

26. Antonia, with breakfast, who handed me on to Soo Pinney, lunch, who retired after Edward Stone with picture, & Jenni, arrived. Strange, now to be alone, in a house so full of kindness.

---

7 Pat Howard had been widowed and re-married. Her new husband was Brian Bullen.

1978

January

6. Fell several times – not at my best.

7. Antonia visited with scheme for Bedding me.

8. Antonia p.m.
   (12:i; Virago[1] 2 forewordes [sic]. poems to Julius.)[2]

   [in bottom margin]
   Mon. [9th] Nurse Lockley.

---

1 Virago Press were republishing *Mr Fortune's Maggot* and *The True Heart* in paperback.
2 Julius Lipton. See note 7, page 373.

Index

Trevelyan, R.C., 98
Truman, Harry S., 165
Turpin, Richard, 226(+n), 229, 291

Untermeyer, Jean Starr, 209(+n)
Untermeyer, Louis, 43n, 47n

Valéry, Paul; *Variété*, 5
Vaughan, Bridget *see* Warner, Bridget
Vaughan, Juliet, 272
Vaughan, Reginald, 272
Vaughan Williams, Ralph, 176, 197, 248–9, 250(+n), 255
Vaughan Williams, Ursula, 248–9, 254, 255
Vietnam War, 307

Wadham, Dorothy ('Doffles'), 26(+n), 236
Wagner, Richard; *Tannhauser*, 300
Walther, Bruno, 53
Walton, Carol, 293(+n), 308, 339
Warner, Bridget (*later* Vaughan), 24n, 26–7, 31, 45, 67, 272(+n)
Warner, Dorothy, 14(+n), 23–4, 26–7, 29, 30–1, 45, 48, 54–5, 67, 83, 100(+n), 133, 272
Warner, Elizabeth, 190(+n)
Warner, Flora (*née* Moir; STW's paternal grandmother), 11n, 154(+n)
Warner, George Townsend ('Russie'; STW's father), 3, 22, 231, 256(+n), 271
Warner, Nora (*née* Hudleston, *later* Eiloart; STW's mother), 3, 20, 22, 42–3, 80, 88, 90–1, 98, 156–8, 162, 177, 354
Warner, Oliver, 14(+n), 27, 31, 48, 67, 83, 85, 100n, 185, 190(+n), 191
Warner, Robert Townsend (STW's uncle), 80(+n), 234
Warner, Sylvia Townsend: childhood, 3, 88; musicology, 3, 17–8, 34–5, 38, 44, 55, 62, 88, 210; and money, 3, 11, 66, 87–8, 90, 98–9, 101, 122, 152, 167, 177, 232, 277; as writer, 11, 13, 52, 53, 65–6, 98, 151, 182–3, 192, 211, 223, 232–3, 253, 280, 284, 287, 298, 305, 315, 340; and Percy Buck, 3, 12, 22, 29, 31, 34, 37, 44–5, 52, 53, 56, 60–2, 73, 86–7; and the Great War, 25, 95; and diary, 30, 301; and astro-physics, 35–6, 45, 47–8, 136, 160, 251–2, 271; and composing, 46; appearance, 49, 198, 203, 208, 239, 241, 348, 357; and feminism, 50, 250; relationship with Valentine Ackland, 69–70, 71–2, 74–5, 77, 79, 80–1, 87–8, 90–2, 94, 142–7, 150, 154–5, 158, 161–2, 164, 200, 203–4, 215, 231, 256, 294, 319, 327–8, 336–9, 340–59, 364, 366; and abortion, 89; and Elizabeth Wade White, 93, 102, 116, 133–4, 142, 145, 148–9, 150–3, 158–9, 161, 163, 188, 287; and Communism, 93, 101, 112, 245–6; and the *New Yorker*, 93, 101–2, 114, 122, 151, 165, 167, 171, 174, 181, 197, 232, 247, 277, 291, 298, 315; and war work, 108–9, 112–9, 121–4; and homosexuality, 205–6, 260–1; WORKS: *After the Death of Don Juan*, 93, 307; *Boxwood*, 236(+n);

Contre Sainte-Beuve (by Marcel Proust, tr. by STW as *By Way of Sainte-Beuve*), 131, 212–6, 219, 222–3, 225, 227, 229, 230–1, 235–6, 245, 259; *Corner that Held Them*, 117, 120, 122–3, 125, 127–8, 131, 152; *La Cote Sauvage* (by Jean-Louis Huguenin, tr. by STW as *A Place of Shipwreck*), 274(+n), 279; *Elinor Barley*, 42; *The Flint Anchor*, 131, 181(+n), 182–3, 187, 190–2, 198, 200, 205–6, 211; *Innocent and the Guilty*, 349; *Kingdoms of Elfin*, 372, 376; *Lolly Willowes*, 3, 16, 287, 305; 'Lost Summer', 188(+n); Miscellaneous articles, 10, 11, 15, 45, 54, 55, 88, 95–6, 98, 102, 167, 284, 337, 341, 346; *Mr Fortune's Maggot* 3, 13, 52, 211, 316; *Opus 7*, 53, 60–3; Poems, 6, 9, 10, 13–4, 19, 29, 43, 45, 48, 65, 74, 78, 88, 120, 140, 353; *The Salutation*, 52–3, 91; 'The Sea Change', 163(+n), 168, 171; *Some World Far from Ours*, 46(+n); Stories, 17, 65, 78, 114, 119, 124, 131, 140, 144, 147, 151, 153–4, 158, 165–7, 171, 173–4, 179, 181, 197, 220, 222, 232, 237, 262, 264, 266–7, 270, 275–6, 278–9, 280, 285, 287–8, 290–3, 297–300, 305, 309–10, 312, 315, 323, 338–40, 347–9, 350(+n), 359, 362, 369–70, 372–3, 375; *Stranger with a Bag*, 299, 300–1, 313; *Summer Will Show*, 93; *T.H. White*, 290–8, 301, 303–7, 312; *Time Importuned*, 3; *The True Heart*, 3, 9, 11, 17, 20–2, 24, 28, 35; *Tudor Church Music*, 3, 16–7, 19, 51, 55, 210, 260; Unfinished novels, 41, 151, 166, 169, 210–11; *The Weekend Dickens*, 91(+n); *Winter in the Air*, 223;
Warren, Dorothy, 72n, 75(+n), 76(+n), 82n, 83–4
Webb, Geoffrey ('Wobb'), 6(+n), 19, 36, 39
Weekes, Father, 222(+n), 224, 226, 228
Weil, Simone; *Attente de Dieu*, 181
Welch, Denton; *Voice from a Cloud*, 179
Welitsch, Ljuba, 166
Wells, H.G., 48
West, Rebecca, 362
Westrup, J.A., 7(+n)
Whistler, Laurence, 238
White, Elizabeth Wade, 40(+n), 93, 102, 115, 131, 133–6, 139, 140, 142–6, 148–159, 163, 167–8, 174, 179, 182, 187–8, 204, 217, 267, 287, 301, 304, 341 (*see also* Warner, S.T. and Ackland, Valentine)
White, Eric Walter, 361(+n)
White, Robert, 38(+n)
White, T.H., 131, 284, 290, 295 (*see also* Warner, S.T.: Works)
Wilson, Steuart, 176
Winfrith Atomic Reactor, 223, 225, 234
Wong, Anna May, 90(+n)
Wooldridge, H.E., 35(+n), 44
Woolf, Leonard, 32n, 254, 262, 286–7, 301, 309n
Woolf, Virginia, 32n, 50(+n), 110, 113, 250
Woollcombe, Joan (née Ackland; VA's sister), 178(+n), 255–6, 262, 265, 327
Woolsey, Gamel, 59(+n)
Wordsworth, Andrew, 88
Wordsworth, Georgia, 330(+n), 362n
Wordsworth, Robin, 362–3, 365